# WITHDRAWN
## UTSA LIBRARIES

D1737639

# LISTEN, DAUGHTER

# THE NEW MIDDLE AGES

BONNIE WHEELER, *Series Editor*

*The New Middle Ages* presents transdisciplinary studies of medieval cultures. It includes both scholarly monographs and essay collections.

## PUBLISHED BY PALGRAVE:

# LISTEN, DAUGHTER

## THE *SPECULUM VIRGINUM* AND THE FORMATION OF RELIGIOUS WOMEN IN THE MIDDLE AGES

*Edited by Constant J. Mews*

palgrave

LISTEN, DAUGHTER
© Copyright Constant J. Mews, 2001. All rights reserved. No part
of this book may be used or reproduced in any manner
whatsoever without written permission except in the case of brief
quotations embodied in critical articles or reviews.

First published 2001 by
PALGRAVE™
175 Fifth Avenue, New York, N.Y. 10010 and
Houndmills, Basingstoke, Hampshire RG21 6XS.
Companies and representatives throughout the world.

PALGRAVE is the new global publishing imprint of St. Martin's
Press LLC Scholarly and Reference Division and Palgrave
Publishers Ltd (formerly Macmillan Press Ltd).

ISBN 0-312-24008-2 hardback
ISBN 978-0-312-24008-0
**Library of Congress Cataloging-in-Publication Data**
available from the Library of Congress.

A catalogue record for this book is available from the British Library.

Design by Letra Libre, Inc.

First edition: November 2001
Transferred to Digital Printing 2011

Library
University of Texas
at San Antonio

# CONTENTS

# SERIES EDITOR'S FOREWORD

The *New Middle Ages* contributes to lively transdisciplinary conversations in medieval cultural studies through its scholarly monographs and essay collections. This series provides focused research in a contemporary idiom about specific but diverse practices, expressions, and ideologies in the Middle Ages; it aims especially to recuperate the histories of medieval women. *Listen, Daughter: The* Speculum virginum *and the Formation of Religious Women in the Middle Ages,* a focused collection of essays edited by Constant J. Mews, is the twenty-third volume in this series. Several spiritual, political, and aesthetic traditions are confronted in the various manuscripts of the *Speculum virginum,* all of which attest not only to the burgeoning of female monastic life in the High Middle Ages but also to its probable impact on male religious formation. What did it mean for the increasingly large numbers of women drawn to religious life to find ease with "authority" in all its guises—from the intense interiority of the quest for personal perfection to the progressive exterior rigidity of (seeming) conformity to empowered men? The chapters in this volume interrogate this problem as presented in the manuscripts of the *Speculum virginum* from the perspectives of history, literature, musicology, aesthetics, and theology, thus allowing readers to understand more fully the rich, coherent, and distinctive identities that medieval religious women (individually and in groups) forged for themselves. As Mews points out, the volume invites us to recognize more fully the range and contexts of the medieval traditions of spiritual formation, especially those deployed by the many legions of the "Brides of Christ."

*Bonnie Wheeler*
*Southern Methodist University*

# ACKNOWLEDGMENTS

Special thanks are due to numerous individuals and institutions for their assistance with the research that has led to this volume. In particular, the Australian Research Council played an important role in financing research and teaching relief essential between 1997 and 1999. Thanks are given to the British Library to reproduce folios from the Arundel 44 MS. I am personally indebted to all the contributors to this volume for their involvement in discussing and reviewing drafts of individual chapters, over a prolonged period. What began as a project involving a group of Australian scholars—Sabina Flanagan, Janice Pinder, Kim Power, Julie Hotchin, and Catherine Jeffreys—expanded into a collective research effort that embraced three continents and enabled a number of scholars, often without easy access to well-resourced libraries, to share their research. It has also been a privilege to bring into the project Professor Jutta Seyfarth of Cologne and to discuss with her numerous disputed questions raised by the *Speculum virginum*. This project could not have been accomplished without the ten years she spent editing the treatise. I am also immensely grateful to Professor Alfred Haverkamp for organizing an outstandingly successful conference in honor of Hildegard of Bingen, held at Bingen under the generous auspices of the local municipality. That conference provided an unparalleled opportunity for discussion of the broader significance of both the *Speculum virginum* and women's religious life in Germany in the twelfth century. It also enabled me to meet Felix Heinzer of the Württembergische Landesbibliothek with whom I had many fruitful discussions about the *Speculum* and the abbey of Hirsau. Professor Franz Felten kindly assisted Julie Hotchin and me in research undertaken at Mainz. In Sweden, Arne Jönsonn has also helped with details relating to Birgitta of Sweden. I am grateful to Maryna Mews for her careful assistance in editing the volume and indeed to all who have shared in this project.

*Constant J. Mews*

# EDITORIAL NOTE

A ll references are to the part and line number of the *Speculum virginum* in Jutta Seyfarth's edition, CCCM 5 (1990). For consistency, the letter *u*, when used as a consonant within Latin words, is printed as *v* rather than as *u*, as in texts printed within the Corpus Christianorum series. Titles of the most frequently cited texts are given in Latin, while others are cited through an English translation, with the original Latin title provided in notes. Scripture references are cited according to the Vulgate translation of the Bible.

# ABBREVIATIONS

| | |
|---|---|
| *AASS* | *Acta Sanctorum quotquot tote orbe coluntur, vel a Catholicis scriptoribus celebrantur* (Paris, Brussels, 1863–). |
| CCCM | Corpus Christianorum Continuatio Mediaeualis (Turnhout: Brepols, 1967–). |
| CCSL | Corpus Christianorum Series Latina (Turnhout: Brepols, 1954–). |
| CSEL | Corpus Scriptorum Ecclesiasticorum Latinorum (Vienna, Leipzig: Teubner, 1866–). |
| MGH SS | Monumenta Germaniae Historica. Scriptorum Series (Hannover: Hierssemann, 1833–). |
| PL | Jacques-Paul Migne, Patrologia Latina (Paris: Garnier, 1844–64). |
| *RTAM* | *Recherches de théologie ancienne et médiévale.* |
| *SAEMO* | *Sancti Ambrosii Episcopi Mediolanensis Opera* (Milan: Biblioteca Ambrosiana and Rome: Città Nuova Editrice, 1979–). |
| *SAOO* | *Sancti Anselmi Opera Omnia,* 6 vols. (Edinburgh: Nelson, 1946–61). |
| *SBO* | *Sancti Bernardi Opera,* ed. Jean Leclercq, 8 vols. (Rome: Editiones Cistercienses, 1957–75). |
| Schr | Sources chrétiennes (Paris: Cerf, 1944–). |
| Seyfarth | Jutta Seyfarth, Introduction, CCCM 5 (1990) [pages cited with asterisk]. |
| *SV* | *Speculum virginum,* ed. Jutta Seyfarth, CCCM 5 (1990). |

# INTRODUCTION

*Constant J. Mews*

*Audi filia et vide et inclina aurem tuam et obliviscere populum tuum et domum pa-tris tui et concupiscet rex decorem tuum.*
*[Listen, daughter, and see, and incline your ear, and forget your people and your fa-ther's house, and the king shall desire your beauty.] Ps. 44.11–12*

These words of the Psalmist provide a particularly appropriate way to begin thinking about the *Speculum virginum [Mirror of Virgins]*. Traditionally interpreted as an injunction to the Church to prepare itself as a Bride to meet the Son of God, they had a particular resonance for women who sought to dedicate themselves to the religious life. The perfect soul was understood as a supremely beautiful woman who leaves her father's house for her spiritual beloved. To a modern mind, this might seem a very alien way of imagining spiritual life. The injunction implies that God is male and that the perfect woman is fully obedient to her lover. Yet these words can also be heard as a "wake-up call," urging rejection of worldly security and attentiveness to the voice of the Beloved. This is the way they were understood within a medieval religious environment.

This injunction of the Psalmist, urging the bride to meet her beloved, plays a particularly important role in the *Speculum virginum*, a text that it-self played a central role in shaping the identity of religious women between the twelfth and early sixteenth centuries.[1] The *Speculum virginum* is an extended dialogue, in which a virgin of Christ called Theodora provokes her spiritual mentor, Peregrinus or "Pilgrim," to explain the meaning of her way of life and of her obedience to God. The large number of surviving manuscripts of the *Speculum virginum*, both in its original Latin text and in vernacular translations, attests to its importance in defining a vision of the spiritual life in the High and Late Middle Ages. Yet although there has been growing interest in the achievement of women mystics during this period of European history, much less attention has been given to those texts, such as the *Speculum virginum,* that were so influential in forming the attitudes and way of life of religious women. The originality of what the author of the *Speculum virginum* was trying to achieve should not be underestimated. It was written in response to a quite new situation that was emerging within the monastic life, the recent foundation of large numbers of communities of religious women throughout Germany and France. As Heloise observed to Abelard in the early 1130s, the Rule of St. Benedict had addressed itself uniquely to men.[2] The *Speculum virginum* presented itself as a guide that concerned itself with the true meaning of the life of a woman who had dedicated herself to the religious life. It did so by urging that she listen to her spiritual adviser and thus to the voice of God.

The terms *virgo* and *virginitas* are much more complex concepts in medieval culture than in contemporary discourse, in which "virgin" and "virginity" tend to be used in a purely physical sense. The primary meaning of *virgo* is that of a woman not subordinated sexually to a man and therefore free to devote herself to God.[3] *Virgo* can also refer to a woman of marriageable age without direct regard for physical state. Less frequently, it is applied to a man perceived as sexually pure, like John the Evangelist or John the Baptist.[4] In a society that considered sexual intercourse as conferring rights of ownership by a man over a woman (it being assumed that the entire human person was contained in male seed), consecrated virginity provided a path by which a woman was freed from the obligations of marriage. We need to be attentive to the different ways in which virginity could be invoked as a concept. As Cindy L. Carlson and Angela Lane Weisl have recently argued with respect to both virginity and widowhood, the category of "virgin" was an ideal that served a range of social functions, both in defining virtue and in locating possibilities for temptation.[5] While the *Speculum virginum* certainly valorizes the virginal state as superior to both marriage and widowhood, its central concern is not to exhort women to maintain physical virginity but to keep them focused on the quest for moral perfection. In its own way, the *Speculum* contributes to a subtle reevaluation of the meaning of virginity. It uses vivid dialogue, visual imagery, and music to suggest new ways of developing the inner life within the framework of some very traditional assumptions about gender.

The chapters in this volume reflect in different ways on the significance of the *Speculum virginum* and the broader issues of dialogue and religious formation for women in the twelfth century and beyond. The publication in

1990 of Jutta Seyfarth's critical edition, the first ever to be produced, has opened up many new paths of research. Before it appeared, only a few scholars had paid any attention to the *Speculum virginum*.[6] While there has since been a growth of interest in the religious culture of medieval women, the literature of spiritual formation has attracted relatively little attention. The *Speculum virginum* in particular is still little known.

The first scholar to identify its author was Johannes Trithemius (1462–1516), the bibliophile abbot of Sponheim who devoted so much of his life to exploring the traditions of Hirsau, a great abbey in southwest Germany that played a key role in promoting religious reform during the late eleventh and early twelfth centuries. Trithemius described the author as a monk of Hirsau known as "Peregrinus" or "Pilgrim," but in fact called Conrad.[7] The testimony of Trithemius about Conrad of Hirsau is impossible to verify firsthand, as most of the manuscripts on which he relied were scattered or destroyed during the conflicts that ravaged this part of Germany during the sixteenth and seventeenth centuries. The *Speculum* languished in almost complete neglect between the seventeenth and nineteenth centuries, with no edition being published.

In the twentieth century, interest in the *Speculum virginum* was initially raised by two art historians, Arthur Watson and later Martha Strube.[8] The first scholar to investigate its text was Matthäus Bernards, who presented much of his research into its manuscript tradition and theological perspectives in a dissertation, published in 1955 under the ambitious title "*Speculum virginum*. The Spirituality and Spiritual Life of Woman in the High Middle Ages."[9] Bernards did not explore the historical circumstances behind its composition but was more interested in establishing its significance within medieval religious thought as a whole. Because he concentrated so much on demonstrating literary and theological parallels between the *Speculum* and other medieval texts (many from a later period), he never clarified what was particularly distinctive about its theological or pedagogical perspective and did not focus on its visual imagery.[10] One scholar who extended the research of Bernards was Eleanor Greenhill. She argued in 1962 that the *Speculum virginum* belonged to a tradition of twelfth-century commentary on the Song of Songs and reflected the influence of Hugh of St-Victor (d. 1141).[11] Close study of the numerous corrections and rubrics in the London copy of the *Speculum virginum* (British Library, Arundel 44, belonging to Eberbach by the late twelfth century) subsequently led her to put forward a strong case that one of the four scribes involved in its redaction was its author.[12]

The *Speculum virginum* has been relatively little studied in relation to medieval monastic culture. Dom Jean Leclercq did not mention the work at all in his immensely influential study, *The Love of Learning and the Desire for God.* He did comment briefly on its final *Epithalamium* as an example of monastic literature of desire, without mentioning that it provided the conclusion to the *Speculum.*[13] On the other hand, Leclercq drew at length on the *Dialogue on the Authors* (also attributed to Conrad of Hirsau by Trithemius) to argue that medieval monastic education embraced the study of the pagan classics, assuming that the *Dialogue* articulated a "typical" monastic education.[14] Leclercq's thesis was that monasticism fostered a contemplative, humanistic culture very different from what he considered to be the analytic technique of scholasticism. He drew heavily on polemical writings from the twelfth century contrasting the peace of the cloister with the hubbub of the schools to make his point. Above all, Leclercq focused on the writing of Bernard of Clairvaux as epitomizing "monastic theology"—a current of contemplative theological reflection that went back to the Fathers of the Church and was practiced by monks. Leclercq's implicit criticism of scholastic theology as too analytic, and his pleading for a return to contemplative spirituality was influential in reshaping Catholic thought during the 1960s and 1970s. Although in later life Leclercq did pay more attention to the role of women in monasticism, this was largely to defend St. Bernard from what he considered to be unjustified charges of misogynism.

The *Speculum virginum* has also been largely bypassed in studies of the involvement of women in religion during the Middle Ages. In 1935 Herbert Grundmann produced a groundbreaking study of women's participation in heretical movements and new religious orders during the late twelfth and thirteenth centuries, but steered away from considering their involvement in movements of monastic reform in an earlier period.[15] In consequence, he gave the impression that the flowering of women's involvement in religious life began only with Jacques de Vitry (ca. 1160/70–1240) and Marie d'Oignies (d. 1213). Since then, much attention has been given to the achievement of women mystics from the mid-twelfth century to the later Middle Ages in developing a distinct "feminine spirituality."[16] The interaction between these women and their male spiritual advisers, who played such a role in shaping their lives, as indeed the process of spiritual formation has not been as well studied. The cultural assumptions that Latin writers automatically drew on in the twelfth century to talk about women were heavily patriarchal. There is no scholarly consensus, however, on the extent to which these assumptions were challenged in the period.[17]

In recent decades, the study of women's involvement in monasticism has blossomed, although within English-language scholarship perhaps more in relation to France and England than to Germany. Simple stereotypes about religious women need to be reexamined.[18] It has been demonstrated that a significant number women's communities in the twelfth century pursued a Cistercian way of life, even if they were not formally affiliated to the order.[19] While there was always a tradition of hostility toward allowing women to enter male enclosures, Cistercian abbeys such as Eberbach acquired responsibility, especially from the late twelfth century, for ministering to communities of religious women.[20] The number of manuscripts of the *Speculum virginum* from male Cistercian houses, especially from the late twelfth century, reflects this involvement.

Barbara Newman has been one of the few scholars to consider the literature of spiritual formation for religious women. In a study that emphasizes how the ideal of virginity offered to women offers a more static image of the spiritual life than offered to men, she observes that the *Speculum virginum* constitutes perhaps the most remarkable example of this literature of spiritual encouragement.[21] In 1985 Urban Küsters published an important interdisciplinary study of twelfth-century vernacular commentary on the Song of Songs, the *St. Trudperter Hohelied,* which related both to the *Speculum* and to the involvement of women in religious houses influenced by the Hirsau reform.[22] His study combined literary and historical analysis, to explore the specific context of female religious communities within which vernacular writing emerged. The innovative qualities of the *Speculum virginum* were also discerned in Einar Jonsson's study of "mirror" literature as a literary genre.[23]

Perhaps the most frequently studied nun from twelfth-century Germany is Hildegard of Bingen (1098–1178). In the English-speaking world, Peter Dronke, Sabina Flanagan, and Barbara Newman have all helped to make Hildegard's writings more widely known in a way that rejects simpleminded popularization. Critical editions and good-quality translations of most of Hildegard's major writings have begun to appear. In much popular literature, however, Hildegard still tends to be presented as an exceptional figure, at odds with the dominant culture of her time. Not enough attention has been given to a significant shift that was taking place within the environment of reformed monasticism at the time she was growing up at Disibodenberg. Here, as at many abbeys influenced by the Hirsau reform, it was not unusual for religious women to live alongside a male monastic community. Volmar's friendship with Hildegard was decisive in enabling her to emerge as a writer and teacher. Given that there can never be any "pure" voice of medieval women, uninfluenced by interaction with an overwhelmingly masculine clerical culture, research needs to focus on the quality of interaction and dialogue between men and women within monastic life. The dialogue presented in the *Speculum virginum* conveyed an influential model of what such interaction could be like.[24]

In part, this volume developed out of a sense that the feast of publications and conferences devoted to Hildegard leading up to the ninth centenary of her birth in 1998 was reaching saturation point. Discovering Jutta Seyfarth's edition of the *Speculum virginum*, published in 1990, led me to realize that Hildegard's achievement had to be understood as part of a much more complex and diverse movement of religious reform taking place throughout Latin Christendom in the late eleventh and early twelfth centuries. It became clear that the *Speculum* needed to be studied on its own terms, not just in comparison to the writings of Hildegard. It also became apparent that any future inquiry would have to combine the skills of historical, literary, and theological research with those of art history and music if its significance and monastic context were to be fully understood.

I had also spent many years studying one of the most famous and controversial examples of literary dialogue between a man and woman from the twelfth century, the correspondence of Abelard and Heloise. My scrutiny of a collection of extracts from 113 Latin love letters copied out by a monk of Clairvaux in the fifteenth century led me to conclude that they shed valuable light on the interaction of these famous lovers in the twelfth century, long before they resumed their exchange in the early 1130s within a monastic environment.[25] Although Heloise was unusual in the extent of her literacy and erudition, it was not unheard of for women of her generation to seek to engage in discussion with men, both in the secular and in the religious sphere. In my study of the love letters, I was primarily concerned with male-female interaction within a secular context. It was also important to study such interaction within a monastic environment. Traditional ideas of dialogue as a purely masculine literary phenomenon were being transformed by the possibility that it was legitimate for women to dialogue with men, so long as certain modesties were preserved. Such experimentation provoked alarm from those who feared that excessive familiarity between the sexes would subvert established ideas of order and morality. The author of the *Speculum virginum* was fully aware of the risks involved in excessive physical intimacy between women and men. Nonetheless, he thought that such dialogue could be transformed to a positive end. He provides for Theodora something very similar to what Heloise demanded from Abelard.

This volume brings together recent research into this broader question of dialogue and interaction between men and women in the religious life. The *Speculum virginum* provides a peculiarly appropriate medium through

which to explore these issues. Because the work operates in many different dimensions, literary, theological, visual, and auditory, it needs to be an-
alyzed from a variety of different angles. It was also necessary to understand
the broader vitality of the phenomenon of interaction between men and
women in the religious life. As a number of chapters make clear, this interaction was a two-way process. Understanding the *Speculum virginum*
might also help illuminate the achievement of those women who sought
to go beyond its teaching.

In my own chapter, I revisit the claims of Trithemius that the *Speculum
virginum* was written by Conrad of Hirsau and suggest that it presents an
original synthesis of the religious life, whose sources of inspiration can be
traced back to currents of pedagogical innovation promoted by William of
Hirsau in monastic houses throughout Germany. It was one of a number
of pedagogically innovative writings by a monastic teacher fascinated by
the capacity of dialogue to probe a wide range of questions about the
monastic life. The *Speculum virginum* illustrates how traditional monastic
values were being articulated in new ways in the twelfth century in response to a changing world.

Jutta Seyfarth is the scholar whose industry in providing a critical edition of the *Speculum virginum* has provided the foundation on which all subsequent research into the work must depend. In chapter 2 she distills her
painstaking research into an unusually rich and fascinating manuscript tradition. There are few works of medieval literature where the earliest textual
witnesses are so closely interrelated yet present such a rich insight into the
process by which a textual tradition is established. Editing the *Speculum* was
no easy task. Seyfarth presents the complexity and fascination of its manuscript tradition as well as the uncertainties that surround its authorship.

In chapter 3 Julie Hotchin expands on some of the issues raised by Seyfarth in relation to the involvement of women in the monastic reform
movement in twelfth-century Germany. She provides an overview of one
of the most distinctive features of the reform movement promoted by
William of Hirsau and a circle of like-minded contemporaries, the involvement of women in monastic life. This movement traces its roots back
to the late eleventh century, when zeal for recovering "the apostolic life"
brought many new challenges to conventional understanding of the
monastic ideal. While Hildegard of Bingen has attracted much attention in
recent years, the dynamism and complexity of the process by which communities of religious women developed alongside male religious communities has been little understood. Hotchin's chapter demonstrates the
tensions involved in the participation of women in a way of life traditionally defined by men, in both Benedictine and Augustinian contexts. By the
mid-twelfth century, Hirsau was losing its role in provoking reform within

monastic life to a much better organized reform movement, that of the Cistercian order. It is not insignificant that most surviving copies of the Latin text of the *Speculum virginum* should be Cistercian in origin. The originality of the *Speculum* can be explored from many different directions. In chapter 4, a study of its teaching on the Virgin Bride, Kim Power identifies both its debt to the Fathers of the Church, in particular to Origen and Ambrose, and its innovative handling of a number of distinct themes. Its Mariological doctrine, heavily influenced by the ideas of ninth-century theologian Paschasius Radbertus, presents a far "higher" view of the status of the Virgin, as preexisting at the beginning of time, than anything imagined by any of the Latin Fathers. Its imagery of nuptial union would be of immense influence in shaping Marian piety over the next three centuries. The esteem attached to a life of virginity in this period cannot be understood outside the context of this understanding of the Virgin as a cosmic presence pervading human history.

In 1997 Morgan Powell completed an important dissertation at Princeton University in which he studied the model of religious instruction in the *Speculum virginum* so as to demonstrate far-reaching parallels between its audio-visual aesthetic and the poetic conception of various early vernacular texts. In chapter 5, Powell pays particular attention to the role of auditory and visual images in the *Speculum*. The work itself, he argues, was composed to be delivered aloud, by a male preacher addressing a community of female religious either individually or in groups. Powell argues that the work's pictures, far from being appendages, are integral to its use and conception, and provide the basis for a sophisticated aesthetic argument that relies on simultaneous consideration of the spoken word and the image. He argues convincingly that the opening of part three of the *Speculum virginum*, a free elaboration of Psalm 44.11–12 ("Listen, daughter, and see") formed the prologue to an earlier eight-book version of the work that highlighted the importance of auditory and visual means of communication. Powell sees the *Speculum* as an innovative pedagogical treatise for the use of monastic teachers in their preaching to and spiritual direction of religious women, one that provided women with alternative access to and participation in the revelation of religious truth.

One aspect of the *Speculum virginum* that has never been given adequate attention is the music that is preserved in the closing *Epithalamium [Bridal Song]* in the earliest manuscripts of the work. The process of understanding advocated by its author is based not just on meditating on visual images of the spiritual life but on participating within a liturgy through which the "daughters of light" can obtain a foretaste of that union with Christ which is the ultimate goal of their lives. Catherine Jeffreys, who has herself specialized in studying the music of Hildegard of Bingen, presents in chapter 6 an analysis of the music preserved in the *Speculum*. She argues that its distinctive tonal features, quite different from those that characterize Hildegard's melodies, illustrate a broader phenomenon evident in the twelfth century, the desire of each religious community to establish a distinct identity for itself through music.

Many features of the *Speculum virginum* become much more apparent when it is compared to other examples of the literature of religious formation, from the same period. In chapter 7 Janice Pinder compares the *Speculum* to two other twelfth-century texts, both of great interest in their own right, the *De claustro animae [Cloister of the Soul]* of Hugh of Fouilloy and the anonymous *De modo bene vivendi [On the Manner of Living Well]*. Her exposition of the contrast in the essentially solitary imagery of the *Speculum* and the more public imagery of the *De claustro animae* highlights the gendered aspect of theorizing about the religious life for women as distinct from literature addressed to women. Her comparison of the *Speculum* with the little-studied *De modo bene vivendi*, however, provides a fascinating insight into the way in which only certain aspects of the *Speculum* were thought to be useful. Not all writing about the spiritual life necessarily followed such strictly gendered assumptions, a feature illustrated by the fact that the *De modo* survives in a version addressed to a brother as well as to a religious woman. Its title is one that can be apply to both men and women. The reduced emphasis it gives to virginity and bridal imagery suggests that the *Speculum virginum* did not provide the only way in which monks could think about the religious life.

The use of dialogue as a pedagogical device to help explain the rational basis behind existing institutions and beliefs was widespread in the twelfth century. In chapter 8 Sabina Flanagan considers the use of dialogue as literary technique in a wide range of dialogue texts from the period. Not least the most intriguing feature of the *Speculum virginum* lies in the way its author brings techniques normally devised for instructing boys and young men in a range of topics into the education and edification of religious women.

While the *Speculum virginum* is certainly the largest treatise of its kind addressed to women in the Middle Ages, it is far from the only composition directed toward the formation of religious women from this period. Elisabeth Bos, in chapter 9, considers a range of this literature, often epistolary or homiletic in form from England and France in the twelfth century, and shows how fundamentally similar are its concerns to those of the *Speculum*. She argues that far from simply exhorting women to preserve their existing state of virginity, the prime concern of such literature was to promote growth in interior virtue rather than to dwell on virginity as a physical condition to be preserved at all costs.

The *Speculum virginum* set a new benchmark for developing a coherent vision of the religious life through dialogue and visual imagery. Yet in its own way, this vision followed traditional gendered assumptions about the contribution that women could make to the religious life. It privileged moral purity over intellectual speculation. In her study of the *Hortus deliciarum [Garden of Delights]* of Herrad of Hohenbourg, presented in chapter 10, Fiona Griffiths analyzes a treatise that goes much further than the *Speculum* in providing a visual synthesis of scholastic theology, drawn from principles of both reason and scripture. Like the *De modo,* it pays less emphasis to bridal imagery than the *Speculum.* Herrad was a remarkable woman, able to transform the arguments of a wide range of sometimes very recent authors into what must have been one of the most magnificent illuminated manuscripts of the twelfth century, now the focus of careful work of reconstruction. The *Speculum* may have provided a precedent in provoking communities of religious women to develop a distinct visual culture, a theme that Jeffrey Hamburger has developed in relation to women's religious communities in the thirteenth and fourteenth centuries.[26] Griffiths's comparison of the *Hortus* with the *Speculum* reveals what can happen when a woman is no longer simply the disciple but herself becomes the teacher.

The manuscripts of the *Speculum virginum,* both Latin and vernacular, provide a fascinating lesson in the profound continuities that underpin religious life during the High and Late Middle Ages. In chapter 11, Urban Küsters explores the great revival of interest in the work that took place above all in the Netherlands during the late fourteenth and fifteenth centuries among the Brethren of the Common Life, a movement that played such an important role in fostering the "Modern Devotion." He shows the close connection between the manuscripts of the translation made into Middle Dutch, *Der Spieghel der Maechden [Maidens' Mirror],* and a tendency toward greater institutionalization of a movement that had initially defined itself in the late fourteenth century by not committing itself to any specific rule. The intense focus on interior morality in the *Speculum virginum,* coupled with its criticism of external show and noble birth, fitted well into the values of the Modern Devotion. The text legitimized the way of life of religious women who otherwise presented a threat to ecclesiastical authority by living outside a traditional monastic framework.

These chapters all point in their own way to further issues demanding exploration. Does the discussion with Theodora reflect a genuine shift in the pattern of religious debate in the twelfth century, or is it in fact reinforcing traditional masculine authority within a sphere previously neglected by ecclesiastical tradition? The chapters suggest that the answer may lie somewhere between these two poles. The *Speculum virginum* established a precedent for writing about the religious life for women upon which other writers, male and female, would seek to improve. As Jutta Seyfarth argues, more research is needed into the iconography of the sequence of images preserved within the *Speculum*, but this must be in relation to its broader pedagogical strategy. Still awaiting investigation are other treatises by the same author, notably the *De fructibus carnis et spiritus* and the unedited *Allocutio ad Deum*, of which Robert Bultot printed only excerpts in an appendix to his edition of the *Dialogus de mundi contemptu vel amore*. There is also the larger question of the role of visual explication as a teaching device within twelfth-century literature as a whole. What role did women's communities play in the development of new attitudes toward religious life both in the twelfth century and later?

The literature of spiritual formation, often anonymous or by authors who are little known, offers a still largely untapped field of study. While the *Ancrene Wisse [Guide for Anchoresses]* has already begun to attract the attention it deserves within Middle English studies, this is only the tip of an iceberg of new writing about the religious life between the twelfth and fifteenth centuries.[27] The extension of religious life from an elite circle within the early medieval period to relatively large numbers of women in the twelfth century demanded the development of a new kind of literature. Narrow attention on a few famous women, such as Heloise and Hildegard in the twelfth century, or Birgitta of Sweden and Margery Kempe in the later medieval period, can obscure awareness of the broader issues involved when large numbers of women participate in religious structures traditionally defined by men. The literature of spiritual formation has the potential to reveal much about both tensions and creative possibilities within the religious life.

There is a profound ambiguity in the phrase "Listen, daughter" as used in the *Speculum virginum*. At one level, it is the voice of authority enjoining obedience and submission. At another, it is a call to step out of what is familiar and to use one's senses to imagine oneself as a bride who must prepare herself to meet her beloved. Now, at a time when the literature of self-improvement is as popular as it has ever been, it may be worth considering why the *Speculum virginum* enjoyed the popularity that it did for so many centuries. Is it simply another example of male control over women? The full story of the interaction between male spiritual guides and the women they were deputed to serve has yet to be written.[28]

## Notes

1. Jutta Seyfarth, ed. *Speculum virginum* CCCM 5 (1990). In her introduction, paginated with asterisks (pp. 56*–123*), Seyfarth describes thirty-six Latin manuscripts of *SV* and twenty-six copies of vernacular translations (mostly into Middle Dutch); see Seyfarth, chapter 2, and Urban Küsters, chapter 11 below, and Powell (chapter 5, n. 3) for two further Latin manuscripts.

2. For an excellent study of Heloise's critique of the Rule of Benedict, see Linda Georgianna, "'Any Corner of Heaven': Heloise's Critique of Religious Life," in *Listening to Heloise. The Voice of a Twelfth-Century Woman*, ed. Bonnie Wheeler (New York: St. Martin's Press, 2000), pp. 187–216, a revised version of the article originally printed under the same title in *Mediaeval Studies* 49 (1987): 221–53.

3. Isidore of Seville defines a *virgo* as someone "who does not know a man" and distinguishes the general category of *mulier* into the categories of "virgin" and "married woman," *De differentiis verborum* 588–90, PL 83: 68B. *Virgo* could refer to a "woman free to be married," even though she might have been married in the past and was not technically a virgin in the modern sense; J. F. Niermeyer, *Mediae Latinitatis Minus* (Leiden: Brill, 1997), p. 1111.

4. Jerome, *Tractatus LIX in Psalmos*, Ps. 127, ed. G. Morin, CCSL 78 (1958): 262. Paschasius Radbertus develops the theme in *De assumptione sanctae Mariae virginis* 14–16 (circulated as a letter of Jerome to Eustochium), ed. A. Ripberger, CCCM 56C (1985): 116, the likely source for *SV* 5.500 and 7.657.

5. Cindy L. Carlson and Angela Lane Weisl, "Introduction," in *Constructions of Widowhood and Virginity in the Middle Ages*, ed. Carlson and Weisl, (New York: St. Martin's Press, 1999), p. 5.

6. Seyfarth reviews this scholarship in the introduction to her edition, pp. 8*–13*.

7. On Trithemius, see Mews, chapter 1 below.

8. Arthur Watson, "The *Speculum virginum* with Special Reference to the Tree of Jesse," in *Speculum* 3 (1928): 445–69, and "A manuscript of the *Speculum virginum* in the Walters Art Gallery," in *Journal of the Walters Art Gallery* 10 (1947): 61–74; Martha Strube, *Die Illustrationen des Speculum Virginum* (Düsseldorf: G. H. Nolte, 1937).

9. Matthäus Bernards, *Die Handschriftliche Überlieferung und die theologischen Anschauungen des Speculum virginum* (Diss.: Bonn, 1950). This dissertation, preserved in typescript in Cologne, Diozesanbibliothek, contains much valuable detail about manuscripts not included in his *Speculum Virginum. Geistigkeit und Seelenleben der Frau im Hochmittelalter* (Cologne: Böhlau, 1955; 2nd ed. 1982).

10. See n. 9 above.

11. Eleanor Greenhill, *Die geistigen Voraussetzungen der Bilderreihe des Speculum virginum*, Beiträge zur Geschichte der Philosophie und Theologie des Mittelalters 39.2 (Münster: Aschendorff, 1962), pp. 8–9, 129–31.

12. Eleanor Greenhill, *Die Stellung der Handschrift British Museum Arundel 44 in der Überlieferung des Speculum virginum*, Mitteilungen des Grabmann Instituts der Universität München 10 (Munich: Max Hueber Verlag, 1966).

13. Jean Leclercq, *The Love of Learning and the Desire for God: A Study of Monastic Culture*, trans. Catherine Misrahi (New York: Fordham University Press, 1961), p. 60; first published as *L'Amour des lettres et le désir de Dieu. Initiation aux auteurs monastiques du moyen âge* (Paris: Seuil, 1957).

14. Leclercq, *The Love of Learning*, pp. 117–20.

15. Herbert Grundmann, *Religious Movements in the Middle Ages: The Historical Links between Heresy, the Mendicant Orders, and the Women's Religious Movement in the Twelfth and Thirteenth Century, with the Historical Foundations of German Mysticism*, trans. Steven Rowan (Notre-Dame, IN: University of Notre-Dame Press, 1995).

16. For an excellent collection of recent studies, see Juliette Dor, Lesley Johnson and Jocelyn Wogan-Browne, eds., *New Trends in Feminine Spirituality: The Holy Women of Liège and Their Impact* (Turnhout: Brepols, 1999).

17. See the different chapters in David Townsend and Andrew Taylor, eds., *The Tongue of the Fathers: Gender and Ideology in Twelfth-Century Latin* (Philadelphia: University of Pennsylvania Press, 1998).

18. Penelope Johnson, "The Cloistering of Medieval Nuns: Release or Repression, Reality or Fantasy" in *Gendered Domains: Rethinking Public and Private in Women's History*, ed. Dorothy O. Helly and Susan M. Reverby (Ithaca, NY: Cornell University Press, 1992), pp. 27–39; see also chapter 3 by Julie Hotchin below.

19. Constance H. Berman, "Were There Twelfth-Century Cistercian Nuns?" *Church History: Studies in Christianity and Culture* 68 (1999): 824–64. See also John A. Nichols and Lillian Shank, eds., *Hidden Springs: Cistercian Monastic Women*, Cistercian Studies Series 113A-113B (Kalamazoo, MI: Cistercian Publications, 1995), vols. 1–2.

20. Franz R. Felten reviews recent literature in "Zisterzienserinnen in Deutschland. Beobachtungen und Überlegungen zu Ausbreitung und Ordenszugehörigkeit," in *Unanimité et diversité cisterciennes. Filiations, réseaux, relectures du XIIe au XVIIe siècles. Actes du quatrième colloque international du CERCOR Dijon, 23–25 septembre 1998*, Centre Européen des recherches sur les congregations et ordres, Travaux et Recherches (Lyons: Publications de l'Université de Saint-Etienne, 2000), pp. 345–400, and more fully in "Der Zisterzorden und die Frauen," in *Weltverachtung und Dynamik*, ed. Harald Schwillus and Andreas Hölscher (Berlin: Lukas Verlag, 2000), pp. 5–135. On Eberbach in particular, see Yvonne Monsees, "Zisterzienserinnenklöster unter geistlicher Leitung Eberbachs," *Forschung und Forum* 3 (1989): 3–17.

21. Barbara Newman, "Flaws in the Golden Bowl: Gender and Spiritual Formation in the Twelfth Century," *Traditio* 45 (1989/90): 111–46, and reprinted in her volume of essays, *From Virile Woman to WomanChrist* (Philadelphia: University of Pennsylvania Press, 1995), pp. 19–45.

22. Küsters, *Der verschlossene Garten,* pp. 60–63.
23. Einar Mar Jonsson, *Le Miroir: Naissance d'un genre littéraire* (Paris: Les Belles Lettres, 1995).
24. I discuss Hildegard's debt to the Hirsau reform in "Hildegard of Bingen, Visions and Religious Reform in Twelfth-century Germany" in Rainer Berndt, ed., *Im Angesicht Gottes suche der Mensch sich selbst. Hildegard von Bingen 1098–1998,* Erudiri Sapientia 2 (Berlin: Akademie Verlag, 2001), pp. 325–42.
25. Constant J. Mews, *The Lost Love Letters of Heloise and Abelard: Perceptions of Dialogue in Twelfth-Century France* (New York: St. Martin's Press, 1999).
26. Jeffrey Hamburger, *Nuns as Artists: The Visual Culture of a Medieval Convent* (Berkeley: University of California Press, 1997), and *The Visual and the Visionary: Art and Female Spirituality in Late Medieval Germany* (New York: Zone Books, 1998).
27. See, for example, *Ancrene Wisse: Guide for Anchoresses,* trans. Hugh White (Harmondsworth: Penguin, 1993), and *Anchoritic Spirituality: Ancrene Wisse and Associated Works,* trans. Anne Savage and Nicholas Watson (New York: Paulist Press, 1991).
28. The publication of a Latin-German version of the *Speculum virginum,* ed. and trans. Jutta Seyfarth, Fontes Christiani 30.1–3 (Freiburg: Herder, 2001) will undoubtedly assist in making this work better known.

# CHAPTER 1

## VIRGINITY, THEOLOGY, AND PEDAGOGY IN THE *SPECULUM VIRGINUM*

*Constant J. Mews*

This chapter introduces the *Speculum virginum* as an original synthesis of teaching about women's religious life, composed in Germany in the first half of the twelfth century. It considers the evidence of a twelfth-century library catalogue of Hirsau, that it was written by a monk of Hirsau, known as Peregrinus, subsequently identified by Johannes Trithemius in the late fifteenth century as Conrad of Hirsau. The Speculum virginum was one of a number of pedagogically innovative writings by a prolific author, who delighted in creating fictional dialogues to provide instruction about the purpose of the religious life. The *Speculum virginum* puts forward the image of Theodora as a female disciple of Peregrinus, who instructs her in the meaning of true virginity and the correct relationship between flesh and spirit within the religious life. It provides a theology of the religious life for women that would be very influential in the Latin West until the eve of the Reformation.

The literature of spiritual formation tends to be neglected in surveys of medieval culture. Such writing is often assumed to be essentially pietistic and devoid of the intellectual rigor associated with treatises addressed to young men in the schools. Yet the *Speculum virginum*, an extended dialogue about the spiritual life for religious women, demands to be heard. Why was it that a treatise composed during the same decade that Heloise asked Peter Abelard for guidance about the religious life should be so widely studied between the mid-twelfth century and the very eve of the Reformation?

Some insight into the reasons for the long-term success of the *Speculum* may be found in the comments that Heloise made to Abelard at the outset of her third letter. She asked him for an account of the origins of the religious life for women as well as for a Rule specifically addressed to women, "which we perceive not to have been done by the Fathers."[1] No major treatise had emerged within ecclesiastical tradition as a definitive exposition of the principles of religious life for women comparable to the Rule of St. Benedict. The growing participation of women in religious life during the late eleventh and twelfth centuries created a demand for literature of edification that addressed their situation. While numerous small treatises were addressed to religious women in this period, the *Speculum virginum* stands apart not just in size but in theological sophistication. This is the work of a monastic teacher eager to provide his peers with instruction that they could usefully employ in their preaching to communities of religious women.

## The Author of the *Speculum virginum*

We know little for certain about the author of the *Speculum*. Our most detailed account is supplied by Johannes Trithemius (1460–1517). In his *Annales Hirsaugienses,* written between 1509 and 1514, Trithemius supplied a slightly more detailed account than he had given in his early writings:

> Also in these times there shone at the abbey of Hirsau the monk Conrad, who, hiding his name out of humility, calls himself Peregrinus [Pilgrim] in his writings. Formerly a listener and disciple of blessed William, he was a most learned man in every discipline and no less venerable in the observance of religion. He wrote many distinguished works under the name of Peregrinus, of which the following survive: a distinguished work which he titled *Mirror of Virgins,* eight books; a great volume on the Gospels for the cycle of the year; about the life of the spirit and the fruit of death, one book; and another which is titled *Matricularius,* one book; *Didascalon,* one book; *On Music and the Difference of the Tones,* one book; *On the Praises of St. Benedict* in heroic verse, one book. He also composed elegantly various homilies and several letters, which it would be excessively prolix and tedious to mention individually. For many years he was in charge of the schools in this abbey; he also educated several important and very learned disciples. He eventually died in his eightieth year and is buried as a servant of Christ with his predecessors in the main church.[2]

In 1492, the first time Trithemius mentioned the *Speculum virginum,* he identified its author simply as Peregrinus, "subtle in genius and truly eloquent in speech, concise, and very beautiful in words, but so full and brilliant in his opinions that he does not seem to be inferior to any of the ancients."[3] By 1494, for reasons that he does not explain, Trithemius was asserting that this author's true name was Conrad.[4] In the passage of the *Annales* quoted above, he added a few details that he had not mentioned earlier, such as that Conrad had once run the school at Hirsau and was buried as an octogenarian in the main church.

What are we to make of these claims, given Trithemius' reputation for idealizing the monastic past?[5] Trithemius was an assiduous scholar and note-taker who came across many manuscript books that have since disappeared. He had a particular devotion to Hildegard of Bingen (1098–1179), whose writings he helped make more widely known.[6] Encouraged to write the history of Hirsau by the abbot of Bursfeld, formerly the abbot of Hirsau, Trithemius looked at Conrad of Hirsau as embodying a fusion of monastic erudition and piety such as he wished to see restored in his own day.[7]

In the London (Eberbach) manuscript of the *Speculum virginum,* a prefatory letter is introduced simply with the rubric "C., last of the poor of Christ, to the holy virgins N. and N.: may you follow the joy of blessed eternity."[8] The name *Peregrinus* or Pilgrim reflects the author's attachment to the idea that we are all pilgrims in this world, longing for an eternal home: "All the saints of Christ coming either before or after the advent of Christ were always pilgrims and poor, and did not allow the path to be embraced in love as a homeland, as a stable resting place or as the glory of the world."[9] That he is a monk is evident from his frequent allusions to the monastic life. He also refers regularly to "the common life" *[vita communis],* a major theme of the Rule of St. Augustine, which emphasized that the apostles held all things in common.[10] At the end of part eight, Peregrinus reveals his Benedictine roots when he describes the path of humility as like climbing a dangerous ladder: "Do you not have a form of this kind of ladder passed on by our holy shepherd Benedict, whose Rule you strive to observe? For he says that the sides of this ladder constitute a form of heavenly discipline, providing steps for our body and soul."[11]

The name of Peregrinus is mentioned at the end of a twelfth-century list of ecclesiastical authors copied at Hirsau "with the greatest labor and maximum expense in the time of the aforementioned father William (1069–1091) and his successors, Bruno (1105–21), Volmar (1121–1157) and Manegold (1157–1165), without doubt an incomparable treasure: Josephus, Origen, Tertullian, Cyprian, Hilary, Augustine, Jerome, Orosius, John Chrysostom, Athanasius, Cassian, Cassiodorus, Isidore, Bede, Alcuin, Raban Maur, Haimo, Anselm of Canterbury, Peter Damian, Hermann, Bernold, William of Hirsau, a certain monk of Hirsau, known as Peregrinus."[12] The three authors mentioned immediately before Peregrinus were all distinguished German monastic figures of the eleventh century: Hermann of Reichenau (1013–1054), Bernold of Constance (d. 1100), and William of Hirsau (1026–1291). A second list follows, perhaps appended subsequently, in which various other texts are mentioned without attention to chronological order. Quite independently of Trithemius, Peter Wagner, abbot of Thierhaupten, reported ca. 1484: "Peregrinus, a monk of Hirsau, a man of outstanding genius, wrote many things, but what they are specially, I did not discover."[13]

Peregrinus' reputation at Hirsau is also confirmed by Johannes Parsimonius, its second evangelical abbot, who transcribed many manuscripts and inscriptions that have otherwise since disappeared.[14] Peregrinus was apparently one of the many teachers depicted on the wall of its summer refectory, constructed around 1500. Parsimonius records that various sayings attributed to Peregrinus, including two from the *Speculum virginum*, were inscribed on beams in the dormitory, alongside other quotations from the Fathers of the Church.[15] Parsimonius also attributes more works to Peregrinus than Trithemius.[16] Besides an eight-book version of the *Speculum virginum*, both mention *A Dialogue about Contempt or Love of the World*,[17] a treatise *On the Fruits of the Flesh and of the Spirit*,[18] an *Introduction to the Authors*,[19] a treatise on music and the tones, a cycle of homilies for the liturgical year, and a poetic life of St. Benedict in duple meter. Parsimonius attributes to this author an extended discussion of the Old and New Testaments, presented as a debate *[Altercatio]* between Paul and Gamaliel.[20] He also mentions certain other writings that have not so far been identified: books about St. Augustine, St. Paulinus, and St. Nicholas; commentaries on the Psalms, on Kings, and on the Gospels; a treatise *On the Grades of Humility;* epigrams on the Psalms and the Prophets; and songs about Job.[21] Parsimonius saw the *Speculum virginum* as only part of the output of a very prolific author.

In the 1960s Robert Bultot was able to confirm through detailed textual analysis that Trithemius was correct in identifying that one author wrote these different treatises.[22] He established that in two manuscripts from Eberbach and Cologne, the *Dialogue about Contempt or Love of the World* is followed by a number of texts by the same author, notably *On the Fruits of the Flesh and the Spirit* (wrongly printed among the works of Hugh of St-Victor) and a small text that accompanies an illustration of both the flesh, depicted as female, and the spirit, depicted as male, rising to God.[23] This passage, largely identical to a passage near the beginning of part eight of the *Speculum* (*SV* 8.8–25), also occurs within a visual narrative of the Gospels copied ca. 1175 in Regensburg.[24] There then follow two sizable and still-unstudied compositions, an *Address to God* and *About Inquiry of the Truth*, or *Sententie morales*.[25] While these treatises address a male audience, the *Speculum* reshapes these themes into a dialogue between a man and a woman.[26] Throughout all this literature runs the theme that the true monastic life is fully consistent with reasoned reflection on both Scripture and the world. Harmony rather than discord should prevail between flesh and spirit. In the dialogue between a monk and the secular cleric, the monk counters the cleric's justification for loving the world with an explanation that the world is not bad in itself but always has to be subordinated to the spirit.

The attitudes taught by Peregrinus in these writings are consistent with what we know about the monastic and intellectual concerns encouraged by William of Hirsau. A monk of St. Emmeram, Regensburg, William was celebrated both for his learning and for his zeal for reform, and was fond of literary dialogue as a way of developing an argument.[27] In his treatise on music, William criticized the theories of both Boethius and Guido of Arrezo for not appreciating the authority of ancient Greek theorists.[28] He presents these in the form of discussion with Otloh of St. Emmeram (ca. 1010–1070), who himself was much concerned about the correct use of pagan learning, but never became a public figure.[29] As abbot of Hirsau from 1069 to 1091 William reformed monastic life at many other houses throughout Germany. Ulrich of Zell praised William for eliminating the practice of parents offering their children to the monastic life simply because they were crippled or deformed in some way, rather than because of any conscious choice on the children's part. William's biographer singled out the importance he attached to poverty and simplicity in the monastic life and his unwillingness to accept any of the traditional gestures of submission accorded the abbot of a great monastery.[30] Although William drew on a number of the observances of Cluny, he did not emulate its practice of having a single abbot exercise authority over subordinate daughter houses. Zwiefalten, St. George, Petershausen as well as all other abbeys founded or reformed from Hirsau during the late eleventh and early twelfth centuries were constitutionally independent. They could adapt the liturgy of Hirsau each in their own way.[31] William attached great importance to building up libraries within all the monasteries that he founded or reformed.[32] In houses influenced by the Hirsau reform, the study of pagan authors came to occupy a central role in the monastic educational curriculum. The intellectual culture of Hirsau, however, simply extended patterns of education that William had absorbed at St. Emmeram in the mid-eleventh century, as theorized by Otloh. In his treatise on the instruction of both clerics and lay people, Otloh had developed the theme that it was important to develop imagery from nature if the unlettered were to be instructed in religious truth. The *Speculum virginum* continues this tradition.[33]

The concern of the *Speculum* with the pastoral care of women echoes the enthusiasm of William of Hirsau for the notion that women were as able as men to follow a strict life of detachment from the world.[34] As Urban Küsters has shown, it was a distinct feature of many of the houses influenced by William's reforms that women lived in communities physically adjacent to those of men.[35] At Zwiefalten, for example, founded from Hirsau in 1089, a separate community of women existed with its own *magistra* only a few hundred meters from the men's community. By 1138 the abbey housed some 70 monks, 130 lay brothers and 62 nuns (one of whom, Mathilda de Nifen is reported as having copied many of its manuscripts).[36] At the abbey of Disibodenberg, Jutta (1092–1136) and Hildegard (1098–1179) lived in an enclosure in close proximity to monks, installed by the archbishop of Mainz sometime before 1108. While the Rule of Benedict never concerned itself with the situation of female recluses living alongside monks, many houses influenced by the Hirsau reforms considered that such a practice actually enhanced the reputation of the community.

The literary and thematic concerns of the *Speculum virginum* so closely reflect those encouraged by William of Hirsau that it seems difficult to doubt the testimony of both the Hirsau library catalogue and of Trithemius that its author was a monk of Hirsau. It is quite possible that he could once have been a student of William of Hirsau and that he lived from about 1080 to 1150. This monastic author belonged to the same generation as Peter Abelard (1079–1142). In many ways, "Peregrinus" was responding to concerns similar to those raised by Heloise. He shared Abelard's belief that the true religious life was fully consistent with the demands of reason and should be available to women as much as to men. Whether his real name was Conrad, as Trithemius surmised, cannot be established with certainty. It cannot be doubted, however, that he was a significant monastic writer who synthesized many new ideas about both virginity and theology in the form of dialogue between himself and Theodora. In his own way, he was helping establish a new tradition of spiritual writing, one that addressed both women and men.

## The Argument of the *Speculum virginum*

The *Speculum virginum* emphasizes throughout that the virgin must always aim at the cultivation of humility and charity. This is fundamentally the same ethical path as Benedict urges on monks in his Rule. However, where the Benedictine Rule is written with only men in mind, the *Speculum* offers the image of a questioning but attentive woman as a model for other virgins of Christ to emulate in learning about their vocation. The *Speculum*

presents traditional teaching about the cultivation of humility and the ultimate goal of union with God through the form of lively dialogue and vivid
illustration. In a prefatory letter, attached after the work was completed, the
author describes the *Speculum* as a sign of "mutual love . . . so that you may
advance in the grace of the eternal spouse and that you may mourn less
about our absence." The letter concludes with a suggestion that the dialogue provides a substitute for being present in person: "In the mirror that
I have sent you consider the expression of your hearts; consider that if you
cannot understand everything which is written, not a small part of learning
is to listen to and love one who does understand" (*SV* Epist. 103–4).

The *Speculum* may initially have been written for a monastic pastor to read
aloud to religious women rather than to be read silently by women religious.
Monks could also draw benefit from its teaching by identifying themselves as
virgins of Christ. All known manuscripts of the Latin text come from male
religious communities.[37] They also all reproduce an identical series of *Nota*
signs in the margin (helpfully reproduced in the critical edition) that assist the
reader to identify the most significant parts of the argument. The *Speculum* engages in explaining the meaning of a life consecrated to virginity with the didactic clarity of a teacher firmly persuaded of the role of questioning dialogue
as a way of arriving at greater understanding.

The theme raised at the outset of the *Speculum virginum*, that inspired
words can constitute a mirror through which individuals can learn truths
about themselves, is deeply rooted in Christian tradition. Gregory the
Great makes a similar comment about the purificatory function of the
basin forged by Moses from the mirrors of women and used by Aaron and
his sons for ritual ablution (Exod. 38.8, 40.29).[38] While Augustine himself
had written a *Speculum* for the moral edification of the faithful,[39] the *Speculum virginum* gives much greater attention to providing a reasoned explanation of how virgins of Christ can come to self-understanding.

The author's driving argument throughout the work is that the goal of
the virgin of Christ is not the preservation of physical virginity but
progress in humility and true purity. "For what use is the flower of chastity,
if the fruit of action is lacking in purity of the body? . . . Therefore the
beauty of virginity is a kind of flower from the integrity of the body, but
the flower is not prevented from flowering when the virgin shows the
beautiful flower by good actions in divine praise" (1.289–97). Traditional
exhortations to virginity, from the patristic period to the early twelfth century, tended to focus on the purity of the angelic life and the absolute importance of spurning the life of the world.[40] In this perspective, the
preservation of physical virginity was essential to any attempt to regain the
life of the angels. The *Speculum* differs subtly from these traditional exhortations in developing a theology that emphasizes how the life of the flesh

has to be regulated by that of the spirit. Just as the *Dialogue about Contempt or Love of the World* teaches that true contempt for the world is based on understanding of the world, so the *Speculum virginum* teaches that true rejection of the world is a spiritual rather than a physical process. Aware of the dangers presented by excessive intimacy between men and women, the author emphasizes that the real threat to the religious life comes not from sexual pollution but from pride and complacency.

Part one of the *Speculum* argues that the true virginal life is a flower that has to bring forth fruit. It opens with a visual representation of the so-called "tree of Jesse," an image that explains how from the stock of Boaz and David came the Virgin, "like the branches of a terebinth" (Eccli. 24.22) from whom flowered her Son and thence the sevenfold gifts of the spirit (figure 1).[41] Peregrinus explains to Theodora the process of metaphor as a whole: Speaking of such verses as "Mountains of Israel, extend your branches and flower and bring forth fruit" (Eccli. 24.22), he explains:

> They create for a rational creature analogies drawn from non-rational and non-feeling things, so that we are least excited to progress by what is lesser, for which examples from what is elevated do not suffice. The nature of things has been offered as an example to humanity, as if to be used. For the donkey of the master has become the mistress [*magistra*] of one whose eyes have been so clouded by the shadow of blindness that he does not see what is evident to cattle. The flowering creature is witness of the perfect creator; while you hasten to him seeking your beginning, you imitate his order in the manner of a creature in its normal course (1.371–79).

Peregrinus' point is that the true religious life is not about rejecting nature but about understanding nature as a guide [*ductrix*] to the invisible things of God (1.386).

Peregrinus explains the vocation of the virgin in the most rational terms possible. His assumption that the state of being a virgin is inherently superior to that of being married or a widow is itself very traditional in patristic writing. However, by having Theodora ask questions about the religious life, or about the meaning of difficult passages in Scripture, the author searches for arguments based on reason rather than authority, in exactly the same way as St. Anselm of Canterbury (1033–1109) had sought to transform discussions of theology. Theodora's role is to offer Peregrinus a foil by which he can explain that the reader should not dally on the literal meaning of the flowers of Scripture at the expense of understanding their deeper mystical sense (1.505–8).

The author is as much concerned with enjoining purity of mind on those monks involved with ministering to women as on the women themselves: "For he feeds captured eyes on mud who is pleased more by beauty of body than of soul. What detestable madness! How many leaders, daughter, are there in the midst of the maiden tambourine players who do not promote them in discipline, but weaken them because, forgetful of the care of souls, they see nothing with their eyes open because of their physical desires" (1.566–69). Their problem lies not in the material world but in their incapacity to live according to reason. Theodora is given the phrase "God saw all that he made and they were truly good" (1.658–59) in order to allow Peregrinus to reflect that "the beauty of the world attests the Maker of everything in the nature of things by virtue of truth" (1.673–75). There is an echo here of the thought of Hugh of St-Victor (d. 1141) in the author's claim that the twin fulcrum of all things lies in the nature of all things as established by God [conditio rerum] and human redemption (1.685–95). The inspiration here, however, is perhaps more likely to be Gregory the Great than Hugh.[42] As if aware of a counterargument that emphasizes the universality of sin, the author has Theodora exclaim: "But I cannot wonder why the same prophet assigns cohabitation of a young man with a virgin to that most delightful and peaceful city, saying, 'The young man will dwell with the virgin and your sons shall dwell in you' [Isa. 62.5] when in this world such living together gives rise to no small danger, if the fear and love of Christ do not intervene. It is a mad thought to suspect anything of this kind in that kingdom, where the flower of uncorrupted nature is quite immutable and does not wish or can have such corruption" (1.766–74). Peregrinus then argues that in the heavenly Jerusalem there is no stain whatsoever in men and women living together in a pure conscience. He wants to push Theodora to greater understanding: "With open eyes, you see nothing. I sometimes want you to be a goat, not a mole. By nature, sight makes one animal sharp, whereas the darkness of the natural earth confuses the other" (1.797–99). The true meaning of this dwelling together of young men and women he explains as the union of Christ and the Church. This union of male and female is not just the goal of history but the original state of humanity as described in Genesis. To explain that the true virginal life is about growth in virtue, he concludes part one with an image of the virtues as flowers, nurtured by the four rivers, or four Gospels, that flow through Paradise.[43]

Having laid out general principles in the first part, the author devotes part two to defending the value of strict enclosure, the goal of which is to stop mental distraction. Theodora puts forward scriptural injunctions about "going out" that might seem to contradict the principle of enclosure in order for Peregrinus to show how sensuality always has to be subject to rationality in the human person. To explain his point, he tells a story of how a young cleric attached to a monastery became so eager to see and speak to one of the virgins that he crept into her bed when they were at prayer, only to be struck dead. Peregrinus goes on to explain that the sinful cleric was not permanently damned for his behavior. The nun in question engaged in so much prayer on his behalf with the other nuns (who had previously praised God for his being struck down) that a pious woman eventually saw in a vision that he had been freed from purgatory. Another example Peregrinus offers is that of Susanna, lusted after by the elders who watched her (2.347–71). The moral that Peregrinus drives home is that the goal of true virginity is interior virtue: "Do not glory, daughter because you carry the name of virgin, but rejoice *truly*[44] in this, that you have offered yourself for him, as a virgin in the reward of virginity. For it is praiseworthy not to be a virgin, but to have made a vow of purity of both flesh and spirit to him, who is both son of a virgin and spouse of virgins" (2.442–44). He advises avoiding excessive conversation with men (a practice Theodora observes is widespread), because it can disturb the hearts of those who talk (2.465–71).

As Morgan Powell demonstrates in the fifth chapter of this volume, the beginning of part three, introduced by Psalm 44.11–12, "Listen, daughter . . ." was the original beginning of the *Speculum*. Peregrinus reflects on the dignity of a virgin's calling and explains that what follows is a mirror by which virgins of Christ can consider, by reasoning and example, who they will be in the future. He then launches into an exhortation to remember always the presence of Christ and to love everyone in Christ. External decoration is as nothing, compared to this inner goal: "There may be among the virgins of Christ a virgin subtle and splendid in beauty, art, and genius, regular in prayer, but deceived by empty glory or lightness of behavior, distracted by various lusts, curious about everything with a vain mind, a spoiled lover of pleasures, surely you will not pronounce her to be of virginal integrity and a follower of the lamb? . . . Believe, virgin of the Lord, that one who looks within considers not only the integrity of the chaste body, but the virtue and intention of the heart. A penitent and humble widow pleases God more than an insolent and proud virgin" (3.226–31, 234–38).[45] Peregrinus is particularly opposed to those virgins who publicly commit themselves to chastity but have actually spurned the love and fear of God (3.343–49). He castigates those "who have the name of holiness" and live in houses next to monasteries, but who "secretly prostitute themselves and by this the whole Church is scandalized" (3.351–58). Every passage in Scripture that relates to false beauty is used to contrast the proud virgin with the true bride of Christ.

Part four is about pride and humility. It begins with two contrasting visual images, one showing how vices all emanate from pride, the other how virtues all spring from love, in turn the fruit of humility (figures 2 and 3). The author includes a detailed analysis of both the virtues and vices, drawing on a separate treatise, *On the Fruits of the Flesh and of the Spirit* (not written as a dialogue), to show how women have to confront the same moral questions as men.[46] Identical passages occur in his *Dialogue about Contempt or Love of the World,* except that references to monks are replaced by those to virgins. While the issues of behavior with which he is concerned are not particularly gender specific, he does seek out images of strong women in Scripture and classical antiquity who can serve as role models in the pursuit of virtue. Drawing largely from Orosius, he reminds Theodora of a range of powerful women who overcame male tyrants: Jahel conquering the king of the Madianites; Judith being victorious over Holophernes; Semiramis of Babylon; Thamar, queen of the Scyths; the Amazons; and the queens Marpesia and Lamphetus, who ruled their kingdoms with great discipline (4.103–609; figure 4). Theodora encourages him to give these and other examples to demonstrate the capacity of the virgin of Christ, assuming devotion to be a virile quality: "You proceed in a most pleasing course to us, adding by words and examples strength of a virile spirit to women's hearts" (4.610–11). As in part three, Peregrinus warns that if the most brilliant, noble, and learned virgin does not have true humility, she cannot be pleasing to Christ (4.752–58). Humility in turn is simply the basis for the charity, "the flower and fruit of eternity" (4.832), that she needs to show to all people.

This leads Peregrinus in part five to present Mary, "leader of the virgins" [*princeps virginum*] as a focus of devotion. Extending the high Mariology in the treatise of Paschasius Radbertus about Mary's Assumption, always circulated as a letter of Jerome, Peregrinus describes her as the wisdom of God existing before creation. He sees her as a figure who can be discerned throughout history, whether as the garden of Paradise, the ark of Noah, the tabernacle of the Old Testament, or the vessel of the Incarnation (5.33–161). He even goes so far as to describe Mary as "reconciler of the world" [*reconciliatrix mundi:* 5.369–70], an expression not used by any of the Fathers, but consistent with the high status accorded Mary in reformed monasticism at the time.[47] Mary embodied the wisdom by which all creation was ordered, through which one could learn about God (5.199–234). She was the supreme achievement of the Creator (5.472–73). Peregrinus identifies Mary as one of the wheels of the four-wheeled chariot [*quadriga*] led not just by Mary and Christ but also by John the Baptist and John the Evangelist. Traditionally the four wheels (or horses) of the *quadriga* of Aminadab (Song of Songs 6.11) were interpreted either as the four evangelists or sometimes as the four virtues. Mary was now put on a par with these three other figures.

Peregrinus' goal in promoting the example of Mary is to exhort virgins of Christ to remain true to their vocation and not be seduced by those who wish to pollute body and soul (5.634–63). He has Theodora put a question that is not dissimilar to the point that Heloise was putting to Abelard in her letter of complaint about the way the religious life was being interpreted: "Since Scripture says that all things are pure to the pure (Tit. 1.5), I wonder whether these or any things created for man are forbidden to the saints. For although the apostle says 'Do not get drunk on wine, in which is debauchery,' I do not think that it is of the nature of wine to be a vice of this kind, but to be harmful when someone drinks to excess" (5.664–68). This is an opinion with which Peregrinus, like Abelard, agrees. Abstinence is wise only because people cannot control themselves. The goal of union with Christ is perfect love [caritas]: "Do you see that the perfection of love is the purification of sinners, the love of the inner light arisen in Christ?" (5.861–63) Peregrinus also reminds Theodora of the example of Agnes, Lucia, Cecilia, Agatha, and of the 11,000 virgins to spur her on to the essential virtues of chastity, charity, and humility. One cannot exist without the others: "Chastity without charity is a lamp without oil. Take away the oil and you have extinguished the lamp" (5.1004–6).[48] His complaints are directed as much against those charged with looking after religious women as with the women themselves. "Woe is me, how many monasteries of virgins in our times seem to be tottering in this disease in that judges and priests of a former time are shown to be represented, by whose perverse sense of lust, holy virgins are deluded and deserve from them eternal shame and punishment, from whose example they ought to hope for the grace and glory of light" (5.1057–62). A long sermon is included here excoriating male pastors who follow the flesh more than the spirit (5.1049–1183). Peregrinus always seeks to resolve these situations by dwelling on interior disposition. Theodora suggests in conclusion that "among men and women exercising the practice of piety in equal profession, knowledge of divine presence is necessary, without which the rule of all discipline and regular life collapses" (5.1239–42). The wise virgin needs to watch out for false shepherds (5.1285–87).

This leads Peregrinus to reflect on the familiar theme of the wise and the foolish virgins. The difference between them lies in their intention (6.119): "virginity of the flesh is of no use without integrity of the mind (6.176–77) . . . For humility is the mother of charity, which is signified through the oil; charity is the glory or reward of holy humility" (6.183–84). He singles out the continuous vigilance needed to discern between good and evil, virtue and vice, spirit and flesh (6.802–4) and to warn against those who display the appearance of holiness but are far removed from it in their minds (6.808–10, 823–25). Christ had been shown to dwell as much in married women and in widows as in virgins.

Peregrinus is aware that this seems to conflict with traditional patristic teaching about the hundredfold reward for virgins, compared to the thirtyfold reward for the married and the sixtyfold reward for widows.[49] Part seven of the *Speculum* is devoted to justifying this doctrine by arguments drawn from reason and pagan antiquity. Peregrinus dwells on the familiar theme of the trials of the married state and the freedom brought by virginity, but, like Abelard in his writing for Heloise, justifies his argument by pagan examples. Theodora asks: "Talk in this way, I beg, about the marriages of the gentiles, so that we may be stirred to caution by examples taken from them" (7.243–45). He similarly has no difficulty in finding examples of virtuous widows from Scripture and antiquity *[in ethnicismo]* to get Theodora to agree that widowhood is preferable to a second marriage (7.532–34). He supports traditional monastic teaching by appealing to precedents from pagan antiquity. Peregrinus similarly defends virginity by quoting from the examples from pagan antiquity supplied by Jerome and Orosius (7.705–98). When Theodora asks why rewards should be different for virgins, widows and married folk, the only argument that Peregrinus can come up with is that varying effort demands varying reward. Her position is the voice of reason: "I weigh up the difference in merits and rewards of these three grades, but no virtue is to be conceded to them in deserving the fruit of reward unless the spirit dominates the flesh in everyone. For it seems to me that the flesh is the cause of victory among the good, just as it is of struggle" (7.858–64). Peregrinus defends the traditional ranking of virgins as above married people and widows, but explains that spiritual reward always is earned by the life of the spirit rather than by position in society.

In part eight, Peregrinus continues the debate in terms of a comparison with what he sees as the crucial distinction, between the flesh *[caro]* and the spirit or breath *[spiritus]* that gives true life to that flesh. As earlier in the *Speculum*, the author expands on ideas that he had raised in his discussion of the virtues and the vices, *On the Fruits of the Flesh and the Spirit*.[50] Whether addressing women or men, the author's concern is to define the right relationship between the flesh and the spirit. Traditional monastic writing followed the Pauline emphasis, often picked up by Augustine, that flesh and spirit were always in conflict (Gal. 5.17). In the *Speculum*, Theodora hints at the argument that Peregrinus seeks to present, that flesh and spirit are not contrasting principles but both essential to creation: "As I see it, these steps that you put forward, namely something good and something better, flesh and spirit, if they follow their paths in right order, they lead indubitably to their beginning *[principium]*, namely that best step, which is God himself. For if, as you say, the spirit is subject to reason, the flesh to spirit, the complete person *[totus homo]* is subject to the Creator"

(8.100–105). Although the image (figure 5) that accompanies this discussion is often titled "the struggle of flesh and spirit," it in fact illustrates how reason and wisdom, both linked to the arms of Christ, assist both flesh and spirit, separated by free will, to rise to the top of the ladder to greet Christ. While at the ladder's base is the "vain deceiver," above this is the figure of the Law, bearing the command "thou shall not lust" [non concupisces]. Characteristic of the gendered structure of this thought, flesh, described as a good thing [caro: bonum], is presented as female, while spirit, something better [spiritus: melius] is depicted as male.[51] In classical Augustinian theology, the perfect union of flesh and spirit is considered as unique to the person of Christ, and only through grace is humanity able to overcome this conflict. It was extended by Bernard of Clairvaux in his reflection on how the individual soul is able to be healed through being visited by the Word of God. Peregrinus is much less interested than Bernard in the psychology of the individual soul or in notions of original sin. Instead he develops the theme that the true religious restrains herself to recover the perfect harmony of flesh and spirit of humanity in its original form. In some respects, his thinking is similar to that of Hugh of St-Victor. Peregrinus gives much less attention than Hugh, however, to the role of sacraments as vehicles of grace through which the soul is able to return to completeness. His approach is a more consciously ascetic one, putting weight on the need for the individual to subordinate worldly impulses through reason and awareness of truth: "Reason rules in vain over vice, or spirit over the flesh if that soul by which the body is animated is not subdued to truth. Therefore knowledge of truth is the matter or task of the soul who advances to God through faith and love, away from worldly relations" (8.250–52).

Rather than valuing the role of ecclesiastical structures and rituals, Peregrinus prefers to emphasize that the true religious is only a pilgrim in this world (8.426–87). As earlier in the Speculum, he complains about those who do not understand their calling: "Daughter, there are many virgins who have changed their habit to seek Christ, they submit their necks to monastic rules, but they do not consider much by what order or principle turning to the religious life should proclaim a beginning to conversion. . . . Many virgins or widows, when they reach the haven of monastic peace, measure the promising beginnings of their religious life by the peace of the life they have found; by this they have attained not so much the shore of great peace, but shipwreck and the judgment of death" (8.595–98). The analogy that Peregrinus prefers is that of growth in the natural world:

> Peregrinus: . . . Flowers are the beginnings of conversion, fruits are the exercise of effort and perseverance. Do you not know from what any things generated in the soil take their strength?

Theodora: Mildness of the air, fruitfulness of the soil, now showers, now sun, now heat, now cold.

Peregrinus: Thus the converted human being takes growth by the peace or effort of righteousness, and turns all things struggling against the holy will to a reward by virtue of patience. (8.628–35)

His message to the virgin of Christ is that she should not take any comfort from her status. The essence of the virginal life is "chastity of spirit and body, [and] strength of patience in observance of the evangelical law, through which one arrives at the glory of divine love" (8.719–21). True virginity is thus interior rather than external (8.725–26). Only at the end of this discussion, does Peregrinus introduce an image known to anyone familiar with the Rule of Benedict, that of the ladder of humility. Having introduced this image at the beginning of part eight, Peregrinus now reminds Theodora that she had read about a virgin who glimpsed this ladder in a vision in the deeds of the martyrs. By alluding to Perpetua's vision of a ladder that climbed to heaven, he provides a female authority figure for an image more widely known as the ladder of humility described by St. Benedict, "whose Rule you strive to follow" (8.756–62).[52]

Part nine begins with a more dramatic visual image of the ever-present dangers that beset the virgin soul as she rises to God, assisted by reason and wisdom. Although it shows personified figures, probably reason and wisdom, resisting the devil, a male figure who bears two swords has climbed the ladder and is threatening the virgin soul even as she is about to greet Christ. In the accompanying text, Peregrinus expounds more fully the meaning of this notion that the bride of Christ is never at rest but continuously has to fight off dangerous temptations that beset her. These temptations are not sexual. Rather they concern worldly glory and complacency with the external structures of the religious life: "If you follow a naked Christ with voluntary poverty, why do you delight in fine foods, and extravagant clothes as if renouncing the world was about mixing delightful poultices in the cloister? Neither the mother of the Lord went out to battle in this way with Thecla and the other martyrs, nor did the Amazons fight the virile sex in this way, with their shields thrown away" (9.194–99).[53] The warnings that he gives could be given just as much to monks as to virgins. Peregrinus emphasizes not religious experience but the complacency of many religious: "Listen, daughter, many men wish to be wise, but they do not know how that wisdom ought to be sought. For they seek outside themselves what is rather within themselves" (9.487–89).

The final temptation is raised by Theodora: "But I ask what is to be said about those who, raising their brow about lineage, exceed the limit of grace among other sisters, distinguishing their condition and through this detracting from common nature by private self-glorification?" (9.499–502) This question allows Peregrinus to distinguish between false and true nobility: "The greatest nobility of man is a noble spirit, one who cultivates virtues and is an enemy of vice. . . . True nobility is therefore to be measured more in the spirit than in the glory of parents" (9.510–11. 523–25).

Theodora makes a revealing observation not unlike one made by Hildegard in *Scivias* in relation to boys offered to the religious life: "How many adult women we see in monasteries repenting of their sacred vow, shown to have been proclaimed by parental concern or monastic discipline at a tender age. They wish wrongly in vain for what they cannot have, because they serve God with an ungrateful mind; what fruit for their effort will they have, I ask?"[54] In such cases the widow is clearly to be preferred to the virgin (9.678–79). "Human conscience is the place of damnation or reward" (9.681–82). Peregrinus advises recalling the presence of God to rise above all distraction (9.950–51) and urges Theodora: "If you want to have peace, take care to not to denigrate anyone, not to condemn, not to judge" (9.1089–90). He concludes by taking her through various steps of the way of life of a virgin, all of which focus on interiority: purity of mind and body, rejection of external luxury, inclining the heart to love of Christ, reflecting with Mary on the Word of God, and then continuing in perseverance without complacency (9.1168–1206). At length he comes to Theodora's question about the virgin who has fallen from her state: "But what shall I say about fallen virgins? What I read, what I feel, I do not dare proclaim. But I shall speak. Fixed remedies have been determined for all criminal sins, that is murder, theft, adultery and others of this kind, but for veiled virgins, committed to Christ by the pontifical ring, brides of the Lord kept in the protection of the angels, nothing is defined by the holy fathers about satisfaction" (9.1236–42). Peregrinus insists that one should not despair about a fallen virgin. "Let her rise in virile fashion, further let her stand strongly, let her beat faithfully at the source of life, and let her be as vigilant about obtaining pardon as she was negligent beforehand about her ruin" (9.1247–49). This leads him to dwell on the working of grace, which is greater than any sinner.

In the original eight-book version, equivalent to *SV* 3.1–10.397, the *Speculum* concluded with an extended prayer in which Peregrinus gives thanks to God for revealing himself in such a wonderful way through creation. In the enlarged version, this prayer begins part ten. Although not a formal theological discussion, the prayer articulates a theme that had underpinned the *Speculum* as a whole, that it is through inquiry into truth that the mind is excited to inner things. By moving from external images, the mind can move to interior understanding (10.93–99). Much of the prayer's text is identical to the *Allocutio ad Deum,* on which it may be based.[55]

In parts eleven and twelve, Peregrinus lifts the discussion to a new level by exploring the meaning of the seven pillars of wisdom. The final image (figure 6) of the house of wisdom, shows how the gifts of the spirit flow from Christ, in turn generated from the Virgin and the stock of Jesse. It connects to the image presented at the opening of the *Speculum* (figure 1). He also returns to his imagery of flowers and fruit as images of the virtues, sketched out in part one. All things have their *principium* in this sevenfold spirit, through which the mind is raised toward God (11.152–74). Peregrinus is defining the nature of knowledge as much as offering exhortation: "Wisdom is the intellectual knowledge of eternal things, learning indeed is rational knowledge of temporal things. The former belongs to contemplating divine things in God, the latter to disposing human things for God; what is to be preferred to this, is to be entrusted to your judgment" (11.432–36). Peregrinus reflects on theological discussion taking place outside the cloister but is wary of its depth: "How many Christian philosophers dispute about heavenly things, how true and how subtle is what they understand by their own learning about good things to come, yet they do not learn by their studies to taste for themselves what they know" (11.438–47). He is concerned that rational enquiry should be pursued at the expense of a personal experience of divine wisdom. Theodora is given the wise word, when she is asked whether she thinks sinful eloquence is to be preferred to holy simplicity: "On the contrary, it is not to be equaled, because I approve the silence of the simple soul more that the noise of eloquence in pompous words" (11.525–26). Peregrinus then asks her if she has been into a church, "illuminated by the beauty of glass" to make her realize that nothing beautiful could ever be seen without light (11.656–69). The analogy provides an excellent synthesis of his fundamentally very simple yet consistent pedagogical technique and theological vision. While Hugh of St-Victor structures his teaching around the notion of sacrament, Peregrinus accords particular value to our recognition of the manifold gifts of the spirit. Visual examples such as about the glass in a church come naturally to his aid. Theodora puts it simply: "Your opinion is most true, that whatever good the soul possesses, it holds by the approach of divine light, which shines" (11.675–76). Only at this point in the *Speculum* does Peregrinus discuss the nature of the unity of the human and divine in Christ (11.797–829). He reflects on his major theme, the gifts of the spirit (11.830–1013). In part twelve, he relates these to the petitions voiced in the Lord's Prayer. Christ is thus presented not as the object of devotion but as the medium through which the Christian soul seeks to be filled by the Holy Spirit.

The *Speculum virginum* concludes with a bridal song *[Epithalamium]* of the virgins of Christ, a hymn of praise that celebrates the goal of religious life in terms of the union of the beloved with her beloved, the bride and the bridegroom of the Song of Songs. It celebrates the rich flowers in that garden of Paradise in ways that recall the allegorization that Peregrinus had provided in part one of the *Speculum*. By being written to be sung as alternate verses, by one side of the choir to another, the community ritually reenacts the final union in Paradise. The first letter of each verse of the bridal song spells out an antiphon celebrating both the Father by whose grace the Mother stands as a rose for all time and the virginal Bride, whom God has kept hidden since the beginning of time. The role of the true virgins of Christ is to prepare themselves for this perfect union, by cultivating humility, patience, and, above all, love.

## Conclusion

The obscurity in which Peregrinus cloaks his identity is significant. He was not someone who wanted to play a major role in ecclesiastical politics or to promote new structures of religious life. He was a moralist, with an intensely personal vision of the world. As someone committed to returning to the values of an idealized early Church, he shared much in common with Hugh of St-Victor and Bernard. In presenting his arguments in the form of questioning dialogue, he was like St. Anselm. At the same time, his vision of religious life was markedly different from theirs. He was not particularly interested in doctrinal debate or in applying Aristotelian logic to theological questions. Because he wanted to present what he understood to be the true teaching of St. Benedict to women committed to the life of virginity, he did not need to spend time on issues with which they were not particularly concerned. He wanted to share with these women the same values that he wanted to convey to his monks, in other treatises. Like Abelard, he saw women who devoted themselves to religion as capable of achieving a degree of moral integrity denied those who immersed themselves in worldly politics.

The continuing popularity of the *Speculum* in the later Middle Ages undoubtedly has much to do with its focus on the need for simplicity of life. It proclaimed that women could imitate the values of the early Church by retreating from the world. In the later Middle Ages, the brothers and sisters of the common life found inspiration in an earlier wave of piety that had transformed the fortunes of so many monastic houses in the late eleventh and early twelfth century. The reform of monastic life promoted by William of Hirsau was one of the many movements in religious life in this period that influenced a new way of thinking about religious life, as important in its day as pietism in the eighteenth century. The large number of women's monastic communities established or reformed in this period provoked new reflection on what values both women and men in such communities ought to pursue. The *Speculum virginum* was a composition, combining literary dialogue, visual art, and music in a way that responded creatively to this new situation.

Even if Peregrinus was indeed a monk of Hirsau, as the Hirsau library catalogue reports, Hirsau did not remain at the forefront of reform after the mid-twelfth century. The reforming zeal that animated the monks of Hirsau during the time of William of Hirsau and his successor, Abbot Gebhard, inevitably changed with the advent of Henry V in 1105 and official approval for movements of monastic reform. In 1105, when Bruno, a canon of noble birth and *matricularius* of the cathedral of Speyer, came to replace Gebhard (elected bishop of Speyer), there was no universal agreement about the choice.[56] Under Bruno's successor, Volmar, consecrated in 1121 at the abbey of St. Alban in Mainz by Archbishop Adalbert, Hirsau increased its wealth, but lost a number of its monks to communities where the observance was more strict, such as the Cistercians. Sometime between 1130 and 1143 Abbot Volmar obtained papal support for insisting that such monks should return to their mother abbey.[57] Some monks of Hirsau approached Hildegard with complaints about their abbot in 1153/54, prompting her to exchange letters with Abbot Manegold after his election in 1156. The abbey was entering a period of slow decline that would not be arrested until a moment of renewed monastic vigor in the fifteenth century.[58] Trithemius' research into the writings of Peregrinus or Conrad of Hirsau was part of a broader narrative about a monastic community that had known both greatness and decline.

Peregrinus' comments in part nine of the *Speculum virginum* about the difference between true and false nobility had a particular relevance at a time when the role of noble birth in recruitment to religious life was under much debate. At Hirsau itself, Abbot Volmar's tendency to align himself closely with local nobility was disliked by those monks who emphasized the importance of poverty and humility. By the mid-twelfth century, the impetus for reform was shifting away to reformed Augustinian houses such as Andernach and Frankenthal and to the Cistercians, as at Eberbach. At Andernach, Tenxwind's criticism (ca. 1150) of what she considered elitist policies being pursued by Hildegard of Bingen reflects a wider reaction against reforming values that she felt were being betrayed by Benedictines who identified too closely with the existing social order. By the thirteenth century, mendicant friars and Cistercian monks were taking the lead in being involved in ministering to communities of religious women.[59] The values of interiority and austerity promoted in the *Speculum virginum* exercised a particular appeal within a Cistercian milieu.

The *Speculum virginum* presents an ideal of austere simplicity for the virgin of Christ living within the confines of the cloister. The treatise offers far more, however, than just an extended exhortation to sexual purity and rejection of the world. It employs innovative pedagogical techniques to develop a theology of the religious life, centered on imitation of the Virgin as Bride of Christ and a vision of the fundamental harmony between flesh and spirit, the material and the spiritual. Rather than dwelling on the divide between flesh and spirit, Peregrinus explains how the flesh needs to be subject to the spirit. The image of the woman who devoted herself to inner purity provided him with an ideal model of Christian behavior. The visual images that provide the framework for the *Speculum virginum* help the person who views the treatise to understand this message. When Hildegard of Bingen developed her own, particularly original way of explaining the relationship between the physical and the spiritual in terms of the viridity [*viriditas*] underpinning creation, she may have been reacting against the more structured way of thinking presented in the *Speculum*.[60] In his own way, Peregrinus was providing an authoritative model from a male perspective of how a teacher should instruct religious women in the path of virtue and understanding. It was a model that enjoyed enduring influence within many religious communities throughout Europe from the mid-twelfth century to the eve of the Reformation.

## Notes

1. J. T. Muckle, ed. "The Letter of Heloise on Religious Life and Abelard's First Reply," *Mediaeval Studies* 17 (1950): 242; *The Letters of Abelard and Heloise,* trans. B. Radice, (Harmondsworth: Penguin, 1974), p. 159.

2. Johannes Trithemius, *Annales Hirsaugienses,* Munich, Bayerische Staatsbibliothek Clm 703, fol. 190: "Claruit his quoque temporibus [i.e., the abbacy of Volmar, 1121–1157] in hirsaugiensi cenobio Conradus monachus qui nomen suum ex humilitate occultans peregrinum in suis se lucubrationibus nuncupat. Beati Wilhelmi quondam auditor atque discipulus, vir in omni sciencia scripturarum doctissimus et non minus religionis observantia venerandus: qui sub nomine peregrini scripsit multa preclara opuscula: de quibus extant subiecta. Ad theodoram sanctimonialem opus insigne quod prenotavit speculum virginum li. viii. In evangelia per circulum anni volumen magnum. De vita spiritus et fructu mortis li i. Et alius qui prenotatur matricularius li i. Didascalon li i. De musica et differentia tonorum li. i. De laudibus sancti Benedicti carmine heroico li. i. Sermones quoque varios omelias simul et epistolas plures eleganter composuit: quorum mentionem facere singulatim nimis prolixum foret ac tediosum. Multis annis monachorum scolis in hoc cenobio prefuit: et plures discipulos

insignes atque doctissimos educavit. Obiit tandem octogenarius cum patribus suis in maiori cenobio ut servus Christi sepultus."

3. Trithemius, *Catalogus illustrium virorum Germaniae* [Mainz, 1495], ed. Marquard Freher, *Opera Historica* (Frankfurt, 1601; reprinted Frankfurt: Minerva, 1966), 1: 136–37: "ingenio subtilis et eloquio valde disertus, brevis et pulcherrimus, sed copiosus et nitidus in sententiis, adeo, nulli priscorum videatur inferior." For full discussion of the passage in Trithemius, *De illustribus viris ordinis sancti Benedicti* [1492], first printed in Cologne 1575 but not included in Freher's edition of the *Opera Historica* (1966), see Constant J. Mews, "Monastic Educational Culture Revisited: The Witness of Zwiefalten and the Hirsau reform," in *Medieval Monastic Education*, ed. George Ferzoco and Carolyne Muessig (London: Leicester University Press, 2000), pp. 182–97.

4. Trithemius, *De scriptoribus ecclesiasticis* [Basel, 1494], *Opera Historica*, ed. Freher, 1: 276; although Trithemius repeats the claim that *SV* had eight books, he provides the incipit of the twelve-book version, "Collaturo tecum...." See also *Chronicon Hirsaugiense* [1495–1503; Basel, 1559], ed. Freher, 2: 90–91.

5. On Trithemius, see Klaus Arnold, *Johannes Trithemius (1462–1516)*, 2nd ed. (Wurzburg: Ferdinand Schöningh, 1991), and Noel Brann, *The Abbot Trithemius (1462–1516): The Renaissance of Monastic Humanism* (Leiden: Brill, 1981). On his so-called forgeries see Nikolaus Staubach, "Auf der Suche nach der verlorenen Zeit: Die historiographischen Fiktionen des Johannes Trithemius im Lichte seines wissenschaftlichen Selbstverständnisses," in *Fälschungen im Mittelalter. Internationaler Kongress der Monumenta Germaniae Historica München, 16–19 September 1986*, ed. Horst Fuhrmann (Hannover: Hiersemann, 1986), 5 vols., 1: 263–307.

6. Michael Embach, "Trithemius als Propagator Hildegards," in *Hildegard von Bingen in ihrem historischen Umfeld. Internationaler wissenschaflicher Kongress zum 900 jährigen Jubiläum 13–19 September 1998, Bingen am Rhein*, ed. Alfred Haverkamp (Mainz: Philipp von Zabern, 2000), pp. 561–98.

7. On Trithemius' close connection to the abbot of Hirsau, see Arnold, *Johannes Trithemius*, p. 46 and Brann, *The Abbot Trithemius*, pp. 82–83, 107–111.

8. *SV* Epist. 1–2: "Ultimus Christi pauperum C. virginibus sacris N. N. Gaudium assequi beatae perennitatis." Not all MSS carry this rubric, Seyfarth, p. 40*.

9. *SV* 8.475–77; cf. 1 Cor. 5.6–8; *SV* 6.855–56; 8.273–76; 8.437–46.

10. The *vita communis* is referred to in *SV* 2.63, 125–29, 177; 8.595, 611, 716; 9.22, 497, 634, 659. On the *vita communis*, see *SV* 3.54; 4.421–25; 8.165, 223.

11. *SV* 8.759; Benedict, *Regula* 7.6–9, *La Règle de S. Benoît*, ed. Adalbert de Vogüé, Schr 181 (Paris: Cerf, 1972).

12. Gottfried Lessing edited this catalogue within "Des Klosters Hirschau. Gebäude, übrige Gemälde, Bibliothek und älteste Schriftsteller," in *Werke*, ed. Albert von Schirnding, 8 vols. (Munich: Carl Hanser, 1974), 6:

491–507, especially 498–99, reprinted by Gustavus Becker, *Catalogi Bibliothecarum Antiqui* (Bonn: M. Cohen, 1885), p. 219. The catalogue is found in the Wolfenbüttel but not in the Tübingen copy of Parsimonius' notebook (see n. 14 below). On the library of Hirsau, see Felix Heinzer, "Buchkultur und Bibliotheksgeschichte Hirsaus," in *Hirsau St Peter und Paul 1091–1991*, ed. K. Schreiner, Forschungen und Berichte der Archäologie des Mittelalters in Baden-Württemberg, Band 10/2 (Stuttgart: Konrad Theiss, 1991), pp. 259–96.

13. Bernards, p. 15, and more fully in his dissertation, *Die Handschriftliche Überlieferung*, p. 429 (Introduction, n. 9 above), quoting from Wagner's *Congestum monachorum illustrium:* "Peregrinus, monachus Hirsaugiensis, vir praecellentis ingenii, scripsit multa, sed que sint specialiter, non inveni." Whether completed in 1484 (according to Bernards) or in 1493, as claimed by Arnold, p. 117 n. 20 (n. 5 above), Wagner was writing without knowledge of Trithemius.

14. On Parsimonius, see Waldemar Kramer, *Johannes Parsimonius. Leben und Wirken des zweiten evangelischen Abtes von Hirsau (1525–1588)* (Frankfurt: Waldemar Kramer, 1980). His notebook is now Wolfenbüttel, Herzog August Bibliothek Wolfenbüttel Cod. 134.1 Extravagantes, fols. 2–194v. A sixteenth-century copy is held at Tübingen, Universitätsbibliothek Mh 164. I am indebted to Felix Heinzer of the Württembergische Landesbibliothek, Stuttgart, for pointing out that Parsimonius copied out an important history of Hirsau on fols. 2–4 of the Tübingen copy, "transcribed from a certain Hirsau manuscript," that confirms otherwise unsubstantiated claims made by Trithemius about the early history of the abbey.

15. Tübingen, Mh 164, fol. 40. Two are from the *Speculum virginum* (9.492 and 418–20); there was also an unidentified quotation: "Peregrinus. Iam Dei regnum possidere incipit, cui in amore aeternorum praesens gloria vilescit." His image was on the wall nearest the kitchen, according to a note in the margin of fol. 31.

16. Lessing, ed. *Werke* 6: 505.

17. Robert Bultot, ed.*Dialogus de mundi contemptu vel amore, attribué à Conrad d'Hirsau. Extraits de l'Allocutio ad deum et du De veritatis inquisitione. Textes inédits*, Analecta Mediaevalia Namurcensia 19 (Louvain: Editions Nauwelaerts, 1966).

18. Parsimonius conflates two works distinguished by Trithemius, the *Matricularius* or *Dialogus de mundi contemptu vel amore* (inc. "Cum manifestum sit") and *De vita spiritus et fructu carnis* or *De fructibus carnis et spiritus* (inc. "Cum omnis divine pagine sermo id intendat"), erroneously printed among the works of Hugh of St-Victor in PL 176: 997–1010.

19. R. B. C. Huygens, ed., *Accessus ad Auctores. Bernard d'Utrecht. Conrad d'Hirsau, Dialogus super Auctores* (Leiden: Brill, 1970), pp. 71–131.

20. Seyfarth, p. 39*; see *Altercatio Synogogae et Ecclesiae*, printed anonymously in *Index Bibliorum*, ed. D. Chuonrado Pelopus (Cologne: Novasianus, 1537). See Robert Bultot, "L'auteur de l'Altercatio Synagogae et Ecclesiae

Conrad de Hirsau?" *RTAM* 32 (1965), 263–76. It had been attributed to Conrad in 1511 by a monk of Hirsau called Johannes Rapolt (Stuttgart, Landesbibliothek IV, 27, fol. 1) who says that he found it in the manuscript entitled *matricularius*, suggesting that this manuscript also contained Conrad's *Dialogus de mundi contemptu vel amore.*

21. In his *De scriptoribus* (n. 4 above), Trithemius gives the incipit of these treatises: *De musica et tonis:* "Musica est secundum cuiusdam"; *Homiliae in evangelios per cyclum anni:* "Quia in litera veteris testamenti"; *De laudibus S. Benedicti,* metrice, lib. 1: "Luce velut solem."

22. Bultot, nn. 17 and 20 above and n. 26 below.

23. Oxford, Bodleian Library, Laud Misc. 377, fol. 83v, copied at Eberbach ca. 1200 and Cologne, Historisches Archiv GB 4o 206, from the first half of the fifteenth century (from the brothers of the Holy Cross). See Bultot, *Dialogus,* 31–33 (n. 17 above). This folio of the Eberbach MS is illustrated alongside that of the Eberbach *SV* by Nigel Palmer, *Zisterzienser und ihre Bücher. Die mittelalterliche Bibliotheksgeschichte von Kloster Eberbach im Rheingau* (Regensburg: Schnell und Steiner, 1998), pp. 78–79. In the Cologne copy, the flesh is personified as male rather than as female. This image in the *K* copy of *SV* is reproduced in plate 11 of Seyfarth's edition.

24. Cheryl Goggin reproduces this page of the *De laudibus crucis* (Munich, Bayerische Staatsbibliothek, Clm 14159, f. 6) in her dissertation, "The Illuminations of the Clairvaux Speculum virginum" (Troyes, Bibliothèque municipale, MS 252) (Ph.D. diss., Indiana University; Ann Arbor, MI: University Microfilms International, 1982), fig. 247. Goggin argues (pp. 117–37) that a copy of *SV* related to that of Clairvaux influenced the Regensburg illuminations. See also Greenhill, *Die Stellung,* p. 25 n. 5 (Introduction, n. 13 above) with references to the earlier discussions of A. Boeckler, *Die Regensburg-Prüfeninger Buchmalerei des 12. und 13. Jahrhunderts* (Munich: A. Reusch, 1924), pp. 33–46. It is possible that the *De laudibus* might be another composition by Peregrinus. Prüfening had been reformed by Hirsau in the early twelfth century.

25. Bultot edited only extracts from the *Allocutio ad Deum de diversis beneficiis homini impensis* and the *De veritatis inquisitione* from Oxford, Bodleian Library, Laud Misc. 377 fols. 44v–55v and 55v–115v as an annex to his edition of the *Dialogus,* pp. 79–90 (n. 17 above).

26. Bernards identifed textual parallels between the *Speculum virginum* and a number of the texts edited or discussed by Bultot, "Um den Zusammenhang zwischen 'Speculum virginum', 'Dialogus de mundi contemptu vel amore' und verwandten Schriften," *RTAM* 34 (1967): 84–130. Bernards decided that the generally more succinct version found in the *Dialogus,* the *Allocutio,* and the *Sententie morales* was culled from *SV* rather than the other way around. His evidence is, however, very slender; the opposite solution is perhaps more likely for the *Dialogus* and *Allocutio.* The *Sententie morales,* on the other hand, shares numerous parallels with *SV* on which it could be based. Further study is needed.

27. *Willehelmi abbatis Hirsaugiensis,* MGH SS 12 (1856): 209–25. His treatises *De Musica* and *De arte astronomica* are edited in PL 150. See also William of Hirsau, *Musica,* ed. Denis Harbison, Corpus Scriptorum de Musica 23 (Rome: American Institute of Musicology, 1975).

28. *Musica* 15, 18, ed. Harbison, 41, 48.

29. Robert Bultot emphasizes the originality of William's conception of nature in "'Quadrivium,' 'Natura' et 'Ingenium naturale' chez Guillaume d'Hirsau (d. 1091)," *Rivista di filosofia neo-scolastica* 70 (1978): 11–27. His argument (n. 2) that *Othlohus* is not Otloh relies on outdated assumptions that Otloh was hostile to the liberal arts. Otloh employs musical metaphors extensively in his *Dialogus de tribus quaestionibus* 41–45, PL 146: 117A-123D.

30. *Vita Willehelmi abbatis Hirsaugiensis* 22, MGH SS 12: 219.

31. On their constitutional structure, see Hermann Jacobs, *Die Hirsauer. Ihre Ausbreitung und Rechtsstellung im Zeitalter des Investiturstreites* (Cologne-Graz: Böhlau, 1961). On their freedom to develop liturgical patterns originally formulated at Hirsau, see Felix Heinzer, "Hildegard und ihr liturgisches Umfeld," in the proceedings of the musicological conference held at Bingen, September 18–20, 1998, ed. Wulf Arlt (forthcoming).

32. Heinzer, "Buchkultur und Bibliotheksgeschichte Hirsaus," in *Hirsau. St Peter und Paul,* pp. 259–96, esp. pp. 270–71 (n. 12 above).

33. *Liber ad admonitione clericorum et laicorum,* PL 146: 243C-262C. See, for example, Otloh's comments (257AB) on the capacity of the heavens (through the sun, moon, and stars) and the earth (through various pleasant flowers and grace, trees and fruits, the beauty of precious stones) to provide instruction about God.

34. Comments made by Otloh about the capacity of a worldly woman to become pleasing to God as well as about a monk who was worried what other monks might think about seeing them together as brother and sister suggest that such concerns predate the Hirsau reform. *Dialogus de tribus quaestionibus* 49, PL 146: 130C-131A; see too *Liber de tentationibus suis,* PL 146: 47D-49A.

35. Küsters, *Der verschlossene Garten. Volkssprachliche Hohelied-Auslegung und monastiche Lebensform im 12. Jahrhundert,* Studia Humaniora 2 (Düsseldorf: Droste, 1985), pp. 71–88, and "Formen und Modelle religiöser Frauengemeinschaften im Umkreis der Hirsauer Reform des 11. und 12. Jahrhunderts," in *Hirsau. St. Peter und Paul,* pp. 195–220 (n. 12 above),

36. Berthold, *Chronicon* MGH SS 10: 160; *Necrologium Zwifaltense,* in *Necrologia Germaniae. 1. Dioceses Augustensis, Constantiensis, Curiensis,* ed. Baumann (1983): 244, 253.

37. Hermann speaks of women who will either hear or read his treatise, *Opusculum de conversione sua* 12, ed. Gerlinde Niemeyer, MGH Quellen zur Geistesgeschichte des Mittelalters 4 (Weimar: Böhlau, 1963), p. 108: "O vos ergo devote et sancte mulieres, quecumque ista legeritis vel lecta audieritis. . . ." An extract from *SV* is also contained in this manuscript (Rome, Biblioteca Vaticana, Vat. Lat. 504), copied in the second half of the twelfth century, perhaps from Dünnwald, a Premonstratensian community near

Cologne; Seyfarth, p. 89*, and Mews, "Hildegard of Bingen, the *Speculum virginum* and Religious Reform," in *Hildegard von Bingen,* ed. Haverkamp, p. 244, n. 23 (n. 6 above). On the oral presentation of *SV,* see Powell, chapter 5 in this volume.

38. Gregory the Great, *XL Homiliarum in Evangelia libri duo* 1.17.10, PL 76: 1143D-1144A.

39. Augustine, *Speculum,* ed. F. Weihrich, CSEL 12 (1887): 3–285.

40. This is the case with Letter 42, addressed to Adelidis, abbess of Barking by Osbert of Clare, *The Letters of Osbert of Clare, Prior of Westminster,* ed. E. W. Williamson (Oxford: Oxford University Press, 1929), pp. 153–79. A fascinating illustration of how the women of Barking transmuted these exempla is given in translations by Jocelyn Wogan-Browne and Glyn S. Burgess, *Virgin Lives and Holy Deaths: Two Exemplary Biographies for Anglo-Norman Women* (London: J. M. Dent, 1996).

41. For a detailed survey of this image, see Margot Fassler, "Mary's Nativity, Fulbert of Chartres, and the *Stirps Jesse:* Liturgical Innovation circa 1000 and Its Afterlife," *Speculum* 75 (2000): 389–434.

42. The antithesis between *conditio* and *reparatio* is closer to Gregory than to Hugh of St-Victor (who prefers the term *restauratio*); cf. Gregory, *Moralia in Job* 35.17, CCSL 143B (1985): 1785; *In librum primum Regum* 4.26, CCSL 144 (1963): 309.

43. Part one may originally have continued after this image with what is now *SV* 2.1–62, as an original explicit is included here in the margin of *L.*

44. The word *valde* (truly) is added in the margin of *L* for emphasis, apparently after *K* was copied; some other MSS misread where the additional would should go (2.443).

45. Cf. Augustine, *Enn. In Psalmos* 75.16, CCSL 39 (1956): 1049: "melior virgo humilis, quam maritata humilis; sed melior maritata humilis, quam virgo superba."

46. On the *De fructibus carnis et spiritus* (n. 18 above) as the source of *SV* 4.98–273, I follow the arguments of Greenhill (n. 24 above) rather than of Bernards. A possible source is Gregory, *Moralia in Job* 31.45, ed. Marc Adriaen, CCSL 143B (1985): 1610–12. See also Adolf Katzenellenbogen, *Allegories of the Virtues and Vices in Mediaeval Art,* Studies of the Warburg Institute 10 (London, 1939).

47. Ortlieb of Zwiefalten describes how William of Hirsau had monks enter "the temple of the Queen of heaven" singing *Ave maris stella, Chronicon,* MGH SS 10 (1852): 78–79; William's disciple Theoger had the new church dedicated to Mary decorated with many pictures, *Vita Theogeri abbatis S. Georgii et episcopi Mettensis* 13, MGH SS 12 (1856): 453.

48. St. Bernard quotes the same passage in Letter 42, *de moribus et officio episcoporum* 9, d. Leclercq, *SBO* 7: 108.

49. Jerome, *Comm. in Matthaeum* 2, ed. D. Hurst and M. Adriaen, CCSL 77 (1969): 106; *Letters* 49.3, 123.8, ed. Hilberg, CSEL 54: 354; 56: 82; Paschasius Radbertus, *Expositio in Matthaeo* 7, ed. B. Paulus, CCCM 56A (1984): 703.

50. There are at least two recensions of the *De fructibus* (n. 18 above). That found in the Leipzig, Universitätsbibliothek MS 148, and Salzburg MS, Studienbibliothek V.1.H 162, is distinct from that found in Oxford, Bodleian Library, Laud Misc. 377, and Cologne, GB 4o 206, also closer to *SV* in part four. The Salzburg MS carries the name *Hhunradus* on fol. 81v, but it is not clear whether this indicates the author or an owner; see Ernst von Frisch, "Über die Salzburger Handschrift von Hugo von St. Victors Opusculum de Fructu Carnis et Spiritus," in *Festschrift für Georg Ledinger,* ed. Albert Hartmann (Munich: H. Schmidt, 1930), pp. 67–71. Bernards identifies nineteen manuscripts of the work, *Die handschrifliche Überlieferung,* pp. 437–38 (Introduction, n. 9 above). I am grateful to Jutta Seyfarth for allowing me to study her transcription of the Salzburg MS. More research is needed to resolve these questions.

51. The image is plate 11 in Seyfarth's edition. In the belly of flesh is the inscription *vis illius* [its force], two words left out of Seyfarth's transcription of the rubrics on p. 136★. I am grateful to Barbara Newman for discussion of this image.

52. *Regula Benedicti* 7.6–9. This image was also reported as having been seen in a vision by the chronicler of Petershausen; see Mews, "Hildegard, Visions and Religious Reform in Twelfth-century Germany," forthcoming in Rainer Berndt, ed., *Im Angesicht Gottes* (Introduction, n. 24 above).

53. Amazons are also singled out for praise in *SV* 4.581–85. The source could be Orosius, *Historiarum* 1.15, ed. Marie Pierre Arnaud-Lindet (Paris: Les Belles Lettres, 1990–91).

54. *SV* 9.634–38; cf. Hildegard, *Scivias* 2.5.43–45, ed. Führkötter and A. Carlevaris, CCCM 43 (1978): 211–14.

55. Bernards noted numerous parallel passages between this part of *SV* and the *Allocutio* in "'Speculum virginum' und verwandte Schriften," 91–95 (n. 26 above).

56. *Historia Hirsaugiensis,* MGH SS 14: 258.

57. *Württembergisches Urkundenbuch,* 4 vols. (Stuttgart, 1883; repr. Aalen, 1974), 4: 348, no. 49.

58. Hildegard, Letters 119–36; *The Letters of Hildegard of Bingen,* trans. Joseph L. Baird and Radd K. Ehrman (New York: Oxford University Press, 1998), 2: 64–77. See Lieven van Acker and Hermann Josef Pretsch, "Der Briefwechsel des Benediktinerklosters S. Peter und Paul in Hirsau mit Hildegard von Bingen. Ein Interpretationsversuch zu seiner kritischen Edition," in *Hirsau. St. Peter und Paul,* ed. Schreiner (n. 12 above), 2: 157–72.

59. John Freed, "Urban Development and the 'Cura Monialium' in Thirteenth-Century Germany," *Viator* 3 (1972): 311–27. On female communities founded by Eberbach in the late twelfth and thirteenth centuries, see Palmer, *Zisterzienser und ihre Bücher,* pp. 19–21 (n. 23 above).

60. Mews, "Hildegard of Bingen, the *Speculum virginum* and Religious Reform," in *Hildegard von Bingen in ihrem historischen Umfeld,* ed. Haverkamp, pp. 237–67 (n. 6 above).

# CHAPTER 2

# THE *SPECULUM VIRGINUM:*
# THE TESTIMONY OF THE MANUSCRIPTS

*Jutta Seyfarth*

*(translated by Janice M. Pinder)*

This chapter introduces the manuscripts of the *Speculum virginum*, with particular attention to considering the significance of the British Library manuscript, Arundel 44 *(L)*, and what the manuscripts might reveal about the identity of its author. It places this fictional dialogue between a religious guide and a female disciple within the context of reforming currents in the twelfth century that attached great importance to the involvement of women in religious life. While the Arundel manuscript was given to the Cistercian abbey of Eberbach by the late twelfth century, the Cologne manuscript of the Speculum virginum, copied either directly from *L* or (as is suggested here) from its exemplar, probably came from the Augustinian abbey at Andernach, founded in 1128 by Richard of Springiersbach and his sister Tenxwind, with the support of a priest called Conrad. Another early manuscript of the *Speculum* is associated with a sister house of Andernach, at Frankenthal.

There are two main reasons why scholars have become more aware of the *Speculum virginum* in the last decade. The first is external, namely that a critical edition of the whole text has been available for scholarly discussion only since 1990.[1] The second has to do with the content presented in the work, a dialogue of instruction between the spiritual teacher Peregrinus and the nun Theodora, pursuing questions that started to attract fresh attention in the changed consciousness of the late twentieth century.

In what follows an attempt will be made, after a brief summary of historical and scholarly perspectives, to give an overview of the manuscript tradition and to ask what contribution the testimony of the manuscripts can make to the two main unanswered questions about the *Speculum virginum:* What place can be assigned to the manuscript Arundel 44 *(L)* in its transmission, and what does the testimony of the manuscripts allow us to say about the identity of its author?

The *Speculum virginum* needs first to be situated in the spiritual and cultural currents of its time. The text must be seen against the background of the great upheavals that characterize the twelfth century as a whole.[2] In that regard, the question of the position of women is of central importance. This question, dating from before the current interest in gender studies, is stimulating research to an unusual degree, causing renewed engagement with old questions, and giving rise to a multitude of possible directions from which to try to explain the exciting phenomena of the twelfth century.[3]

In this context, the *Speculum virginum* is extraordinarily welcome as a text that offers new assumptions and therefore a new point of entry into the questions of the age. The work can be dated to the middle of the twelfth century. Since neither the author nor other individuals involved with the text are known, it evades easy historical classification. Scholarly literature on the work has until recently generally been limited to discussion of isolated questions.[4]

Such an approach is especially unsatisfactory since in the *Speculum virginum* other media come into play alongside text in dialogue form. As pictures and songs with musical notation are an inseparable part of the overall concept, an assessment of the work as a whole is needed.[5] Furthermore, the *Speculum* not only provides material relating to the behavior of both sexes toward each other but enables a picture to be formed of the way didactic content was conveyed, from teaching practice to the delivery of knowledge.[6]

The establishment of this picture begs the question of the historical reality reflected by this text. How real or fictional is the lesson that takes place in the 480 exchanges between the priest Peregrinus and the nun Theodora?[7] Is the dialogue a literary technique used to convey the didactic content, or does it correspond to a lived experience? Have we in the *Speculum* a handbook for the spiritual instructor?[8] Alternatively, is it a manual from which a virgin of Christ can benefit independently in finding the way to inner perfection?[9] Is it a compendium, able to convey spiritual content in a particularly accessible form and therefore suitable as a book for mealtime readings or private meditation?[10]

The Cistercian order, which developed little notion of responding to the needs of religious women in the twelfth century, consistently refused to sanction contact between the sexes. The Cistercians were much more fundamentally opposed to any incorporation of female communities, whether in the form of organized convents or in less structured communities, like those that often developed around single recluses.[11] Already in the first Cistercian statutes, chapter seventeen states "that in our order living with women is forbidden."[12]

There was quite a different reaction from the founding community of the other reforming orders, such as the regular canons or the Premonstratensians, who could be regarded as supporters and promoters of the institution of the double monastery.[13] A recent study has shown that the monasteries following the Hirsau reform in southern Germany had a decided preference for this organizational model, still at its height under Abbot William (1026–1091) in the last two decades of the eleventh century.[14] At the beginning of the twelfth century it developed in such a way that each period and region has to be differentiated clearly and general conclusions can be drawn only with great care from individual observations. It is this reform circle that has passed down to us the biblical justification for the cohabitation of men and women *ob amorem dei.* The Petershausen Chronicle, which dates from between 1134 and 1156, writes, with reference to Acts 1.14, "it should therefore not be a cause for blame, but rather for praise, that religious women [*sanctimoniales feminae*] are accepted into the monastery, so that both sexes, separated but in the same place [*uno in loco*] may be led to their salvation."[15]

It is in this area of tension over the differing value placed on the cohabitation of men and women that the *Speculum virginum* gains its topicality, as it mirrors the historical situation in its themes and terminology. As a virgin of Christ Theodora belongs to a monastery, referred to as *claustrum* or *monasterium* and in which she lives in physical and voluntary enclosure (2.69–74). The usefulness of her enclosure and the dangers threatened by any meeting with persons of the opposite sex is the subject of most of the second part. Reciprocal glances, small gifts, and above all frequent conversations (2.461–70) between persons of both sexes have hidden dangers and are to be avoided; time spent together must be ended by sunset,[16] to avoid giving rise to unfavorable talk, so that the shepherds of the virgins of Christ may not turn into marauding wolves.[17] A lengthy passage (5.1185–1287) discusses the dangers that also threaten men and women who share the same commitment and way of life if they do not have a lively awareness of God's presence.[18] Too great a proximity brings the danger of conflagration; if only a single wall separates the sexes and there is no fear or love of God, the community is laid open to calumny and sin (5.1243–51).

The question arises of whether the lengthy discussion of the problem in the *Speculum* allows us to draw any conclusion about the incorporation of a female monastery and about the particular rule of life being followed. Is the "single wall" so precisely meant that we must postulate buildings that are architecturally one?[19] On one hand, the dialogue between "master" and "disciple," "father" and "daughter," seems to be a practice that is taken for granted; the two have an absolutely equal chance of obtaining the same place in heaven, if they combine love and fear of God.[20] On the other hand, the author never tires of pointing out the dangers of a community of men and women.

It is difficult to be content with the general finding that the work belongs to the reform efforts of the twelfth century. Can the area of its origin be more narrowly pinpointed? Does the thesis, debated at length among scholars, that Conrad of Hirsau is its author point to the Benedictines, or more specifically to the Hirsau reform movement? [21] Or does its spiritual home lie in the Cistercian order, whose strong presence in the midst of this century cannot be overlooked and is even reflected in the manuscript transmission of the *Speculum virginum*? How is its relation to the regular canons, whose engagement in pastoral care for women is a matter of historical fact, to be evaluated? Faced with these questions, it seems a good idea to summarize once again the testimony of the manuscripts and to list the salient elements of their description and provenance, at least permitting a clear distinction between fact and hypothesis. The number of surviving manuscripts that contain the *Speculum virginum* is impressive.[22] There are twenty-seven Latin manuscripts, not including seven fragments, excerpts, and references to manuscripts that have disappeared.[23] Of these, one third date from the twelfth century and the start of the thirteenth,[24] a sign of the evident immediate resonance of the work when it first appeared. In particular, we can consider the two earliest manuscripts:

*L*—London, British Library, Arundel 44. 129 folios, 27/18.5 cm. Gatherings of four folios (eight leaves), marked with Roman numerals from III (17v) to XVIII (137v). In addition there are two single folios in Arundel 501, fols. 32 and 33. Four scribes worked on this manuscript, of which hand A was responsible for large sections (fols. 1r–17v; 99r–102r among others) and for the corrections. The manuscript contains almost the entire text of the *Speculum,* including the *Epithalamium* and the entrance song, in addition to the marginalia and the pictures.[25] The listing of vices and virtues (*SV* 4.99–273) is absent from the body of the text and was added at the end of the manuscript. A rubric on fo. 30v (4.99) informs the reader to look at the end of the work: *Diffinitiones ipsarum virtutum et viciorum require in fine libri ad hoc signum.*

*K*—Cologne, Historisches Archiv der Stadt Köln, W 276a. 95 folios, 27/17.5 cm. Gatherings of four folios (eight leaves), numbered from IIII (8v) to XV (95v), some cut off at the lower edge. The manuscript is incomplete.

Some three gatherings are missing from the beginning, as are three or four gatherings from the end, as well as one folio between the modern folio numbers 16 and 17.[26] A single folio, D 182, also belongs to this manuscript. The text as it stands has no gaps, however, and the songs, marginalia, and pictures are all to be found where expected.

Both of these manuscripts, which for us represent the earliest available state of the text of the *Speculum virginum,* can be dated only indirectly. A reliable *terminus ante quem* is provided by the manuscript *V* (Rome, Biblioteca Vaticana, Cod. Pal. lat. 565), copied in 1155 in the Augustinian priory of St. Mary Magdalene in Frankenthal.[27] Since *V* was certainly copied directly from *K,* the latter must be from an earlier date. A *terminus post* for the dating cannot of course be established with the same precision, but some internal evidence (a possible allusion to a sermon of Bernard of Clairvaux in 9.917, reference to the comedy "ridiculous Geta" in 2.43, allusion to stained glass windows in 11.662) points toward a period around 1140.[28] The palaeographic evidence is consistent with this conclusion.

On the provenance of both manuscripts, which provide no information about their place of origin, the following can be ascertained: Manuscript *L* came into the possession of the Cistercian abbey of Eberbach in Rheingau, founded in 1131. From there, along with a whole bundle of other manuscripts from Eberbach, it came through the troubles of the Thirty Years' War into the possession of the Earl of Arundel and finally into the care of the British Library in London. Nigel Palmer, in his recent pioneering study of the library holdings at Eberbach, has confirmed that Arundel 44 belonged to Eberbach, at the same time making clear that the manuscript was probably not produced there.[29] On fol.1r it bears an owner's name, *Hugo magister,* also found in other manuscripts from the Arundel and Laud collection.[30] Palmer concludes that this group of manuscripts had belonged to a monk of Eberbach called Hugo, who had gained the title of master after a period of study in Paris and had brought the manuscripts back from there with him.[31] In Eberbach the text of the *Speculum virginum* could have found a use in pastoral care from the end of the twelfth century onward.[32] The abbey of Eberbach was the first of a long list of Cistercian houses at the forefront of its transmission.[33]

Manuscript *K* comes, almost certainly, from the house of canonesses of St. Mary in Andernach on the Rhine. This provenance is substantiated by a charter from Andernach, attested but apparently lost when the manuscript was rebound, and is not contradicted by the subsequent path of the manuscript in the nineteenth century.[34] The founding of the house of canonesses in Andernach in 1128 needs to be seen against the background of an astonishing presence and expansion of the Augustinian canons of the strict observance in the territory of the ecclesiastical provinces of Cologne and Trier. A decisive figure was Richard of Springiersbach, under whose firm leadership as provost *[praepositus]* of the convent not only did Springiersbach develop into a center of the canonical movement, but numerous other male and female convents sprang up, held together in a firmly governed association. Richard founded Andernach for his sister Tenxwind and gave her the priest Conrad as spiritual adviser on the spot: "Under the most careful protection and watchful concern of these three people" *[sub horum itaque trium cautissima tutela et pervigili solertia]*, the monastery underwent such an expansion that by 1138 its membership had to be limited to one hundred women.[35]

The *Speculum virginum* fits well into these historical circumstances. The *Speculum* manuscript *V,* a direct copy of *K,* originated in the scriptorium of the priory of Augustinian canons in Frankenthal. This priory, founded in 1129, was turned into a double monastery through the addition of a female convent in 1135. In the same year the monastery in Springiersbach chose canon Bertolf as reforming abbot. These closely related circumstances yield nothing that permits an identification of the *Speculum* author within the canonical movement. While the density of the evidence is striking, no definite attribution can be claimed.[36]

The provenance and classification of the other Latin manuscripts does not need to be discussed here. They can all be arranged into a stemma that forms in essence four branches, to which the manuscripts may be successively assigned with certainty by common errors.[37] On the whole the textual transmission is very uniform and, with the exception of the different placing of the catalogue of vices and virtues (*SV* 4.98–273), shows hardly any differences in the form of the text. The pictures also largely follow this unbroken transmission, within which slight differences could also bring about a different emphasis. A recent work in historical theology has made clear that the idea handed down from Jerome of the scheme of rewards for the different states (virgins, widows, married) clearly underwent a change in the conception of the pictures in the manuscripts of the *Speculum virginum* by the time of the Zwettl copy in the thirteenth century.[38]

Against the background of this general description of the manuscript transmission, two controversial questions relating to manuscripts *L* and *K* remain to be discussed. These are whether Arundel 44 is to be regarded as the author's autograph, and whether it is possible to reach a conclusion about the identity and place of origin of the author.[39] It is undisputed that manuscripts *L* and *K* deliver a largely identical text, which in *L* underwent numerous corrections by scribe A, while *K* passed the text on almost unaltered to *V.* This must be pointed out, because for the purposes of comparison the missing parts of *K* are supplied from *V.*

Manuscripts *L* and *K* are very different in outward appearance. While the scribe of *K* writes in a very careful, even minuscule hand, corrects unobtrusively, and is apparently working with a finished image of the page in mind, the script of *L* is marked by such careless treatment in this respect that it appears to be a working copy. Nevertheless, only the examination and critical weighing up of the textual variants will permit a judgment to be made. In *L* and *K* (and in *V* for the missing parts of *K*) there are eighty-seven odd words, scribal errors, and variants, that are common to both manuscripts and then corrected in *L* by scribe A. Even if not all examples carry the same weight, they remain convincing in their totality. A few selected examples may show that the corrections can be a matter of simple completion, grammatical improvement, or clarification of content.

In *SV* 9.431 it is stated that the pious should trust in the Word of God. *L, K,* and *V* all write *sic verbum dei pio commissum* [thus the Word of God entrusted to the pious]. In *L* scribe A adds *cordi* [heart] above the line after *pio,* to text written in his own hand. From then on, all manuscripts of the three branches that descend from *L* write *sic verbum dei pio cordi commissum* [thus the Word of God entrusted to the pious heart] on the same line, while the branch that descends from *K* continues to transmit *sic verbum dei pio commissum.*

*SV* 9.599 speaks about the difference between demons and human seducers, who trap people in the snares of sin in different ways: "Inter demonem et hominem peccati persuasores hoc interest, quod alter suggestione laqueos tendit, alter aperto malo proximum necare contendit" [Between a demon and a human being, there is this difference that one puts forward snares by suggestion, the other strives to kill a neighbor by obvious evil]. While *L* and *K* leave out the grammatically indispensable *hoc interest* [there is this difference], scribe A adds to *L* here a sign in the margin. Both variants are transmitted in the respective branches.

*SV* 5.102–103 says of Mary that "you will find her among the judges and kings coming out from the line of kings and coming forth from the Jews like a rose among thorns." *L* and *K* initially write: "repperis eam . . . de Iudeis quasi spinam erumpentem" [you will find her . . . like a thorn coming from the Jews]. Scribe A corrects this, through crossing out and writing above the line *quasi de spinis erumpentem rosam* [like a rose coming from thorns]. He thus corrects the meaningless image resulting from an obvious omission, of a thorn bursting into flower, to the key comparison with the rose.

A final example shows how scribe A's careless technique of correction can give rise to different readings. For *SV* 2.443, *L* and *V* (here standing for *K,* from which this part is missing) have *in hoc gaude* [rejoice in this]. Scribe A corrects this in *L* to "rejoice truly in this" by placing a sign below the line and adding *valde* [truly] in the margin under this sign. In doing this scribe A has so placed the sign that it could be taken as referring to *laudabile* on the next line: "Non enim te virginem esse laudabile est, sed quia votum vovisti puritatis" [It is truly praiseworthy for you not to be a virgin, but because you have made a vow of purity both of the flesh and the spirit]. Accordingly, *T1, T2,* and *B* have, like *V,* in hoc gaude, but then *T1, T2,* and *B* have the nonsensical "Non enim te virginem esse valde laudabile est" [It is not truly praiseworthy for you to be a virgin], while *Z* and *W* give the correct readings *in hoc valde gaude* and then *virginem esse laudabile est.*[40]

This finding, which there are sufficient further examples to corroborate, admits only two conclusions: Either *L* and *K* are copies of the same manuscript, now lost, or *K* was copied from *L* before it was corrected.[41] The latter possibility seems out of the question, or at the very least improbable in relation to situations like *SV* 8.272–76, where scribe A adds the entire quotation from Paul under a sign in the margin, while in *K* it is written without interruption straight into the text. If *K*'s exemplar had been the uncorrected *L,* then the quotation from Paul would have to be missing in *K.*[42] So it must be postulated that it was present in the manuscript that served as exemplar to both, was copied by *K,* overlooked by *L,* and restored through scribe A's correction.

The same process must be assumed for the analogous situation of the omission of the catalogue of vices and virtues, *SV* 4.98–273. Scribe A marked 4.98 with a sign in the margin and the note: *Diffinitiones ipsarum virtutum et viciorum require in fine libri ad hoc signum* [Look for the definitions of the virtues and the vices themselves at the end of the book, at this sign]. All the manuscripts depending on *L* retain this peculiarity and in each case put the catalogue of vices and virtues at the end of the text, while *K* and the other manuscripts that are independent of *L* simply integrate it into the text. The discovery of the two single leaves in Arundel 501 has now furnished proof that this catalogue was also originally to be found at the end of Arundel 44.

The close comparison of the manuscripts of the first generation imposes the conclusion that in Arundel 44 we do not have before us the original of the *Speculum virginum,* but—together with *K*—a very early, probably even the first copy of a version that is now lost. That this was not simply corrected, in the simple sense, by scribe A, but actually revised, is beyond doubt. This does not mean, however, that he can be awarded the status of author.[43] It nevertheless must be stated clearly that it is the form taken by the *Speculum virginum* in Arundel 44 that has to be accepted as the standard that would be received and transmitted, and that therefore its central importance in the history of the transmission of the work is not to be denied.

The critical apparatus confirms the hypothesis of an earlier version. In the work itself traces can also be found that indicate a particular order in the process of creation. These clues can be enumerated briefly here. The division of the work into twelve parts, enumerated exactly and identified by their content in the introductory letter, is brought into question by indications that it originally consisted of a smaller number of books, occasionally identified as either eight (according to Trithemius) or ten (a Zwettl library catalogue).[44] Possible reminiscences of such another division are found in statements that do not match the final system. Thus in *SV* 2.475 we find *secundo libro demus inicium* [let us provide a beginning in a second book] where according to the final division it should have been *tertio libro* [in a third book]. For *SV* 6.853, manuscripts *L, K, V, T1, T2, B,* and *H* have *quinto libro nostro demus exordium premissa figura* [let us provide an introduction with a prefixed picture in our fifth book] to introduce a picture that in fact introduces part seven.

Another paradox is that the words of Peregrinus at the end of part nine (9.1286–99) signal not only the conclusion of the intellectual argument but also an action of thanksgiving. He says (9.1295): *Et hic finis dialogi nostri et totius operas nostri, expleta tamen gratiarum actione cum oratione* [And here is the end of our dialogue and all our work, completed with a thanksgiving and a prayer]. In fact, the *actio gratiarum* follows in part ten. It stands out from the preceding text in being arranged no longer in dialogue form but as a hymn of thanks. At the end of this prayer is the lapidary statement: *Explicit speculum virginum* (*SV* 10.397). Yet in direct contradiction to this *explicit* the dialogue is taken up again in the following lines to discuss a new topic, namely the seven gifts of the Holy Spirit. The join between lines 10.397 and 10.398 clearly preserves the traces of the process of creation and provides evidence that in this work apparently earlier and later parts were put together to form a new whole.[45]

Finally let us consider the transition between parts two and three. The author portraits placed there (an almost identical repetition of the author portraits on folio 2v in *L*, before the beginning of part one), have no reason to be in that position. They make sense only if they stand at the beginning of a text. The custom of documenting authorship with an author portrait *before* the start of the text was firmly established in biblical tradition (from David to the evangelists). This is also consistent with the phrase *Audi filia et vide* (*SV* 3.2) from Psalm 44 [Listen, daughter, and see] being the original beginning. The initial A does not seem to be distinguished particularly from the initial letters of the other books by size or decoration, but this does not prevent us conjecturing that, because of the unmotivated placement of the author portraits and the inconsistent numbering of the books, an earlier version of the *Speculum virginum* began at this spot.[46]

In conclusion, it must be stressed again that while this "first version" may be significant for the process of the work's creation, it has no relevance for the later tradition. Here the twelve-book version with introductory letter, *Epithalamium* [Bridal song], and associated pictures is definitive; it is the version passed on by *L* and *K* in almost identical form and transmitted by the groups of manuscripts that depend on them, in *L* after correction by scribe A.[47] It has already been stressed that this corrected version, given by Arundel 44, experienced the greatest success, without it being possible to grant manuscript *L* the status of autograph exemplar in this web of affiliations. In our present state of knowledge no convincing answer can be expected to the question as to which of the versions of the text is truly "authentic."

There remains the question of the author of the text and the religious order to which he belonged. That the author, as far as he is generally named, is primarily designated with the name of the male partner in the dialogue, that is Peregrinus, cannot be questioned. Whether Peregrinus is to be understood as an eloquent pseudonym or the actual name of the author was a question the humanist Johannes Trithemius tried to resolve in his fashion. He reported that the author of the *Speculum virginum* was the monk Conrad, who out of humility hid behind the pseudonym Peregrinus.[48]

Johannes Trithemius, in his early years the abbot of Sponheim, later of the monastery of St. Jacob in Würzburg, was not brought up at Hirsau. As someone in the vanguard of the reform at Bursfeld and an eloquent humanist, he received a commission to write the history of the monastery of Hirsau from the abbot Blasius, who came to Bursfeld from Hirsau in 1495 and was interested in history. The reliability of Trithemius' writings—those that relate to Hirsau are above all the *Chronicon insigne monasterii Hirsaugiensis* (1495–1503) and the *Annales Hirsaugienses* (1509–1514)—is contested.[49]

Whether Trithemius is trustworthy chronicler in the information that he gives about the author of the *Speculum virginum* is a matter of opinion. In his various writings on the history of the monastery of Hirsau, Trithemius not only equates Peregrinus with Conrad, a monk of Hirsau,[50] but also provides a list of his works, with the shelf number and *incipit* of each work.[51] Since this information has proven to be partly true, partly false, no decisive judgment on the reliability of the abbot of Sponheim can be drawn from this.[52] But we can say with certainty that the name Conrad for the author is not substantiated before Trithemius, that is before 1494, and that contemporaries also consistently gave him the credit for this "discovery."[53]

Peregrinus, one of the partners in the dialogue, was evidently also used as the author's name. On the spine of the original vellum binding of *A2* (Arras, Bibliothèque municipale MS 916) was written *Peregrinus. Speculum virginum,* which may go back to the cataloguing of the library of St. Vedas-tus. In a manuscript from Hohenfurth, Peregrinus is named as author in the reference given for a citation,[54] and at the beginning of the letter in the Düsseldorf manuscript the sender refers to himself as *Peregrinus, Christi pauperum servus.*[55] Of equal weight is the entry in the Oxford manuscript Bodleian Laud Misc. 377, dated to soon after 1200, which contains the col-lection of the *Speculum* author's minor works. On fol. 2v it has: *Liber sancte Marie in Eberbach. Peregrinus minor.*[56] This evidence is corroborated by the Eberbach library catalogue, in the inventory *oculus memoriae,* which lists the shelfmark "h 22: *Peregrinus minor. Initium: Cum manifestum sit.*"[57]

It seems obvious to make a connection between these notices and infor-mation from the catalogue of Hirsau, which was compiled after 1165.[58] It states: *libri cuiusdam monachi Hirsaugiensis cognomento Peregrini* [books of a cer-tain monk of Hirsau known as Peregrinus]. The information is limited to this short notice; there is nothing further on the titles or content of these *libri.* The catalogue has come down to us only in a sixteenth-century copy, for which the protestant abbot Johannes Parsimonius (1525–1588) is responsible.[59]

Some questions remain at the end of these observations. Was the Hir-sau monk named Peregrinus, attested in the catalogue, the author of the *Speculum virginum?* Was the Peregrinus attested as the author in the Oxford manuscript from Eberbach a monk at Hirsau? Was Conrad, according to Trithemius' testimony also Peregrinus, a monk at Hirsau and the author of the *Speculum?* The surest way of determining the spiritual home of the *Speculum virginum* is without doubt by engaging with the content of the work itself. Here there is abundant material in text and script, pictures, and songs. In his recent work on the library at Hirsau, Felix Heinzer attempted to show a relationship between an 1134 missal from Hirsau and the pic-ture of the *quadriga* [chariot] in Arundel 44.[60] Unfortunately, the Hirsau leaf has disappeared and the comparison can be made only on the basis of an old photograph, which makes the conclusion less reliable. However, the composition dominates this picture so strongly that one is tempted to sug-gest that it came from the same workshop or borrowed features that were stipulated when commissioning the picture. But it certainly follows from this that, in principle, a thorough interpretation of the pictures may yet contribute something about the composition of the work and in even greater measure for the analysis of the content of the text.

### Notes

1. Jutta Seyfarth, ed. *Speculum virginum,* CCCM 5 (1990).
2. The fundamental study on this question is still Herbert Grundmann, *Reli-gious Movements in the Middle Ages: The Historical Links between Heresy, the*

*Mendicant Orders, and the Women's Religious Movement in the Twelfth and Thirteenth Century, with the Historical Foundations of German Mysticism,* trans. Steven Rowan (Notre Dame, IN: University of Notre Dame Press, 1995).

3. See, for example, Barbara Newman, *Sister of Wisdom, St. Hildegard's Theology of the Feminine* (Berkeley: University of California Press, 1987); Urban Küsters, *Der verschlossene Garten. Volkssprachliche Hohelied-Auslegung und monastiche Lebensform im 12. Jahrhundert,* Studia Humaniora 2 (Düsseldorf: Droste, 1985); Morgan Powell, "The Mirror and the Woman: Instruction for Religious Women and the Emergence of Vernacular Poetics 1120–1250" (Ph.D. diss., Princeton University, Ann Arbor, MI: University Microfilms International, 1997). The artistic activity of nuns, although centered on the fourteenth and fifteenth centuries, is studied by Jeffrey F. Hamburger, *Nuns as Artists: The Visual Culture of a Medieval Convent* (Berkeley: University of California Press, 1997).

4. For the history of the reception of the *Speculum virginum,* first given scholarly attention by the Maurists in 1730, see Seyfarth, pp. 8*–15*.

5. For an assessment of the song within the overall conception of the work and a critical edition of the music, see chapter 6 by Catherine Jeffreys in this volume. A performance of the songs took place in August 1998 in the former Cistercian abbey of Eberbach and on September 19, 1999, in the basilica of St. Martin in Bingen.

6. Most spiritual writing is male dominated, reflecting the position of women in the Church. In the *Speculum,* however, Theodora appears throughout as an equal partner in the dialogue with Peregrinus; independent utterances lend concreteness to her portrayal (*SV* 1.358–61; 1.797–801).

7. This offers an extraordinarily rich body of material for investigation of the interaction of dialogue, which has remained a fictional representation of oral reality in the eyes of scholars: see Peter von Moos, "Zwischen Schriftlichkeit und Mündlichkeit Dialogische Interaktion im lateinischen Hochmittelalter. Sonderforschungsbereich 'Mündlichkeit und Schriftlichkeit,'" *Frühmittelalterlicher Studien* 5 (1991): 300–14.

8. Morgan Powell (see above, n. 3) strongly favors this view of the text's function. He bases his thesis on a close analysis of the text, in which he also includes the origin of the pictures for the purpose of instruction, and understands the prominent use of the psalm verse "Audi filia et vide" as a literal call to the female pupil to listen and look. Other passages in the text support this thesis and suggest such a use, because they are unequivocally directed to the spiritual instructor of virgins. Thus there are direct addresses to the *custos vasorum domini* (*SV* 5.1079), *custos celestis depositi* (5.1106), *miles Christi* (5.1113), *serve Christi* (5.1121), and *amici dei* (5.1162). Whether this thesis does justice to Theodora's role in the dialogue, however, must remain an open question. Passages throughout the dialogue show her as an independent partner in the conversation. See above, n. 6.

9. Arguments can also be advanced in favor of this kind of use, for instance various passages in the introductory letter such as: "misi vobis libellum

quoddam mutui amoris insigne, in quo mentem exerceatis, ad sponsi aeterni gratiam proficiatis minusque de absentia nostra doleatis" [I have sent you a little book as a kind of token of mutual love. In it you may exercise your mind, grow in the grace of the eternal bridegroom, and grieve the less at my absence] (*SV* Epist. 31); or "In speculo, quod misi, vultus cordium vestrorum attendite" [Scrutinize the faces of your hearts in the mirror I sent] (*SV* Epist. 102).

10. The demand for literature of this kind for reading or study by individual members of the faithful was high; we have sufficient information about it from library catalogues and records of borrowing.

11. The role of being a recluse became widespread in the twelfth century and was more than ever used by women, who were often called to special holiness. Hildegard was not the only one who began her religious career in this way. See Küsters n. 14 below and Hotchin, chapter 3 in this volume.

12. The fact that individual female Cistercian houses still existed in the twelfth century does not contradict the general tendency to reject interaction, rooted above all in Bernard's attitude; Maren Kuhn-Rehfuss, "Zisterzierinnen in Deutschland," in K. Elm, P. Joerissen, and H. J. Roth, eds., *Die Zisterzienser. Ordensleben zwischen Ideal und Wirklichkeit* (Cologne: Rheinland-Verlag, 1981).

13. Michel Parisse refers to the extraordinary difficulty in forming a valid definition of the double monastery taking into account its legal form and appearance, in *Lexicon des Mittelalters* (Zürich: Artemis, 1986), 3: 1257. See also Kaspar Elm and Michel Parisse, eds., *Doppelklöster und andere formen der Symbiose männlicher und weiblicher Religiosen im Mittelalter,* Berliner historische Studien 18 (Berlin: Dunker und Humblot, 1992).

14. Urban Küsters, "Formen und Modelle religiöser Frauengemeinschaften im Umkreis der Hirsauer Reform des 11. und 12. Jahrhunderts," in *Hirsau St Peter und Paul 1091–1991, Forschungen und Berichte der Archäologie des Mittelalters in Baden-Württemberg,* Band 10/2, ed. Klaus Schreiner (Stuttgart: Konrad Theiss, 1991), 2: 195–220.

15. Petershausen was a Benedictine monastery near Constance, which had been reformed from Hirsau. *Casus monasterii Petrishusensis* 24, praef. Cap. 8–9, MGH SS 20 (1868): 622; see Küsters, "Formen und Modellen," p. 210, and Hotchin, chapter 3 in this volume.

16. *SV* 9.1160: "ut sexum diversum conferentem concludat solis occasus."

17. *SV* 5.1029: "ne pastores Christi ancillarum lupi rapaces sint animarum."

18. *SV* 5.1029: "inter viros et feminas pari professione cultum pietatis exercentes necessaria est divinae praesentiae cognitio, qua a mente pariter conversantium remota perit totius disciplinae vel regularis vitae magistra."

19. Parisse (n. 13 above) gives the example of Watton in England, where a wall divided the church in two in order to keep the men and the women apart, *Lexicon* 3: 1257.

20. *SV* 5.1193: "sic parem meritis non imparibus in caelis sortientur locum magister et discipula, pater et filia, qui summi patris et magistri timorem et amorem diviserunt inter se mente sincera."

21. Felix Heinzer suggested that the MS *L* came from Hirsau in "Buchkultur und Bibliotheksgeschichte Hirsaus," in *Hirsau. St. Peter und Paul, 1091–1991*, ed. Schreiner (n. 14 above) 2: 270–71. For earlier literature on Conrad of Hirsau see Seyfarth, p. 37*.

22. For an exact description of the manuscripts and all questions of detail, see the introduction to my critical edition, Seyfarth, pp. 56*–123*.

23. Morgan Powell (chapter 5, n. 3 in this volume) has been able to add to this list two further Latin manuscript fragments from Tortosa, Spain. Even if the manuscripts are comparatively late (fourteenth and fifteenth century), they prove once more how astonishingly widely disseminated the work was.

24. On the peak of its reception in the fifteenth century, which produced mainly vernacular translations and was associated with the *Devotio moderna*, see Irene Berkenbusch, *Speculum virginum. Mittelniederländischer Text. Edition, Untersuchungen zum Prolog und einleitende Interpretation*, Europäische Hochschulschriften 1/1511 (Frankfurt: Peter Lang, 1995), and Küsters, chapter 11.

25. The few missing sections can be filled in from the two folios from Arundel 501.

26. Since the missing text can only have taken up about seventeen leaves, the first gathering must have been incomplete or used for something else. The same is true for *L*, where, judging from the length of the transmitted text, the gathering number III on fol. 17v can only be explained by an incomplete first gathering.

27. Aliza Cohen was able to show in her work on the Frankenthal scriptorium that Cod. Pal. lat. 565 was produced directly after the Worms Bible, which is dated in a colophon to 1148. Aliza Cohen-Mushlin, *A Medieval Scriptorium. Sancta Maria Magdalena de Frankendal*, Wolfenbütteler Mittelalter-Studien 3 (Wiesbaden: Harrasowitz, 1990).

28. A detailed discussion of the arguments for the 1140 date can be found in Seyfarth, pp. 32*–37*.

29. Nigel F. Palmer, *Zisterzienser und ihre Bücher. Die mittelalterliche Bibliotheksgeschichte von Kloster Eberbach im Rheingau* (Regensburg: Schnell und Steiner, 1998), pp. 77–78.

30. Seyfarth, p. 58*.

31. Palmer, *Zisterzienser*, pp. 72, 76, 146.

32. At the end of the twelfth century, the abbot of Eberbach had the right to appoint the superior of two female Cistercian houses. Palmer, *Zisterzienzer*, p. 79, and Blasius Huemer, "Verzeichnis der deutschen Cisterzienserinnenklöster," *Studien und Mitteilungen zur Geschichte des Benediktinerordens und seiner Zweige* 37 (1916): 1–47.

33. Seyfarth, p. 58*. A definite Cistercian provenance can be ascertained for manuscripts from Himmerod (*H* Baltimore, Walters Art Gallery W 72), Clairvaux (*T1* Troyes, Bibliothèque municipale MS 252), Mores (*T2* Troyes, Bibliothèque municipale MS 413), Igny (*B* Berlin, Deutsche Staatsbibliothek MS Phillipps 1701), Zwettl (*Z* Zwettl, Bibliothek des Zis-

terzienserstift Cod. Zwetl. 180)), and Ebrach (*W* Würzburg, Universitäts-bibliothek M.p.th. f. 107). Palmer (*Zisterzienser,* p. 80) argues plausibly that the content of the text and pictures fits well into Cistercian spirituality, without it being necessary to posit that the manuscript originated within the Cistercian Order.

34. For further arguments for a provenance from Andernach, see Seyfarth, p. 62*.

35. *Fundatio monasterii sanctae Mariae Andernacensis* MGH SS 15.2 (1888): 968–70

36. Perhaps the testimony on Conrad should be reviewed again; his memory was kept alive with an inscription in the chapter house of Andernach: "Conradus fulsit vita quasi gemma polita / istud ovile regens hic multo tempore decens / felix migravit, quem grex suus hic tumulavit." *Die Kunstdenkmäler des Kreises Mayen,* Kunstdenkmäler des Rheinlandes 17 (Düsseldorf, 1941), 1: 151.

37. The stemma found in the edition is now also reproduced by Palmer, *Zisterzienser,* p. 77.

38. Bernhard Jussen, "Jungfrauen, Witwen, Verheiratete. Das Ende der Konsensformel moralischer Ordnung," in *Kulturelle Reformation. Sinnformationen im Umbruch 1400–1600,* Veröffentlichen des Max-Planck-Instituts für Geschichte 145 (Göttingen: 1999), pp. 97–127, esp. pp. 109–111.

39. Eleanor S. Greenhill, *Die Stellung der Handschrift British Museum Arundel 44 in der Überlieferung des Speculum virginum.* Mitteilungen des Grabmann-Intitüts der Universität München 10 (Munich, 1966). Greenhill comes out in favor of seeing scribe A of Arundel 44 as the author of the *Speculum virginum,* under whose pen the text literally took the form presented today in the London manuscript and on which all the other manuscripts depend. She relies mainly on the placing of the *explicit* and *incipit.*

40. This case can be verified in illustration I of the edition: Seyfarth, facing p. 144*.

41. An important point for this argument is provided by *SV* 9.373–484, where the dialogue partners in *L* and *K* are designated initially as *Magister* (M) and *Discipula* (D). In both manuscripts these letters are erased and replaced by *P* and *T;* in manuscript *K* the correct initials are first used one exchange earlier (*SV* 9.485, 487). Unfortunately there is a printing error in the edition: for *SV* 5.396, 439, and 463 the manuscript siglum *D* should read *M* (Trier).

42. Further examples may be added, such as *SV* 1.555; 3.219. [*Editor's note:* Another possibility is that some corrections to *L* were made before *K* was copied from *L* while others were added later.]

43. Determining the role of scribe A and therefore the resolution of the autograph question hangs on the close examination and evaluation of the corrections undertaken by scribe A. On this see Seyfarth, pp. 129*–132*.

44. The 1620 library catalogue from Zwettl speaks of ten books: Vienna, ÖNB Cod. 9520, fol. 7r: "Speculum virginum Peregrini presbyteri ad Theodoram

virginem in 10 Partes distinctum et imaginibus illustratum MS. Item eiusdem expositio de septiformis spiritus sancti gratia. In fine epithalamium Christi virginum alternantium."

45. The attempt not to let the join remain as a break, but integrate it into the overall concept, becomes clear in the words of Peregrinus (SV 10.398): "Ecce Theodora, tandem per prolixiores sermonum circuitus speculum virginum pro posse nostro monstrando potius quam fabricando exhibuimus et ad stationem finiti operis Christo favente fessi pervenimus" [Behold Theodora, eventually through rather prolix wandering of speech, we have displayed a mirror for virgins, by showing rather than by constructing it, as far as we are able, and have wearily arrived at the end of the finished work, through the favor of Christ].

46. This conjecture is made in Seyfarth, pp. 62★ and 20★. This is argued further by Morgan Powell, chapter 5 in this volume.

47. For the closeness of L and K the reader is referred once more to the codicological research, which identifies gaps at the beginning of both manuscripts. See above, n. 26.

48. Chronicon insigne Monasterii Hirsaugiensis ord. S. Benedicti per Ioannem Trithemium (Basel, 1559), p. 116: "nomen suum ex humilitate sub Peregrini vocabulo abscondit."

49. The complex question of how the historical writing of Trithemius is to be judged, as much in its historiographic orientation as in the facts it reports, is discussed at length in Klaus Schreiner, "Geschichtsschreibung im Interesse der Reform. Die Hirsauer Jahrbücher des Johannes Trithemius (1462–1516)," in Hirsau. St. Peter und Paul, 1091–1991, 2: 297–324. See also Mews, chapter 1.

50. On the role of the letter C in the heading of the introductory letter in L and the manuscripts dependent on it, see Seyfarth, p. 40★.

51. Robert Bultot, "Konrad von Hirsau," in Die deutsche Literatur des Mittelalters. Verfasserlexicon, 2nd ed., 5 (1985), 204–8 and Seyfarth, p. 38★.

52. To reach a judgment on the reliability of the information reported by Trithemius, it is necessary to fall back on the notes of the Hirsau abbot Johannes Parsimonius, studied by Lessing during his time as librarian at Wolfenbüttel, and the excerpt by the monk Johannes Rappolt. These diverse sources are discussed in Seyfarth, pp. 37★–40★, and by Mews, "Monastic Educational Culture Revisited: the Witness of Zwiefalten and the Hirsau reform" in Monastic Education in the Middle Ages, ed. George Ferzoco (London: Leicester University Press, 2000), pp. 182–97.

53. Entries in some of the manuscripts (H, I, A2, G) confirm that people were aware that the Conrad thesis could be traced back to Trithemius. Thus the Innsbruck manuscript (Cod. 742, fol. 58v) has: "Sequens opus tribuit Trithemius Conrado Monacho Hirschaugiensi ordinis Sancti Benedicti, diocesis Spirensis, quem vocat virum in divinis scripturis eruditissimum et in secularibus valde peritum, philosophum, rhetorem, musicum et poetam insignem venusti sermonis nulli veterum inferiorem. Nota: Trithemius

huic dialogo Peregrini et Theodorae tribuit tantum octo libros, dum in nostra ista editione sunt duodecim. Initium operis etiam Trithemii est quod in nostra editione sequitur post prefationem: Collaturo tecum, o Theodora ss. Sanctus Conradus claruit sub Conrado imperatore anno domini 1140."

54. "Hec Peregrinus in speculo virginum libro IX circa finem"; see Seyfarth, p. 105*.

55. Seyfarth, p. 88*.

56. There is a reproduction of this note in Palmer, *Zisterzienser,* p. 275.

57. Seyfarth, p. 41*.

58. Gustavus Becker, *Catalogi Bibliothecarum Antiqui* (Bonn: M. Cohen, 1885), p. 220.

59. Heinzer, "Buchkultur" (see above, n. 21), p. 263. Heinzer stresses the difficulty of making any statement about the library at Hirsau on the basis of the "very summary and moreover incomplete catalogue" as information about its holdings are sparse.

60. Heinzer, "Buchkultur," (see above, n. 21), p. 269.

# CHAPTER 3

# FEMALE RELIGIOUS LIFE AND
# THE *CURA MONIALIUM* IN
# HIRSAU MONASTICISM, 1080 TO 1150

*Julie Hotchin*

This chapter explores the historical context of the *Speculum virginum* through investigating the expansion of religious life for women in houses founded or reformed by monks of Hirsau in the late eleventh and first half of the twelfth century. Under the influence of William of Hirsau and his immediate disciples, there was a dramatic growth of interest in reestablishing the *vita apostolica* as a way of life in which women could participate alongside men. Many monastic houses influenced by these reforms incorporated groups of women living as recluses alongside a male monastic community. Inevitably the participation of women in a way of life traditionally defined by men created tensions. The *Speculum virginum* can be seen as vindicating a way of life that might easily provoke criticism from outsiders. Male commentary on female religious life was a process through which they could actively constitute their own male religious identity. The popularity of this treatise within male communities, involved in pastoral responsibility for religious women, reflects a continuing need for men to be instructed in the way they had to relate to religious women.

The structure of the *Speculum virginum* as an instructional dialogue between a male teacher and his female student is a literary depiction of a contemporary historical phenomenon: the growing demand for men to provide pastoral care of religious women, or *cura monialium*. The rapid growth in the number and size of women's communities throughout Germany from the end of the eleventh century presented challenges to traditional monastic structures. Not the least of these was how monks were to provide spiritual direction to women without compromising the integrity of their own religious calling. The *Speculum* circulated in a region where large numbers of women were living a religious life subject to the pastoral care of men, circumstances that made the production of such a work not only possible but necessary.[1]

The *Speculum* is one example of a burgeoning literature addressing the ideals and practice of religious life for women. A significant portion of these texts were didactic in nature, comprising what has been called "literature of formation" intended to guide the large numbers of women seeking a religious life in the models of comportment expected of them.[2] Other texts emerged out of a specifically institutional necessity: how to regulate women in monastic life at a time when the explosion in numbers of women's religious houses challenged traditional notions of that life. Not all of this literature was aimed solely at a female audience. The treatment of the relationship between a male teacher and his female student presented in the *Speculum virginum* instructs male spiritual guides *[pastores]* in the codes governing their interactions with women as well as prescribing the behavior appropriate for a woman dedicated to life in the cloister. As a guide for men responsible for the pastoral care of women, the *Speculum* is eloquent testimony to the contemporary preoccupation with negotiating the boundaries of the relationships between the sexes.

It is notable that a substantial literature treating the mixed religious life of men and women emanates from monastic authors within Germany, where the presence of women living a religious life alongside men was commonplace among communities espousing evangelical ideals. This phenomenon was prominent within the Hirsau circle, an affiliation of monasteries inspired by the ideals of monastic life promoted by William of Hirsau (1026–1091). Nearly two decades ago, Urban Küsters observed that the writings of monastic authors, within the Hirsau circle in particular, contain a wealth of material dealing in different ways with the problem of female religiosity, in works directed to women, in narratives about women, or addressing the theme theoretically.[3] These writings reveal a male monastic worldview in which the presence of women was regarded not as an ephemeral adjunct to male houses, as women have often been represented in monastic historiography, but as an integral element of their religious ideal.[4] This worldview did not translate, however, into equality of treatment. Gendered assumptions about female nature continued to shape and differentiate women's material circumstances within the Hirsau circle. Female religious life was promoted as part of this monastic revival, but women were expected to conform to male expectations governing their space, relationships, and manner of religious observance. This chapter is an introduction to the ways in which the spiritual ideals and self-consciousness of Hirsau monks shaped the development of women's religious life within one of the most popular monastic movements in twelfth-century Germany.

## The *Vita apostolica* and Religious Life for Women

One of the most striking features of the religious revival of the end of the eleventh century to contemporaries was the sheer number of new religious communities and forms of religious life adopted by men and women across Europe. In his chronicle entry for 1091, Bernold of Constance (d. 1100), a monk in the southern German abbey of St. Blasien, relates in glowing terms the evangelical piety and social ferment wrought by this spiritual awakening:

> The common life flourished at this time in many places in the kingdom of the Germans *[in regno Teutonicorum]*, not only among clerics and monks living in a very religious way but also among lay men, who devoutly offered themselves and their property for that same common life, and who, although they were neither clerics or monks in their habit, were considered in no way unequal to them in merits. For they made themselves their servants for the sake of the Lord, imitating him who came "not to be ministered unto but to minister" (Matthew 20.28) and who taught his followers to come to greatness by serving. So these men renounced the world and devoutly offered themselves and their property to communities of both clerics and monks leading regular lives, so that under their obedience they might deserve to live communally *[communiter vivere]* and to serve them.[5]

Bernold's description is replete with the images used by monastic reformers to frame their actions in imitation of Christ and the apostles. These expressions of personal spiritual awakening were self-consciously and deliberately modeled on the early Church as described in Acts of the Apostles. The most influential account of the life and activity of the apostles was that in Acts 2.42–47 and 4.32–37, which depicted a highly cohesive community, its members "one in heart and mind," living together with shared property, common ceremonies and a unified purpose.[6] The communal life of the apostles, the *vita apostolica*, was widely held as the model for monastic life. The description in Acts 1.14 of women joining with the brothers in the earliest Christian community differed, however, from existing monastic models in that it included women as well as men. This image of men and women joined in prayer was replicated within many of the new religious groups, such as those described by Bernold:

For an innumerable multitude not only of men but also of women flocked at this time to this form of life, to live communally under the obedience of clerics or monks, and they devoutly performed the load of domestic services in the manner of maidservants to them. In these same villages many daughters of farmers strove to renounce marriage and the world so as to live under the obedience of some priest. Even married women did not cease to live religiously and to obey religious men with greatest devotion.[7]

This account illustrates both the variety and imprecise nature of religious life adopted by these women. It is not clear whether they were drawn to existing monastic communities, possibly accompanying their menfolk, or whether they were part of new, informal groupings of pious laypeople seeking a spiritual life under the guidance of a priest.[8] This practice was widespread, and continued to attract comment well into the twelfth century. Some thirty years or so after Bernold's account, a canon in Liège referred to the women who "sweetly take up Christ's yoke with holy men or under their guidance" in his unfinished commentary on the various orders and forms of religious life practiced at the time.[9] Both commentators emphasize the central role of clerical authority in guiding the spiritual enthusiasm of these women. In particular, Bernold stressed that the clerics and monks providing spiritual direction themselves lived the communal life regularly [regulariter], that is, according to the discipline of a rule. A canon lawyer and ardent supporter of papal reforming efforts, Bernold reinforces his praise of these novel forms of religious life by inserting the text of a decree of Urban II affirming the legitimacy of groups such as he describes living the communal life.[10] His account of women willingly submitting to clerical authority, in spite of the somewhat innovative circumstances, may be interpreted as a defense of what was viewed in many ecclesiastic circles as a highly dubious practice.

Bernold himself was well placed to observe this phenomenon. At the time of writing his chronicle, he was a monk at the abbey of St. Blasien in Swabia, one of the rapidly growing number of monasteries sharing the reforming aims and spiritual ideals of the abbey of Hirsau. St. Blasien was another center of reform in southwest Germany, maintaining close links with other abbeys responsible for directing female religious life.[11] Earlier, in his chronicle entry for 1091, Bernold commemorated the death of William of Hirsau, the man widely hailed as the renovator of monastic life in Germany. He praised the abbot of Hirsau for his ardent support of papal reforming aims and for his fervent promotion of the monastic way of life, including the foundation or reform of many monasteries in the southwest of Germany.[12] William was renowned for his pastoral concern for women. Haimo, in his vita of the reforming abbot, described how he instructed, edified, and taught virgins, widows, and women as well as bishops, clerics, monks, and the "poor of Christ."[13] Two beneficiaries of the abbot's interest in female religious life were Herluca (d. 1127/8) and Paulina (d. 1107). Both women, venerated within Hirsau circles as models of female piety, received counsel from William about the establishment of their own religious life. Herluca sought William's advice about the most appropriate place to settle as a recluse, and Paulina, a widow who eventually achieved her aim of living as a recluse after the death of her third husband, sought assistance from William in establishing a monastery at Paulinzella in Thuringia.[14]

William was but one of a constellation of influential reformers in the southwest who actively promoted female religious life. He and his friend Ulrich of Zell, fellow abbot Siegfried of Schaffhausen, and bishop Altmann of Passau were praised as leading advocates of the monastic revival by the Augustinian canon and propagandist for papal reform, Paul of Bernried (d. 1146/50).[15] Altmann (d. 1091) founded the Augustinian house of Rottenbuch for men and women around 1073. Rottenbuch, the first house of Augustinian canons in Germany, developed into an influential centre of reform, closely linked to Hirsau, in southern Germany and modern-day Austria.[16] Siegfried (d. ca. 1098), abbot at Schaffhausen, supervised the female community that had developed around the recluse Ita of Nellenberg.[17] Ulrich of Zell (d. 1093) was claustral prior of the Cluniac priory for women at Marcigny and established a priory for women at Boleswiler, a short distance from his own foundation at Zell.[18] Abbot Theoger of St. Georgen in the Black Forest, not mentioned in this group, was also highly influential in promoting women's religious life. Although Hirsau was recognized as the leading abbey in the affiliation of monasteries that shared Abbot William's reforming ideals, St. Georgen took a more active role in directing women's religious life throughout southwest Germany (see figure 3.1).[19] Paul's choice of these four men for particular praise reflects his personal associations as well as the diversity of the monastic revival in southern Germany. This grouping also illustrates the close affinity between reformers of Benedictine and Augustinian houses, for whom the external differences of observance were less important than the similar spiritual aspirations and political allegiances that brought them together. Moreover, their interpretation of monastic life as replicating the *vita apostolica* fostered the creation of structures in which women, whether as Benedictine nuns or as Augustinian sisters, could also participate in the communal life lived in imitation of the apostles.

Two of the most ardent justifications of the practice of women sharing a religious life alongside men emanate from abbeys in southern Germany: Muri and Petershausen. The author of the *Acta Muriensa* invokes the authority of the patristic period in his praise of the custom of men living alongside women as "an example to us of the life of the holy fathers, who also gathered women to themselves for the love of God."[20] A monk at Petershausen similarly praised this practice in his preface to the abbey's chronicle. Monastic life lived in proximity to women was conceived to be replicating the actions of the apostles: "they all joined together constantly in prayer, with the women and Mary mother of Jesus and with his brothers" (Acts 1.14). The chronicler adds that this model was emulated in contemporary monasteries, where a similar commitment to prayer meant that "nearly all day and night is taken up in the work of God." In relation to nuns, he notes that "devout women fight for God equally with holy disciples, and for that reason this example is not blameworthy, but greatly worthy of praise, if women are received in monasteries as nuns in service of God, so that each sex, separated from the other, may be saved in the one place."[21] The presence of women within the monastic community formed a vital part of the monks' own identification with the early Christian communities as described in Acts. Küsters has identified the development of these mixed communities as a genuine component of the Hirsau monks' reforming consciousness and apostolic self-understanding. The presence of cloistered women provided monks with an outlet for the pastoral duties associated with the active life [vita activa], while the women devoted themselves to the highly esteemed contemplative life [vita contemplativa].[22] The position as spiritual adviser to religious women enabled the men in these communities to mirror Christ's relationships with the women in his following, just as Abelard imagined himself in his writing for Heloise.[23]

The influence of William's abbey of Hirsau ranged primarily through southwest Germany and into modern-day Austria in an extensive network of affiliated houses. Several of these abbeys were recognized as leading centers of reform, sending monks, and in some cases nuns, to other monasteries to introduce the Hirsau customs. The status of a house as a reform center was not legally based but reflected the charismatic appeal of its abbot and the piety of its inhabitants. Hirsau itself, St. Georgen, Schaffhausen, Petershausen, and Admont were all abbeys where the rigor of observance was viewed as a model to be emulated by other houses.[24] Abbeys adopting the Hirsau observance also extended into Thuringia (Paulinzell, Reinhardsbrunn) and as far north as the Weser valley (Corvey, Lippoldsberg).[25] During the height of Hirsau monasticism, from about 1080 to 1140, the foundation or reform of a male abbey was often accompanied by a daughter house for women. This was particularly the case for houses associated with the reform centers of Hirsau, St. Georgen, and Admont. The Hirsau observance was introduced to Petershausen by Abbot Dietrich, and soon after his arrival in 1116 women are mentioned at the abbey.[26] Zwiefalten, founded in 1089, included women from the outset.[27] St. Georgen, founded in 1083, developed into the most important Hirsau foundation. It originally appears to have been a double monastery, but the women were moved to Amtenhausen shortly after its foundation. Female communities were regularized at Ottobeuren (1104) and Admont (1115) upon the arrival of monks from St. Georgen who became abbots there.[28] Admont, which grew into one of the most renowned houses for women, also supervised a daughter female community at St. Georgen am Langsee (founded 1122) and the double house at Seeon from 1115. The strength of this development led Küsters to conclude that "the connection, establishment and extension of a double monastery was thus not a contingent, isolated action of an individual monastery but part of the systematic monastic politics of the affiliated group."[29] The women's community either formed part of a double monastery with the monks or was established as a dependent priory under the direction, legal and spiritual, of the abbot. Independent houses for women, observing the Benedictine Rule and subject to the authority of a bishop instead of an abbot, had no place within this monastic revival.

This trend was mirrored in the region broadly encompassed by the diocese of Trier, which experienced the greatest growth in the number of women's communities from the turn of the twelfth century. This increase in the number of houses for women reflects the expansion of Augustinian orders—primarily through the reform center of Springiersbach, but the Premonstratensian houses of Arnstein and Rommersdorf and the abbey of Marbach also supervised female religious communities.[30] Springiersbach was founded by the recluse Benigna around 1100. Under the leadership of her children, Richard and Tenxwind, it developed into the most popular new order for men and women in this region. Significantly, it was the first house to offer women the opportunity to live according to the Rule of Augustine in the diocese. Although originally a mixed community, in 1128 Tenxwind moved the women to Andernach, where she supervised a large community as *magistra* of around one hundred women.[31] Perhaps the most significant indicator of the preeminence of Springiersbach in Trier was the transfer of the important Benedictine house of St. Irminen to the authority of the abbot of Springiersbach in 1148. This transfer of the last autonomous female house in the region underscores the dominance of the Augustinian movement in Trier. No independent house for women was founded in Trier or its environs after 1050; the houses that were founded from about 1100 onward were all associated with Augustinian canons. By the mid-twelfth century no house for religious women remained unaffected by the influence of monastic reform in this region. Existing houses were brought under male control, and all new ones were founded under the aegis of a male abbey.[32]

The prevalence of Augustinian canons in Trier as ministers of the *cura monialium* reflects a trend widespread across Germany by the mid-twelfth century. Women's religious communities were increasingly placed under male authority, and the men in those positions of authority, particularly from the 1130s, were Augustinian canons. By this date, the influence of Hirsau had begun, so that except in southern Germany, where the tradition of double houses continued into the later Middle Ages, canons were increasingly selected to replace monks as provosts of nuns.[33] Even on the rare occasion when an independent female house was founded, a canon was nominated as provost for the women. This was the case at Ichtershausen, founded in 1148 by the noblewoman Friderun with the support of her relative Archbishop Henry of Mainz, where the nuns were described as living according to the Cistercian observance, although their provost was to be a discreet and devout man chosen from the order of regular canons.[34] Herrad of Hohenberg also successfully secured the spiritual services of canons for her monastery. She was instrumental in the foundation of two houses of canons, St. Gorgon and Truttenhausen, who ministered to the women at Hohenbourg. These foundations freed her community from dependence on the Benedictine monks of Ebersheim and granted Herrad an unusual degree of autonomy over her monastery.[35]

The expansion of female monasticism in Germany was strongly influenced by the emergence and development of new male religious orders. Women were prominent in the reform movement as founders and members of new religious houses. They were also among the most active and influential supporters of William and his reforming colleagues.[36] Hirsau monasticism fostered the development of female religious life as part of a monastic community of both sexes, either by founding a female community or bringing an existing informal group of women under the direction of an abbot. The distinctive feature of Hirsau and the new Augustinian orders was their drive to incorporate, enclose, and regulate feminine religiosity within their monastic structures.

## Monastic Arrangements for the *Cura Monialium*

The demand for monks to provide pastoral care for women increased significantly as women joined the religious life in growing numbers during the twelfth century. Men who previously may have acted as spiritual mentors to individual women were now confronted with the need to provide spiritual direction to often large communities of women on a permanent basis. The female element of mixed communities within the Hirsau circle may have represented an integral aspect of the monks' own religious calling, but the structures governing their lives were firmly based in their worldly concerns and expectations. This is apparent in Paul of Bernried's praise of the four forms of religious life [religio] that comprised monasteries founded by Hirsau monks and their Augustinian colleagues: the "tonsured servants of Christ" or monks; the "bearded brothers faithfully serving them" or lay brothers; recluses, described as "virgins enclosed perpetually in singular devotion"; and nuns living in double houses, those "virgins whose movements are guarded by observance of a rule."[37] Paul's description of lay brothers and women as distinct groups within the monastic community reflects the extent of the structural changes experienced by traditional monastic forms in accommodating large numbers of men and women. Female religious life, however, was promoted within certain constraints. Paul carefully delineates the parameters within which women participated in this monastic ethos: enclosed either as recluses or nuns, and guarded by men. In this way the monastic virtues of stability and obedience, and particularly chastity for women, were reinforced through the spatial arrangements governing interactions between men and women in these congregations. As the Petershausen chronicler made abundantly clear, each sex must be separated from the other in order to be saved.

The solitary life of a recluse, enclosed in a cell next to a church or within a monastic precinct, was a popular form of religious life for women. Women living either alone or in small groups attached to male abbeys were a common feature of the religious landscape in the Rheingau region near Mainz and across the southwest of Germany.[38] Recluses in Hirsau circles were often aristocratic women, whose life of poverty and penitential piety embodied the spiritual élan of the period.[39] These women were often wives or female relatives of male founders or patrons of an abbey. Life as a recluse also enabled women who had developed a spiritual friendship with an individual abbot or canon to continue their spiritual development in the vicinity of a male house. These women were often venerated as holy for the exceptional harshness of their life and their ascetic piety. The biographer of Jutta (1092–1136), daughter of the count of Sponheim and enclosed as a recluse at Disibodenberg in 1112, praised her ascetic regime as an exemplary embodiment of monastic virtue.[40]

Life as a recluse offered women a greater opportunity to teach and edify publicly than their cloistered sisters. Jutta's pastoral activity also extended to teaching. Her piety attracted several daughters of the local nobility who sought to emulate her way of life. Her biographer mentions that she "taught ungrudgingly whomever she could," including those women who formed a small religious community under her direction at Disibodenberg. Although not learned in the formal sense of literati, the charismatic spirituality of women such as Jutta inspired the trust and confidence of the people who sought the immediacy of divine authority mediated through these women.[41] Ava of Melk (d. 1127) performed a similar didactic and pastoral role, exhorting her audience to a life of piety through her vernacular poetic rendering of the life of Christ.[42] A striking example of the recluse's ability to counsel someone at a moment of personal and spiritual need is the case of Hermann the Jew. His autobiography contains a moving account of how his encounter with two recluses in Cologne gave him the confidence to convert to Christianity. Their prayer and spiritual counsel proved to be more effective in this instance than any preaching and exhortations of clerics.[43] The recluse blurred the boundaries separating the monastic enclosure from the secular world through her teaching and counsel. Far from living an isolated, solitary life withdrawn in a cell, the recluse was in fact a vital node in the web of social relations and interactions of the monastic community to which she belonged.

The popularity of this form of religious life for women often transformed the recluse's cell into a community, bringing with it greater regulation and removal from the perceived perils of the world. In many instances, the female community living alongside a male house had developed around a woman or women seeking a pious life in imitation of the "poor of Christ" [pauperes Christi]. The female community of St. Agnes at Schaffhausen had its origins in the group of women who gathered around the recluse Ita of Nellenberg.[44] The female community at Disibodenberg had grown to around twenty when Hildegard left to found her own monastery in 1148/50. At Lippoldsberg and Admont women who had gathered to live an informal religious life under the direction of a monk or priest were directed into monastic structures by men who sought to regulate their religious calling.[45] The transition from a small eremitic community to cenobitic life is a common pattern in the history of female monastic houses. Religious life for women independent of monastic structures could be precarious, whereas the support of male patrons offered them greater economic sustainability and longevity for their community. But the promise of stability afforded by an association with a male abbey came at the cost of female autonomy.[46]

Women joining the Hirsau and Augustinian reform movements were most commonly accommodated within double houses or dependent priories. The practice of men and women living together in a single monastery, a tradition going back to the seventh century, was revived at the end of the eleventh century as a practical means of accommodating large numbers of women within monastic structures.[47] The use of the term "double monastery" to describe these communities of men and women has attracted criticism for being used too loosely as a descriptor of the many and varied forms of religious life shared by celibate men and women.[48] The notion of a double monastery may imply a greater degree of organization, size, or regular life than actually existed. The definition of double monasteries used by Sally Thompson in her study of women religious in England is relevant also to the situation in Germany, that is a monastery "consisting of two communities, one of monks and one of nuns, established in the same place but not necessarily within the same boundary, observing the same rule, and together forming a legal entity under one authority."[49] This was the case, for example, at Admont, Zwiefalten, Petershausen, Schaffhausen, Schönau, Muri, and Engelberg, where the nuns were housed in separate buildings from the monks yet were considered an integral part of the community.

The popularity of double houses as a means of enabling men and women to share the religious life accentuated the question of how space was to be structured between the sexes. Female enclosure assumed greater significance during the twelfth century as female sanctity became increasingly associated with sexual purity. At Admont the women's spiritual virtuosity was premised on their strict segregation from the world. A celebrated description of the female community of this double house forms part of the monk Irimbert's (d. 1176) account of the fire that nearly destroyed the monastery in March 1152.[50] The nuns refused to leave their cloister to flee to safety, despite the urging of their abbot. But they were miraculously rescued when the wind changed direction at the last moment. This fortuitous escape prompted Irimbert to reflect on the spiritual merits of the Admont community, including the arrangement of female monastic space. According to Irimbert's account, the entrance to the women's monastery was through a single door, opposite the altar, through which the women passed for only two reasons: profession and burial. Two elder monks and the *magistra* of the women, each of whom held a key to the nuns' enclosure, regulated movement across this threshold. No one was allowed to enter the enclosure except the abbot or prior, accompanied by two or three witnesses, and then only to administer the sacraments to a nun confined to her bed through illness or occasionally to preside over chapter. The nuns adhered to the rule of silence strictly, speaking to no one except at the window of their chapter house, and then in the presence of two or three witnesses, except for confession. Irimbert nevertheless suggests that the rigor of this enclosure, while restrictive, did not preclude sociable interaction across the cloister boundary. While on one hand he describes how the women did not approach the grille to speak unless with the permission of the *magistra,* and then only when they saw the abbot approaching, the nuns enjoyed supervised visits from "spiritual or secular friends." Despite this physical segregation, the women at Admont played an active role in the abbey's intellectual life. Irimbert records how they took down his sermons preached through the window of their chapter house and collaborated with the monks to produce lavish manuscripts.[51]

Male and female communities in double houses, separated physically, formed a spiritual unity: Both sexes followed the same liturgical rhythm, undertook the same ascetic exercises, and fulfilled the same duties of prayer. Irimbert describes how the nuns at Admont mirrored the observance of the monks: "Throughout the entire year, summer or winter, at the sound of the bell, they rose with the brothers for the vigil of matins, and extended the order of vigils through the whole of winter until daylight. They observed the same fasts and the same silence with the brothers through the course of the year."[52] The opportunity for men and women to celebrate the liturgy side by side—albeit separated by walls—was a vivid demonstration of the sense of spiritual unity that could be engendered within this environment. At the Augustinian house of Rolduc in Liège, the sisters joined with the brothers to celebrate mass at the altar in the crypt of the church, a practice, however, that was not welcomed by all observers.[53] Women living as nuns or recluses represented an important element of the monastic *familia*. The necrologies for Muri and Engelberg, both monasteries with significant female populations, list women to be commemorated as "sister (or nun, or laywomen etc) of our congregation" *[soror nostrae congregationis]*.[54] Female recluses are prominent among the names commemorated in necrologies of Hirsau houses. The pattern of commemoration reflects the importance of this form of religious life as a model for other women: Female recluses were more likely to be commemorated within houses where women were present, as at Zwiefalten, Admont, Amtenhausen, and Petershausen.[55] The presence of women within the community formed part of the spiritual self-consciousness of the reformed monk, for whom pastoral responsibility for women enacted a vivid experience of the relationships between Christ and his followers.

Despite the popularity of double houses as a material expression of a spiritual ideal, not all of them were long-lived. At the abbey of Hirsau itself the women who had gathered around the male community were moved to Kentheim by William around 1079.[56] In doing so, William may have been seeking to emulate more closely the Cluniac model, in which women were gathered under the direction of the abbot in the dependent priory at Marcigny.[57] The priory was geographically removed from the male abbey and constituted a separate legal entity but was subject to abbatial, not episcopal, authority. The prohibitions of II Lateran in 1139 against co-celebration of the liturgy provided justification for abbots, troubled by the proximity of the sexes, to relocate the female community of a double house in a dependent priory at a distance from the men. This occurred at Zwiefalten in 1138, at Marbach the women were relocated to a priory at Schwarzentann in 1150; and at Rolduc a dependent priory to house the women who had previously lived near the abbey was founded in 1140. There were increased efforts within the Premonstratensian order from the late 1130s to relocate the female element of double houses away from men. This drive to curtail female participation in the order reached a peak at the end of the twelfth century, when the General Chapter decreed that women were no longer to be admitted into the order. But regardless of these decrees, the enduring appeal of religious life shared between the sexes motivated the continued foundation of double houses into the thirteenth century.[58]

Women may have shared a spiritual unity with their monastic brothers, but their material life was subject to male authority. Religious women were directed by a provost, who acted on behalf of the women in administrative affairs and ministered the sacraments. Female dependence on men for provision of their material needs was regarded as a determinant of female piety. Idung, a monk at the Hirsau-affiliated abbey of Prüfening in Regensburg, justified this arrangement on the grounds that the Rule of Benedict did not specifically cater to women: "Benedict wrote no rule for holy virgins, nor did he need to write one, since monasteries of virgins from that time have been guarded by the rule of abbots." This arrangement was necessary as "brides of Christ are weaker and inferior" than men and therefore had greater need of the protection afforded by enclosure and male supervision.[59] While an image of shared intimacy could shape relationships between men and women in monastic life, in reality the institutional arrangements governing the lives of their members ensured that interactions between the sexes occurred only in strictly controlled ways. The extension of the order and customs of Hirsau to women, who were expected to structure their lives according to a model created for and by men, is a telling insight into the worldview of these monks. Although they held to the image of revived monasticism as a model of the apostolic life, the contemporary expression of that life was premised on a masculine model and shaped by assumptions of feminine fragility.

The position of provost was neither new nor unique to female houses, but it assumed greater significance within this reforming milieu. The provost in reformed houses had full authority and responsibility for administrative, economic, and legal matters that were previously vested in the abbess of an independent house. Female leadership was restricted to the office of magistra who was responsible for the discipline and day-to-day supervision of the women and subject to the provost's authority. It was possible for the women to have a role in the choice of their provost, although the supervising abbot or bishop ultimately approved the decision. The nuns at Lippoldsberg could request the election of a new provost, if their existing one proved unsuitable.[60] Hildegard eventually succeeded in securing the right to choose a monk to act as provost to the women at

Rupertsberg, after lengthy and acrimonious negotiations with Abbot He-lenger of Disibodenberg.[61] Similarly, the foundation charter for the Cistercian nunnery of Ichtershausen confirmed the nuns' right to chose their provost, subject to the approval of the Archbishop of Mainz. Securing the right to choose their provost was an important means for women to retain some control over their material and spiritual existence.

The responsibility for the *cura monialium* was not one to be assumed lightly. Men who acted as custodians of religious women were enjoined to preserve the boundaries separating them from their charges. The threat represented by the permeability of female enclosure was most pronounced in situations where the potential for transgression was greatest. Potent images of near-complete female enclosure emanate from double monasteries where vigilant observance of sexual segregation was deemed essential to protect the virtue of all inhabitants. Architectural historian Loraine Simmons has described this heightened sensitivity about preserving boundaries between the sexes as "proximity anxiety." She demonstrates how the monastic spaces and statutes at Fontevrault were designed to shape the interactions between the nuns and the clerics providing spiritual services to them. Simmons concludes that these boundaries served to "maintain the proper relationship between the women and men, to guard the integrity of the cloister, to mediate their differences and the balance of power between them."[62]

The *Speculum virginum* was the product of a similar environment in which men and women shared a religious life lived in close physical proximity. An acute sensitivity to perceptions of impropriety inform descriptions of the relationship between a magister and his female student in the work. The model of spiritual conversation between the sexes represented in this dialogue stresses the pious intent of the participants and the requirement that their relationship be conducted within a suitably structured space. Peregrinus and Theodora model the ideal relationship between teacher and student as one guided by the "knowledge of divine presence" (*SV* 5.1240–41). Purity of intent alone was not, however, sufficient. Peregrinus advises his female charge that "when men and women come together in holiness, one wall encloses them separately . . . but nevertheless fear and love of God intervenes" (5.1243–48).

The character of the men responsible for the *cura monialium* receives extended treatment in the *Speculum virginum*. The author's concern with the nature of the interactions between teacher and student is most apparent when he addresses the potential abuse of this privileged relationship. The danger of sexual transgression inherent in contact between men and women is the focus of moral exhortation and dire warning in a number of passages in the work (*SV* 1.543–69; 5.1030–1287), but perhaps its most engaging treatment is the story of a young cleric related by Peregrinus in *SV*

2.260–374. The cleric was one of a number assigned to minister to a community of nuns who are described as maintaining their vows through the fear of God and monastic discipline. Succumbing to temptation, he attempts to violate the nuns' dormitory but is struck dead. Although this example amplifies the dangers of illicit sexual relations between the sexes, the misogynist overtones characteristic of many critics of the mixed religious life are challenged in the tale. The cleric, whose intemperate desire for the nun caused him to violate the women's enclosure, and not the nun herself, is the subject of condemnation. Elsewhere in the work Peregrinus is critical of similar rash behavior of clerics who abuse the privileged position conferred by their office, lamenting that this was all too common in his own day. The danger presented by contact between the sexes was as real as the relationship was necessary: Religious women relied on the teaching and example of their male spiritual guides. Religious women are warned to be on guard against clerics who act like "rapacious wolves" (5.1029) in threatening the chastity of the women entrusted to them. In addition to providing a model of comportment for female readers, the Speculum virginum also guides men in the conduct of their relationship with their female charges.

The anxieties expressed by the Speculum author about the nature of the relationship between the sexes echo contemporary preoccupations. The threat of sexual impropriety occurring in these relationships focused attention on the character of those men who were chosen to minister to women. Clerics selected to act as provosts for female communities were commonly described as "religious men" [viri religiosi], and abbots were urged to ensure that women under their authority were provided with a spiritual director whose character was beyond reproach.[63] The anxieties and difficulties faced by men responsible for providing pastoral care to women are evident in Irimbert's eulogy of monastic virtue at Admont. He concludes his account of the fire with a passionate defense of the life and morals of the Admont community, monks, lay brothers, and women, rejecting the accusations of detractors who interpreted the fire as divine retribution.[64] Irimbert appears to have been responding to local criticism of the continued presence of women at Admont, an arrangement that at the time of the fire was regarded in many circles as highly problematic and suspicious. The image he constructs of the women at Admont, their strict enclosure and the intensity of their devotions, is one that embodies the virtue and discipline of the entire community. Irimbert represents a model of the ideal relationship between religious women and their male teachers that underscores the spatial separation and comportment necessary to conduct the relationship. With a similar intent as the Speculum author, he directs his words to a male audience, this time his brothers at Admont, as a warning to them not to fail the women in their care.

## Conclusion

The concern in the *Speculum virginum* with the nature of relationships between religious women and the men who provided their spiritual direction echoes the common difficulties and problems faced by men engaged in the *cura monialium*. The *Speculum* is one of a number of works treating the structure and governance of female religious life that were not aimed solely at women but also addressed a male audience. These works were intended as guides for men in the performance of their pastoral responsibilities. As such, they provided models of the ideal structuring of relationships—of authority, comportment, and space—required between men and women sharing a religious life.

The study of literature produced by and for religious women has emphasized how women negotiated their relationships with their male mentors and spiritual advisers—at times in concert, at other times in conflict with them. Art historian Jeffrey Hamburger has drawn our attention to the fact that works written by and for women existed in relation to each other: "to the extent that each type of text shaped the other, neither should be read in isolation. The two bodies of literature, like their authors, co-existed within a dynamic and polemical context."[65] Male commentary on female religious life was a process through which they could actively constitute their own male religious identity. Descriptions of the regulation of the female cloister and praise of virtuous women can also be read as a defense of a model of monastic life that was increasingly subject to criticism. Images of nuns guarded by a cloister wall speak of male desire to maintain this separation in situations where restricting contact may have been neither straightforward nor simple. Praise of a disciplined and virtuous community of women was also an affirmation of the men who sustained that ordered and sacral environment. Images of feminine virtue promoted by monks in double houses speak as much, if not more, of their own concerns than they do about the women represented by them.

As the spiritual benefits accruing from engaging with holy women were increasingly valued, the physical accessibility of these women was reduced. Access to the private, inner spiritual rewards offered by holy women was regulated by the walls of their enclosure and their male spiritual directors. The enduring popularity of these deep personal spiritual relationships, and of the meditative quality of holy women during the latter twelfth and thirteenth centuries, testifies to the continued appeal of the image of caring intimacy between men and women in the religious life. The parallel popularity of the *Speculum*, particularly within male communities with pastoral responsibilities for women, reflects a continuing need to instruct them in the comportment required of men in their contact with religious women.

Map 1   The spread of the Benedictine reform movement of William of Hirsau in the
eleventh and twelfth centuries.

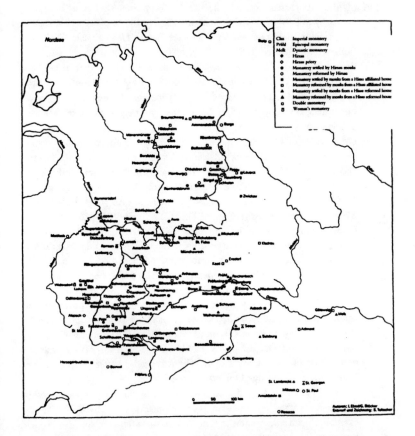

Adapted from Immo Eberl, ed., *Kloster Blaubeuren 1085–1985. Benediktinisches Erbe und Evan-
gelische Semnartradition. Katalog zur Ausstellung der Evangelischen Seminarstiftung und des Haup-
stadtarchivs Stuttgart, 15 Mai bis 15 Oktober 1985* (Sigmaringen: Jan Thorbeke, 1985)

**Notes**

I would like to thank Franz Felten, Fiona Griffiths, Stephanie Tarbin, and Constant Mews for discussion of many issues and comments on earlier versions of this chapter.

1. Matthäus Bernards estimates the number of women's religious houses in Germany to have increased from about 150 in 1100 to 500 by 1250, *Speculum Virginum. Geistigkeit und Seelenleben der Frau im Hochmittelalter* (Cologne: Böhlau, 1955; 2nd ed. 1982), p. 1.

2. Barbara Newman, "Flaws in the Golden Bowl: Gender and Spiritual Formation in the Twelfth Century," *Traditio* 45 (1989/90): 111–46, reprinted in *From Virile Woman to WomanChrist* (Philadelphia: University of Pennsylvania Press, 1995), pp. 19–45, and chapter 7 by Pinder and chapter 9 by Bos in this volume.

3. Urban Küsters, *Der verschlossene Garten. Volkssprachliche Hohelied-Auslegung und monastiche Lebensform im 12. Jahrhundert* (Düsseldorf: Droste, 1985), and "Formen und Modelle religiöser Frauengemeinschaften im Umkreis der Hirsauer Reform des 11. und 12. Jahrhunderts," in *Hirsau. St. Peter und St. Paul. Teil II Geschichte, Lebens-und Verfassungsformen eines Reformklosters*, ed. Klaus Schreiner (Stuttgart: Konrad Thiess, 1991), pp. 195–220.

4. Roberta Gilchrist is critical of historians who tend to judge women's monastic houses "as failures according to the model of male monasticism" and perceive them to be less important, politcially and economically, poorly supervised, and poorly documented. She challenges the practice of comparing women's monasticism to the model of their male counterparts, arguing that nunneries were founded for different social purposes and adopted different structures to men; see *Gender and Material Culture: The Archaeology of Religious Women* (London: Routledge, 1994), pp. 22–25.

5. Bernold of Constance, *Chronicon*, MGH SS 5 (1844): 452–53. The translation is that of Giles Constable in *The Reformation of the Twelfth Century* (Cambridge: Cambridge University Press, 1996), p. 80.

6. Constable discusses how the common usage of these concepts expressed the self-understanding of reformers in *Reformation*, pp. 125–67. To cite one example, Siegfried, Archbishop of Mainz, in a charter for the regular canons of Ravengiersburg in 1074 described them as living "according to the example of those men who, in the primitive church, as is read in the Acts of the Apostles, said nothing was theirs but all things were common to them"; *Urkundenbuch zur Geschichte der jetzt die preussischen Regierungsbezirke Coblenz und Trier bildenen mittelrheinischen Territorien*, ed. Heinrich Beyer, Leopold Eltester, and Adam Goertz (Coblenz, 1860–1874), 1: 431, no. 374. Herbert Grundmann's classic study still provides a useful introduction and discussion of the energy of the period; *Religious Movements in the Middle Ages: The Historical Links between Heresy, the Mendicant Orders, and the Women's Religious Movement in the Twelfth and Thirteenth Century, with the Historical Foundations of German Mysticism*, trans. Steven Rowan (Notre Dame, IN: University of Notre Dame Press, 1995), esp. pp. 7–21, 75–88.

7. Bernold, *Chronicon,* MGH SS 5: 453.

8. Constable, in *Reformation,* pp. 80–81 (see above n. 5), also discusses contemporary lay communities of men and women in Italy, apparently short-lived, where men and women grouped under an abbot for mutual religious, social, and economic support. Other similar communities consisted of lay penitents, mostly peasants, leading a common life who were served either by their own or a parish priest.

9. *Libellus de diversis ordinibus et professionibus qui sunt in aecclesia,* ed. G. Constable and B. Smith (Oxford: Clarendon Press, 1972), pp. 4–5. This was written in the second quarter of the twelfth century, probably in the diocese of Liège.

10. Bernold, *Chronicon,* MGH SS 5: 453.

11. On Bernold's link to St. Blasien, see Gerold Bönnen, Alfred Haverkamp, and Frank G. Hirschmann, "Religiöse Frauengemeinschaften im räumlichen Gefüge der Trierer Kirchenprovinz während des hohen Mittelalters," in *Herrschaft, Kirche, Kultur. Beiträge zur Geschichte des Mittelalters,* ed. Georg Jenal (Stuttgart: Anton Hiersemann, 1993), p. 372. The female community at St. Blasien was relocated to Berau as a dependent priory of this abbey between 1108 and 1125. The abbey of Muri was reformed by St. Blasien in 1082. The *Acta Murensia* records that abbot Giselbert from St. Blasien sent lay brothers with sisters (*exteriores fratres cum sorores*) to the newly reformed house; Urban Küsters, "Formen und Modelle," p. 210 (n. 3 above). For a brief outline of St. Blasien's connections to other female communities, both priories and double houses, see Küsters, *Der verschlossene Garten,* p. 154 (n. 3 above).

12. Bernold, *Chronicon,* MGH SS 5: 451. Bernold lists the houses where William "instituted regular discipline," including St. Georgen in the Black Forest, Zwiefalten, Schaffhausen, and Petershausen.

13. Haimo, author of William's *vita,* attributes the revival of monasticism in Germany to William's efforts and comments on his sponsorship of female religious life, emulated by reforming abbots within the Hirsau network; *Vita Willihelmi Abbatis Hirsaugiensis,* MGH SS 12 (1856): 218. William settled the women who were attracted to Hirsau at a distance from this foundation at Kentheim in 1079; Küsters, *Der verschlossene Garten,* p. 147.

14. Paul of Bernried, *Vita beatae Herlucae,* AASS, April II, 552–57. *Sigebotonis Vita Paulinae,* MGH SS 30.2 (1934): 910–38. On the significance of Herluca, see Gabriela Signori, "Eine Biographie als Freundshaftsbeweis. Paul von Bernried und seine Lebensbeschreibung der seligen Herluca von Epfach," in *Meine in Gott geliebte Freundin. Freundschaftsdokumente aus klösterlichen und humanistischen Schriebstuben,* ed. Gabriela Signori (Bielefeld: Verlag für Regionalgeschichte, 1995), pp. 60–66. The *vita* of Pauline represents the life of the woman and the foundation history of her monastery as integrally entwined; see Camilla Badstübern-Kizik, *Die Gründungs-und Frühgeschichte des Klosters Paulinzelle,* Uni-Press Hochschulschriften 41 (Münster: Li-Verlag, 1993); and Küsters, *Der verschlossene Garten,* pp. 121–30 (n. 3 above).

15. Paul of Bernried, *Vita Gregorii papae VII* in *Pontificum Romanorum vitae I*, ed. Johann Matthias Watterich (Leipzig, 1862; reprinted Aalen Scientia Verlag, 1966), p. 543. This was the second in a three-part cycle of *vitae* crafted by Paul to promote the ideals of clerical and monastic reform favored within Hirsau and Augustinian circles. The other two subjects of Paul's hagiographic interest were Ulrich of Zell, prior at Cluny and Herluca, the recluse and spiritual friend of Paul: *Vita Udalrici. Ex Vita posteriore*, MGH SS 12 (1856): 253–67.

16. Altmann's biographer also relates how he erected seven chapels to various saints, to which recluses were attached, and a hospital with canons to minister to them; *Vita Altmanni episcopi Pataviensis*, MGH SS 12 (1856): 228–43, esp. 237. On the influence of Rottenbuch and its close relationship to the Benedictine reform centers of Hirsau and St. Blasien, see Roswitha Wisniewski, *Das frühmittelhochdeutsche Hohe Lied–sog. St. Trudperter Hohes Lied* (Frankfurt am Main: Peter Lang, 1995), pp. 31–38.

17. Schaffhausen was founded by the comital family of Nellenberg in 1049. In 1073 Count Eberhard entered the monastery as a *conversus*, and Ita became a recluse there. William of Hirsau introduced the Hirsau observance to Schaffhausen ca. 1079/80. Shortly after, in 1082, Abbot Siegfried organized Ita and the women who had joined her into the Benedictine community of St. Agnes, under his direction. Küsters, "Formen und Modelle," pp. 202–4 (n. 3 above).

18. The *vita* of Ulrich refers to his relations with the female community of Boleswiler, situated not far from the male house at Zell; Küsters, *Der verschlossene Garten*, p. 106, n. 30 (n. 3 above). *Vita S. Udalrici prioris cellensis*, MGH SS 12 (1856): 262. At William's request Ulrich provided him with a copy of the *consuetudines* of Cluny, on which the abbot of Hirsau based his customary for that abbey.

19. On Theoger's spiritual leadership of the women at the priory of Amtenhausen, see *Vita Theogeri* 1.25–26, MGH SS 12 (1856): 459–62. Of the seventeen monasteries reformed by St. Georgen, ten were double houses or female monasteries; Romuald Bauerreiss, "St. Georgen im Schwarzwald, ein Reformmittelpunkt Südostdeutschlands im beginnenden 12. Jahrhundert," *Studien und Mitteilungen zur Geschichte des Benediktiner-ordens und seine Zweige* 53 (1935): 47–56.

20. *Acta Murensa*, ed. P. Martin Kiem, *Quellen zur Schweizer Geschichte* 3 (Basel: Allgemeine Geschichtsforschende Gesellschaft der Schweiz, 1883), p. 60; cited in Küsters, *Der verschlossene Garten*, p. 144 (n. 3 above).

21. *Casus monasterii Petrishusensis*, MGH SS 20 (1868): 625.

22. Küsters, "Formen und Modelle," pp. 210 and 143 (n. 3 above).

23. Mary M. McLaughlin, "Peter Abelard and the Dignity of Women: Twelfth-Century 'Feminism' in Theory and Practice," in *Pierre Abélard–Pierre le Vénérable. Les courants philosophiques, littéraires et artistiques en occident au milieu du XIIe siècle. Abbaye de Cluny 2 au 9 Juillet 1972*, ed. Jean Jolivet (Paris:

CNRS 1975), pp. 287–333 emphasizes this point in her analysis of Abelard's relationship with the women at the Paraclete.

24. Nuns from Schaffhausen introduced the Hirsau observance to Lippoldsberg around 1100; Michel Parisse, "Die Frauenstifte und Frauenklöster in Sachsen vom 10. bis zur Mitte des 12. Jahrhunderts," in *Die Salier und das Reich. Band 2, Die Reichskirche in der Salierzeit,* ed Stefan Weinfurter (Sigmaringen: Jan Thorbeke, 1991), pp. 465–501, esp. 487–91. The nuns at Admont lead the reform of several women's houses; Bauerreiss, "St. Georgen" (n. 19 above).

25. The spatial dispersion of Hirsau monasteries is illustrated in map 80 in Josef Engel, ed., *Grosser Historischer Weltatlas* II Mittelalter (Munich: Bayerischer Schulbuch-Verlag, 1970).

26. *Casus monasterii Petrishusensis* 18–20, MGH SS 5 (1868): 220ff.

27. Ortlieb, *Chronicon* 20, MGH SS 10: 88ff. In 1138, the number of choir nuns at Zwiefalten almost equaled the number of monks. Berthold records that at that time, the abbey comprised 70 monks, 130 lay brothers, and 62 nuns of noble origin; Berthold, *Chronicon* 43, MGH SS 10: 276ff.

28. Küsters, *Der verschlossene Garten,* pp. 147–50 (n. 3 above) for St. Georgen and its affiliations.

29. Ibid., p. 153. When an abbey was reformed along Hirsau lines, an abbot was selected from one of the reform centers, the Hirsau *ordo* (or customs) introduced and a women's house established. Although a large number of monasteries were influenced by the customs of Hirsau they did not form an organized monastic association, or order, in a legal sense. For a detailed listing of Hirsau affiliated women's houses in southwestern Germany; ibid., pp. 147–54.

30. Franz Felten provides a detailed analysis of the development of women's monasticism for the Rhineland region in "Frauenklöster und-stifte im Rheinland. Ein Beitrag zur Geschichte der Frauen in der religiösen Bewegung des hohen Mittelalters," in *Reformidee und Reformpolitik im Spätsalisch-Frühstaufischen Reich. Vorträge der Tagung der Gesellschaft für Mittelrheinische Kirchengeschichte vom 11. bis 13. September 1991 in Trier,* ed. Stephan Weinfurter, Quellen und Abhandlungen zur Mittelrheinischen Kirchengeschichte Band 68 (Mainz 1992), pp. 189–300. He discusses Arnstein and Rommersdorf at pp. 266–67. See also Bönnen et al, "Religiose Frauengemeinschaften," (n. 11 above). Manegold of Lautenbach was appointed provost of the Augustinian house catering to both sexes at Marbach in 1094. His wife became *magistra* of the women's community, which was relocated to Schwarzentann around 1150. For Marbach, see Elsanne Gilomen-Schenkel, "Engelberg, Interlaken und andere autonome Doppelklöster im Südwesten des reiches (11.–13.Jh). Zur Quellenproblematik und zur historiographischen Tradition," in *Doppelklöster und andere Formen der Symbiose männlicher und weiblicher Religiosen im Mittelalter,* ed. Kaspar Elm and Michel Parisse (Berlin: Duncker & Humblot, 1992), pp. 121–23.

31. Bönnen et al., "Religiöse Frauengemeinschaften," pp. 396–98 (n. 11 above). Two other daughter houses attracted similar popularity: charters for Stuben (1137) and Schönstatt (1226) reveal that these houses were also restricted to one hundred women. On the foundation of Andernach and references to Tenxwind's learning, see *Fundatio Sanctae Mariae Andernacenses*, MGH SS 15.2 (1888): 969. Alfred Haverkamp discusses Tenxwind and her interpretation of the Springiersbach observance in "Tenxwind von Andernach und Hildegard von Bingen," in *Institutionen, Kultur und Gesellschaft im Mittelalter. Festschrift für Josef Fleckenstein zu seinem 65. Geburtstag*, ed. L. Fenske, W. Rösener and Th. Zotz (Sigmaringen: Jan Thorbeke, 1984), pp. 515–48.

32. Bönnen et al., "Religiöse Frauengemeinschaften," pp. 387–90 (n. 11 above). This close association of women with canons was mirrored in the diocese of Salzburg, where between 1120 and 1150 practically all houses of canons had a *claustrum* for regular canonesses; Küsters, *Der verschlossene Garten*, p. 154 (n. 3 above).

33. Michel Parisse describes similar trends developing in Saxony for the same period, "Frauenstifte und Frauenklöster in Sachsen" (n. 24 above).

34. *Mainzer Urkundenbuch II, Die Urkunden seit dem Tode Erzbischof Adalberts (1137) bis zum Tode Erzbischof Konrads (1200)*, ed. Peter Acht (Darmstadt: Selbstverlag der Hessichen Historischen Kommission, 1968–71), p. 190, no. 98. This charter is an important source for the early history of women and the Cistercians in Germany.

35. See chapter 10 by Fiona Griffiths in this volume.

36. Beatrix Wilms emphasizes this aspect of female involvement in reform in Germany; *Amatrices Ecclesiarum. Untersuchung zur Rolle und Funktion der Frauen in der Kirchenreform des 12. Jahrhunderts*, Bochumer Historische Studien, Mittelalterliche Geschichte 5 (Bochum: Studienverlag Dr. N. Brockmeyer, 1987).

37. Paul of Bernried, *Vita Gregorii*, p. 543 (n. 15 above).

38. Trithemius of Sponheim reflected on the widespread popularity of this practice in the region near Disibodenberg and Sponheim in his *Chronicon Monasterii Sponheimense*, in *Johannis Trithemii Opera Historica*, ed. Marquard Freher (Frankfurt: 1601; repr. Frankfurt/Main: Minerva, 1966), 2: 247–48. A translation and introductory comments can be found in *Jutta and Hildegard: The Biographical Sources*, ed. and trans. Anna Silvas (Turnhout: Brepols, 1998), pp. 42–45. Otmar Doerr's study of recluses in southern Germany underscores the popularity of this form of religious life for women in Hirsau circles; *Das Institut der Inclusen in Süddeutschland* (Münster: Aschendorff, 1934).

39. Küsters, *Der verschlossene Garten*, pp. 135, 138, 141–42.

40. "The Life of Lady Jutta the Anchoress" in Silvas, *Jutta and Hildegard*, pp. 70–71.

41. Silvas, *Jutta and Hildegard*, pp. 72–73 (n. 38 above). Anneke B. Mulder-Bakker discusses the role performed by recluses in instructing the laity in "The *Reclusorium* as an Informal Centre of Learning," in *Centres of Learn-*

*ing: Learning and Location in Pre-Modern Europe and the Near East*, ed. Jan Willem Drijvers and A. A. McDonald (Leiden: Brill, 1995), pp. 245–54.

42. Ernst Ralf Hintz, "Persuasion and Pedagogy in the Works of Frau Ava," in his *Learning and Persuasion in the German Middle Ages* (New York: Garland Publishing, 1997), pp. 103–37.

43. Karl F. Morrison, *Conversion and Text: The Cases of Augustine of Hippo, Hermann-Judah, and Constantine Tsatsos* (Charlottesville: University Press of Virginia, 1992).

44. Küsters, "Formen und Modelle," pp. 203–4 (n. 3 above).

45. Parisse, "Frauenstifte und Frauenklöster in Sachsen," pp. 487–91 (n. 24 above) briefly discusses the early history of Lippoldsberg. Abbot Wolfold, on his arrival at Admont from St. Georgen in 1115, organized the women living there at the time into a monastic enclosure. Jacob Wichner's history of the women's community at Admont is still useful; "Das ehemalige Nonnenkloster O.S.B. zu Admont," *Wissenschaftliche Studien und Mitteilungen aus dem Benediktiner-Orden* 2 (1881): 75–84 and 288–319.

46. Sharon Elkins, in *Holy Women of Twelfth Century England* (Chapel Hill: University of North Carolina, 1988), p. 52, claims that women traded personal independence for material protection and the benefit of stability provided through association with a male abbey. Some male historians of female religious life in Germany have tended to represent the shift from an informal, unstable anchoritic lifestyle to the institutional stability of cenobitic life as a positive one for women; Küsters, *Der verschlossene Garten*, p. 161 (n. 3 above), and Bönnen et al., "Frauengemeinschaften," pp. 387–88 (n. 11 above).

47. On double monasteries, see Stephan Hilpisch, *Die Doppelklöster. Entwicklung und Organisation* (Münster: Aschendorff, 1928), and Elm and Parisse, eds., *Doppelklöster* (n. 30 above).

48. Sharon Elkins argues that in twelfth-century England, double monasteries were only one of many arrangements in which men and women affiliated with each other; *Holy Women*, p. xviii (n. 46 above). Felten points out that double houses have been poorly treated by German scholars of Hirsau monasticism; "Frauenklöster und -Stifte," p. 242, n. 232 (n. 30 above). Gilomen-Schenkel argues for a reconsideration of their history in "Engelberg, Interlaken und andere autonome Doppelklöster," pp. 115–33 (n. 30 above).

49. Sally Thompson, *Women Religious: The Founding of English Nunneries after the Norman Conquest* (Oxford: Oxford University Press, 1991), p. 55.

50. Bernard Pez, *Bibliotheca ascetica antiquo-nova* (Regensburg, 1725) 8: 454–64. As at Admont, the claustration of the nuns at Amtenhausen, a female priory supervised by the monks of St. Georgen, was represented in ideal terms: "There was such great separation from men, that once [she] had entered the monastery she rarely went outside except to bury a dead sister"; *Vita Theogerii* 1.25, MGH SS 12: 460. For Irimbert, abbot of Admont from 1172 to 1176, see Johann Wilhelm Braun, "Irimbert von Admont," *Frühmittelalterliche Studien* 7 (1973): 266–323.

51. Alison I. Beach, "Claustration and Collaboration between the Sexes in the Twelfth-Century Scriptorium," in *Monks and Nuns, Saints and Outcasts: Religion in Medieval Society*, ed. Sharon Farmer and Barbara H. Rosenwein (Ithaca, NY: Cornell University Press, 2000), pp. 57–75.

52. Pez, *Bibliotheca Ascetica* 13: 459 (n. 50 above). The Cluniac customs allowed for a return to sleep in the time between matins and lauds during the long winter nights. The practice of extending vigils through the night described here would have been a particularly harsh requirement to sustain.

53. *Annales Rodenses*, MGH SS (1859) 16: 706. The canon who wrote the *Annales* regarded the women at the community as intrusive and potentially scandalous, but despite the efforts of a succession of abbots to remove them, they were not relocated until 1140.

54. Gilomen-Schenkel discusses the significance of the necrologies of Muri and Engelberg in "Engelberg, Interlaken und andere autonome Doppelklöster," pp. 125–28 (n. 30 above). Her analysis illustrates the sheer size of these houses, a large proportion of whom were women. At Muri the ratio of women to men was four to five during the period from 1140 to 1220, and at Engelberg during the fourteenth century women outnumbered men by two to one. Likewise, the women at Admont are described as "our sisters" by Abbot Wolfold in a charter confirming the monks' obligations to provide for the women economically; J. Zahn, ed., *Urkundenbuch Herzogtums Steiermark*, 1. Band 798–1192 (Graz, 1875), no. 171, p. 170.

55. Küsters, *Der verschlossene Garten*, p. 137–38, n. 154 (n. 3 above). Doerr, *Institut der Inclusen* (n. 38 above).

56. Ulrich of Zell comments that William removed the women from his monastery, *Antiquiores consuetudines Cluniacenses monasterii*, PL 149: 635A–637C. For the identification of Kentheim, see Küsters, *Der verschlossene Garten*, p. 147, n. 192 (n. 3 above), citing *Annales Sindelfingenses*, MGH SS 17: 300.

57. On Marcigny, see Joachim Wollasch, "Frauen in der *Cluniacensis ecclesia*," in *Doppelklöster*, ed. Elm and Parisse, pp. 102–3 (n. 30 above). Wollasch argues that at Cluny and Marcigny, monks and nuns formed a monastic community, legally and economically.

58. For an overview of the official stance of the Premonstratensians toward women, see Felten, "Frauenklöster und -Stifte," pp. 290–91 (n. 30 above); Thompson, *Women Religious* (n. 49 above), pp. 135–37, and Carol Neel, "The Origins of the Beguines," in Judith M. Bennett et al., eds., *Sisters and Workers in the Middle Ages* (Chicago: University of Chicago Press, 1989), pp. 241–60, esp. p. 251.

59. Idung of Prüfening, *Argumentum*, ed. R. B. C. Huygens, "Le moine Idung et ses deux ouvrages, 'Argumentum super quatuor questionibus,'" *Studi Medievali* 13.1 (1972): 354, 361.

60. The personalities and manner of election of successive provosts are described in the history of the house, *Chronicon Lippoldesbergense*, MGH SS

20 (1866): 546–56. See also Walter Heinemeyer, "Die Urkundenfälschungen des Klosters Lippoldsberg,Teil 1," *Archiv für Diplomatik* (1961): 69–203.

61. Acht, ed., *Mainzer Urkundenbuch II,* (n. 34 above), no. 231, p. 417. See my M.A. thesis, "Saintly Expectations and Earthly Networks: The Construction of Hildegard of Bingen's Sanctity" (Monash University, 1997, chapter 3); and John Van Engen, "Abbess: Mother and Teacher," in *Voice of the Living Light: Hildegard of Bingen and her World,* ed. Barbara Newman (Berkeley: University of California Press, 1998), pp. 30–51.

62. Loraine Simmons, "The Abbey Church at Fontevraud in the Later Twelfth Century: Anxiety, Authority and Architecture in the Female Spiritual Life," *Gesta* 31.2 (1992): 99–107, esp. 102, 105.

63. The men selected to serve the nuns at Ichtershausen and Rupertsberg were described as *viri religiosi.* The monks of St. Georgen supervising the women at Amtenhausen were described in the same way in the *Vita Theogeri* 1.25, MGH SS 12: 460. The papal legate Octavian directed an exhortatory letter to abbot Rudolf of Reinhardsbrunn around 1152 concerning the spiritual direction of the women there; Friedel Peeck, ed., *Die Reinhardsbrunner Briefsammlung* (Munich: Böhlau, 1978), MGH Epistolae Selectae 5: 17, no. 17.

64. Pez, *Bibliotheca ascetica* 22: 464 (n. 50 above).

65. Jeffrey Hamburger, "'On the Little Bed of Jesus': Pictorial Piety and Monastic Reform," in *The Visual and the Visionary: Art and Female Spirituality in Late Medieval Germany* (New York: Zone Books, 1998), pp. 383–84.

# CHAPTER 4

# FROM ECCLESIOLOGY TO MARIOLOGY: PATRISTIC TRACES AND INNOVATION IN THE *SPECULUM VIRGINUM*

*Kim E. Power*

This chapter explores the influence of patristic teaching about the Virgin Bride, particularly that of Ambrose of Milan, on the ascetic teaching and theology of the Speculum virginum. It also identifies the influence of Paschasius Radbertus, a ninth-century theologian, whose treatise on the Assumption of the Virgin always circulated under the name of Jerome, as responsible for shaping a far "higher" view of the status of the Virgin, as preexisting at the beginning of time, than anything imagined by any of the Latin Fathers. The Speculum author develops Paschasius' teaching about the Virgin Bride into an extended reflection on the moral virtues of humility and charity that all virgins of Christ should imitate. The esteem attached to a life of virginity in the Speculum cannot be understood outside the context of this understanding of the Virgin as a cosmic presence pervading human history.

We might compare the author of the *Speculum virginum* to the biblical scribe who brings things both old and new from his storehouse. We can identify some of his legacy easily, although we do not necessarily know whether he read the primary texts himself or received them through an intermediary. In many cases, we encounter an eclectic blend of patristic texts, symbolism, and liturgical developments that were harmonized well before the *Speculum*. Paschasius Radbertus' defense of Mary's assumption in the ninth century is a particularly influential example. He knew Ambrose of Milan's corpus well and wove much of the patristic tradition with liturgical texts.[1] Moreover, Paschasius' text was attributed to Jerome and so was heavily invested with the authority of tradition.

Yet the Speculum is distinctly the work of an innovative theologian arguing his case for two contentious issues: spiritual relationships between consecrated men and women and a quantum leap in Mariological doctrine. To make these points effectively, he had to engage with patristic texts that opposed the former argument but that might provide grounds for the latter. We also see the effect of the development of Marian cult between the sixth and the twelfth centuries when texts from the Canticle became privileged Marian texts in the Assumption liturgy, thus laying the foundation for Peregrinus' high Mariology. This chapter focuses on these innovations in part five of the Speculum virginum, in which major themes are developed related to the sacred marriage between God and humanity.

## Patristic Sources

Peregrinus deliberately situates himself within the patristic tradition of nuptial imagery. Ambrose of Milan had described his first sermon on virginity as a mirror for virgins, written in 378.[2] Peregrinus underlines that it was the Fathers who had revealed the "sweet delights" of the eternal bridal chamber. In her useful concordance of patristic sources, Jutta Seyfarth noted the influence of many major Latin writers but did not single out the eastern theologian Origen of Alexandria, or his western disciple, Ambrose of Milan, the authors who influenced medieval nuptial spirituality most strongly.[3] For two centuries after Christ, the title of Bride was reserved for the Church. Origen argued that each soul participated in the sacred marriage individually.[4] Christianity never wavered from this insight, although Origen's orthodoxy was questioned in 399. Then, when consecrated virginity became the Christian ideal during the fourth century, other eastern theologians equated virgins with souls. Ambrose was the conduit through which this eastern theology reached the West. In his texts, the virgin becomes the incarnation of the Church and inherently, the ideal soul.[5] Ambrose was the first to apply the Canticle to Mary, as the model virgin, so that she too became a symbol of the Church.[6] He was also the first to draw moral implications from the Canticle for the cloistered life. Ambrose was therefore the more orthodox source of nuptial spirituality, although he was Origen's faithful disciple, for he had already made his mark on Paschasius' Marian treatises. If Hirsau was indeed the site of production, then we know the author had access to Origen and Ambrose as well as to Jerome and Augustine.[7]

In earlier periods, the Canticle had been hotly contested ground. Since the second century, it had been used to justify the goodness of marriage against arguments for sexual renunciation. Ambrose had believed passionately that asceticism permitted human beings to regain the angelic life lost by Adam and Eve, a life characterized by its ardent and erotic spiritual union with the divine. Jerome and Augustine resisted such a sensual and realized eschatology. With rare exceptions, Augustine used the Canticle only when forced to respond to Donatist polemics. For him the Church, her virgins, and Mary were virgin mothers rather than virgin brides. Maternity implies consummation, but the latter should be discreetly veiled. Such tensions arose when consecrated virgins were included under the umbrella of the Bride. What held metaphorically for the Church did not always translate easily to the situations of real women.

Peregrinus chose to adopt one of Ambrose's key nuptial texts, Canticle 4.12: *A garden enclosed is my sister, my Bride*. This metaphor was especially powerful because such a garden already existed at the heart of religious life, built into monastic architecture.[8] Peregrinus depicts his treatise as an idyllic pastoral, wherein the virgin's gathering of mystical flowers to weave her crown of glory is both an allegory of her desire for Christ and an implicit promise of her reward (Epist. 64–66). This subtle nuptial symbolism frames his whole treatise, which begins in a garden and finishes with a wedding song.[9]

Part one also echoes several ascetic patristic texts, yet Peregrinus turns them to his own ends. He is a researcher rather than a plagiarist. Nor does his use of the imagery have any of the polemical thrust or the overdetermined interpretation of earlier allegorical interpreters. For example, Peregrinus conflates Isaiah 56.4–5 (the eunuchs who keep God's Sabbath) with Canticle 4.12 (the enclosed garden) and Revelations 14.4 (undefiled virgins who follow the Lamb), a fusion of texts not found in his patristic sources. The paradoxical equation of enclosure and following the Lamb signals that he had a spiritual rather than a literal pilgrimage in mind. Thus, he deftly identifies the garden as the Church and places monastics (both spiritual eunuchs and undefiled virgins) within her walls, ascribing the highest possible status to them (*SV* 1.12–21). We cannot place too great a weight on his juxtaposition of open fields and enclosed gardens. Patristic authors sometimes distinguished between the enclosed garden as symbol of the weaker, feminized soul and the open fields as that of either men's souls or virile female souls (3.436).[10] In the *Speculum*, however, Mary, not Jacob, is the exemplary field. As such, she typifies the Church, and therefore the ideal soul, witnessing that the feminine within the souls of both sexes is redeemable (*SV* 1.91).[11]

Peregrinus also follows Origen and his heirs in identifying the Bride of the Canticle as the Queen of Psalm 44.10–15 (Psalm 45.10–15 in modern Bibles),[12] subtly coloring the pastoral imagery of the Canticle with that of the royal household (*SV* 2.474; 4.275, 369, 443; 6.667).[13] Significantly, he opens part three, which Morgan Powell has argued constitutes the original beginning of the *Speculum,* with a citation from this psalm that can only be a deliberate echo of Jerome's introduction to his letter 22 to Eustochium: *Hear O daughter, and see and incline your ear . . . and the king will desire your beauty* (Ps. 44.11–12).[14] Seventeen lines later Peregrinus describes consecrated virgins as the Father's "pledges of love," borrowing Ambrose's description of his virgin ward at the beginning of *De institutione virginis* (*SV* 3.1–2, 19–24).[15] If Powell is correct, then clearly the author intended to align himself with these authorities from the outset. In the revised version, *SV* 1.217 not only refers to Psalm 44 but to Proverbs 8.32–35, a text found several times in Ambrose's *De virginibus.*[16] Proverbs here parallels Psalm 44 but is addressed to men.

It is significant that the *Speculum's* advocacy for male-female dialogue is directly opposed to Augustine's example. Once ordained, Augustine had avoided private speech with women on principle. Evoking Jerome and Ambrose was excellent strategy, for they were influential allies. Jerome respected women as scholars and worked closely with Eustochium and her mother, Paula, who were his patrons. Ambrose had a close relationship with his older sister and frequently discussed important events with her. He believed that consecrated virgins and all ascetic, celibate women, even if they were married, were freed from the curse of Eve, because they bore spiritual children with joy, not physical children with tears. Jerome restricted this blessing to consecrated virgins.[17] Both men would offer support for Peregrinus' advocacy of male-female dialogue.

Yet methodologically and theologically, Peregrinus favored the more optimistic allegorical and intertextual readings of Origen and Ambrose over Jerome's systematic exegetical analysis. Furthermore, Peregrinus makes these biblical and patristic sources uniquely his own by reading them through a filter constructed from the Wisdom literature and Johannine texts, especially 1 John. Mimicking Johannine language in his elucidation of Christ's relationship with Mary, Peregrinus imbues his text with the authority of Scripture, a technique used most effectively by Augustine in his *Confessions.*

## The Genre of the *Speculum virginum*

The *Speculum* is structured as a somewhat one-sided dialogue, with Peregrinus showing a decided preference for monologues. This structure admits the use of several different genres: biblical exegesis, moral exhortation, narrative, and doctrinal argument. Nevertheless, it is presented as a conversation, which we do not find in patristic sources. The hypothesis that this text reflects changes in social structures and the acceptance of women's voices is seductive. Still, we need to consider whether the *Speculum* is a transparent depiction of monastic life or an idealized portrait of a pastoral relationship. Ascetic patristic treatises often began as sermons or letters. In many, women constitute the "Other," the ambiguous feminine within a man's own soul.[18] In other cases, epistles on ascetic discipline became opportunities to engage the support of influential women in theological debates. The dialogue structure is found more often in polemical texts, written as dialogues between a bishop and his congregation or the author and his opponent.[19] In each case the text includes material the author wishes to rebut. Often it is only through such strategies that we can recover anything that resembles the arguments of the author under attack. It is but a short step to create a persona for the voice of the "Other," although women rarely speak for themselves in early Christian texts.[20]

Does Theodora indicate that Peregrinus offers real support for women's inclusion in theological enterprises, or is he co-opting her to further his authorial agenda?[21] Putting words into a woman's mouth creates an aura of reality otherwise unattainable. It helps women identify with the speaker and therefore internalize her example. Peregrinus' technique is so persuasive that the reader frequently needs to remind herself that this is his script for Theodora, not the voice of Theodora herself.[22]

There is no doubt that in the *Speculum* the ordained cleric is the teacher. Although Theodora is a sympathetic portrait, tensions abound. Peregrinus' quip that he prefers Theodora to skip on the heights rather than root around in the earth blindly like a mole is a loaded remark that needs to be read in the context wherein physical pregnancy was an allegory of spiritual fertility (*SV* 5.7–11, 599–606). In medical discourse, although women's ovaries were known to exist, they were considered virtually nonfunctional, and compared to the eyes of a mole. Women could only nurture life, not author it—an argument used to define women as lacking the capacity for authority in patristic texts.[23] In the *Speculum virginum*, this analogy also functions on a spiritual level. Theodora is expected to become virile, but she has to be taught how (5.925).

In addition, Theodora consistently sets up the "dumb question," permitting Peregrinus to develop his argument in stages and to preempt potential objections. As he tends not to chastise Theodora herself, presumably he directs these comments to the text's wider audience (5.13–17, 118–122). Significantly, although Peregrinus encourages Theodora to use her reason, he refuses to teach her how to interpret Scripture's mystical meanings, because that is too difficult for her. Rather than seeking to ascend the spiritual heights, which one might expect to be within the limits of a nimble "goat," she and her sisters should humbly imitate Mary's faith and chastity (1.797–99; 5.235, 6.289–310).

This brings us to the claim to authoritative integrity inherent in allegorical exegesis. Only the virtuous could move beyond the literal meaning of Scripture to its moral and mystical interpretations. As believers increased in wisdom, their illuminated souls would penetrate Scripture's historical meaning to discern first the ethical, then the mystical meanings hidden within it. Indeed, it is truer to the nature of patristic allegory to say that interpreters did not so much understand different meanings within the text but different capacities for understanding it.[24] Therefore, when Peregrinus cautions the eponymous Theodora against seeking to grasp mystical meanings, he implies that she lacks the wisdom to do so. Clearly, pretensions to virility only extend to accepting what she is taught, not aspiring to teach herself or, implicitly, others. Other authorial assumptions about gender and virtue appear in justifications of enclosure in these same passages. Women are warned about Dinah, who invited her own rape, and the consequent social disorder when she left her father's tent to visit foreign women (Gen. 34). Men are warned about the heroic Samson, undone by Delilah, the woman who is synonymous with seduction and betrayal (Judges 14–16; *SV* 2.100–106).[25]

This ranking of virtue found legitimization in 1 Corinthians 13.11–12, when interpreted in a world that had structured itself as a spiritual hierarchy (*SV* 3.2–5). In this life, some Christians are the spiritual equivalent of children, who can only "consume" milk not meat. These read according to the flesh, that is, historically or literally. Others can be fed meat—moral and mystical meanings. Yet even with the light of Christ illuminating the shadows, most Christians can see God only in a dark mirror. Peregrinus' Epistle indicates that 1 Corinthians 13.11 is a key to his thought (Epist. 53–55). It is only in relation to Paul's metaphor that the play on *speculum* as Scripture, illumination, and the interpreter's voice can be fully realized. These constitute the "dark mirror" itself, the only way to see God while on earth. This emerges clearly in 5.896–99, where model virgins already united to the Bridegroom reflect the radiant and undimmed vision promised by Paul. Peregrinus' *Speculum* is the mirror in which his virgins will see the face of Christ, as clearly as their nature and virtue permits. His intended audience, chaplains to women, could use the *Speculum* to form nuns in Christ's image, an image they delineate through their exegesis, their prescription of virtue, and their exhortations to ascetic discipline.

Although any allegorical interpretation is also an implicit claim to virtue, the author is painfully aware that this claim is not always legitimate. Other clerics are damned as the "new Judas . . . a new offshoot of the Antichrist"; as "wolves in sheep's clothing"; and profane teachers causing scandal (*SV* 2.260–302; 5.1029, 1067–68).[26] Even here, though, women may bear some blame for this, as they are like thorns that will pierce the secret places of the mind with a sharp sword (2.303–4). In this passage the author explicitly alludes to patristic use of Proverbs 6.27 (in which visiting a neighbor's wife is compared to carrying fire) to condemn celibate men and women living in the same house or in close proximity. Peregrinus' combination of fire and thorn imagery suggests that his prime target was Jerome, a vociferous opponent of brother-sister households, who believed they were an open invitation for the devil to ignite the thorns of lust.[27] Peregrinus needed to provide counterarguments, and his deliberate engagement with patristic authorities met several goals.[28] It established his theological credentials and showed that he was not naïve about temptation. He warned of traps for experienced players, even as he anticipated counterarguments in order to affirm that normative spiritual relationships were graced and healthy (2.311, 9.1160–66).[29]

Theodora plays a significant role in allowing Peregrinus to develop these arguments. Theodora's persona cannot offer us reliable access to women's experience of the monastic life, let alone that of one specific woman. Rather, his dialogue with the *inclusa* scripts the appropriate relationship, instructing nuns and clerics how to remain morally safe when playing with spiritual fire (5.13–17, 118–122, 696). The *Speculum's* dialogue is the medium of the message. Through the performance of dialogue, through contemplation of the illuminations, the Word is made flesh.

### Bridal Imagery in Part Five
### of the *Speculum virginum*

Part five, the axis of the *Speculum*, is elegantly structured around its accompanying illustration, which depicts a *quadriga*, or four-wheeled chariot, carrying the holy virgins whose marriages with the Lamb have been consummated through their martyrdoms. The chariot's "wheels" are the central characters in part five—Jesus, the sacrificial Lamb of God; Mary; John the Baptist; and John the Evangelist.[30] Their relationships are complex. Each has a special personal relationship with the Lamb. Mary is his mother. John the Baptist is his cousin, sanctified before his birth by the Word within Mary's womb (Luke 1.36–45).[31] John the Evangelist is the beloved disciple, so close to Jesus in the Gospels (John 13.23). The two Johns are coupled as symbols of the two testaments. Each has a link to Mary. One is her cousin (Luke 1.36), the other the man with whom she lived after Christ's Crucifixion (John 19.26–27).

Each of the four is a mirror of the ideal virgin. Jesus is the archetypal Christian virgin, the seed and source of all others (*SV* Epist. 64; 1.1–3).[32] Mary teaches humility, virginity of mind and body, and devotion to her son. She is also the glorious promise of the joy awaiting the faithful virgin in eternity. For Peregrinus, however, Mary is more than an exemplary human being, as will be discussed later. John the Baptist has two important functions. As a true Jewish prophet, he affirms Christianity's Jewish heritage while also modeling the penitential disciplines required of the monastic (5.508–52, 605–33, 637–64, 739–63).[33] John the Evangelist, whom Peregrinus calls "our theologian," is the ideal disciple, most beloved and greatest of the evangelists. In fact, John is the only person described as the Bride of Christ in part five. Reclining on the breast of Christ at the Last Supper, he is a figure of the Church at the heavenly banquet and of the faithful at Communion (5.535, 859–905).[34] This use of a male figure for the Bride at Eucharist offers male religious involved in ministering to religious women an especially beloved disciple with whom they could identify.[35] The virgin martyrs, already in the chariot, may depict souls feminized in relation to their divine spouse. However, they are named and identified with historical figures, which certainly indicates that women themselves are capable of heroic virtue. Part five concludes with a long harangue on the proper conduct of clerics that is clearly directed more to pastors than virgins. Yet so effortlessly is this particular ethical material woven into the text that this can easily be overlooked. As Peregrinus develops his argument, he combines a beautiful vision of heavenly joy with moral exhortations on fasting, prayer, and, above all, love. His tone is rarely minatory. Rather, moral and spiritual advice is filtered through the Wisdom literature and even more so through I John. Love is the preeminent virtue. The virgin's compassionate and pure love for, and commitment to, her monastic community is the only authentic criterion that she loves the God she cannot see (5.425–27, 434, 463–64, 542, 777–905, 931, 991, 1002–8).

## A Radical Mariology

The *Speculum* author clearly had little choice but to set his Mariology within the context of nuptial symbolism. As we saw earlier, an allegorical reading of the Canticle had been normative since Origen. As Ambrose depicted Mary as the ideal Virgin Bride and identified her with the corporate Church, she could not escape being Christ's Bride as well as his mother. Like Augustine, however, Peregrinus masks overt nuptial symbolism wherever possible when Mary is his focus. In early patristic readings of the Canticle, rabbinic nuptial symbolism had developed a distinctly Christian trajectory when the paradisal garden also became the site of Christ's suffering and resurrection, wherein the cross became Eden's tree of life restored. In the *Speculum,* the figure of the Lamb subtly conveys this sacrificial dimension of the garden.[36] Yet, the author does not follow Jerome and Augustine who used Mary's body to symbolize birth and death—womb and tomb.[37] His emphasis is on the eternal garden as a Kingdom, as it was in Ambrose, but now Mary is its Queen, not the Church.

Peregrinus' floral motif was entirely traditional, achieving a nuanced melding of patristic authors that would have carried a strong symbolic freight for theologically literate monks.[38] In addition, embedded in the nuptial imagery are patristic tropes, such as the belief in death as the consummation of holy marriage (5.939–61), the identification of procreativity as a male prerogative, and the identification of soul with mind (5.434, 464, 645, 764–72, 839–45). The last is important in a context where women's minds are considered inferior to men's. The *Speculum* uses nuptial imagery very discreetly. In keeping with this, the Lamb imagery, or that of the Christ child, veils that of the Bridegroom. Yet although Peregrinus adopts strategies to mask Mary's role as Bride, he describes her early in part five in this way: "This daughter, mother and virgin, dove, sister and beloved is the eternal bride of the King. She is the singular mother of the one God . . . because she is the supreme and peacemaking mediator" (5.33–42). This title blends patristic ecclesial metaphors with ascetic beliefs that the saint had a special capacity to mediate the power of God.[39] Although Paschasius had previously described Mary's role as the mediation of truth and virtue (presumably in the person of Jesus), earlier sources do not address her as *mediatrix*.[40] The *Speculum* also applies Canticle 8.10 (a text formerly applied to the Church or the bishop) to Mary, to emphasize that she brings peace (5.113–14).[41] The statement that Mary contains all sacraments within her melds her with the Church just as elegantly. This was not an empty claim. Peace was a very important value for the *Speculum's* author, because peace of mind and a peaceful (chaste) body were essential to the virginal enterprise (5.977–83).[42]

In *SV* 5.105–14 Peregrinus returns to the Canticle in a surprising and somewhat bizarre context. Mary lies beside her son's manger, marveling at him. In her mouth Peregrinus places a jubilant speech, collated entirely from the Canticle (scriptural verses here italicized):

*Let him kiss me with the kisses of his mouth!* [Cant. 1.2] *My beloved is to me a sachet of myrrh lying between my breasts.* [1.13] *Behold, you are beautiful my beloved.* [1.15] *As beautiful as an apple tree among the trees of the wood so is my darling among the young men;* [2.3] *my beloved is mine and I am his.* [2.16]. In addition, *I have found him whom my soul loves. I held him and never let him go until I take him to my mother's house and my mother's bedroom.* [3.4] *I am a wall and my breasts are towers, so I become in his presence as one bringing peace.* [8.10][43]

The author's careful combination of texts draws the imagination away from Mary the Bride to Mary the mother, crooning over her infant. This is a completely different strategy from that of the Fathers. It retains Augustine's emphasis on Mary's virginal motherhood while managing to preserve Ambrose's nuptial symbolism.[44] Ambrose himself only used Canticle 1.13 twice, and then to refer to Christ and his Church, although he frequently used the other passages, always interpreting them allegorically, if ardently. Christ's kisses were consolations or illuminations of the soul, for example. Ambrose only applied the Canticle to Mary once, interpreting Mary's womb as the bowl in which Wisdom united Christ's humanity and divinity.[45] Similarly, Jerome, following Origen, interpreted the Bride's breast as the truest part of her heart, where the Word resided.[46]

The *Speculum* author is far more daring. He has introduced the nuptial symbolism into the human relationship of mother and son, although the son's infancy is another way of masking the implied sexual relationship. This literary strategy would come to dominate artistic representations of Mary in the enclosed garden. These include symbols of betrothal or marriage, yet Christ is invariably a child. One major exception though is the mosaic in the apse of Sancta Maria Trastevere. There the Virgin, clothed in queenly gold, sits next to her grown son who embraces her as she holds a scroll of Canticle 2.6.[47]

The liturgical use of the Canticle for Marian feasts helped prepare Christian audiences for such exegetical tactics.[48] The Assumption feast was especially important, for it had been part of the Church calendar since the seventh century, although Paschasius Radbertus had still had to vehemently defend the argument that Mary was the principle referent of the Canticle in the ninth.[49] Certainly it explains why texts from that liturgy are privileged as the foundation for Peregrinus' new material in the *Speculum*. Unquestionably, the *Speculum* takes seriously Paschasius' encouragement that Christians may be brought to praise Mary "for her own worth."[50] Such an exhortation suggests that her significance does not lie solely in her role as virginal mother. She is significant in her own right. In part five, Peregrinus explains just what that means to him.

Mary's significance is highlighted from the first sentence of part five, where, in the language of litany and liturgy, Peregrinus instructs Theodora to study:

> this heavenly behavior, the example of God's mother, the ornament of holy beauty, the mirror of holy virginity, in whom blossomed the signs of virtue, that is humility and virginity. She merited to conceive the Word, whom heaven and earth cannot contain, enclosing him in the sanctuary of her uterus; he was begotten without a human father and he came forth for the salvation of all. This mother, this virgin, mother of mothers, virgin of virgins, gave birth without injuring her modesty and after the birth she re-

mained a virgin, preserving her integrity. Mary is the root of the eternal flower, she is the flower and fruit of eternal blessing. (*SV* 5.1–10)

Such acclamation reveals just how far Marian doctrine had traveled from late antique conflicts over whether Mary could or should be called "Mother of God." The council of Ephesus compromised by awarding her the title "God-bearer" *[genetrix dei]*.[51] It was not until the late sixth century that this title appeared in nonpolemical contexts. Then it quickly became a trope, usually qualified by "blessed" or "holy" *[beata dei genetrix]*.[52] Given this general usage, the absence of the title in the *Speculum* is notable. Instead, Mary is Mother of God *[mater dei]* (5.7, 40, 123–7, 264). This may simply indicate that the title *mater dei* is no longer problematic. Yet for the author of the *Speculum*, no title is too august for Mary. Her exalted status is never in doubt from the moment that Theodora pleads to be taught how to imitate her (5.13–17). Despite having called Mary the "mirror of virgins," a title that is traceable to Athanasius,[53] Peregrinus warns her that it is difficult, even presumptuous, to try to understand Mary, because she was assigned a fullness of divine grace that the mind cannot grasp (Ecclus. 3.22; *SV* 5.21–30). Perhaps this is why he begins with a litany of titles instead of explanations (5.44–79).[54] Drawing on patristic metaphors for the Church, he calls Mary the heavenly bridal chamber of God and humanity,[55] radiant moon,[56] the golden urn of the tabernacle,[57] the Paradise in which the flower from the patriarchal roots blossoms, and the blossoming rod of Aaron.[58]

The *Speculum* goes far beyond these ecclesial titles, subtly using traditional language about Mary's election as a springboard for the author's radical assertion that Mary existed in heaven prior to her human birth.[59] This is a direct reversal of patristic thought. Patristic use of "chosen" *[electa]*, or even "chosen prior to her birth" *[praelecta]*, indicated God's prior knowledge of the woman he would choose at the appropriate time and God's ability to endow her with the graces she needed to fulfill the divine will. Peregrinus asserts that not only was Mary Queen of heaven even in her earthly life, but her heavenly rank preexisted in some way before earth's creation. Here the author has ascribed to Mary an ancient title accorded to Ishtar, the Canaanite goddess. Such a daring move would have scandalized the very prophets he quoted to prove his argument (Jer. 7.18; *SV* 5.99–104). While it was more usual to acclaim her as Queen of the world *[regina mundi]*, some of the author's contemporaries also call her Queen of heaven.[60] Almost certainly, both usages result from the application of Psalm 44 to Mary, an extension of Origen's ecclesiology applied to virgins as early the fourth century.[61] Another factor was possibly an extrapolation of the title Queen of the world, which would seem natural once her assumption into heaven was accepted. Paschasius' assertion that

Mary was divine and ineffable because virginity had been deified in her could also have influenced the author's shift from patristic authors' insistence that Christ was the archetypal divine virgin[62] Nevertheless, Paschasius remained within the tenor of patristic thought and terminology, seeing Mary's deification as a grace given her and using the language of election. The *Speculum,* on the other hand, prefers to claim new ground,[63] claiming Mary had been present throughout salvation history: in Paradise; in Noah's ark;[64] with the wandering patriarchs; amid judges and kings.[65]

Peregrinus continues to structure his dialogue to drive his argument. Thus, Theodora's persona perceptively unmasks the agenda hidden in Peregrinus' mystical interpretation: that Mary existed before time began (*SV* 5.118–22). Peregrinus had not staked his claim in precisely those terms, but the literary device allows Theodora to put the words in his mouth. His response is unexpected. Mary herself shall answer. When she does, she is revealed as Wisdom, the first creation of God, who delighted to dwell among us: "The Lord took possession of me in the beginning of his ways, in the beginning, before anything had been made. Ages ago I was appointed, from eternity, before the earth existed. When there were no depths I was conceived, etc." (Prov. 8.22–31, quoted in *SV* 5.125–28). This was an audacious move, given Wisdom's role as God's master workman in creation and John's gospel describing God's creative Word becoming Wisdom incarnate in Jesus (John 1.1–18). Hence Theodora's continuing concern introduces a somewhat terse dialogue, as she consistently demands proof of Peregrinus' extraordinary claims. Peregrinus' response is convoluted and often tortuous, until Theodora enables him to explain, by posing four key questions, each of which need to be examined in turn.

### The Preexistence of Mary as Wisdom

The astute reader will note that these questions are all variations on a theme, necessitated by Peregrinus' frequent retreat into mysteries hidden in divine Providence (Col. 2.3). Consistently, his key argument is that Providence holds both present and future and that all things exist in the wisdom of God's Word. This is unexceptional, again requiring only God's foreknowledge. But given his identification of Mary with Wisdom, his argument links Mary even more closely with her Son, because as Mary-Wisdom, she is hidden in Christ-Wisdom. Peregrinus clearly saw this implication, immediately defending the proposition that Mary was *always* with her Son, as the Son was with the Father (*SV* 5.130–39).

Theodora perceives that this demands Mary's preexistence, allowing Peregrinus to argue that as Wisdom, Mary was with the Word before his Incarnation. Again, he appealed to God's immutable will, in which all things exist before they come into being. Therefore, the causes of all things human existed before time, and his claim that Mary and her Son were always united sacramentally is justified (5.141–61). This argument for Mary's preexistence as opposed to pre-election may draw on certain patristic accounts of a double creation, derived from the two creation stories in Genesis 1–2. Such accounts distinguished between God creating quasi-Platonic forms for all things that would ever be created (Gen. 1), before they were actualized in the creation of the material world and incarnated in human beings.[66] This tradition allows Mary to have existed always in the mind of God, but it does not justify Mary's uniqueness.

So it is not surprising that Theodora still questions, although Peregrinus has her accept his statement that these mysteries are too profound to be understood—an assertion that she is not competent to challenge, as the *Speculum* has already established. She asks him what meaning they hold for the Church or soul. This is an important question, directly related to the *Speculum*'s function as a teaching aid. If Mary is Wisdom, what does this imply for those who imitate her? Peregrinus reverts to the trope of Christ's marriage to the Church, virgin or soul. Following Origen, he interprets Genesis 2.24 as revealing Christ's leaving his Father to be one flesh with his Church. Then he falls back on mystery again. The inherent contradiction is that the *Speculum* creates one persona who understands the mystery enough to teach it and another astute enough to perceive his defects. Peregrinus then returns to his original thesis. Mary was not with her Son eternally as his human mother. Rather she existed within the divine prescience, as a kind of conception of her incorporeal substance that would take flesh at the preordained time (*SV* 5.162–89). The result is the same. Mary's uniqueness is still not established. Hence Theodora's third question.

Peregrinus responds with a long peroration on the inseparability of God and Wisdom. He argues that Wisdom is part of the Trinity and that just as the Father was with the Son, when all things were made, so he was in his Incarnation, which initiated a new creation (Rev. 21.5). Mary's motherhood takes on added significance in this context. Where God's first creation was effected through Wisdom, so his re-creation also occurs through Wisdom—unexceptional Johannine theology—except that Mary, not the Word, is here identified as Wisdom (*SV* 5.199–235). The dialogue justifies this claim in two ways. The first appeals to tradition, introducing the patristic trope of Mary's womb as the bridal chamber of God and humanity (cf. Ps. 118). This and similar texts, Peregrinus tells Theodora, are allegories about Mary's possession of Christ and his of her. Pertinent to this is the necessity for the Son of God to have possessed his mother from the beginning to ensure that the matter from which his body would be formed would be perfect. The vital change to tradition is his assertion that without Mary, Jesus could not have "begun his way" (5.240–46).[67]

His second strategy is rhetorical. This passage describing Jesus' relationship with his mother is so powerful because it is couched in the language and style the evangelists used to explain Jesus' relationship with the Father woven with allusions to the Canticle and Luke's infancy narratives:

> How does his mother know our lamb? The mother knows the son, the Son knows the mother [cf. Luke 10.22; John 10.15]; Mary knows Christ: Christ knows the virgin. Just as the Son is *chosen from his companions* [Cant. 2.3], so the mother *is blessed among all women*. Through his light she unveils a clearer discernment of mutual knowledge and through the prerogative of celestial dignity an enlightened understanding of the other was growing in both [Luke 1.28; *SV* 5.456–60].[68]

This exegetical tour de force is dependent on a Johannine understanding of love. Peregrinus can write this way only because Mary is Wisdom and therefore quasi-divine. Yet he is reluctant to explain further, although does insist that the mother glorifies her son—another biblical allusion loaded with meaning, for the theme of God's glorification of Mary also runs through part five (lines 326, 405–6, 467). When Theodora continues to question him, Peregrinus admonishes her at length that a mystical reading is too complex for her. Her model is Mary's humility, her witness to wisdom, and the discipline of the Holy Spirit.

Theodora's question about Mary's presence in Paradise allows Peregrinus to segue into a stereotypical comparison of Mary and Eve. He deploys the usual topos before declaring that Mary was in Paradise because God said he placed enmity between the serpent and the woman (Gen. 3.15). Through Mary, God has crushed the serpent. Therefore, as the graced harbinger of the eternal Paradise, she was present when the promise was made. Consequently, says Peregrinus, she will be found in heaven as she was on earth—clearly echoing the Lord's Prayer here (Matt. 6.10). Finally, he shuns argument altogether, instead heaping metaphoric titles on Mary. Their cumulative effect is extraordinary, as this excerpt from his lengthy panegyric demonstrates:

> She is the door shining with heavenly light, the glory of the heavenly court, the singular home of the Holy Spirit, and tabernacle of the eternal sun. Herself the love, beauty, and form of virginity, she contains all the sacraments of the Church within her. She gave birth to the shoot from the root of Jesse on earth, and before time began, she was proclaimed the mother of Christ in heaven. She is daughter of Zion and Jerusalem, born from a royal house; the handmaid of Christ, mother and lady of the faithful, Queen of the heavenly militia, reconciliatrix of the world, shrine of the Holy Spirt . . . the

flower and fruit of virginity, the morning star more splendid than the moon, superior to the angels (themselves purer than ether); the reparatrix provided for the lost of the world, operatrix of virtue, and lover of humanity. She was hidden in the patriarchs, revealed by the prophets, the root of the flower in the synagogue, the fruit of the root in the Church (*SV* 5.362–78).

Shortly after he adds, "She is the perfect and irreproachable work of the greatest artist. . . . Of all creation, she is most worthy of praise, who is lady of the angels, the deliverance of humanity, the jewel of virginity (5.472–76). In sum, she is Queen of virtue (5.482). These passages are so dense that we cannot do justice to the author's command of patristic tropes and images. The "closed door" (cf. Ez. 44.1–3), alluded to at the beginning, was first used in the fourth century against those who denied Mary's virginity before, during, and after Christ's birth.[69] Patristic descriptions of ascetics as the heavenly militia, of virgins as the heavenly Jerusalem, and of Mary as the court of the King lie behind Mary's heavenly queenship and glory, including her acclamation as Queen of angels.[70] Other titles echo Ambrose's description of the Church in his *Commentary on the Gospel of Luke:* "Behold the mother of all mothers, behold the house of the Spirit, behold the city, which lives forever because it does not know death. She is the city of Jerusalem, which is now seen on earth, but which will be carried off above Elias—for Elias was one . . . whom death could not grasp . . . for she is loved by Christ as if glorious, holy, immaculate, without stain . . . this is the hope of the Church."[71]

Mary has here already fulfilled Ambrose's eschatological hope for the Church. From this perspective, Mary now manifests the glory that the earthly virgin can only yearn for. However, in the *Speculum,* Mary outshines the Church. She is intermediary *[reconciliatrix],* renewer *[reparatrix],* and creator *[operatrix].* These are active, public roles, not ascribed to women in antiquity. Reconciler is least controversial, as Mary's role as intercessor and patron is consistent with tropes from the late patristic and early medieval liturgy. *Reparatrix* is ambiguous. It may be intended to convey her graced obedience to God, to bear the Word. Ambrose accepted that as mother, Mary mediated between heaven and earth. The Word was poured from heaven into Mary and from Mary to the world.[72] Yet to describe Mary as the deliverance of humanity and superior to the angels seems to imply a more active role. *Operatrix* is unambiguously active. She is "creator of virtue." In patristic sources, Tertullian understood the spiritual soul to have an active role in redeeming the body, while Ambrose applied *operatrix* to the Holy Spirit as God's creative power. Yet even Ambrose was emphatic that Mary's role was that of passive vessel.[73] The *Speculum* justifies this title in the nexus of symbols clustering around Wisdom.

In the Jewish Scriptures, Wisdom and the Spirit of God are allied, being agents of God's will, the immanence of divine presence as mother, fashioner, renewer, and source of order. In Christian Scripture, love, peace, patience, kindness, and goodness are also gifts of the Spirit (Gal. 5.22). In patristic texts, Wisdom is seen as the virtue that leads to authentic love of God. It is the source of pure virginity and faith, attributes also defined by Gregory of Nyssa as "the life of the Spirit."[74] However, for patristic authors, Christ was invariably Wisdom. Hippolytus had believed Mary was anointed by Wisdom, and he used the wisdom imagery of Proverbs 9.5 as a metaphor for Christ uniting himself to humanity.[75] Ambrose developed this interpretation, linking Proverbs with Canticle 7.1–2. He established a trajectory that led to the Mariology of the *Speculum* by claiming that Mary was the mirror of the ideal Bride. Wisdom was also one of the consecrated virgins' spiritual children,[76] and some esteemed virgins were seen as disciples of Lady Wisdom.[77] As they were exhorted to imitate Mary, we can see how this tradition would also have facilitated Mary's representation as Lady Wisdom incarnate, so infused has she been with the Holy Spirit. Nevertheless, by declaring Mary to be preexistent Wisdom, the *Speculum* author was making a leap of faith.

## Mary, Mirror of Virgins

In keeping with his treatment of Mary as Bride, Peregrinus' depiction of the nun as bride is very discreet. "Virgins of Christ" is his preferred address. Although the *Speculum* does portray Theodora and her companions as Christ's *sponsae,* only once does it use the term *sponsa* to address her directly (*SV* 8.589).[78] Even then it depicts her as a lovelorn Bride. Theodora objects, saying that she experiences the embrace of her heavenly spouse, whereupon Peregrinus reminds her that she shares the spiritual barrenness of the whole human race (Cant. 2.6; *SV* 1.704–11, cf. 1.27). Ambrose might summon a virgin whom he is consecrating with "Come be made pregnant by God!" Peregrinus by contrast mutes the eroticism, although he does speak of Mary being impregnated by the Spirit (5.408). Addressing Theodora, he conflated Paul's earthen vessel (2 Cor. 4.7) with the pearl of great price in Matthew's Gospel 13.6, exhorting her to remain vigilant over her mind and body so she would not be destroyed (*SV* 5.645).[79]

It is only in his discussion of virgin martyrs as exemplary virgins that we find Christ the Bridegroom and a clear sexual subtext. In the *Speculum,* just as in the writings of Ambrose, the deaths of virgin martyrs are vividly depicted as consummations of their marriage to Christ. To introduce these model virgins, Peregrinus even copies Ambrose's rhetorical strategy in *De virginibus.* When Theodora objects that Mary is too august a model, too perfect a mirror, Peregrinus uses virgin martyrs as "mirrors" too, to prove women's capacity for great virtue (5.908, 967).[80] The distinction between the virgin martyrs and Theodora and her sisters suggests that Peregrinus worked within a less realized eschatology than Ambrose. The *inclusa* should not consider her marriage as consummated until she had proven herself beyond doubt. Her devotion and discipline, her love and fidelity, would effect in her what physical suffering had effected in the virgin martyrs. In this, he had strong precedents in Origen and Gregory of Nyssa. The former distinguished between the Bride or Church and her handmaid souls, and the latter taught that virginity deifies those who share her mysteries.[81] Thus these women, like Mary, are co-regnant with Christ in heaven (5.948–49). However, other factors might also have influenced Peregrinus' use of nuptial imagery. Several passages in the *Speculum* attest that Peregrinus was well aware of sexual temptations between male and female religious, so he may have intended to avoid problems that Ambrose's explicit sexual imagery might cause. Like almost all texts addressed to women, admonitions to virginity of mind, humility, and simplicity pepper his treatise. Yet he does not follow his mentors blindly. He allows his imagination full flight in lauding Mary, and he does depict the virgin martyrs in erotic terms, unfortunately tainted by the images of sexual violence. This creates the ambiguity of a man exhorting women to modest enclosure while holding up their violated bodies to public scrutiny (5.912–74).[82]

## Conclusion

How are we to account for such a high Mariology? However exalted Mary was in patristic treatises, she was never divinized or depicted as Wisdom. Late antique authors often described her as a spiritual martyr, but never as her son's co-worker. Ambrose was adamant on this point, while Augustine was uncompromising in his assertion that only masculinity could symbolize Christ's Wisdom. For Augustine, Mary could represent the temporal virtues of faith, humility, and obedience but never wisdom.[83]

To find such a paradigm we have to go back to Philo, who represented Wisdom as the mother of creation, as God is the Father of the universe.[84] None of the Christian Fathers followed Philo directly in this, but Origen presented an interesting variant. Origen believed that God's first creative acts produced the souls of the Word and the Bride. When the Bride's soul fell from heaven through sin, the Word accepted incarnation to reclaim her for heaven.[85] Hence Origen could describe the redeemed Church as the celestial mother who makes peace between heaven and earth.[86] Here we see a distinct congruence between Origen's ecclesiology and Peregrinus' Mariology. However, Origen's theology was susceptible to Christian criticism of

Platonic influences, for Plato's paradigm, in its purest form, demanded the fall of preexistent souls into human bodies, a doctrine rejected at the end of the fourth century. This is where Peregrinus is so creative. By reinterpreting the Bride as eternal Wisdom, who is perfection herself, the *Speculum* avoids Origen's imputed heresy while reinstating the Bride in heaven. As preexistent Wisdom, she is one with the creative Word. As Mary, she gives birth to the Word made flesh, who will redeem humankind so beloved of Wisdom.

The question remains: Why such high Mariology? It is not essential to Mary's primacy as either virgin or mother. The answer, I think, can only be speculative. The role of noble women in the Middle Ages would have been one factor, as writers and artists had a tendency to depict heaven in terms of contemporary political structures. Certainly later authors would argue that as a queen had equal rights to a king, so Mary shared power equally with God.[87] When earthly queens were significant public figures, the Queen of heaven must outshine them all yet be the model of exemplary feminine behavior.

The nature of Peregrinus' intended audience and the need to legitimate contact between consecrated men and women is another factor. Women who imitate Lady Wisdom rather than Dame Folly do not present a sexual threat. The image of feminine Wisdom melds nicely with his frequent references to the wise and foolish virgins in part six (Matt. 25.1–13).[88] The glorious figure of Mary was also an implicit promise to pastors and their "lambs." What she now is, they will be. Furthermore, it offered a priest a desirable image of the feminine, a way of perceiving his own soul as a spouse of Christ, modeled on the example of John, the most beloved disciple.

The pattern of the *Speculum* is clearer now. Its judicious blend of Jerome's stringent morality, Augustine's moderate ascetic practice, and Origen's and Ambrose's paradisal nuptial imagery is expertly done. Centuries of monastic life have worn the gilt off Ambrosian gingerbread. There is a sober awareness of the problems of community life and the failures that can occur. Not to mention the sad fact that these virgins are no longer threatened by pagan men but sometimes by the very men who direct them.

The *Speculum virginum* is nonetheless optimistic. It offers a mirror of sanctified and glorified models dwelling in heavenly paradise, wherein its audience may see their faces reflected as the brides of Christ. It also charts the pilgrim's journey. For the devout religious, it will be a smooth one, for it is guided by Christ, his mother, the ideal prophet, and the ideal disciple. At its heart stands the figure of Wisdom. Mary's identification with Wisdom places her as Mother within the Trinity. Jesus is then truly the Son of Wisdom, the ultimate extension of this very Johannine theme. The *Speculum virginum* represents, too, a certain primacy of the feminine in the new creation. The new Adam is born from the new Eve, and not Eve from Adam. In the Burgsteinfurt illumination, Mary walks at her Son's side. She is what today's world would call a proactive woman. Undoubtedly, the reception of the *Speculum* played an important role not only in assisting the development of Marian cult but also in shaping ecclesiology. Where once ecclesiology had determined the depiction of Mary, now Mary determines the image of the Church.

## Notes

1. E. Ann Matter, "Introduction," *De partu virginis,* CCCM 56C (1985): 15.
2. Ambrose, *De virginibus* 2.6.39, ed. E. Cazzaniga, SAEMO 14/1 (1989): 198–200.
3. Seyfarth, pp. 396–98.
4. Origen, *In Canticum Canticorum* 1.5.10–1.6.1–5, ed. Luc Brésard and Henri Crouzel, Schr 375 (1991): 246–52. On Origen's originality, see Friedrich Ohly, *Hohelied-Studien: Grundzüge einer Geschichte der Hoheliedsauslegung des Abendlandes bis um 1200* (Wiesbaden: Franz Steiner Verlag, 1958), pp. 24–25.
5. Franca Ela Consolino suggests that Ambrose may have drawn on Basil's *Commentary on Psalm 44,* "Dagli *Exempla* ad un Esempio di Comportamento Cristiano: il *De Exhortatio Virginitatis* di Ambrogio," *Rivista Storica Italiana* 74 (1982): 405, 408–9. Ambrose, *De virginibus* 2.6.40–42, SAEMO 14/1 (1989): 20; *De institutione virginis* 9.62, 14.82, 17.109–11, SAEMO 14/2 (1989): 158, 172–74, 188–90.
6. Ambrose, *De institutione virginis* 13.81–83, 14.87–17.93, SAEMO 14/2: 168–76.
7. For Hirsau's library holdings see Mews, chapter 1, n. 12, in this volume.
8. The garden loggia at Montecassino was even called "Paradise." Giovanni Spinelli, *L'Abbazia di Montecassino* (Milano: Silvana Editoriale, 1982), p. 109. For a general survey of the monastic garden, see Maria Adriana Giusti, ed., *Il Giardino dei Monaci* (Lucca: Macia Pacini Fazzi Editore, 1991). For Ambrose's interpretation of the garden, see Power, "The Secret Garden: The Meaning and Function of the Hortus Conclusus in Ambrose of Milan's Homilies on Virginity" (Ph.D. diss., La Trobe University, Bundoora, 1997).
9. There are over fifty passages on the *hortus* in the *Speculum.* The word *hortus* itself is used nineteen times in *SV* 1 alone; often there are allusions to the Canticle's paradisal themes, which evoke the enclosed garden; see *SV* 1.8, 17–35, 238.
10. On the soul's fragility, see Ambrose, *De Isaac* 5.48, CSEL 32/1 (1897): 672.7–673.9; *De virginibus* 1.45, SAEMO 14/1: 144. Note that in *De virginibus* 2.6.43, the soul ascends from her field to her tower; in 3.4.17 the soul is a fertile field with many crops like the Church, SAEMO 14/1: 202, 222.
11. See Ambrose, *De virginibus* 1.8.45, 3.7.34–35, SAEMO 14/1: 144, 236–8; *De virginitate* 6.34, 15.94–96, ed. E. Cazzaniga, SAEMO 14/2 (1989): 36, 74–78.

12. For Origen, see Ernst Dassman, "*Ecclesia vel Anima:* die Kirche und ihre Glieder in der Hoheliederklärung bei Hippolyt, Origines und Ambrosius von Mailand," *Römische Quartalschrift für christliche Altertumskunde und für Kirchengeschichte* 61 (1966): 129–37.

13. Seyfarth lists only those occasions when Peregrinus cites Ps. 44.10–15 in full. She does not note where Peregrinus abbreviates it to *Audi* or *Audi filia* alone. Given the early emphasis on the full text, later abbreviations echo the full pericope. We find five instances in *SV* 5 alone: 5.634, 685, 729, 927, 1011. In addition, we find *filii audite me . . . audite disciplinam* in a citation of Prov. 8.32–35, *SV* 5.308–9 and *Ecce filia* at 5.902.

14. Morgan Powell, "The Mirror and the Woman: Instruction for Religious Women and the Emergence of Vernacular Poetics 1120–1250" (Ph.D. diss., Princeton University; Ann Arbor, MI: University Microfilms International, 1997), pp. 176–77 and chapter 5 in this volume.

15. Jerome, Letter 22.1, trans. F. A. Wright, *Select Letters of St. Jerome* (London: Heinemann, 1933), p. 52; Ambrose, *De institutione virginis* 1.1, SAEMO 14/2: 112; Ambrose's vivid depiction of the bridal chamber is found in *De virginibus* 2.6.40–41, SAEMO 14/1: 200.

16. Ambrose, *De virginibus* 1.8.46, 2.2.7, 2.6.43, SAEMO 14/1: 144–6, 168–70, 202.

17. Jerome, Letter 22.18, 21, trans. Wright, pp. 90, 98; Ambrose, *De institutione virginis* 4.27–29, 5.32, SAEMO 14/2: 128–30, 132–4. See my discussion of the way Ambrose uses this to promote his own ascetic agenda in "The Rehabilitation of Eve in the *De institutione virginis* of Ambrose of Milan," *Religion in the Ancient World: New Themes and Approaches,* ed. Matthew Dillon (Amsterdam: Adolph Hakkert, 1998), pp. 367–82.

18. See my study of Augustine's correspondence with women in *Veiled Desire: Augustine on Women* (New York: Continuum, 1996), chapter 9.

19. One example is Ambrose's dialogue with his congregation over asceticism, which could spill over into serious conflict. See his criticism of a widow's remarriage in *De viduis* 9.57–59 and his subsequent apology in *De virginitate* 8.46. *De viduis,* SAEMO 14/1: 292–94; *De virginitate* 14/2: 44.

20. Methodius had done this in his *Symposium,* modeled on Plato's *Symposium.* Virgins at a dinner party offer varying opinions on marriage and virginity, with the prize going to the woman who eulogizes virginity as the highest virtue. See n. 8 above.

21. Elizabeth Clark has demonstrated how the role of the bishop was constructed so that all men were feminized as the body of Christ, of which the cleric was the temporal head. "Sex, Shame and Rhetoric: En-gendering Early Christian Ethics," *Journal of the American Academy of Religion* 59 (1990): 221–45.

22. An excellent patristic example is Ambrose's *De institutione virginis,* in which much of Ambrose's sermon is put in the mouth of Juliana, a wealthy consecrated widow, who had invited Ambrose to dedicate a basilica she had built in Florence. He uses her not only to speak for the primacy of vir-

ginity over marriage but also to dramatize the trials of marriage, "even to a good man." *Exhortatio virginitatis* 2.12, 3.13–4.27, especially 4.24, SAEMO 14/2 (1989): 208, 210–18.

23. Ambrosiaster, *Questions on the Old and New Testaments,* Question 45, sections 21 and 26, ed. Alexander Souter, CSEL 50 (1908): 82.

24. Kim Power, *The Secret Garden,* p. 36 (n. 8 above).

25. See Jerome, Letter 22.25, trans. Wright, 108.

26. See a similar passage in John Cassian, *Conferences* 18.16, ed. E. Pichery, Schr 64 (1959): 32–33.

27. Patricia Cox Miller explores this dynamic in "The Blazing Body: Ascetic Desire in Jerome's Letter to Eustochium," *Journal of Early Christian Studies* 1 (1993): 21–46.

28. Cyprian, *De habitu virginum* 3, CSEL 3/1: 189.11–22, presents virginity's beauties in a positive light. Virgins are "the flower of the tree of the church, the beauty and adornment of spiritual grace, the image of God reflecting the holiness of the Lord, the more illustrious part of Christ's flock." Origen's is an exquisitely wrought depiction of the Bride and Groom in his Commentaries and Sermons on the Canticle.

29. Such a possibility is inherent in Ambrose's statement that faithful virgins hold within themselves Christ's fire, which confers eternal life. *De institutione virginis* 11.74, SAEMO 14/2: 164.

30. The *quadriga* owes a debt to the Platonic chariot of the soul, which Ambrose merged with Elijah's chariot. This aspect does not emerge in the illumination in the Burgsteinfurt Archive, which shows a four-wheeled chariot without horses, CCCM 5, Plate 8. Instead, the wheels are driven by the four principal figures. The Cologne manuscript, however, depicts Mary and both Johns standing on wheels. Mary holds the Christ child, and a wheel is under his feet also. Thus, we have the wheels within wheels of Elijah's chariot.

31. John the Baptist is a significant figure in Ambrose's *De virginibus.* He has more power dead than most men alive. On his birth: 2.2.12; on his death: 3.6.25–30, SAEMO 14/1: 174–76, 228–34.

32. Ambrose, *De virginibus* 1.3.13, SAEMO 14/1: 116.

33. John the Baptist had previously filled this function for patristic authors: Ambrose, *De virginitate* 3.11 and *De institutione virginis* 1.4, 7.50, SAEMO 14/2: 20 and 150; Gregory of Nyssa, *De virginitate* 6, ed. Michel Aubineau, Schr 119 (1966): 338.1–348.41.

34. Ambrose also describes John as the most spiritual disciple, *De institutione virginis* 7.46–48, SAEMO 14/2: 144–48.

35. In Peter Chrysologus' *Sermo* 127.2, ed. A. Olivar, CCSL 24B (1982): 782, there is a similar description: "John, the student of virtue, teacher of life, the essence of holiness, model of practice, mirror of virgins, renowned for his modesty, exemplar of chastity and penitence" (*Iohannes virtutum schola, magisterium vitae, sanctitatis forma, norma morum, virginitatis speculum, pudicitiae titulus, castitatis exemplum, poenitentiae*).

36. Ambrose had reserved the Lamb metaphor for reference to Christ's suffering or the Eucharist. For him, virgin martyrs were also sacrificial lambs: *De virginibus* 1.2.5, 1.2.8–9, SAEMO 14/1: 106, 108–110; *De virginitate* 11.60 and *De institutione virginis* 16.99, SAEMO 14/2: 52 and 180.

37. Jerome, Letter 48.21, PL 22: 510B; *Adversus Iovinianum* 1.31, PL 23: 265D; Augustine, *De trinitate* 4.5.9, ed. W. J. Mountain, CCSL 50 (1968): 172–73.1–25. Augustine did not connect Mary directly to the Canticle's garden as Jerome did.

38. Compare *SV* 1.88, 200, 269–787, 297; 5.103, 348, 489, 505, 727–30, 922–24, 976–99, 1011–16, with Origen, *In Canticum Canticorum* 16–22, 3.4.7, 4.1.13, Schr 376: 520, 684–94; *Homiliae in Canticum* 4, and *Homiliae* 2.2, Schr 37: 80–82, 106–8; Ambrose, *De virginibus* 1.8.40–48, 3.4.17, 3.4.16, 3.7.34–35, SAEMO 14/1: 140–48, 221–22, 236–38; Gregory of Nyssa, *De virginitate* 23.5, Schr 119: 542.7–8.

39. See, for example, John Cassian, *Conferences,* 2.11 and 18.16, ed. E. Pichery, Schr 42 (1955): 121–22, and Schr 64 (1959): 31.

40. Paschasius, *De assumptione* 13, CCCM 56C: 115. See liturgical examples and discussion in Éric Palazzo and Ann-Katrin Johansson, "Jalons liturgiques pour une histoire du culte de la Vierge," *Marie: Le culte de la vierge dans la société médiévale,* ed. Dominique Iogna-Prat, Éric Palazzo, and Daniel Russo (Paris: Beauchesne, 1996), pp. 15(44, esp. p. 36. Hilda Graef states that Paul the Deacon (d. 799) was the first Latin writer to describe Mary as a mediator between God and humankind. He was dependent on Greek sources. *Mary: A History of Doctrine and Devotion,* 2 vols. (London: Sheed and Ward, 1963–65), 1: 161, 171.

41. Ambrose applies Cant. 8.10 to the Church in *De virginibus* 1.8.49, SAEMO 14/1: 148. Before this, Athanasius used Mary as a model of the peace of heart that typifies virginity, *Letter to the Virgins* 259, L. Th. Lefort, "Saint Athanase: Sur la virginité," *Le Muséon* 42 (1929): 135.

42. See John Cassian, who believed that the peaceful soul possessed the kingdom of God, *Conferences* 18.16, Schr 64 (1959): 32.

43. Ann W. Astell discusses this mother-son relationship from a Jungian perspective. She tends to be uncritical of psychoanalytic theory's ahistoricism and gender stereotyping. See *The Song of Songs in the Middle Ages* (Ithaca, NY: Cornell University Press, 1991).

44. Ambrose, *Expositio Ps. 118* 3.7–8, SAEMO 9 (1987): 128–30. Even when referring to Mary's human motherhood, Augustine privileged the faith in her heart over the womb that carried Jesus. *De virginitate* 3, PL 40: 398.

45. Ambrose, *De Isaac* 3.8, CSEL 32/1: 648.5; *De virginibus* 2.6.42, SAEMO 14/1: 200; *De institutione virginis* 14.89–90, SAEMO 14/2: 172–74.

46. Origen, *In Canticum* 1.1.1–15, 2.10.1–11, Schr 375: 176–86, 446–52; Jerome, *Adversus Iovinianum* 1.30, PL 23: 263BC.

47. Graef, *Mary,* p. 244 (n. 40 above) discusses Amadeus of Lausanne (d. 1159), who appears to have been even more audacious in depicting the erotic re-

lationship between Mary and her son. The text appears to be heavily dependent on Ambrose. See n. 45.

48. Here I am dependent on two excellent studies of the development of Marian liturgy. Palazzo and Johansson (n. 40 above) demonstrate that from its first inception, the feast of the Assumption was a Marian feast, not a Christological one. In the same volume, Claire Maître establishes that Marian liturgy did not emerge from the feasts of the virgins, but that the common of virgins was modeled on Marian feasts. Texts for Mary were chosen from psalms praising the Temple and from earlier feasts of Christmas and the Purification, "Du culte marial à la celebration des vierges," in *Marie: Le culte de la vierge,* ed. Iogna-Prat, Palazzo, and Russo, pp. 44–63 (n. 40 above).

49. Paschasius, *De assumptione* 9 and 15, CCCM 56C: 135 and 153.

50. Paschasius Radbertus, *De assumptione* 3.13.99–106, CCCM 56C: 115.

51. *Genetrix dei* was the customary Latin translation of the Greek *theotókon.* This nuanced language distinguished the motherhood of the human Jesus from motherhood of his divine nature. Mary bore God but was mother only to Jesus' humanity. Even Augustine insisted on this distinction. Power, *Veiled Desire,* p. 175 (n. 18 above).

52. Paschasius used it seven times in *De assumptione* 14–19, CCCM 56C: 150–62.

53. Athanasius, *Letter to the Virgins* 244, Lefort, p. 88 (n. 41 above).

54. Peter Damian offers a similar passage in *Sermon* 46.10, ed. I. Lucchesi, CCCM 57 (1983): 281.

55. The bridal chamber of God and humanity is an interpretation of Ps. 19.6 frequently found in Ambrose. A typical interpretation is *Hymn* 4.14, PL16: 1474: Augustine followed Ambrose's interpretation in *Enarrationes in Psalmos* 18.6.6; it is found in Paschasius, *De assumptione* 9, 15, CCCM 56C: 135–36, 153.

56. According to Marie-Louise Thérel, Mary was linked with the moon in Christian art by the sixth century, *Les Symboles de "l'Ecclesia" dans la création iconographique de l'art chrétien du IIIe au VIe siècle* (Roma: Edizioni di Storia e Letteratura, 1973), Plate 26. Paschasius' *De assumptione* 8, CCCM 56C: 129, may have influenced the author of *SV.*

57. *SV* 5.58–59 follows patristic interpretation of the tabernacle as purity of mind and body. That is, Christ dwells in the pure mind, contained within the urn that is the pure body. See the commentaries of Origen translated by Rufinus, *In Numeros Homiliae* 10.3, ed. W. Baehrens, Corpus Berolinense 30 (Berlin, 1921): 74; *In Exodum Homiliae* 9.4, ed. Baehrens, Corpus Berolinense 29 (1920): 242; Gregory of Nyssa, *De virginitate* 18.2–4, Schr 119: 468–76.

58. The root of Jesse became one of the tropes for the feast of the Assumption. Palazzo and Johansson, "Jalons liturgiques pour une histoire du culte de la Vierge," p. 38 (n. 40 above).

59. Images of election are applied to Mary by Ambrose, *Expositio evangelii secundum Lucam* 2.14, CCSL 14: 37.213; Ambrose, *De institutione virginis* 5.33, SAEMO 14/2: 134.

60. *Regina caeli* does appear in several medieval texts. Bernard of Clairvaux, *Sermones* [Pentecost] 2.4 and *Sermones [Assumption of the Blessed Virgin Mary]* 4.1, *SBO* 5: 168.1, 244.20; Aelred of Rievaulx, *De institutione inclusarum*, line 759, ed. C. H. Talbot, CCCM 1 (1971): 637–82.

61. Ambrose designated virgins spouses of the eternal King in *De virginibus* 1. 37, SAEMO 14/1: 138. Augustine called the City of God Queen of heaven in *De civitate Dei* 17.16, ed. Bernard Dombert and Alphonse Kalb, CCSL 48 (1955): 582. Late antique representations of Mary with her child, which depict her as a Byzantine empress, may have provided a visual influence.

62. Paschasius, *De assumptione* 3, CCCM 56C: 115–17.

63. *SV* uses *mater electa* only once, 5.124, and uses instead "preordained" on two occasions, 5.51, 186.

64. Ambrose used the ark as a type of the body in *De Noe* 6.13, CSEL 32/1: 422; *Exameron* 6.9.72, SAEMO 1 (1979): 414. Thérel states that Ambrose also used the ark as a type of the Church, *Les Symboles,* p. 114 (n. 56 above). As ecclesial symbols were being applied to Mary, Peregrinus' argument strengthens the metaphor when applied to Mary.

65. Regarding judges and kings, see Paschasius, *De assumptione* 5, 9, CCCM 56C: 123, 133; see, for example, Augustine, *De civitate Dei* 17.15–16, ed. Emmanuel Kauffman, CSEL 40 (1962): 246–51.

66. On Origen's thought, see John Dillon, "Origen and Plotinus: The Platonic Influence on Early Christianity," in, *The Relationship between Neoplatonism and Christianity,* ed. Thomas Finan and Vincent Twomey (Dublin: Four Courts Press, 1992), pp. 7–26.

67. Ambrose suggests a similar mediation, which is, however, Christ's choice, not a necessary condition for his incarnation. Ambrose was intent on emphasizing that Christ needed no help in his saving work. Ambrose, *De institutione virginis* 7.49–50, SAEMO 14/2: 148–50. *Exp. evang. secundum Lucam* 10.132, CCSL 14: 383, 1260; *De obitu Valentiniani* 39, PL 16: 137B; *Epist. extra collectionem traditae* 14 [63], ed. M. Zelzer, CSEL 82/3 (1982): 294.

68. In *SV* 5.450–54, Peregrinus bases his argument on the natural relationship between lambs and ewes. Two centuries later, Richard of St. Laurent would use the same strategy, applying to Mary the language of the Lord's Prayer; Graef, *Mary,* p. 266 (n. 40 above).

69. Tertullian and Origen, in fact, had argued against Mary's virginity during the birth (*in partu*) and Irenaeus has been read this way. Charles W. Neumann certainly accepts that even Jerome came late to virginity *in partu* while always arguing for it before and after the birth. From Neumann's perspective, any divergence from virginity *in partu* is not taken as evidence of differing traditions or the development of Marian doctrine but as an error due to heresy. Thus he explains away both Tertullian and Origen. *The Virgin Mary in the Works of Ambrose* (Fribourg: University Press, 1962), pp. 105–12. The *porta clausa* was first deployed against Jovinian by the Roman synod. Ambrose's use of it in *De institutione* against Bonosus may have influenced a parallel passage in Jerome's Letter 48.21 (ca. 393/94). Dom

Gori, SAEMO 14/2: 155 n. 115, cites the study by J. A. De Aldama, "La condemnación de Joviniano en el Sinodo de Roma," *Epheremides Mariologicae* 13 (1963): 114–15.

70. Ambrose, *De virginibus* 1.3.11–13, 1.8.51, 2.2.10–17, SAEMO 14/1: 110–18, 150, 172–78; *De institutione virginis* 2.79–80; cf. 17.105, SAEMO 14/2: 166–68, 186. He may have been influenced by Origen's interpretation of Ps. 44, *In Cant.* 3.10.4–7, Schr 376: 590–94. Also, Gregory of Nyssa, *De virginitate* 2.1.12, 2.3.3, 4.8.10, 14.4.15, Schr 119: 264, 268, 330, 560; Athanasius, *Letter to the Virgins* 26, ed. Lefort, p. 156.

71. Ambrose, *Exp. evang. secundum Lucam* 2.88, CSEL 14: 1226–32.

72. Ambrose, *De institutione virginis* 8.52, 13.82–84, SAEMO 14/2: 152, 168–70.

73. Ambrose, *De Spiritu Sancto* 1.13.132, 2.9.92, PL 16: 762, 794C; *De institutione virginis* 7.49–50, 10.67–68, 17.113, SAEMO 14/2: 148–50, 162, 192; *De fide* 1.1.8, ed. O. Faller, CSEL 78/8 (1962): 7; *Exp. Ps. 118* 18.25, ed. M. Petschenig, SAEMO 10 (1987): 252. Neumann argues that because Ambrose said that Mary risks martyrdom under the cross, he understood her to be co-redemptrix. He dismisses Ambrose's own clear statement that Christ needed no helper although Mary wished to support him, as "letting himself be carried away." *The Virgin Mary*, p. 265 (n. 69 above). However, Ambrose let himself get carried away in similar fashion in *Sec. Lucam* 10.132, CCSL 14: 383, and *Epist. extra coll.* 14, CSEL 82/3: 294.

74. Gregory of Nyssa, *De virginitate*, 13.3, Schr 119: 430.9–20; Ambrose, Letter 7.37, ed. Otto Faller, CSEL 82/1 (1969): 62.

75. Hippolytus, *Fragment on Proverbs* 9.1, trans. Alexander Roberts and James Donaldson, revised A. Cleveland Cox, Ante Nicene Fathers 5 (Peabody, MA: Hendrickson Publishers, 1994): 175; *Fragment on the Song of Songs* 1–2, trans. S. D. F. Salmond, Ante Nicene Fathers 5: 176; cf. Athanasius, *Letter to the virgins* 257, ed. Lefort, p. 125.

76. Ambrose, *Exp. evang. secundum Lucam* 10.25, CCSL 14: 353.

77. Ambrose, Letter 7.36, CSEL 82/1: 61.369. Gregory of Nyssa described his sister, Macrina, in these terms.

78. In *SV* 5.876–890, Peregrinus uses *virgo Christi* ten times.

79. Cf. Ambrose, *De institutione virginis* 17.109, SAEMO 14/2: 188.

80. Cf. Ambrose, *De virginibus* 2.2.6 and 15, 3.21, SAEMO 14/1: 168 and 176, 182.

81. Origen, *In Canticum* 1.6.1–5, Schr 375: 250–52; Gregory of Nyssa, *De virginitate* 1, Schr 119: 256.16–258.24.

82. Cf. Ambrose, *De virginibus* 1.2.8 (Agnes), 2.3.19 (Thecla), 3.7.34 (Pelagia), 3.7.38 (Soteris), SAEMO 14/1: 108, 180, 236, 240.

83. Augustine, *De trinitate* 12.12–14, CCCM 48: 371(75. For Mary as Augustine's emblem of faith, see *Veiled Desire*, pp. 179–80, 196–97 (n. 18 above).

84. Philo, *The Worse Attacks the Better* 54, 115–117 and *Allegorical Interpretation* 14.49, trans. C. D. Yonge, *The Works of Philo*, new ed. (Peabody, MA: Hendrickson Publishers, 1993), pp. 118, 125, 43.

85. Origen, *In Canticum* 1.1.1–5, 2.8.4–9, Schr 375: 176–81, 408–12; *Homiliae I in Canticum* 1.3.4, Schr 37: 80–82. See Henri Crouzel, *Virginité et marriage chez Origène* (Bruges: Desclée de Brouwer, 1963), pp. 17–24, esp. pp. 19–21.

86. Origen, *In Canticum*, Prol. 4 passim; 2.1.27–53, Schr 375: 146–72, 276–92; Ambrose, *De virginibus* 1.8 45, SAEMO 14/1: 144.

87. See Graef, *Mary*, p. 269, on Richard of St. Laurent (n. 68 above).

88. Athanasius used such a comparison in his *Letter to Virgins* 255, ed. Lefort, pp. 122–23.

# CHAPTER 5

# THE *SPECULUM VIRGINUM* AND
# THE AUDIO-VISUAL POETICS OF
# WOMEN'S RELIGIOUS INSTRUCTION

*Morgan Powell*

This chapter considers the role of auditory and visual images in the *Speculum*. It argues that the treatise was composed to be delivered aloud by a male preacher addressing a community of female religious either individually or in groups. The illustrations in the treatise, far from being appendages, are integral to its use and conception and provide the basis for a sophisticated aesthetic argument that relies on simultaneous consideration of spoken word and image. The original beginning of the *Speculum virginum* can be seen in the opening of part three of the *Speculum virginum,* a free elaboration of Psalm 44.11–12 ("Listen, daughter, and see"). The commentary on these verses highlights the importance of auditory and visual means of communication. This pedagogically innovative treatise offered a new way by which spiritual directors could present traditional teaching, providing women with alternative access to and participation in the revelation of religious truth.

There are few more remarkable cases of religious women, or "daughters" of the Church, listening to divine instruction than that of Birgitta of Sweden (ca. 1303/73). While living first (1344–1349) as a widow at the Cistercian monastery of Alvastra, in Sweden, and then at Rome, her harkening to heavenly voices resulted in a large body of "Revelations." This included a Rule for the Order of the Holy Savior that she established with Cistercian assistance and became one of the major monastic orders of the Late Middle Ages, commonly known as the Birgittines. My concern is with a less celebrated instance of Birgitta's listening, in which she harkens not to her heavenly but to her spiritual father, her mentor and confessor, the Cistercian prior of Alvastra, Peter Olavi (d. 1390), who himself reported the event as a witness in her canonization proceedings:

> The same witness reported that, when one day at the said monastery he was reading aloud to the said lady Birgitta from the book called the *Speculum virginum,* in which the monk Peregrinus confers on all the virtues with the virgin Theodora, then the lady Birgitta, while he was speaking and while he looked on, as the witness asserted, was raptured in the spirit, and when she returned to herself she said, "I have just heard a voice in the spirit saying to me that virginity merits the crown, widows draw near to God and marriage is not barred from heaven, but rather obedience admits all to glory."[1]

This account is well known in the secondary literature on the *Speculum virginum.*[2] It is the only account we have of actual use of the text, the first medieval treatise devoted to the female monastic life and a work that, judging from its broad and rapid dissemination as well as its longevity, was both avidly and widely used.[3] But the pastoral care of women, of which Peter's activity is one instance, and which the *Speculum virginum* portrays in idealized form, is generally treated in the negative when it is mentioned at all in medieval written sources—another example of the silencing of women's presence in the institutions of the Church. While Birgitta's experience is recounted here as evidence of her sanctity, her place among God's elect, it is worth scrutinizing for the assumptions and conventions it may reveal as well as for what it may tell us of the use of texts, specifically the *Speculum virginum,* in women's spiritual instruction.

My subject here is the use of the *Speculum virginum,* the place of its text and images in monastic reading practice. This question as well as its corollary, who the users/readers were, has scarcely received mention in previous research. But if we are to understand the basic feature that makes this work so extraordinary, its cycle of images and their relationship to a program of women's monastic instruction, then these questions must be our starting point. In what follows I offer a summary view of my own research and conclusions on these questions.[4] Birgitta's experience forms not only a point of departure but also a touchstone for this inquiry. As will be seen, despite the two intervening centuries and Birgitta's own status as a visionary, Peter's and Birgitta's use of the *Speculum virginum* is most notable for its consistency with the other evidence; more surprisingly, an experience of the aural and visual presence of the divine such as Birgitta's, far from being a miraculous exception, is implicitly claimed by the work itself as the object of its orchestration of text and image.

Birgitta does not read the book that inspires her rapture. Her instructor acts as mediator between her experience and the written text, reading aloud from it as she listens. The complete text of the *Speculum virginum* in the version we possess today begins with a dedicatory letter, or *Epistula,* in which an anonymous author C (in some manuscripts, N) presents his finished work to the anonymous virgins N and N. The medieval use of N to stand for a name to be determined by the occasion suggests that the communication figured in the *Epistula* is a fiction serving to introduce the work.[5] This conclusion accords with our knowledge of the work's actual owners: Of the ten manuscripts that date from the first century after its completion (ca. 1140), there is only one for which there is any indication of provenance from a women's community.[6] On the other hand, the best and possibly even autograph copy, MS Arundel 44 in the British Library, London *(L),* belonged in the twelfth century to a certain "magister Hugo" of the Cistercian abbey of Eberbach on the Rhine.[7] No less a Cistercian spiritual center than Clairvaux produced three other early copies of the work, one for its own use and the other two for its (men's) daughter houses of Mores and Igny.[8] In the later transmission, which includes fourteen more manuscripts that contain, or once contained, the entire text, the exception proves the rule: There is one manuscript that can be traced to the Birgittine house Sion in Cologne; all other indications point to provenance from men's communities.[9] But Birgitta conceived her order in part as an institutionalization of the very relationship that the manuscript transmission of the *Speculum virginum* implies: men using the text for their pastoral care of women, much as Peter undertook with Birgitta. Birgitta's unique organization of the monastic community called for joint, if not "double," communities of not more than sixty women, whose pastoral needs were to be met by a neighboring house of not more than twenty-five men.[10] The design and regulation of the Birgittine order reflect in many points both Peter Olavi's experience in the *cura monialium* and the Cistercian model for its practice.[11] It would appear that the *Speculum virginum* initially recommended itself to Birgitta's order for the same reason that her own use of the text, as described by Peter, accurately represents the model of instruction that the work was designed to serve.[12] The *Speculum* is a model, handbook, and sourcebook for male *magistri* engaged in the instruction of women's communities.[13]

That a work entitled "The Virgins' Mirror" should never have belonged to women's communities does not surprise in terms of the conventions of its own time, however it may disappoint our expectations.[14] While many women became Latin literate, and some among these used their ability to sensational effect, here again the exception proves the rule: No less prolific a writer and example of women's learning than the abbess Hildegard of Bingen repeatedly described herself as an unlearned laywoman in order to inscribe her voice within the strictures of Church authority and convention.[15] Women, like layfolk, were summarily classed as *auditores,* a term that was often used synonymously with *illitterati,* or *laici,* in opposition to the preaching, literate cleric. The classification need not accurately reflect an individual's level of learning or ability to read.[16] The terms instead designate a position in an immutable order of things. These same conventions are echoed in the text as justification for its existence and of its innovative form as a text-image compilation. In fact, only the dedication of the *Epistula* implies any inconsistency with the text's construction of its audience as ignorant of letters *[ignorantes litteras],* poor or slow "readers" at best, limited in their ability to read in the contemporary sense, that is to engage in serious study of the Scriptures or to grasp unassisted more than their literal meaning.[17] This characterization recurs several times as a way of justifying the inclusion of a new picture: As the dialogue progresses, Peregrinus, the instructor, spontaneously produces his pictures as aids to Theodora's understanding and repeatedly interjects apologetic remarks that, more often than not, conceal more ambitious ideas on the real value and role of the images.[18] The repeated allusion to difficulty with *scriptura* as a justification for *pictura* is part and parcel of the same conventions I have just outlined, and found its authority in Gregory the Great's epistolary response to the overzealous iconoclasm of Bishop Serenus of Marseilles.[19] Gregory made the argument that *picturae,* or Church art, were for the lay and unlearned what Scripture was for the clerical, lettered elite; this equation thereby acquired an authority that continued to be cited through the end of the Middle Ages.[20] The *Speculum virginum* thus constructs its audience according to a system of binary oppositions that place—by reason of assumed natural affinity—women, listening, and pictures on one side of God's order and men, preaching or reading, and Scripture on the other.[21]

It is not my objective here to investigate the extent to which the historical circumstances in women's communities of the twelfth century correspond to the author's characterization of his audience. To a great degree, the same conventions to which the work appeals doubtless also dictated how it was used, as the manuscript transmission suggests. But the work's appeal and the potential impact of its model of women's instruction is readily grasped by recalling in general terms its historical position.

While the twelfth-century Church knew a long tradition of the illustration of certain liturgical works (the Apocalypse and the Psalms, for example), the *Speculum virginum* is among the earliest examples of the development of an original composition imbricated with a program of images. Among these, it stands out both in the ambitious nature of its project and in the sophisticated understanding and implementation of its imagery. Both these characteristics are the result of one thing: The *Speculum virginum* represents an attempt to codify a practice of instruction for religious women that was in greatly increasing demand, and may already have been widely in use, at the time of its composition. Beginning in the late eleventh century, the number of women entering the monastic life and the number of new foundations for women increased enormously in both France and Germany, so that the resources of the existing orders were increasingly strained by the women's pastoral needs.[22] The notion of women as "natural illiterates" no doubt provided a welcome justification for a resultant lack of training in *grammatica* and *litterae*. That is, the conventions that justify the salient features of the work conveniently correspond to the historical circumstances, and this fact in itself allows the author/compiler to codify his instructional practice as a universal model for broad dissemination.

In the various manuscripts of the *Speculum* both the frontispiece and the so-called author-portraits (found between parts two and three) portray a situation very like what Peter describes to Birgitta's tribunal: A male instructor holds forth a book, usually open, or a scroll, and appears to propound or read from it for his attentively listening pupil. Whether in text or image, the work consistently portrays the instructor as the reader or the voice of the text and the woman as recipient of his mediation of Scripture. This reception of Scripture is the real object and subject of the instructional dialogue. Where women's reading is explicitly referred to, emphasis is sooner placed on its rudimentary character, and nothing beyond the recital of Scripture in the office is implied. In fact, the verb *legere* refers in the text exclusively to Scripture.[23] It is this "reading"—a process of gathering and assimilating *Scripturae* to the self—to which the entire work is addressed. The *Speculum virginum* is not so much a book to be read as it is an alternative method of monastic reading, the *lectio divina* as redesigned to be suitable to the station and capacities of women—as Church authority saw them. The voice of the instructor becomes the voice of Scripture, or Christ himself, and his auditor "reads," in the fully transformational monastic sense, through him:

*Peregrinus:* Attende igitur vocem Christi, in voce legem Christi, ut in Christo per Christum vincas hoc, quod fuisti. Amor Christi naturam a solito cursu reflectit, naturae legem dissipat, ut non sit homo, quod fuerat.
*Theodora:* Vocem istam de te audiam, legem de te legam. (*SV* 12.321–25)

[*P.:* Hear, then, the voice of Christ, in His voice, the law of Christ, so that in Christ and through Christ you overcome what you once were. The

love of Christ turns the natural disposition away from its habitual path,
eradicates the law of nature, so that its recipient is no longer the person
she once was.

*T.:* This voice let me hear through you, this law let me read through you.]²⁴

In this way, the seemingly conservative nods to convention, whereby
women remain auditors and viewers, perform as the smokescreen for the
innovation this work represents, an innovation that is replete with reper-
cussions in women's spirituality, the religious use of images, and text-image
forms throughout the remainder of the Middle Ages: It undertakes to
transform the *lectio divina* into an audio-visual performance, an instructor's
manipulation of voice, physical presence, and visual perception that is to
deliver a sensory experience of the Logos.²⁵

If the significance I thereby claim for the *Speculum virginum* has escaped
earlier scholars, it is only partly a result of their approach and concern with
other questions. The work has always seemed to lack a statement of its understanding of the roles of text and image, voice and presence in instruction. The prologues to other early and later works that incorporate
images—an increasingly frequent phenomenon from the early twelfth
century onward—generally offer a straightforward statement and justifying
explanation of this fact.²⁶ Not infrequently these statements are for their
own part little more than nods to convention and may reveal little and obscure much. The *Speculum virginum* provides something different and altogether more persuasive. Its prologue is not a collation of conventional
arguments but a demonstration of the method in action; the argument for
audio-visual presentation is projected into its portrayal of instruction—
even as it now occurs not at the beginning of the work but at the beginning of part three:

"Audi filia et vide et inclina aurem tuam et obliviscere populum tuum et
domum patris tui. Et concupiscet rex decorem tuum" [Ps. 44.11–12]. Audi
sanctae ecclesiae filia, "uni viro Christo Iesu virgo casta desponsata" [cf. 2
Cor. 11.2] et consignata, audi sponsum tuum ad æterna dona te vocantem,
vide premia premonstrantem, sequere precedentem. Audi, inquam, legibus
divinis intendendo, vide legibus ipsis non vi vel necessitate, sed ratione, vol-
untate et amore ferventer obtemperando, audi quid sponsus precipiat, vide
quid promittat, ut sic dirigaris ad precepta, quo pervenias ad promissa. (*SV*
1.1–10)

["Listen, daughter, and see, and bend your ear, and forget your own people
and the house of your father. So shall the King desire your beauty." Listen,
daughter of holy Church, chaste virgin betrothed and promised in everlasting fidelity to Jesus Christ, hear your Bridegroom calling you to eternal

gifts, see the rewards he shows you beforehand, so that you follow him who leads. Listen, I say, by attending to the divine laws, see by fervently obeying those laws not from force or necessity, but from reason, free will, and love. Listen to what the Bridegroom requires, and see what he promises, so that you are directed to his teaching, in order that you may attain what is promised.]

This passage, an extended elaboration on a theme offered by the eleventh verse of Psalm 44, the epithalamic or wedding-song psalm, was once the opening of a completed eight-book version of the *Speculum virginum,* as I shall clarify below. In its original position, it echoed unmistakably the opening of the prologue to the monastic archtext, the Rule of St. Benedict: "Listen, carefully, my son, to the master's instructions, and attend to them with the ear of your heart" [Obsculta, o fili, praecepta magistri, et inclina aurem cordis tui].[27] The author thus anchored the opening of his introduction to the female monastic life firmly within Benedictine tradition—with equally pointed variation from that tradition. I will return to this point shortly. In the final twelve-part version of the work, this passage became the opening of part three. The author by then was willing to obscure at least partially his Benedictine authority, but not only this: In its final form the *Speculum* dispenses altogether with a *textual* presentation of its audio-visual poetics (the added *Epistula* features the titulary *speculum,* but only as visual metaphor), and instead elaborates the role of images and oral delivery in entirely visual form in the frontispiece (figure 1) that precedes part one. Neither the frontispiece nor the *audi filia et vide* opening of part three previously have been recognized to fulfill this function. Together they offer a sophisticated introduction to the author's reflection on his method and means. Here I shall limit myself to a discussion of the original "prologue," now *SV* 3.1–118.[28]

But before I turn to the proto-prologue itself, I shall present in summary form the most immediate evidence identifying it as such.[29] The hypothesis that an eight-book version of the *Speculum virginum* once circulated, if only for a short time, has a historical, if troublesome, witness in Johannes Trithemius. The fifteenth-century humanist and author of several "encyclopedias" of medieval literature described the *Speculum* as containing eight books. Trithemius' description has long troubled scholarship on this work, not least because his own internal inconsistencies allow no clear conclusion.[30] But the manuscript evidence clearly corroborates the existence of an earlier, shorter version.[31] Six of the early manuscripts read "Here ends the *Speculum virginum*" [Explicit *speculum virginum*] at 10.397, the point at which the prayer of part ten concludes, and which was no doubt once the end of the last book. In the later version, part ten continues with a passage that playfully stages the resumption of the dialogue: Peregrinus considers her instruction complete; Theodora disagrees.[32] Parts eleven and twelve are also a later addition. This much had been recognized. But my examination shows that parts one and two, which are in themselves very closely linked in content with parts eleven and twelve, were also later additions. The four new books were composed and added as a unit, with the preceding *Epistula,* to an eight-book whole made up of what is now parts three through ten. The similarity in content and pictures alone between the added parts makes this conclusion probable.[33] But it is also verified within the text.

The end of part two marks a similarly unique rupture in the text as that just mentioned at the end of part ten: The text records both a break in the conversation and a break in its recorded form, the divisions of the finished codex. Immediately before the "proto-prologue" that opens what is now part three, Peregrinus announces a break in the conversation and proposes that it be resumed "in a second book" *[secundo libro],* while in the final count the following "book" is numbered as part three.[34] There is only one other point at which the illusion of continuous dialogue is abandoned to make note of a corresponding codicological division, at the end of part six. Here, too, Peregrinus "gets the numbers wrong," referring to the ensuing book as the *quintus liber,* rather than the seventh.[35] The two anomalies possibly have the same explanation: When the first two parts were added, the entire preexisting body of text could be called the "second book" (as opposed to *pars);* the unusual rupture in recorded text and "spoken" dialogue still marks the break in composition that gave rise to this idea. At about the same time, the author must have begun to refer to the divisions of his text as parts *(partes*—this is the term used in the twelve-part version) rather than as the books *(libri)* that made up the eight-book version. The single preexisting intratextual reference (now at the end of part six) to a break between parts, however, was overlooked, such that in most manuscripts Peregrinus still refers to part seven as the fifth book.[36]

Near the opening of what is now part three there is one textual feature that would seem to disallow this argument—but in fact verifies it—and another that places it beyond doubt. Theodora requests of Peregrinus a *speculum,* in which she and her sisters can observe what is necessary to their monastic lives *(SV* 3.94–104). This is the first mention of the figure of the work's title outside the *Epistula.* But in all collated manuscripts except *L,* Theodora's request contains the mention "rogo te per florem aeternem . . . de quo superius nonnulla contulimus . . ." *(SV* 3.96–97) [I ask you by the flower eternal, of which we spoke earlier at some length]—an apparent reference to the *flos campi,* announced at the opening of part one as the subject of the conversation. *L,* which stands out in the manuscript tradition for the peculiarly decisive and authoritative interventions of its pervasive corrector, gives this phrase in the margin, supplied by the same corrector.[37] The phrase is thus unmasked as the author's (or a very early corrector's) attempt to disguise the fact that part three does not acknowledge the earlier beginning, while sounding every bit like a beginning itself. Finally, only a little earlier in part three, Peregrinus defers a question from Theodora for later discussion (*SV* 3.52–53). True to his word, the subject is revisited in part eight, where he introduces it with the words, "Verum locus oportunus se hic optulit tecum conferendi, de quibus non parum movebaris *in ipsa fronte incepti operis huius*" (*SV* 8.149–51, italics mine) [Indeed, this is the appropriate place to talk to you about those things that moved you not a little *at the very beginning of this work*]. The evidence is clear: The author's original formulation of his project in text and image occurred at the beginning of what is now part three, in its *audi et vide* address.

The opening of the work is spoken in words of Scripture that designate at once the twin media of the method and the identity of their addressee. It cites the epithalamic psalm at the juncture where the singer turns from his praise of the Bridegroom to address the Bride. In addition to inspiring the opening of Benedict's Rule as mentioned earlier, this passage had a long tradition of use in women's instruction, for which the exemplar was Jerome's letters to his spiritual charges, Eustochium and Principia.[38] But just as the complicity between the unique project of the *Speculum virginum* and the biblical text is immediately evident—and exploited in ample repetition of the two verbs that serve to structure the entire opening address—so the difference between Jerome's exegetical treatises and this oral address is readily apparent. Jerome operates in the standard commentary mode, citing Scripture and then commenting on it for his reader—and a reader she clearly is, for Jerome's authorial persona is a writer, and he repeatedly describes his activity as such. But for Theodora, the recipient of the oral address, the voice of Scripture and that of her instructor are not separated into letter and gloss, Scripture and its exegesis. What opens here with a passage from Psalm 44.11–12 and might appear, in written form, to continue as commentary on that passage for the first forty-five lines is not a commentary on Scripture but an elaboration of it in which the voice of the instructor is identical with the voice of the Holy Spirit and with the voice of the Bridegroom. The biblical text is not so much explicated as appropriated to the instructor's purpose: "Audi, inquam. . . ."[39] Its language thus simultaneously describes the relationship between Holy Spirit and Daughter Church and that between instructor and pupil. *Filia* clearly identifies the present listener, who is also the object of the second person addressed in the question "Cuius filia? Vis nosse?" (*SV* 3.14) [Whose daughter? Do you want to know?] The lengthy response makes the allegorical figures indistinguishable from models of her own identity that the listener is to fulfill:

Filia regis regum, filia rectoris creaturarum, immortalis sponsi per fidem sponsa, singularitate dilectionis unica, gratia simplicitatis columba, castitatis dono formosa, soror Christi tam gratia quam natura. . . . Audi filia apostolorum, audi proles et pignus omnium doctorum catholicorum, qui te genuere per fidem, instituerunt per operationem, ornaverunt per virtutem amorem, qui thalamum deliciosae dulcedinis in aeterno decore tibi futurum doctrina demonstrant, ut repetas principium tuum per virtutum custodiam . . . (*SV* 3.14–23)

[Daughter of the king of kings, daughter of the ruler of all creatures, Bride, through faith, of the immortal Bridegroom, one and only in matchless love, dove in grace of simplicity, beauteous in the gift of chastity, sister of Christ as much by grace as by nature. . . . Listen, daughter of the apostles, listen, child and kin of all catholic doctors, who, to engender you through faith, have instructed you with their works, adorned you with the love of virtues, who guide you to the future wedding chamber of delicious sweetness in eternity, so that you may return to your beginning through the custody of virtues . . .]

Peregrinus' interpolations into the biblical text are indistinguishable from it; they serve to render its meaning pregnant and immediate for a specific addressee, his female pupil. Scripture is delivered as sensory experience through a fusion of letter and gloss. In a masterful choice, the author has made the biblical authority for this audio-visual experience one with the message it delivers. The medium is the message.

The same two points, the identity of voice between Scripture and instructor, and the reification of the recipient of the Word in the female viewer and listener, is illustrated by the author's borrowing of Benedict's prologue opening. Benedict, too, relied on the injunction from Psalm 44 to inaugurate the instruction that would serve as the foundation of western monasticism. But he clearly suppressed the visual component of the scriptural text. Moreover, for Benedict, the voice of Scripture is distinct from that of the orally expounding *magister,* who is accordingly identified: "Ausculta, o fili, praecepta magistri, et inclina aurem cordis tui" [Harken, son, to the teaching of the master, and incline the ear of your heart]. The master's teaching echoes, but does not appropriate, the voice of Scripture; accordingly, the son listens, but does not "see," the meaning he is to receive, and even the act of hearing is rather a metaphor for the reception of the truth, which properly occurs in the heart. For the author of the *Speculum virginum* and more importantly, for the model of instruction it portrays, the woman reembodies the addressee of the biblical text. Her hearing and seeing are an immediate reception of its truth.

The instructor's address to his pupil is thus a performance of the voice of Scripture, the same voice that calls the Bride to the Bridegroom. Instruction becomes a kind of sensory seduction, and the text accordingly emphasizes the idea of attraction, both of the voice and of what it promises. The injunction to see is especially and consistently aligned with the idea of attraction in the address. Where the pupil is to hear what the Bridegroom requires, she is to see him and what he promises and thus be drawn to follow him *[sequere precedentem]*. Where the audible message instructs, its visual counterpart is to draw the onlooker irresistibly, or seduce.[40] The consistent alignment of the ideas of physical attraction with the visual privileges the eye with an immediate apprehension of both the Bridegroom and his celestial rewards. In the prayer that concluded the eight-book original version (the content of what is now part ten), the final entry of the Bride *[sponsa]* into heaven is envisioned in the words (spoken to the Bridegroom): "Haurit ibi sancta sponsa tua certissimo visu, quod nunc capit indubitanter auditu, et plus erit de suscepta gratia liberi stuporis quam fuerit in exilio de patria illa profundi rumoris" (*SV* 10.180–83) [There your holy bride will drink in through true sight what she now perceives indubitably by hearing, and so much the greater will be her unlimited wonder over this grace received than was the wonder she felt in exile over the premonition of that homeland]. The ultimate experience of the Godhead occurs through sight and surpasses the earthly experience through the ear. By implication, earthly sight, and the role of the visual in instruction, the viewing of the images, is akin to this ultimate vision as its counterpart in this world, where we see but as in a mirror *[speculum]*, darkly.[41]

The *audi et vide* address demonstrates an audio-visual delivery of Scripture that is to effect the transformation that is the object of all monastic *lectio divina*.[42] It initiates a process whereby, as the text says, a new woman will emerge from the old, a beautiful woman from an ugly one (*SV* 3.33: *nova de veteri, pulchra de vili*). The virgin's progress in the virtues is the beauty she will acquire that is so desirable to the Bridegroom (*SV* 3.41–45). But both here and in the actual implementation of the pictures, this progress is again programmatically advanced as a result of the audio-visual experience. The proto-prologue delivers at the outset the key statement of its audio-visual poetics:

Querit enim Christus "aures audiendi" [Matt. 13.9], querit oculos videndi, id est ut resideat interius, quod sonus innuit exterius, et fructificet ad mentis intuitum, quod trahitur per oculorum aspectum. Audi filia, vide unica, attende sponsa, columba, et soror et amica. (*SV* 3.10–14)

[For Christ seeks the open ears, he seeks open eyes, that is, so that what the sound commends outwardly shall reside within you, and so that what is drawn in through the eyes' gaze may bear fruit to the consideration of the mind. Listen, daughter, see, only one, attend to the Bridegroom, O dove, sister and beloved.]

The listener and viewer receives Christ though her eyes and ears, an interiorization of voice and image. This is the process that is to allow the female listener to become the Bride with whose name she is already called. While this statement could easily be applied to the function of the pictures, the proto-prologue makes no specific mention of them. The relationship of the pictures to the author's audio-visual poetics is revealed in action—a feature that is characteristic of the work as a whole. The focus of attention is always on the effect *[efficatia]* of the whole on the listener/viewer rather than on the elements that bring this about. It is then all the more to be noted that, despite the absence of a foregrounded statement on its multimedial composition, the *Speculum virginum* can be properly understood only when full account is taken of this effect and its construction through image and presence, word and voice.

The author's statements on the effects of Scripture, picture, and *speculum* reveal them as identical in the conception of his method. But the actual implementation of the pictures reveals as well that they become, in conjunction with the oral address, a "Paradise seeing aid" *[paradisum speculatorium]*, to use the words with which Peregrinus tellingly introduces one of them.[43] They are capable of initiating a visual intimation of epiphany. In this aspiration to an immediate experience of the divine presence, the *Speculum virginum* exploits the ostensible "weaknesses" of its female audience to reach beyond the bounds of traditional monastic *lectio*, both in media and in effect. These points are all highlighted, and appropriately so, in the course of part four, which follows the introduction of the first picture in the original version, the Trees of the Vices and Virtues.

The injunction to hear and to see, while repeated over and over again in the opening forty-five lines of part three, does not recur prior to the introduction of the picture between parts three and four. Thereafter, Peregrinus uses it three times to enjoin his pupil to listen to and consider Scripture, as she is to listen to him while looking at the picture (*SV* 4.275, 369, 443). The audio-visual poetics of the prologue are thus implicitly transferred to the entire instructional manipulation of word and image. When Peregrinus first places the double-page image of the Trees of the Vices and the Virtues before Theodora, he enjoins her to ponder the unresolved tension made manifest in this visual realization of mirror imaging, and identifies it as such (figures 2 and 3). The picture is a mirror *[speculum]* and affords the transformational experience immanent in Scripture:

Speculum, filia queris. Ecce quantum profeceris vel defeceris, in alterutro fructu speculari poteris. Hic enim, si te queris, reperis. Speculum dici non potest nisi quod intuentis imaginem representat. Igitur ex consideratione sacrae scripturae te ipsam consule, et aliqua vel virtutum vel viciorum vestigia reperis impressa conscientiae tuae. (*SV* 4.18–23)[44]

[You ask for a mirror, daughter. Here you can behold in the one fruit and the other how much you have progressed and where you are still wanting. Here, indeed, if you seek, you will find yourself. Nothing can be called a mirror unless it reveals the image of its beholder. Therefore, advise yourself through the consideration of Holy Scripture, and you will discover the signs of the vices and virtues impressed on your conscience.]

Picture and Scripture are part of one hermeneutic experience—even one hermeneutic moment, for as the passage shows, there is no discontinuity between the one and the other. In both, the virgin is to seek *herself*, a fact the author insists on by stating the seemingly obvious: Nothing can be called a mirror unless it reflects the image of its beholder. Far from relying on and purveying a "dead" metaphor, that of the mirror as image of the ideal, these statements force recognition of a paradox.[45] In the same way, the physical disposition of the two opposite Trees is intended to induce recognition and even anagnorisis: The hermeneutic gap created opens into a possibility of self-assessment and self-recognition as the viewer situates herself between the poles of the fruits of flesh and spirit *[fructus carnis et spiritus]*, as between the ideal and real images of self—and, as the picture reveals, between "old" and "new" woman, between Eve and Mary as the women whose agency generates the *vetus* and the *novus Adam* visible in the tops of the trees.[46]

The implementation of the pictures thus acts to fulfill the promise made in the *audi et vide* address: It effects the transformation of the old to the new woman, offers her self-recognition and growth in the virtues that will be her beauty before the Bridegroom. This is accomplished only as a result of the picture's effect in concert with the instructor's address, a conclusion that follows not only from the insistent repetition of *audi et vide*, but more so from the recognition that the intended experience of the text and its images must be identical to Theodora's own for the effect it models to be realized. No reader could continuously hold the picture in her gaze and also scrutinize the text, and yet the pictures are ever-present in the background of the conversation. For this very reason, it would seem, they receive only infrequent explicit mention there. The author's text does not regularly provide the verbal equivalent of pointing fingers that would allow a reader to refer his remarks back to the picture. The success of the method, the very experience in which the completion of meaning is accomplished, depends on the simultaneous effect of the aural and visual media. This is the final confirmation of the identity between instruction as portrayed in the *Speculum virginum* and the practice it was meant to serve.

The text of the *Speculum* does not by any means sustain the rhapsodic, performative quality of the *audi et vide* address over the length of its twelve parts. On the contrary, much of Peregrinus' and Theodora's conversation is a down-to-earth, nuts-and-bolts catechism. The opening address is rather a demonstration of the kind of performative moment toward which the dialogue and the instructive process it portrays strive and which they achieve at various points in the course of the twelve parts. These moments deliver the transformation that the text promises and requires as the object of the virgin's monastic life. They characteristically collapse the distinction between Scripture and voice, Bride and virgin, letter and gloss, and even heavenly and earthly vision. Here again the treatment of the first picture in the original eight-book composition serves to demonstrate the method in action, the transfer of the prologue's poetics to the mechanics of word and image in instruction.

As suggested earlier, the Trees of the Vices and Virtues implicitly represent the virgin's own place and development in a cosmic plan. The extremes of the two trees with their roots as the two women, *superbia* and *humilitas,* are the old and the new woman and demarcate the field of identification in which the viewer is to "seek herself." As such—and this characteristic is shared on some level by all the pictures—they stand for the entire instructional project, the virgin's progress through the virtues in her monastic life. The transformation of the old Adam into the new is thus relived by the viewer in her own instructive path from the real to the ideal. The text all but records this fact as a function of the use of, and response to, the pictures themselves. Turning from the left to the right tree, Peregrinus says: "Sed leva relicta, dexteram repetamus, ligno vitae transgressionis stipitem mutemus, paradisum intremus amentitate sua ultra gratiam secularis exuberantiae deliciosum . . ." (*SV* 4.383–85) [But leaving the left side, let us return to the right, let us transform the trunk of transgression into the tree of life, let us enter Paradise, in its delight and by its flowing abundance beyond all the rewards of this world. . . .]. The left tree, that of the original transgression and the object of the preceding discussion, is "changed" into the *lignum vitae,* or the Tree of Virtues. Peregrinus not only identifies this second tree as Paradise, but in entering into discussion of it, he invites his pupil to enter Paradise with him. This experience he then mediates verbally with an elaborate and evocative description of Paradise as a dizzying accumulation of herbal perfumes and flowery spectacle seen as the ultimate delight of the five senses (*SV* 4.384–95). Theodora confirms the success of the audio-visual presentation, but her response is given as one tied to the visual aid of the picture: She is not only overwhelmed by Peregrinus' verbal imagery, she also feels she *sees* its visual counterpart in the picture before her:

O utinam hortum istum deliciarum tam dignis plantationibus floribundum
non tantum videre, verum etiam intrare merear! Puto flores vel fructus horti
istius ad arborem referas, cuius radix humilitate fundatur, summitas vero flore
aeterno, id est novo Adam presidente consummatur. (*SV* 4.396–400)

[Oh, if only I may merit not only to see this garden of delights in all its flowering abundance, but truly to enter there! I believe when you speak of the
flowers and fruits of this garden, you mean the tree that is rooted in humility, its crown completed by the true eternal flower that is the new Adam
who sits there above all.]

Peregrinus confirms this impression and then identifies the picture of Paradise with the virgins and their life. Just as the left tree is transformed into
the right, so the picture, within the instructional process, can portray and
"effect" the transformation of the instructed:

Ita est. Verum non solum flores premissos, id est virtutes, sed et virtutum cul-
tores studiosos hortum istum deliciarum dixerim, ubi omnis plantatio, quam
plantavit pater caelestis, imbre gratiae spiritalis irrigatur. . . . Itaque paradisus,
quem propono, monasticae vitae regula est, hortus iste sanctarum virginum
concors in Christo commanentia est . . . (*SV* 4.401–6)

[That is so. I call not only the flowers before you, that is, the virtues, but also
those who bend themselves to the cultivation of virtues this garden of delights, where every planting the heavenly father has made is watered with
showers of spiritual grace. . . . Accordingly, the Paradise I place before you is
the rule of the monastic life, this garden is the harmonious communal life
of holy virgins in Christ . . .]

What the picture renders immediate is not Scriptural exegesis but an experience of the full meaning of the Word. In the exchange over the Tree
of Virtues, this experience extends beyond the hermeneutic tension between ideal and real to include a direct sensory apprehension of spiritual
truth—a moment of visual perception akin to epiphany.

The scriptural call to the Bride to look on the beauty of the Bridegroom
and his rewards thus acquires its earthly object in the pictures. The Bride's
visual apprehension of divinity on her entry into heaven in part ten is pre-
figured, as it were, by Theodora's visual experience before the picture of the
Tree of Virtues as the *hortus deliciarum*. Thus the repetition of *Audi filia, et vide*
within part four is, true to the instructional method, simultaneously a call to
pay heed to the instructor's presentation and the seductive voice of the
Bridegroom calling attention to his rewards. The full meaning of Scripture
is activated in its relevance to the pupil and the instructive act. The object of

the pupil's aural attention and the object of her gaze is always simultaneously something before her and something beyond this—whether instructor or picture.[47] The specific significance of the pictures for the Bride's vision is for this reason not properly part of the *audi et vide* address. Rather, it emerges as a consequence of the method; the pictures are tools, "seeing aids," and no end in themselves. Both the prologue and the later *Epistula* instead foreground the *efficatia* of the visible on the viewer, the process through which the ultimate vision is experienced intuitively, beyond the picture and within the mind of the viewer as a visualization of the ideal image. This is both "self-image" (*imago dei*) and image of that which is desired, of the Beloved and of Paradise. As the *Epistula* says in justification of the work's title, "Representatur enim in speculo intuentis imago, et licet diversa sint aspectus et respectus imaginarius, utcumque tamen ad id, quod appetit, intuentis informaretur affectus" (*SV* 2.42–45) [The image of the beholder is represented in the mirror, and, while the appearance of the beholder and the reflected image may not be the same, in some way, nonetheless, the emotive disposition of the beholder is formed toward that which it ardently desires]. The role of the pictures and the experience they facilitate is best identified through this aesthetic function of the mirror—just as the author repeatedly maintains.

Before returning to Birgitta in conclusion, a methodological disclaimer is in order. The object of my inquiry has been to examine the *Speculum virginum* on the terms in which it is likely to have confronted its female initiates in the monastic life. For this reason, as well as by way of complementing earlier research and filling in its "blind sides," I have not considered the extent to which the text and its images are original or derivative, their possible sources or predecessors. I am convinced that such originality as the work possesses lies not in saying new things, or even in saying them in new ways. As a manipulator of monastic tradition, the author's task is to adapt and combine to the greatest extent possible existing texts and practices such that they enable a mode of delivery appropriate for a specific audience. Much of what perhaps expands on tradition, and even challenges it, is a result of this concern. The identification of the instructor's voice with the voice of Scripture, that is, the delivery as performance, is in large part a result of the collapsed distinction between *filia* [daughter] as Church and as the instructor's own female pupil. When the recipient of the Word is a woman, daughter, and potential bride, the meaning of Scripture gains a literal dimension that is immanent in the communication itself. So far as our knowledge of the development of women's spirtuality goes, at the time when this text emerges, the author's intent exploitation of this notion is not only innovative, it is a break in a dam that proved impossible to shore up.

In the later Middle Ages, women's experience of scriptural metaphor exhibits an increasingly literal, or material, dimension, and their religious practice proceeds on an increasingly somatic trajectory, as is attested to in their own writings after 1200.[48] As Caroline Bynum has argued in her studies of female spirituality, these developments often can be seen to reflect women's attempts to exploit the opportunities hidden in the chinks between the planks of medieval gender stereotyping.[49] Jeffrey Hamburger's recent studies of the role of art in women's religious practice in late medieval Germany give ample evidence that these principles are most assiduously and ingeniously applied to the integration of visual art in spiritual practice.[50] The author of the *Speculum virginum,* too, responds to the need to develop a women's *lectio divina* by building on the assumptions of women's unsuitability for cognitive reflection on Scripture, of their affinity with the literal, the body, and the senses—and by manipulating these into opportunities for an apprehension of the Word through the performative use of voice, presence, and images. As a model of instruction that was very soon taken up into the enormous expansion of the Cistercian order—to cite only one order in which it was implemented—and is found by the fifteenth century in an area stretching from Sweden to Spain, the conclusion suggests itself that the *Speculum virginum* played a role in forming women's religious practice and the development of medieval art, the importance of which we have only begun to discover.

The report of Birgitta's experience provided by her confessor, Peter Olavi, is an unfortunately isolated occurrence. Only the most exceptional women were granted any consideration in the annals of the Church. But it conforms remarkably to the experience shaped in the pages of the *Speculum virginum* as an idealized transcription of women's religious instruction and a script for future performance. Whether Peter's account is entirely accurate or not, its value remains little changed: Peter's witness is given as evidence of Birgitta's saintliness, and as such its value for our purpose is in a sense enhanced, for it would be of no use in this context to report an experience that would meet with reproof or seem out of accordance with orthodox practice. From this point of view it is intriguing that the text so insistently identifies the specific book and even the figures whose conversation that book represents: "the book called the *Speculum virginum,* in which the monk Peregrinus confers on all the virtues with the virgin Theodora." Peregrinus and Theodora are here models for an experience that is presented in turn as evidence of the veracity and holiness of both Birgitta and Peter's relationship to her. When Birgitta is transported by her "father's" oral delivery of the text into a state of rapture in which she hears "a voice in the spirit" that speaks the true content of her instruction, the authority for her experience is given by the communication that is cited as its inspiration. Far from being an enhancement of that communication as received two centuries later, Birgitta's experience attests instead to the continuous implementation of the model of instruction that the *Speculum virginum* portrays and to the continued understanding of its audio-visual poetics.[51]

## Notes

1. "Item dixit idem testis, quod, cum ipse quadam die legeret in dicto monasterio coram dicta domina Brigida in libro, qui vocatur Speculum virginum, in quo Peregrinus monachus disputat de omnibus virtutibus cum Theodora virgine, tunc domina Brigida ipso teste loquente hoc vidente, ut asseruit, rapta fuit in spiritu, reversa autem ad se dixit: 'Audivi nunc in spiritu vocem dicentem michi, quod virginitas meretur coronam, viduitas appropinquat Deo, coniugium non excluditur a celo sed obedientia omnes introducit ad gloriam.'" Prior Peter made his very thorough deposition (*deposicio copiosissima* as it is entitled in the MSS) on January 30, 1380 "in curia Romana" when he was about seventy-three years old. The event reported took place at Alvastra and can be dated to 1348/49. The passage is found in Isak Collijn, *Acta et processus canonizacionis beate Birgitte*, Samlingar utgivna av svenska fornskriftsällskapet 2: 1 (Uppsala: Almqvist, 1924–31), p. 491 (translation my own). I am grateful to Arne Jönsson for his verification of details pertaining to this event in Brigitta's life and to Peter's deposition. A useful anthology of Birgitta's writings in translation is now available in *Birgitta of Sweden: Life and Selected Revelations*, ed. Marguerite Tjader Harris, Classics of Western Spirituality (Mahwah, NJ: Paulist Press, 1990), pp. 71–98. Some publications refer to her as Bridget and to her order as the Bridgettines.

2. Matthäus Bernards noted that Peter's report is corroborated elsewhere by Matthias of Linköping, Birgitta's theological instructor, in *Speculum virginum: Geistigkeit und Seelenleben der Frau im Hochmittelalter* (Cologne: Böhlau, 1955; 2nd ed. 1982), p. 10, n. 56.

3. Seyfarth's catalogue (pp. 56*–122*; see also chapter 2 in this volume) includes thirty-six manuscripts transmitting the Latin text extending from the twelfth through the seventeenth centuries and twenty-six of the vernacular. I have identified two more Latin manuscripts in Tortosa (Tortosa, Archivo de la Catedral 279 and 283), both of which appear to be fragments of once-complete copies of the text. They are dated to the fourteenth and the fifteenth centuries respectively, by E. Bayerri Bertomeu, *Los Códices Medievales de la Catedral de Tortosa* (Barcelona: Porter-Libros, 1962), pp. 459, 461. The *Speculum virginum* has predecessors in several patristic treatises. Letters of vocation to individual nuns survive from the eleventh century (see chapter 9 by Elisabeth Bos in this volume), but no post-patristic text previous to the *Speculum virginum* undertakes an introduction to the female monastic life that is intended for broad circulation.

4. The full study is found in Chapters 2 to 4 of Morgan Powell, "The Mirror and the Woman: Instruction for Religious Women and the Emergence of Vernacular Poetics 1120–1250" (Ph.D. diss., Princeton University, Ann Arbor, MI: University Microfilms International, 1997), forthcoming as a monograph.

5. Arthur Watson reached the same conclusion in "The Speculum Virginum with Special Reference to the Tree of Jesse," *Speculum* 3 (1928): 445.

6. Cologne, *Historisches Archiv,* W276a, ca. 1150, may be from St. Mary of Andernach, a house of Augustinian canonesses founded by the abbey of Springiersbach. Springiersbach, a double monastery from its inception, and especially its eminent reformer and abbot, Richard (d. 1158), was intensely engaged in the foundation and pastoral care of women's communities; see Seyfarth, pp. 45*–46*, 60*–63* and chapter 2 in this volume.

7. The manuscript bears the inscription "Hugo mag" on f. 1r. This identification is found in several other Eberbach manuscripts (Seyfarth, p. 58*).

8. Troyes, *Bibliothèque municipale,* MS 252, ca. 1200 (from Clairvaux), and MS 413, early thirteenth century (Mores); and Berlin, *Deutsche Staatsbibliothek,* MS Phil. 1701, early thirteenth century (Igny).

9. Darmstadt, *Hessische Landes- und Hochschulbibliothek,* Hs. 738, late fifteenth century.

10. In practice, the number of men often may have been far smaller, as even the experience of the mother house of Vadstena indicates; Georg Schwaiger, ed. *Mönchtum, Orden, Klöster: Von den Anfängen bis zur Gegenwart* (Munich: Beck, 1993), p. 118.

11. This is the conclusion of Tore Nyberg, whose investigation considers both the history of Cistercian involvement with the *cura monialium* and its influence on the Birgittine rule in detail: Tore Nyberg, *Birgittinische Klostergründungen des Mittelalters,* Bibliotheca Historica Lundensis 15 (Leiden: CWK Gleerup, 1965), pp. 11–29. Alvastra was actively engaged in these issues, as several women's communities were in its jurisdiction and care (ibid., pp. 12, 15).

12. The Birgittines' avid reception of the *Speculum virginum* is attested to in several ways. There is the one Latin manuscript from the Birgittine house of Sion, in Cologne; another must have been owned by the order's mother house in Vadstena, for the users there created a concordance to the Latin text in the second half of the fifteenth century that still survives (Uppsala, *Universitetsbibliotek,* Cod. C247). In addition, Birgitta's order produced a Swedish translation of the text, which survives in Stockholm, *Königliche Bibliothek,* A8 (dated 1473–1486); and another manuscript, London, British Library MS Add. 38527 (ca. 1410), which contains the Middle Dutch translation, is from the Birgittine house at Utrecht; see Urban Küsters, chapter 11, n. 16 in this volume.

13. While Bernards, *Speculum virginum,* p. 12, offered this conclusion, it has been ignored since. He noted also the evidence of the text, which at one point lapses into a harangue of Peregrinus' fellow *magistri* that extends for

over a hundred lines of the modern edition, and occasions no break or other mention in the dialogue. See *SV* 5.1078–1183.

14. This statement applies only to the Latin transmission of the text. See below, n. 51.

15. This point was made long ago by Herbert Grundmann in "Die Frauen und die Literatur im Mittelalter," *Archiv für Kulturgeschichte* 26 (1935): 135–36.

16. Hildegard's self-description was paraphrased by a male Cistercian contemporary with the words *laica et illitterata*. On this reference, and on the terms *auditores* and *illitteratae* as descriptors for layfolk, see Herbert Grundmann, "*Litteratus-Illitteratus:* Der Wandel einer Bildungsnorm vom Altertum zum Mittelalter," *Archiv für Kulturgeschichte* 11 (1958): 58–59, 43–44, and passim. Michael Clanchy, *From Memory to Written Record,* 2nd ed. (Oxford: Blackwell, 1993), pp. 226–32, assesses the terms' metaphorical versus their historical value. The significance, beginning in the twelfth century, of the same descriptors for the history of women's mysticism is reviewed by Kurt Ruh, *Geschichte der abendländischen Mystik,* 2 vols. (Munich: Beck, 1993), 2: 64–75.

17. These points are investigated in detail in Powell, *The Mirror and the Woman,* pp. 145–50. It is important here to distinguish between the depth of knowledge Theodora at times displays, and which occasions no remark, and the way the dialogue manipulates her responses to display an ignorance or difficulty she is meant to represent—that is, between the present and the constructed audience. Theodora gives the impression of being simultaneously a "real" woman and coauthor, and the representative female pupil to whom all the conventional assumptions apply. The necessity of play between these two personae is perhaps more suggestive of medieval nuns' real relationship to literacy than is either of them alone.

18. The following example introduces the picture of the Wise and Foolish Virgins: "Quod ergo de hoc capitulo queris, sicut a patribus accepimus, pauca ponenda sunt, premissa tamen figura, ut consodales tuae, si forte quod legunt non intelligunt, vel proficiant ex forma subposita, quia ignorantibus litteras ipsa pictura scriptura est et exemplo excitatur ad profectum, cui littera non auget intellectum" (*SV* 5.1314–19). [What you seek on this passage of Scripture, as we have received it from the fathers, a few things should be said. This picture precedes, however, so that your sisters in communal life may progress through a substituted figure if perhaps they do not understand what they read, for this picture is scripture for those who are ignorant of letters, and they may be incited to improvement by example for whom the letter does not aid understanding.] Other examples are *SV* 1.989–1000 and 10.437–442. See also Powell, *The Mirror and the Woman,* pp. 119–21 and 145–48.

19. For the text of Gregory's letter, see *S. Gregorii Magni registrum epistularum libri VIII-XIV* 11.10, ed. Dag Norberg, CCSL 140 A (1982): 873–76, and on its historical context, Celia M. Chazelle, "Pictures, Books and the Illiterate: Pope Gregory I's Letters to Serenus of Marseilles," *Word and Image* 6 (1990): 138–53.

20. Lawrence G. Duggan, "Was Art Really the 'Book of the Illiterate'?" *Word and Image* 5 (1989): 227–51, provides an overview of the reception of Gregory's dictum. For an inquiry into the play between the historical and metaphorical dimensions of its terms, see Michael Curschmann, "*Pictura laicorum litteratura?* Überlegungen zum Verhältnis von Bild und volkssprachlicher Schriftlichkeit im Hoch- und Spätmittelalter bis zum Codex Manesse," *Pragmatische Schriftlichkeit im Mittelalter,* ed. Hagen Keller et al., Münster Mittelalter-Schriften 65 (Munich: Fink, 1992), pp. 211–29.

21. Where this opposition serves to distinguish the lay from the clerical, the gender dimension still may apply metaphorically. Similarly, when seen in these terms, women become "laymen" within the monastery.

22. The situation in France has recently been clarified by Bruce L. Venarde, *Women's Monasticism and Medieval Society: Nunneries in France and England, 890–1215* (Ithaca, NY: Cornell University Press, 1997), pp. 6–16. Venarde shows that the number of new foundations for women increased sevenfold between 1050 and 1150, with the total number of active monasteries for women increasing from 100 in 1080 to 400 in 1170. Moreover, the most rapid period of growth falls in the second quarter of the twelfth century, when the *Speculum virginum* was composed. Herbert Grundmann described the situation similarly, if with less numerical precision, speaking of France and Germany in *Religious Movements in the Middle Ages,* trans. Steven Rowan (Notre-Dame, IN: University of Notre-Dame Press, 1995), pp. 19–21, 77–78. Küsters offers a detailed account of the socio-historical situation in Germany in *Der verschlossene Garten,* esp. pp. 61–62; see also chapter 3 by Hotchin in this volume.

23. Powell, *The Mirror and the Woman,* pp. 140–45, and Bernards, *Speculum virginum,* pp. 198–99.

24. All translations from the *Speculum virginum* are my own. I would like to thank Constant Mews and Barbara Newman for their helpful suggestions on improving them.

25. A word of clarification is in order here on the language of delivery in instruction, a question I have left aside for economy's sake. It is difficult to assess with any certainty the degree to which the idea of vernacular literacy is still an anachronism in twelfth-century Germany or France. The teaching of reading is still generally acknowledged to have been accomplished only through training in Latin; the words "*litteras*" and "Latin" are often used synonymously in the sources. In order to accord with its own representation of its audience, then, the text would have been delivered not as written but rather through the instructor's own vernacular rendition of its content. In practice, however, the amount of Latin used can have varied according to the capacity of a given audience, and a maccaronic mix may well have been the rule. Giles Constable has recently offered an excellent survey of this question, emphasizing among other points that Latin was often understood aurally to a degree by those who could not read at all, and that Latin was sometimes used first and preferred by audiences who

were not proficient in the language because of the greater "mystery, sonority, and prestige" it was felt to possess: "The Language of Preaching in the Twelfth Century," *Viator* 25 (1994): 131–52, here 139. My own concern is not, however, with the various uses the text in reality could undoubtedly serve, but with the model of instruction and women's "reading" it promulgates. See Powell, *The Mirror and the Woman,* pp. 45–48, 127–31, and 151–53. The practice of delivering texts orally in the vernacular while recording them only in Latin was widespread in the period, although it has received little attention in the secondary literature. See Clanchy, *From Memory to Written Record,* pp. 206–11; Michael Richter, *Sprache und Gesellschaft im Mittelalter,* Monographien zur Geschichte des Mittelalters 18 (Stuttgart: Hiersemann, 1979), pp. 62–63, 91, 92; and Grundmann, "Litteratus," 42–43, 47–48 and passim (n. 16 above).

26. My concern here is with works that were composed with a program of images by the author. The few contemporary examples include the *Expositio in cantica* of Honorius Augustodunensis, composed around 1135. Honorius' picture program is limited to portrayals of the four brides corresponding to the four senses of scriptural exegesis in the Song of Songs, but he nevertheless makes due mention of his pictures in the prologue. On this and other twelfth-century examples of "imagined exegesis" originating in Germany, see Michael Curschmann, "Imagined Exegesis: Text and Picture in the Exegetical Works of Rupert of Deutz, Honorius Augustodunensis, and Gerhoh of Reichersberg," *Traditio* 44 (1988): 145–69.

27. *La règle de S. Benoît,* ed. Adalbert de Vogüé, Schr 181 (Paris: Cerf, 1972), p. 412; trans. from *The Rule of St. Benedict in English,* ed. Timothy Fry, O.S.B. (Collegeville, MN: The Liturgical Press, 1982), p. 15.

28. For a discussion of the frontispiece as final prologue, see Powell, *The Mirror and the Woman,* pp. 206–27. The author portraits immediately preceding *SV* 3 are reproduced in Seyfarth, plate 1.

29. For a fuller account of the textual, palaeographical, and codicological evidence behind my argument, ibid., pp. 517–39.

30. Bernards, *Speculum virginum,* p. 23; Eleanor S. Greenhill, *Die Stellung der Handschrift British Museum Arundel 44 in der Überlieferung des Speculum Virginum,* Mitteilungen des Grabmann-Instituts der Universität München 10 (Munich: Hueber, 1966), pp. 9–10.

31. The problem is complicated by the fact that in 1494, Trithemius described *SV* as containing eight books, but with the *incipit* "Collaturo tecum" (the beginning of part one). It is quite possible, however, that when Trithemius originally described *SV* as a work of Peregrinus in 1492, he knew only of the eight-book version. By 1494 Trithemius may have come across the longer version, with its prefatory letter identifying the author as C., but failed to correct his original reference to eight books. Constant Mews reviews the question of Trithemius' references to the *Speculum virginum* in chapter 1 in this volume.

32. The two other manuscripts collated for the modern edition, Z and W, have modified this explicit to make it accord with the addition of parts eleven and twelve, reading,"here ends the tenth part of the *Speculum virginum*. . . ." Z then goes so far as to make part eleven begin at the same point, while W limits itself to naming the title of the following part: *Part XI the Exposition of the Sevenfold Gifts of the Holy Spirit*. Neither Z or W repeats this explicit/incipit at SV 10.451, where the other collated manuscripts place it.

33. The content of parts eleven and twelve is entirely predetermined by the inscriptions over Christ's head in the frontispiece image that precedes and is in large part the subject of part one. Theodora's requests that give rise to the last two books (*SV* 10.410–15 and 11.1–10) refer specifically to the frontispiece and to a promise, made in part two (2.46–61), to complete its discussion "at the closing of the work"; and the final picture at the beginning of part eleven, the House of Wisdom, clearly repeats the first.

34. The passage in question is followed immediately in all manuscripts by an explicit for the "second part": "Sed in hac allocutione secundo libro demus inicium resumptis viribus per intervallum. Explicit pars secunda" (*SV* 2.474–76) [But let us take up this address in the second book after a rest to refresh our strength. Here ends the second part]. There can be no doubt that Peregrinus intends the content of part three as the resumption of the conversation, as he refers specifically as well to the *Audi filia, et vide* address that opens part three.

35. The "error" persists in all but two of the nine manuscripts collated for the edition at that point.

36. Another possible explanation, which may be corroborated by evidence internal to parts one and two, is that the author originally planned these as one book and only later divided them. Thus, before he made this final division, part three would have been the *secundus liber* and therefore still bears this name in the body text. The reference to part seven as the *quintus liber* could be an uncorrected reference taken over from the eight-book version. The use of *secundus liber* to refer to part three reflects an intermediate stage between this eight-book version and the final twelve-part conception, before the "books" were renamed as "parts." Which of these explanations applies is not of consequence to my argument.

37. L has a unique place in the stemma of the textual tradition between two of the oldest prototypes. If the editor is correct, it is descended from both prototypes that produce the entire textual tradition, having been copied from the one and then corrected by means of the other. Eleanor Greenhill argued that this corrector was the author himself in *Die Stellung der Handschrift British Museum Arundel 44*, passim (n. 30 above).

38. Jerome, Letters 22 and 65, *Sancti Eusebii Hieronymi Epistulae*, ed. Isidorus Hilberg, CSEL 54 (1910): 145ff and 616ff.

39. This technique of biblical citation was typical of monastic commentary in oral delivery. Jean Leclercq terms it "reminiscence," and writes, "Reminiscences are not quotations, elements of phrases borrowed from another. They

are the words of the person using them; they belong to him." *The Love of Learning and the Desire for God: A Study of Monastic Culture,* trans. Catherine Misrahi, 3rd ed. (New York: Fordham University Press, 1982), p. 75.

40. The distinction is doubly reemphasized in Theodora's response: " . . . in hac divina vocatione virgini sanctæ non parum emolumenti constare, si audiat quod precipitur et videat quod promittitur, si auditis obaudierit et sequatur, quod viderit" (*SV* 3.46–49) [In this divine calling no small reward awaits the holy virgin if she will hear what is taught and see what is promised, if she obeys what is heard and follows what she sees].

41. Paul's well-known words in 1 Cor. 13.12 on the mirror are cited prominently and repeatedly in the *Speculum virginum* and in one instance accompany the introduction of a picture (see *SV* 5.896–99).

42. Of the *lectio divina* Leclercq writes, "It is what inscribes, so to speak, the sacred text in the body and in the soul" (Leclercq, *The Love of Learning,* p. 73).

43. "Verum, licet in omni pictura vel artificio ratio prestet operi et sit maior, qui fecit quam quod fecit, volo tamen quendam paradisum speculatorium pre oculis tibi in pictura ponere . . ." (*SV* 1.989–92) [Truly, although in any picture or device the idea surpasses the execution and the creator is superior to his creation, nevertheless I wish to place a certain paradise seeing-aid before your eyes in a picture . . .]. My translation of the author's neologism *speculatorium* as "seeing aid" emerges from my study of the implementation of images in the work as a whole. The image spoken of here is the "Mystical Paradise."

44. A parallel passage to the one quoted here describes the effects of Scripture as *speculum* in the same terms (*SV* 4.678–86). The words *in alterutro fructu* refer to the two pictures. The text refers to the Trees of the Vices and Virtues as *fructus carnis et spiritus,* and not as *arbores virtutum et viciorum* (*SV* 3.748–49, and 4.4–5). It does, however, speak of the images as trees.

45. In her survey article, "Backgrounds of the Title *Speculum* in Medieval Literature," *Speculum* 29 (1954): 113, Sr. Ritamary Bradley claimed that "Peregrinus is not setting forth his own understanding of the title, . . . but is repeating the traditional view." The first claim is decidedly not the case, the second very much so. The author uses traditional elements to shape an understanding of the mirror that is highly specific to his own purposes, and implements it in sophisticated and innovative ways: see Powell, *The Mirror and the Woman,* pp. 136–60. In a study of the mirror as a genre designator from antiquity to the High Middle Ages, Einar Már Jónsson has now argued most forcefully, and in terms that complement my own conclusions, that the densely constructed conception of the mirror in the *Speculum virginum* constitutes a "radical innovation": *Le Miroir: Naissance d'un genre littéraire* (Paris: Les Belles Lettres, 1995), pp. 171, 187–94.

46. The connection between the two trees and Eve and Mary was thoroughly elucidated with reference to the corresponding passages of the text by Eleanor Greenhill, *Die geistigen Voraussetzungen der Bilderreihe des Speculum virginum,* Beiträge zur Geschichte der Philosophie und Theologie des Mit-

telalters 39.2 (Münster: Aschendorff, 1962), pp. 85–88. Her observations remain useful, despite the flawed argument they serve, which saw the *Speculum virginum* as a commentary on the Song of Songs.

47. This is, as well, a general statement on the medieval aesthetic of the visual and the sign or symbol. See Friedrich Ohly, "Probleme der mittelalterlichen Bedeutungsforschung und das Taubenbild des Hugo de Folieto," *Frühmittelalterliche Studien* 2 (1968): 164, and Karl F. Morrison, *History as a Visual Art in the Twelfth-Century Renaissance* (Princeton, NJ: Princeton University Press, 1990), pp. 120–21.

48. This statement is not intended to imply that women's spirituality is somehow impoverished of allegorical understanding. I am refering to the increasingly material manifestation and physical imitation of bridal metaphor in women's devotional practice.

49. See the essays now collected in Caroline Walker Bynum, *Fragmentation and Redemption: Essays on Gender and the Human Body in Medieval Religion* (New York: Zone Books, 1991), especially "'. . . And Woman His Humanity:' Female Imagery in the Religious Writing of the Later Middle Ages," pp. 151–79; and idem, *Holy Feast and Holy Fast: The Religious Significance of Food to Medieval Women* (Berkeley: University of California Press, 1988), pp. 277–94.

50. Now collected into one volume as Jeffrey F. Hamburger, *The Visual and the Visionary: Art and Female Spirituality in Late Medieval Germany* (New York: Zone Books, 1998). Hamburger's conclusions on the nature of the images in the Rothschild Canticles (ca. 1300), reveal where the *Speculum virginum's* implementation of images, as I have presented it here, would lead: *The Rothschild Canticles: Art and Mysticism in Flanders and the Rhineland circa 1300* (New Haven, CT: Yale University Press, 1990), pp. 120, 124, 133.

51. The continuity observed here would appear to depend on the transmission of the Latin text. The transmission of the vernacular versions presents in all salient features a complementary opposite to the Latin: With only isolated exceptions, all vernacular manuscripts representing transmission of the work as a whole can be traced to women's monasteries and contain no pictures. The conclusion presents itself that the two forms of transmission represent two different use paradigms for the work, one depending on the instructor's audio-visual delivery, the other on women's direct use of the text. The implementation of the vernacular versions awaits further study. See chapter 11 by Urban Küsters in this volume.

# CHAPTER 6

# "LISTEN, DAUGHTERS OF LIGHT": THE *EPITHALAMIUM* AND MUSICAL INNOVATION IN TWELFTH-CENTURY GERMANY

*Catherine Jeffreys*

This chapter examines the *Epithalamium* or Bridal Song that concludes the *Speculum virginum* in the earliest manuscripts of the treatise. Its text and music, integrally related to the *Speculum* as a whole, provide the vehicle through which "the daughters of light" can obtain a foretaste of ultimate union with Christ. The structure of the *Epithalamium* parallels that of the Proper for the Office of Lauds in its alternation of antiphon and response. The *Epithalamium* provides a sung response to the text of the *Speculum virginum*. The musical settings adhere to contemporary theoretical norms, such as promoted in the treatises of Berno of Reichenau and William of Hirsau, as well as in the preface to the Cistercian antiphonary (ca. 1147). The songs illustrate a tendency, defended by Anselm of Havelberg in the mid-twelfth century, for religious communities to develop "new ways of psalmody" so as to better express their own liturgical identity.

Behold we see in the Church of God, as they say, certain people emerge who put on unusual habits at their own whim, they choose a new way of living and whether under the name of the monastic profession or under the vow of canonical discipline, they take up for themselves whatever they want, they find for themselves a new way of psalmody, they decide on a new type of fasting and a new regime of food, imitating neither the monks who follow the Rule of Benedict nor the canons who follow the apostolic life under the Rule of Augustine.[1]

In this passage from the first book of the *Dialogues* (ca. 1149), Anselm of Havelberg (ca. 1100–58) presents the perspective of a hypothetical critic of novelty in the Church. The brusque tone of this passage—rendered by throwaway descriptions of monastic tasks and repetition of the word "new"—is deceptive. In his account of new developments in the Church, he repeats the argument and mimics the tone of a hypothetical critic as a way of refuting conservative hostility toward novel practices. Anselm lists corruptions of daily monastic concerns: dress ("unusual habits"), routine ("new way of living"), manual labor ("whatever they want"), abstinence ("new type of fasting"), and diet ("a new regime of food"). Psalmody is located among these daily concerns, reflecting the place of singing among the daily tasks performed by the medieval monastic. His phrase "a new way of psalmody" *(novum psallendi . . . modum)* implies that psalms were recited and responded to in a new way that existed outside established norms as part of a set of "new" and "unusual" monastic practices.

One such "new" and "unusual" practice of psalmody is suggested by the *Epithalamium* to the *Speculum virginum*. The *Epithalamium* begins with 129 metrical and rhyming couplets, prefaced by a rubric that suggests their recitation by alternating choirs: *Incipit epithalamium Christi virginum. Alternatim.* The initial letter of each couplet comprises two neumed acrostic verses, *O qualis es* and *O quam miranda*, prefaced by the incipits "Acrostic choir A" *[Akrostichon Chor A]* and "Acrostic choir B" *[Akrostichon Chor B]* respectively. These verses are followed by three other settings: a truncated version of verses from the Song of Songs (5.9–16 *Qualis est dilectus . . . totus desiderabilis*) describing the divine spouse, the first verse of the five-verse Marian hymn *O sancta mundi domina,* and a newly composed text, *Audite o lucis filiae* [Listen, daughters of light], which describes the coming together of virgins and Christ.

Several facets to the *Epithalamium* suggest that it belongs to the "new way of psalmody" referred to by Anselm of Havelberg. The 129 couplets and the two acrostic verses represent an equivalent to verses and responds, or the transaction that takes place in psalmody (verse + respond). Manuscripts of the *Epithalamium* also preserve references to psalmody through psalm cadences *(euouae = seculorum amen),* although there is no indication as to which psalm belongs with each song.[2] Anselm also implies that a "new way of psalmody" was part of a set of "new" practices, suggesting that novel musical practice arises from new devotional expression. Here the *Epithalamium* seems to be an example of novel musical practice, with an emphasis on music as a response to text, in this case, the *Speculum virginum.*

## Sources of the *Epithalamium*

The neumed *Epithalamium* survives from the earliest period of transmission of the *Speculum virginum.* The copy taken to the Cistercian abbey at

Eberbach during the twelfth century, London, British Library, Arundel 44 *(L)*, copied between 1140 and 1150, preserves the final song of the *Epithalamium, Audite o lucis filie,* at the opening of the work. This song is preserved on twelve staves on the first folio of *L* and includes a psalm cadence *(secuouae = seculorum amen)* written in a later hand to the song. It appears that the complete *Epithalamium* was once preserved in the manuscript. Two leaves from the *Epithalamium* in *L* are included in the miscellany collection in London, British Library Arundel 501 (fols. 32r–33v). Comparison of these leaves with *L* and the complete Clairvaux copy of the *Epithalamium* suggests that one folio is missing between fol. 33v of Arundel 501 and *L.* This provides enough room for the missing seventeen verses from the acrostic and sixteen staves of music, as follows:

[Acrostic
O qualis es—O quam miranda
O qualis est dilectus
O sancta mundi domina]
Audite o lucis filie + psalm cadence

A second copy of the *Epithalamium,* Cologne, Historisches Archiv, Einzelblatt D182, copied before 1150, is thought to have belonged to the Augustinian house of St. Maria, Andernach. The Einzelblatt was originally part of Cologne, Historisches Archiv Hs. W 276a *(K),* but leaves containing the five songs (and in all probability the acrostic) became separated from the text, with the Einzelblatt the only surviving folio of the *Epithalamium.*[3] The Einzelblatt includes three songs: a portion of *Qualis est dilectus,* which survives from midway through verse 5.13; the hymn *O sancta mundi domina;* and *Audite o lucis filie.* Unlike the other sources of the *Epithalamium,* there are no psalm cadences in this copy. It appears that the complete *Epithalamium* was once preserved after the *Speculum virginum* in *K.* Comparison with the complete collection in the Clairvaux copy (*T* Troyes, Bibliothèque Municipale MS. 252, fols. 129r–132v), indicates that twelve staves, or one half-folio, of music is missing. This provides room for the two acrostic verses and the opening verses of *Qualis est dilectus.* This also suggests that *L* and *K* once preserved the same ordering of songs.

The Clairvaux copy of the *Epithalamium* was produced around 1180 to 1200. Another copy, Berlin Deutsche Staatsbibliothek, MS. Phil. 1701 *(B)* fols. 146r–148r, was prepared around 1200 at the Cistercian abbey at Igny. The Clairvaux manuscript is the only surviving copy that includes the complete *Epithalamium* with neumes. The copy from Igny also preserves the entire *Epithalamium* but is unneumed. A further three copies of the *Speculum virginum*—all produced before about 1220—preserve the acrostic but not the *Epithalamium*.[4] The Igny copy appears to have been taken from the Clairvaux copy, with songs preserved in *B* in the same order as in *T*. Psalm cadences are also included in both sources. Unlike the copies of the *Epithalamium* in *K* and *T*, however, the hymn *O sancta mundi domina* is placed after, not before, the song *Audite o lucis filie*:

Acrostic
*O qualis es—O quam miranda* + psalm cadences
*O qualis est dilectus* + psalm cadence
*Audite o lucis filie* + psalm cadence
*O sancta mundi domina*

A feature of the three neumed sources of the *Epithalamium* is that there are no pitch discrepancies between them. There are several neumatic discrepancies, however, between *L* and the Einzelblatt, which suggest that they probably were copied from a common exemplar, not one from the other.[5] The notation in *T*, which is typical of Cistercian books from this era, differs from that of *L* and the Einzelblatt, but each neume in these two early sources is given a notational equivalent in *T*.[6] Comparison between *L*, the Einzelblatt, and *T* reveals that the copy of *Audite o lucis filie* in *T* is a *verbatim* copy of *L*, with complete consistency in neumation and *musica ficta* between these two sources.[7] These observations suggest that the surviving sources of the *Epithalamium* are the result of close written transmission.

## The *Epithalamium* and the Liturgy

Although the sources indicate a close written transmission between the sources of the *Epithalamium*, the differences between them—in particular, the inclusion/absence of psalm cadences and the different ordering of songs between the earlier and later copies—suggest a range of liturgical practices. In addressing the issue of a relationship between the *Epithalamium* and the liturgy at the monasteries in which it was circulated, one useful guide is the first verse of *O sancta mundi domina* (example 1) in the *Epithalamium*. There are at least a dozen sources of this hymn dating from between 1100 and 1300,[8] and at least three different settings of the text survive, including one from Einsiedeln around 1150, which has the same final, the note D,[9] as the version in the Einzelblatt and *T*.[10] The setting of *O sancta mundi domina* preserved in the Einzelblatt and *T* is also used for the hymn *Deus, qui quovis eligis* (Analecta Hymnica 43: 236) in Klosterneuburg MS 1000, copied in 1336. The Einzelblatt and *T* preserve the earliest known version of this melody.[11]

O sancta mundi domina,               O holy lady of the world,
regina celi inclita,                 noble queen of heaven,
o stella maris Maria                 O Mary, star of the sea
virgo mater deifica.                 divine virgin mother.[12]

The presence of the first verse only of *O sancta mundi domina* in the Einzelblatt and *T* suggests that this hymn was already known at the monasteries
in which it was circulated. This is perhaps more pronounced in *T,* in which
the verse appears at the end of the *Epithalamium* and only the first phrase
is neumed. That this eight-syllable, four-phrase setting was transferable also
raises the possibility that it could have been used for the recitation of the
eight-syllable, four-phrase verses of the acrostic, with "Choir A" chanting
the first two phrases, and "Choir B" responding with the final two phrases,
suggesting the "alternating" verse-respond sequence represented in
psalmody. The rubric that might support this—*Incipit epithalamium Christi
virginum. Alternatim*—is lacking in all four manuscripts that include the *Epithalamium* songs. Nonetheless, the potential, referential function of this
hymn is reflected in *T* (and *B*), where *O sancta mundi domina* is an adden-
dum to the previous four songs.

   *O sancta mundi domina* was also sung at Lauds for the Nativity of the
Blessed Virgin Mary, which is cited as a Sanctoral feast day (September 8)
in the *Gemma Animae* of Honorius Augustodunensis (ca. 1070–ca. 1139).[13]
The association of this hymn with the Lauds Office hour offers one way
of relating the practice of psalmody and the *Epithalamium*. In the Einzelblatt (and probably the missing folios from *L*), *O sancta mundi domina* is po-
sitioned between *Qualis est dilectus* and *Audite o lucis filie.* This position
follows the ordering of variable items in a standard monastic Lauds.[14] With
this order in the Einzelblatt, the *Epithalamium* could be rendered as the
Proper necessary for this Office hour.[15] This need not imply that the *Epithalamium* was necessarily performed as part of a Lauds celebration, but it
does offer one redactive possibility for the *Epithalamium* as new song suitable for use in psalmody:

*Deus in adiutorium*
*Gloria patri*
*Alleluia*
Psalmody                              Acrostic (verses + responds)
Psalm 66
Psalm 50
2 variable psalms + responds          *O qualis es + O quam miranda*
Old Testament canticle                *Qualis est dilectus*
Psalms 148–150

Chapter + *Deo gratias*
Short Respond
Hymn                                    *O sancta mundi domina*
Versicle + response
*Benedictus* + antiphon
Kyrie                                   *Audite o lucis filie*
*Pater noster*
Collect
*Benedicamus domino.*

The relationship between the *Epithalamium* and psalmody is also suggested by the psalm cadences in *L* and *T.* The text and neumes to the psalm
cadence that follow *Audite o lucis filie* in *L* are in a different hand from the
song, and psalm cadences are unnotated in *T.* In both manuscripts, a relationship between the *Epithalamium* and psalmody is represented, but psalm
cadences are given without any indication of which psalm was connected
to each song. An important distinction between the Einzelblatt and *L/T* is
the absence of psalm cadences in the former. This represents a distancing
of this copy of the *Epithalamium* from the practice of psalmody.[16]

The placing of the *Epithalamium* at the beginning of *L* suggests a different liturgical association again. Its presence before the *Speculum virginum*
represents the initiation of praise, in particular, with song.[17] This is reflected
in a description of the *chorus* or assembly given by Honorius in his *Sacramentarium* (before 1139), in which lessons associated with different days in
the liturgical year are outlined: "The *chorus* is the gathering of those
singing: it is said of the *chorus* that it stands around the altar in the mode
of a garland and sings *[psallerat]*. The *cantores* are praisers of God rousing
others to praise."[18] In this passage, Honorius puts forward the *chorus* as ini-
tiator of praise (in worship) and the *chorus* accedes to the cantor, who is the
"praiser of God." This is reflected in the *Epithalamium* by the antiphonal
acrostic and the "Choir A" and "Choir B" that initiate praise. In *L,* this
sung praise precedes the *Speculum virginum* text.

The location of *Audite o lucis filie* at the end of the *Epithalamium* in the
earliest sources, the Einzelblatt and *L,* is also significant. It is the only song
in the *Epithalamium* without a written precedent, and it describes a central
theme of the *Speculum virginum,* the desired union of virgins and Christ.
The opening recalls Psalm 44.11: "Audi filia et vide et inclina aurem tuam
et obliviscere populum tuum et domum patris tui," associated with feasts
in celebration of the Virgin.[19] The content and position of the "antiphon"
*Audite o lucis filie* suggests its suitability not only as a conclusion to a collection of songs that expound the theme of the union of Christ and his
Bride but also as a summation of the dialogue between Peregrinus and

Theodora in the *Speculum virginum*. In the earliest sources, the function of this *Epithalamium* comes across as a sung response to a particular circumstance—that of the female monastic to a didactic text—redacted in the earliest sources in the order of proper chants for a Lauds celebration.

## The *Epithalamium* Settings

The songs *O qualis es, O quam miranda, Qualis est dilectus,* and *Audite o lucis filie,* are typical examples of new Latin liturgical song produced in the West during the twelfth century. In all songs, melodic phrases coincide with text phrase beginnings and endings. There is also an emphasis on consonant intervals, or between the final and its fourth, fifth, and eighth degrees, known in medieval theory as the diatessaron, diapente, and diapason respectively.[20]

*O qualis es* and *O quam miranda* indicate an approach to text setting common to all four songs. The position and repetition of notes emphasizes the relationship between the final and its diapente, with each phrase ending on the final (the note c) in *O qualis es* and in *O quam miranda* on either the final, the note F, or the diapente, the note c. (See examples 2 and 3.) The two texts are similarly set, with phrases beginning and ending on the final, and a central phrase of each beginning on the diapente. These two songs are distinguished by the extension of the range of *O quam miranda* to include the diapason above the final.

Akrostichon Chor. A
O qualis es, o quantus, quam
    suavis,
o rerum pater in gratia,
qua stabit eternaliter unica
    mater catholica,
sponsa, columba, interminabili
    munere rosa

Alleluia
Euouae

Acrostic Choir A
O how great and how sweet
    you are,
Father of the universe, in grace
through which the only catholic
    mother will
stand eternally by your
    unending gift—
the bride, the dove, and the rose.

Alleluia
As it was in the beginning, is
    now, and ever shall be, world
    without end, Amen

Akrostichon Chor. B
O quam miranda, quam preclara,
Quam magna multitudo
    dulcedinis tue, domine,

Acrostic Choir B
O how marvelous, how radiant,
how great is the multitude of
    your sweetness, Lord,

Quam abscondisti timentibus te,
  perfectisti autem sperantibus,
  deus, in te

Alleluia

Euouae

which you have hidden for
  those who fear you but
  perfected for those who
  hope in you, O God.

Alleluia

As it was in the beginning, is
  now, and ever shall be, world
  without end, Amen.[21]

As with the acrostic songs, the text to *Qualis est dilectus* is derived from the
written word, here verses 5.9–16 of the Song of Songs, with a similar incipit to *O qualis es.* Some verses of the Latin Vulgate have been abridged,
while the punctuation of the translation has been modernized.[22]

[5.9] Qualis est dilectus tuus ex
  dilecto, quia sic adiurasti nos?
[5.10] Dilectus meus candidus
  et rubicundus, electus ex
  milibus,
[5.11] caput eius aurum
  optimum, come eius elate
  palmarum,
[5.12] oculi eius sicut columbe
  super rivulos aquarum, que
  lacte sunt lote et resident
  iuxta fluenta plenissima,
[5.13] gene illius sicut areole
  aromatum consite a
  pigmentariis, labia lilia
  distilantia murram primam,
[5.14] manus illius tornatiles
  auree plene iacinctis, venter
  eius eburneus distinctus
  saphiris,
[5.15] crura illius columne
  marmoree, que fundate sunt
  super bases aureas, species eius
  ut Libani electus, ut cedri,
[5.16] guttur illius suavissimum
  et totus desiderabilis.
Alleluia.
Euouae

What is your beloved like, that
  you have so adjured us?
My beloved is white and ruddy,
  chosen out of thousands.

His head is the finest gold, his
  hair like palm branches.

His eyes are like doves beside
  brooks of water; they have
  bathed in milk and dwell
  beside plentiful streams.
His cheeks are like beds of
  fragrant spices set by
  perfumers. His lips are lilies
  distilling choice myrrh.
His hands are finely turned gold
  full of hyacinths, his belly is
  ivory set with sapphires.

His legs are pillars of marble set
  upon bases of gold. His
  beauty is choice as the
  cedars of Lebanon,
his throat is most sweet, and he
  is altogether desirable.
Alleluia.
As it was in the beginning, is
  now, and ever shall be, world
  without end, Amen.[23]

As in *O qualis es* and *O quam miranda,* melodic phrases in *Qualis est dilectus* coincide with textual ones, with the final, the note D, and the diapente dominating the melodic structure. (See example 4.) In the setting, there are five repetitions of a progression that passes through the notes (A)-D-a-d-a-D. Also as in *O qualis es* and *O quam miranda,* middle phrases within each of these progressions begin on the diapente, here the note a.

Similar melodic workings to those observed in these three songs are also observable in *Audite o lucis filie.* (See example 5.) As with *O qualis es* and *O quam miranda,* there is a strong rhyming scheme in the text, which in all three songs are delineated by the repetition of the final (the note F in *Audite o lucis filie*) and diapente at phrase ends in the settings. This suggests that the composer of the acrostic was also responsible for the text to *Audite o lucis filie.*

Audite, o lucis filie, advertite
   coheredes regis et salvatoris
   nostri!
Nox precessit, dies autem
   appropinquabit:
Dies interminabilis gracie,
Dies decoris et glorie,
Dies inquam quam fecit
   dominus, in qua celi terreque
   omnis ornatus perficitur,

Quando nativus decor hominis
   victo mortis vinculo
   restauratur,

Quando regis eterni sponsa,
   columba, soror et amica
   sponso suo perfectissimo
   amoris igne copulatur,

ubi sponsa cum sponso letatur
   et una per unum eternaliter
   gloriatur.
Alleluia.
[euouae]

Listen, daughters of light!
   Attend, fellow heirs of our
   king and savior!
The night has passed and the
   day is drawing near:
The day of never-ending grace,
The day of beauty and glory,
The day, that the Lord has
   made, in which all the
   adornment of heaven and
   earth is perfected,
When the native beauty of
   humankind is restored and
   the chain of death is
   vanquished,
When the bride of the eternal
   king, his dove, his sister and
   beloved, is united to her
   bridegroom in the most
   perfect fire of love,
When the bride rejoices with
   the bridegroom, and the one
   glories eternally in the One.
Alleluia!
As it was in the beginning, is
   now, and ever shall be, world
   without end, Amen.

Similar melodic workings to those observed in the previous three songs are represented in the setting of *Audite o lucis filie.* This setting comprises predominantly stepwise movement between the final and diapente, but middle phrases are initiated on the diapente. One notational peculiarity in all four songs is a *porrectus* that proceeds diapente-final-diapente in all songs, over "e[ternaliter]" in *O qualis es,* "quam [magna]" in *O quam miranda,* "e[lectus]" in verse 5.15 of *Qualis est dilectus,* and over "c[olumba]" in *Audite o lucis filie.* Its use in the *Epithalamium*—always on the first syllable of a word—and the similarity in melodic structures among these four songs suggests that a single composer was responsible for them all.[25]

While this composer remains unknown, there are indications that he or she was well educated in the musical arts. The settings of the *Epithalamium* adhere closely to prescribed theoretical norms. An immediate comparison here is with the highly specified instructions for the location of *tritus* (fifth and sixth mode) chants on the gamut given in the Cistercian reform treatises, in particular, the Cistercian preface that accompanied the revised antiphonary (ca. 1147). In the preface, it states: "you should end all chants of the third *maneria,* that is, the fifth and sixth modes, on F and c, assigning F to the greater part of the authentics, but c to almost all the plagals."[26] This recommendation is followed to the letter in *O qualis es,* which has a plagal range from G to g and takes the note c as final, and in *O quam miranda,* which has an authentic range from F to g and takes the note F as final. Cistercian theoretical recommendations, however, are less closely followed in the other songs. The setting of *Audite o lucis filie,* a plagal tritus melody that extends from C to d, coheres with the properties of a tritus plagal chant but is notated with the note F as final, not the note C.[27] The setting of *Qualis es dilectus* belongs to the protus *maneria,* with the note D as final, and can be described as an authentic protus melody (with a range from C to f), although at five points the melody descends beyond the range of an authentic protus melody to encompass the notes A, C, and D. This descent conflicts directly with a recommendation in the preface to avoid "double-ranged" melodies in composition.[28] This instruction was of particular concern in antiphons and responsories as they had *either* authentic *or* plagal psalm cadences assigned to them. In canticles, which were not performed psalmodically, range crossing does not interfere with modal designation.

While the melodic movement in *O qualis es, O quam miranda, Qualis est dilectus,* and *Audite o lucis filie* suggests ex tempore processes, the close written transmission of the *Epithalamium* suggests that these melodies do not represent redactive reworking of improvised material. The placement of melodies on the gamut without evidence of a sustained period of redactional consolidation suggests that the composer was a *musicus* or was schooled in the *ars musica* and familiar with its dictates. Here the range crossing in *Qualis est dilectus,* in particular, highlights a distinction between compositional impetus and the modal classification system used to preserve the *Epithalamium.* Even a composer apparently familiar with the rules governing chant redaction was not restricted by them in expressing musically verses from the Song of Songs.

The use of the note c as final suggests the influence of other German treatises aside from the Cistercian preface, such as Berno of Reichenau's preface to his *Tonary* or William of Hirsau's *Musica,* both of which expound relations between notes that enabled chants to be similarly located at various positions on the medieval gamut. The Cistercian revision of the repertory also incorporated newly composed songs with an emphasis on Marian songs, which betray the influence of the Song of Songs.[29] The *Epithalamium* circulated predominantly among Cistercian houses, with only one copy, the Einzelblatt, housed at a monastery that was not Cistercian. This fact suggests that the *Epithalamium* initially could have been produced in a reformed Benedictine or Augustinian monastery, such as those Anselm of Havelberg's hypothetical critic complained about, even though it came to circulate among predominantly Cistercian communities.

## Conclusion

The references to the practice of psalmody in the *Epithalamium* reflect a basic liturgical transaction: verse and respond. This basic monastic transaction also recalls Anselm's testimony that many new religious communities indulged in new psalmodic practices. Musical traditions in Germany during the twelfth century did not cohere with a particular monastic code of practice; rather individual communities appear to have experienced music in different ways and had various ways of expressing themselves, including through music.

In particular, the *Epithalamium* illustrates how song could function as a liturgical "response" to the written word. This is also the case with the writing of Hildegard of Bingen, whose fourteen *symphoniae* at the conclusion of *Scivias* 3.13, written between 1141 and 1151, summarize the conception of the celestial hierarchy expounded throughout that treatise. This function of song shaped the presentation of the notated collections of her songs, which are devoted to—and ordered according to—the celestial hierarchy described in *Scivias* 3.13. The format of the earliest known redaction of Hildegard's songs also resembles that of the *Speculum virginum:* musical responses to a written work. These two examples suggest a tradition of complementing didactic texts with song in Germany in the mid-twelfth century.

The *Epithalamium* can thereby be taken as embodying the "new way of psalmody" in Anselm's description. As an example of new practice, the *Epithalamium* offers one indication of the ways in which innovative music could reflect the liturgical experiences of medieval monastics, in particular, as part of a wider set of local customs—in this case, the adoption of Marian songs into liturgical practice. It suggests that among communities in Germany during this period, there was an emphasis on novel modes of liturgical expression that incorporated the production of new song.

Example 1   *O sancta mundi domina*—Cologne, Historisches Archiv, D 182 Einzelblatt recto

O sanc- ta mun- di do- mi- na re- gi- na ce- li   in- cli- ta,

o stel- la ma- ris Ma- ri- a   vir- go   ma- ter de- i- fi- ca.

Example 2   *O qualis es*—Troyes, Bibl. Mun. 252, fols. 131v-132r

[O]   qua- lis   es, o   quan- tus quam sua- vis,

o re- rum   pa- ter in   gra- ci- a,

qua sta- bit e- ter- na- li- ter u- ni- ca ma- ter ca- tho- li-   ca,

spon-   sa co-   lum- ba,

in- ter-   mi- na- bi- li mu- ne- re ro-   sa.

al-   le   lu-   ia.   euouae

Example 3   *O quam miranda*—Troyes, Bibl. Mun. 252, fol. 132r

150

Example 4　*Qualis est dilectus*—Troyes, Bibl. Mun. 252, fol. 132r

Example 4    *Qualis est dilectus*—(continued)

(3) D

5:13

ge- ne      il- li- us si- cut a- re- o- le a- ro- ma- tum

con- si- te a pig- men- ta- ri- is,

a                    d

la- bi- a il- li- us li-            li- a dis- til-      lan- ti- a

a

mir- ram pri- mam;

5:14                    a                                        D

ma- nus il-    li- us tor-      na- ti- les au-      re- e

ple-   ne   ia- cin- tis,

(4) D                    a

ven- ter ei- us e- bur- ne- us dis- tinc- tus      sa- phi- ris;

5:15    a        d        a

cru- ra il- li- us co-            lum- ne ma-    ro- re- e,

a

que fun- da- te sunt su- per ba- ses au-          re- as,

D

spe- ci- es ei- us ut    li- ba- ni    e-    lec-    tus, ut ce- dri;

Example 4  *Qualis est dilectus*—(continued)

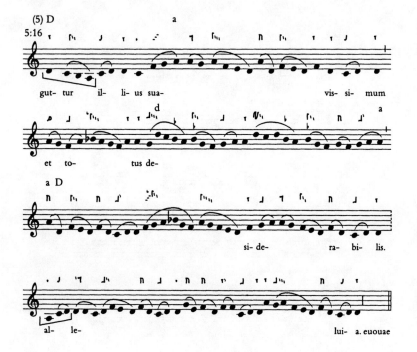

(5) D

5:16

gut- tur  il-  li- us sua-                    vis- si-  mum

et to-        tus de-

si- de-        ra-  bi-  lis.

al-  le-                    lui-  a. euouae

Example 5  *Audite o lucis filie*—London, British Library, Arundel 44, fol. 1r

Au- di- te o lu- cis fi- li- e,

ad- ver- ti- te co- he- re- des re- gis et sal- va- to- ris nos- tri;

Nox pre- ces- sit, di- es au- tem ap- pro- pin- qua- bit:

Di- es in- ter- mi- na- bi- lis gra- ci- e,

Di- es de- co- ris et glo- ri- e,

Di- es in- quam, quam fe- cit do- mi- nus,

in qua ce- li ter- re- que om- nis or- na- tus per- fi- ci- tur,

Quan- do na- ti- vus de- cor ho- mi- nis

vic- to mor- tis vin- cu- lo re- stau- ra- tur,

Example 5   *Audite o lucis filie*—(continued)

## Notes

1. "Ecce videmus in Ecclesia Dei, ut aiunt, quosdam emergere, qui pro libitu suo insolito habitu induuntur, novum vivendi ordinem sibi eligunt, et sive sub monasticae professionis titulo, sive sub canonicae disciplinae voto, quidquid volunt, sibi assumunt, novum psallendi sibi adinveniunt, novum abstinentiae modum, et metas cibariorum statuunt, et nec monachos qui sub Regula beati Benedicti militant, nec canonicos qui sub Regula beati Augustini apostolicam vitam gerunt, imitantur." Anselme de Havelberg, *Dialogues Livre I*, ed. and trans. Gaston Salet, Schr 118 (1966): 36.

2. In antiphonal psalmody, the order of performance is antiphon/psalm, cadence/psalm/psalm, cadence-antiphon.

3. Jutta Seyfarth, ed., *Speculum Virginum*, CCCM 5 (1990): 60–62.

4. These three manuscripts are: Baltimore, Walters Art Gallery W. 72 (from Himmerod); Würzburg, Universitätsbibliothek M. phil. theol. f. 107 (from Ebrach); and Zwettl, MS 180 (from Zwettl).

5. This observation is based on notational discrepancies that represent articulative (including *pressus/virga* and *scandicus/quilisma* distinctions) variants between these two sources.

6. The family of signs used in Cistercian books is commonly regarded as influenced by Laon notation. The signs in *T* also reflect the "Messine" influenced notational systems found in sources produced in southern Germany during the thirteenth century.

7. *Ficta*, from *fictus* [false]. The only "false" note allowed by music theorists at this time was the b-flat, which was used to "soften" or remove the interval of a tritone formed between the notes F/f and b.

8. The earliest source, Verona, Biblioteca Capitolare CIX (102), is the only known source of this text from outside Germany; *Die Hymnen des Thesaurus Hymnologicus H. A. Daniels und anderer Hymnen-Ausgaben*, ed. Clemens Blume, Analecta Hymnica 51 (Leipzig: O. R. Reisland, 1908), pp. 139–40.

9. Pitches are rendered here according to the Guidonian system with "C" as "middle c," i.e.: G A B C D E F G a b c d e f g a' b' c' d'.

10. Einsiedeln, Stiftsbibliothek 366 (twelfth/thirteenth century). Bruno Stäblein, ed., *Hymnen I: Die mittelalterlichen Hymnenmelodien des Abendlandes*, Monumenta Monodica Medii Aevi (Kassel: Bärenreiter, 1995), p. 575.

11. Ibid., p. 575. The *Epithalamium* sources are not taken into consideration in Stäblein's study, in which the Einsiedeln 366 melody is cited as a possible precursor to the Troyes 252 and Einzelblatt melody as documented in Klosterneuburg, Stiftsbibliothek MS 1000.

12. *SV* Epithal. 149–52. The translations have been provided by Barbara Newman.

13. Honorius Augustodunensis, *Gemma Animae* 3.166, PL 172: 689. Honorius was an English canon who (ca. 1109) took up residence at the Alte Kapelle in Regensberg, where he completed the *Gemma animae*, V. I. J. Flint, *Honorius Augustodunensis of Regensberg*, Authors of the Middle Ages: Historical

and Religious Writers of the Latin West 5.2, ed. Patrick J. Geary (Aldershot: Variorum, 1995), pp. 138–39.

14. See John Harper, *The Forms and Orders of Western Liturgy from the Tenth to the Eighteenth Century: A Historical Introduction and Guide for Students and Musicians* (Oxford: The Clarendon Press, 1996), pp. 97–98.

15. The term "Proper" refers to the liturgical items in a mass or office that are particular to the feast day in which they are included.

16. The prioress of the cloister to which *K* probably belonged, Tenxwind of Andernach, criticized the extravagant dress worn on feast days and the exclusion of non-noble women from Hildegard of Bingen's congregation at Rupertsberg in her letter of around 1150. "Tenxwindis Magistra ad Hildegardem," *Epistolarium*, ed. L. van Acker, CCCM 91 (1991): 125–26. The absence of psalm cadences in the Einzelblatt perhaps spares this particular critic of novelty from the hypocrisy of being associated with the unconventional *psalmodic* practices.

17. The presence of the *Epithalamium* in *L* does not appear to be the result of the relocation of folios from the end of the manuscript. The preface to the *Speculum virginum* commences on the verso side of the music folio and the first gathering ends at folio 11 (partway through part one). See Eleonor S. Greenhill, *Die Stellung der Handschrift British Museum Arundel 44 in der Überlieferung des Speculum Virginum*, Mitteilungen des Grabmann-Instituts der Universität München 10 (Munich: Max Hueber, 1966), p. 12.

18. "Chorus est consensio cantantium: dicitur chorus quod initio in modum coronæ circum aras starent et psallerent. Cantores sunt Dei laudatores et ad laudem cæteros excitantes." Honorius, "De Choro," *Sacramentarium* XXXIII, PL 172: 764.

19. *Audi filia* is set variously as a tract, an alleluia, a gradual and verse, and a gradual. None of these settings suggests a relationship with the setting of *Audite o lucis filie*.

20. The "final" traditionally refers to the note on which a chant concludes and is taken as a principal guide to the mode of a chant.

21. *SV* Epithal. 130–37.

22. *SV* Epithal. 138–42.

23. *SV* Epithal. 138–48.

24. *SV* Epithal. 153–63.

25. One guide as to the peculiarity of this diapente-final-diapente *porrectus* comes from comparison with the neumed sources of Hildegard of Bingen's seventy-seven liturgical songs in Dendermonde St. Pieters & Paulusabdij MS. Cod. 9 (ca. 1175) and Wiesbaden, Hessische Landesbibliothek, Hs. 2 (ca. 1179). These manuscripts preserve what is possibly the most extensive range of neumes to survive in a single twelfth-century German source, and the diapente-final-diapente *porrectus* is not included therein.

26. "Porro omnes cantus tertiae maneriae, id est quinti et sexti toni, termines in F vel in C; F maiori arti autentorum, C vero omnibus fere plagalibus attribuens." "Praefatio," *Epistola S. Bernardi. de revisione cantus Cisterciensis et*

*tractatus,* ed. and trans. Francisco J. Guentner, Corpus Scriptorum de Mu-sica 24 (Rome: American Institute of Musicology, 1974), p. 52. The prin-ciple behind this directive concerns the notes B and b around the final, the note F, in tritus plagal chants. The rendering of tritus plagal chants on the note c means that the undesirable tritone between F and b (and B) occurs between c and F/f, which is a consonant interval. See Guy, *Regulae de arte musica* (ca. 1131), *Scriptorum de Musica Medii Aevi* 2, ed. Edmund de Cousse-maker (Hildesheim: Georg Olms, 1963), pp. 150–52.

27. This song incorporates both the notes b *and* b flat. If located on c, where one would expect to find it, f and f sharp are required. The song is thus lo-cated on F rather than on c.

28. "Praefatio," p. 36 (n. 26 above).

29. Chrysogonus Waddell, "The Early Cistercian Experience of Liturgy," *Rule and Life: An Interdisciplinary Symposium,* ed. Basil M. Pennington, Cistercian Studies Series 12 (Shannon: Irish University Press, 1971), p. 97.

CHAPTER 7

THE CLOISTER AND THE GARDEN:
GENDERED IMAGES OF RELIGIOUS LIFE FROM
THE TWELFTH AND THIRTEENTH CENTURIES

*Janice M. Pinder*

This chapter compares the *Speculum virginum* to the *De claustro animae
[Cloister of the Soul]* of Hugh of Fouilloy, a treatise addressed to male religious, and the anonymous *De modo bene vivendi [On the Manner of Living Well]*, addressed to a religious woman but also extant in a version
adapted to religious men. It observes that the *Speculum* offers an essentially solitary model of the religious life, unlike the *De claustro animae*,
which employs much more public imagery. The contrast between these
two treatises illustrates the gendered quality of theorizing about the religious life. By contrast, the *De modo bene vivendi*, a treatise influenced in
part by the *Speculum*, has much less emphasis on virginity and on bridal
imagery. This suggests that the *Speculum virginum* did not provide the only
way in which monks could think about the religious life.

*This little work is entitled* The Mirror of Virgins. *In it a priest, Peregrinus, holds
a dialogue with Theodora, a virgin of Christ, to provide Christ's studious virgins with
a great incentive for the preservation of chastity, an example of disdain for the present life, and a model of desire for heavenly things.*[1]

Thus the author of the *Speculum virginum* introduces the image he has
chosen to encapsulate his work. As he elucidates this idea for his female reader, we see that the author conceives of his work as an image
against which the religious woman can measure her inner self, a reminder

of who she is and what she is supposed to be like: "Now the mirrors of the women are divine words set before the eyes of holy souls, in which they may see at all times how they either please the eternal bridegroom with the beauty of a holy conscience or displease him with the ugliness of sin."[2] Implicit in his words is the notion that the mirror is used habitually, in a constant process of self-evaluation and emendation. He has not constructed the mirror from his own words and ideas, however: Its substance is the divine word [eloquia divina].[3]

This chapter is concerned with the nature of the image that the *Speculum virginum* reflects back to its reader, and hopes to make a contribution to the discussion of the gendering of religious life in the twelfth and thirteenth centuries. In her survey of works of religious advice from this period, which included the texts to be discussed here, Barbara Newman found that, by and large, advice to women was distinguished by an emphasis on virginity, a lack of a notion of spiritual progress, and a lesser attention to communal life than is found in texts addressed to men.[4] These are general trends, which provide a useful framework against which to measure the position of individual texts; close comparative readings may uncover some surprising variations. To this end I shall place the *Speculum* beside two other texts, one addressed to men and one to women: the *De claustro animae [Cloister of the Soul]* of Hugh of Fouilloy (d. ca. 1172/74) and the anonymous *De modo bene vivendi [How to Live Well]*.[5] Like the *Speculum virginum*, these are substantial treatises. Both the *Speculum* and the *De claustro animae* were widely diffused. By comparing the treatment in these three texts of some common themes, I hope to show how differences of orientation are possible even within shared paradigms and at the same time to give some account of the specifically gendered nature of the *Speculum virginum*.

I have chosen the *De claustro animae* both because it was one of the most widely disseminated texts of male religious reform and may therefore be considered representative of a certain view of the religious life for men, and because Hugh of Fouilloy's work in general presents some interesting parallels with the *Speculum virginum*. These are noted by Jutta Seyfarth in her introduction to her edition: dissemination in Cistercian houses, common influence of St. Augustine, and the use of didactic pictures.[6] This use of images as a pedagogical tool is perhaps the most striking parallel. Seyfarth quotes the introduction of Hugh's *Liber de rota verae religionis:* "Therefore, so that I may place a certain kind of mirror before the cloistered, I depict the wheel of prelates at the beginning of this little work."[7] There is certainly a similarity of intention in the use of pictures between this and the *Speculum virginum:* " . . . I wish to put forward before you a kind of paradise seeing-aid in a picture. . . ."[8] An even better parallel can be drawn with Hugh's *De avibus,* or *Aviarium,* which, like the *Speculum,* contains an instructional picture cycle.[9] While this final parallel does not apply to the *De claustro animae*, which contains no pictures, nonetheless it is this work of Hugh's that corresponds most closely to the *Speculum* in conception and intention. The *De claustro animae* is his last and longest work, and in it he sets out the fullest development of his vision of the monastic life for the edification of those trying to live it, just as the *Speculum virginum* sets out a coherent vision of the virginal life as a model for the recluse or nun. It is a treatise in four books, probably written for his canons at Saint-Laurent-au-Bois in Picardy.[10] The first book deals with the temptations of the world and the benefits of the religious life. The second is full of practical advice on the running of a monastery. In the third and fourth books he gives free rein to his preferred form of didactic exposition, allegory. The third treats the inner life of the soul, setting it out as a monastery in which the parts of the building represent virtues and aspects of religious activity, while the fourth book looks to the life to come and describes the monastery that will be established in the heavenly Jerusalem.

The *Liber de modo bene vivendi* is a substantial work of advice for nuns, although by no means as widely disseminated as the *Speculum virginum*.[11] Like the *Speculum*, however, it was one of the books owned and read by St. Birgitta of Sweden.[12] Although it was circulated under the name of Bernard of Clairvaux, as a work written for his sister, the identity of its true author remains unknown.[13] One feature of the manuscript tradition makes it a very interesting case in the intersection of gender and images of religious life. The text in the earlier of the two Madrid manuscripts (871) is addressed not to a woman but to a man. That this version is the result of the adaptation for a male audience of a text intended for women and not the reverse seems clear from the presence in this manuscript of content pertaining only to women in passages such as one on the monastic habit, which includes references to the significance of the black veil.[14] Madrid 871, the earliest datable copy of the text (we do not know the date of the Clairvaux manuscript), was completed in 1267, which means the text can have been composed no later than the middle of the thirteenth century.[15] This would make it somewhat later than the *Speculum* and the *De claustro*.

There are in fact indications that the author knew the *Speculum virginum*. The strongest evidence for this occurs in the preface of the *De modo*, where there is a striking echo of the interpretation of the mirror given in the *Speculum virginum*. The *De modo* begins:

> Now therefore, dearest sister, receive this book, and place it before your eyes like a mirror, and look into it often as into a mirror. For the precepts of God are mirrors, in which souls look upon themselves, and in which they recognize the stains of sin, if there are any; because no one is unsoiled by sin; and

in which they emend the vice of their thoughts, and arrange their face like
the image reflected back at them; for when they turn themselves whole-
heartedly to the precepts of the Lord, they recognize in them without doubt
that in themselves which is pleasing to the heavenly bridegroom, or that
which is displeasing.

In spite of its greater length, there is nothing in this passage that is not in the
corresponding sentence from the *Speculum:* "Now the mirrors of the women
are divine words set before the eyes of holy souls, in which they may see at
all times how they either please the eternal bridegroom with the beauty of
a holy conscience or displease him with the ugliness of sin." The *De modo*
author is simply expressing the same idea in a less concise and less sophisticated style, and could well have taken the *Speculum* passage as his model.[16]

No other passages suggest direct paraphrase, but within the division into
chapters there is a rudimentary dialogue structure. Often after the initial
general exposition of the subject, the sister is given a question that relates the
teaching more directly to her situation or opens the way to a treatment of
particular cases. For example, in the chapter on abstinence, after its purpose
and effects have been expounded, the sister asks how she should chastise her
own body by abstinence. Very occasionally the brother asks a question, as in
the brief dialogue in the chapter on thought *[cogitatione]:* "Beloved sister, do
you wish never to be melancholy?—My brother, yes I do—Then live
well."[17] In the chapter on confession, the sister is given a long prayer of re-
pentance (PL 184: 1248C-50B). The chapters on virginity, continence, and
enclosure seem to be close in content and tone to the *Speculum virginum*, as
do the scattered passages that construct the reader as virgin and identify her
(not just her soul) with the Bride in the Song of Songs. Many other chapters, however, deal with subjects that are not touched on at all in the *Speculum*, notably the practicalities of monastic life such as dress, fasting, silence,
reciting the Psalms, and the sacraments of confession and the Eucharist.

The *De modo bene vivendi* is clearly not a simple rewriting of the *Speculum virginum*. However, given the popularity of the *Speculum*, the framing
of the *De modo* as a mirror in very similar terms, and the other similarities
just noted, it is tempting to think that the author of the later text took
some inspiration from the earlier one. If this is the case, then the *De modo*
suggests that for at least one thirteenth-century author, the image of the
religious life for women provided by the *Speculum virginum* needed sup-
plementing from other sources.

The *Speculum virginum*, the *De claustro animae*, and the *De modo bene vivendi*,
springing as they do from the same broad tradition of ascetic and moral
writing for the professed religious, have some common preoccupations.

One is characteristic of the religious reform literature of this period, a concern with the interior life, with a particular emphasis on the match between inner and outer, mind and body. This concern permeates discussion of every aspect of monastic vocation and behavior dealt with by these texts, but for the *Speculum* it is applied particularly to the notion of true virginity. The second area of common ground is the importance of separation from the world, an essential characteristic of monasticism. Three aspects are of interest in these texts: conversion (the moment of leaving the world), enclosure or regulation of contact with the world once in the monastery, and perseverance in the life that has been chosen. My comparison will begin with the treatment of separation and enclosure, and then move on to examine the theme of virginity and its relative importance.

### Separation from World: Conversion

Separation from the outside world is a central element of monastic life, and all works of religious advice accord it great importance. All three of the authors considered here define their audience as people who have left the world. The author of the *De modo bene vivendi* sets out a very explicit contrast between the monastery and the world, setting up oppositions such as contemplation/labor, holiness/sin, spirit/flesh.[18]

This separation begins with the moment of conversion, the individual's decision to leave the world and seek the sanctuary of the monastery. A number of biblical images were available to give meaning to this moment, and the three texts under consideration here make very different choices. The *Speculum* chooses a specifically feminine image, that of a daughter leaving her family for marriage. Part three (the beginning of the original eight-book version) opens with an explication of Psalm 44.11–12: "Listen, daughter, see, and incline your ear, and forget your people and your father's house, and the king will desire your beauty."[19] Forgetting the father's house is construed as turning away from the temptations of the world and entering into "heavenly discipline," at which point the virgin of Christ begins to please the King (*SV* 3.31–38). This contributes to the construction of the nun's identity as virgin bride and indeed reinforces the identification with the Bride of the Song of Songs in the same passage, where Peregrinus says that on hearing Christ's loving admonition to forget her homeland, the virgin will declare: "draw me after you" (3.28–29). Peregrinus returns to this text in part eight (8.153), to consider more closely the modalities and justifications for departing from the father's house, and here joins it with another biblical image, that of Abraham leaving the land of his fathers (8.169 and 267–68).

The *De modo*, although it is addressed to a woman, does not use bridal imagery at all in relation to conversion, even if it calls on it elsewhere.[20] It devotes two chapters (six and seven) to the subject, outlining two stages: washing away our sins with tears and then contemplating what it is that we seek. Chapter seven opens with Jesus' admonition to his disciples to take up their cross and follow him (Luke 9.23). Other biblical images applied to entering the monastery are escape from Sodom and from Egypt (PL 184: 1212C). Later, in the chapter on perseverance, the sister's conversion to monastic life (evoking the parable of the merchant who sold all that he owned) is presented as buying the kingdom of Heaven with herself as the price (PL 184: 1236D-1237A). In the chapter on effort the moment of conversion is again evoked, this time as taking refuge in God's fortress [castra Dei] (PL 184: 1229D). This is also an area where the author of the De modo stresses the need for inner and outer consistency. Conversion must be of mind and body, and his criticism of those who come to the monastery for material support rather than for spiritual reasons (PL 184: 1210BC) echoes the Augustinian precept that no one should seek goods in the monastery that they would be unable to have outside.[21]

The metaphors used by Hugh of Fouilloy for entry into the religious life are different again from those either of the Speculum or of the De modo. At the very beginning of his treatise, he alludes to the story of Paul's shipwreck (Acts 27, 28.1–9). The sea represents the world, he explains. The ship is secular life and the shipwreck its dangers. The escape of Paul and his companions from the sea stands for renunciation of the world, and the island on which they are washed up signifies the gateway to right living [portum rectae conversationis] (PL 176: 1018D-1019A). The notion of a gateway or doorway is particularly apt in a work whose governing metaphor of the religious life is that of a building. A similar phrase occurs in the description of Solomon's temple in the third book, where the entrance to the temple of right living is through the portico of renunciation (PL 176: 1129BC). The other image used by Hugh is entry as a warrior into the fortress of the Lord (PL 176: 1020A).

The use of the bridal metaphor for conversion in the Speculum virginum sets it apart from the other two texts. The willing departure of the bride for the house of her powerful and desirable husband is in strong contrast to the images of flight and refuge that predominate in the De modo and the De claustro. This line of division does not hold, however, when we turn to the theme of perseverance.

## Separation from World: Perseverance

The Speculum and the De modo both set up a contrast between beginning and perseverance. It is not enough to begin well; the moment of conversion is fulfilled throughout the person's life in the work of pursuing spiritual perfection. Here they are taking up a theme common in monastic writing—indeed, it could be argued that the purpose of all texts of religious formation is to provide support in the living of that life of which conversion is only the beginning.[22] Both use the metaphor of an athletic contest. The *De modo* notes that the prize is promised to those who start out but awarded in the end to those who persevere (PL 184: 1209A), while the *Speculum* warns against relaxing before the race is finished (*SV* 8.1189–93). The *De modo*, in a chapter devoted to perseverance, holds up Paul as an example of someone who began badly and finished well and Judas Iscariot as one who began well and ended badly (1235C). The kingdom of Heaven will be given to those who keep knocking at the door (1236B).

The absence of perseverance can have two meanings in the monastic context: leaving the monastery and returning to the world or sliding into laxness while remaining in the monastery. The *De modo* author devotes some space to the former, urging the sister not to turn back once she has set her hand to the plow. He quotes Isidore at length, saying that those who return to the world from the monastery are like cold ashes, because their dull hearts have allowed the fire of God's charity to be extinguished (1236CD).[23] The author of the *Speculum* does not really contemplate return to the world. For him the danger to the vocation of a virgin is complacency. Alluding to the same shipwreck story that is used by Hugh of Fouilloy to stand for rescue from the spiritual dangers of the world, he neatly turns it on its head; those who think that when they come to the monastery, they have reached a safe harbor and need strive no more, face mortal shipwreck (*SV* 8.611–15). The struggle must continue in the cloister. As well as presenting this struggle as a race, he uses images of battle. The Bride of Christ goes forth not to tranquility but to war (9.22–23, 197). The tenor of all his arguments is to discourage expectation of instant reward, and the other metaphor he uses is of growth in the plant world: The spiritual life is likened to a bush, whose flowers come from conversion, but whose fruit are the product of hard work and perseverance (8.629–30).

The *De claustro animae* does not deal explicitly with the virtue of perseverance, but it is continually alive to the threat of laxness and of outward appearance not matching the inner state. In the first book, Hugh sets up the notion of life in the cloister as a battle with his simile of the castle under siege and his detailing in the first seven chapters of the ways the Devil may seek to gain entry. His sense of what can go wrong with monastic life is practical, and he deals with individual abuses and difficulties in far more detail than either of the other authors. In spite of the martial imagery that frames the first book, the emphasis in the third is with getting on with the business of the inner life, which is contemplation. Here it is the routines and spaces of the monastery itself that provide a metaphor for the interior life of the monk.

## Separation from World: Enclosure

The third set of themes common to these treatises concerns both the practicalities and the philosophy of separation: notions of the cloister and of enclosure. Enclosure can be thought of as a location (the cloister, home of the monk, canon, or nun) or as a state of being (remaining inside). While all three texts stress the exclusion of outside temptations and distractions, and to some extent equate the cloister with an inner space in which communion with God takes place, there are differences of emphasis, and a very different set of images is used in the two women's texts from those found in the *De claustro animae*.

The image of the cloister provides a governing metaphor throughout the treatise. Concerned as he is with the harmony of the inner and outer man, Hugh of Fouilloy writes about the cloister on two levels. He presents both the external arrangements necessary to regulate the life of the outer man so that the inner man may flourish and the regulation of the inner life within a monastery of virtues constructed in the heart. Monks build themselves a cloister in which to keep the outer man, but they ought also to build one to keep the inner man in order.[24]

Hugh writes about the cloister for the outer man at the beginning of the first book, where he mentions where the monastery should be located, and in the second, when he deals with enclosure in his practical advice on the running of a monastery. The cloister for the outer man should be a fortress, safe from the incursions of the enemy.[25] Its buildings should be modest and placed far from the disturbances of towns (PL 176: 1053B).

In the third book Hugh describes the cloister of the soul, where the inner man will dwell. The cloister of the soul is called contemplation. Within it the soul, removed from the disturbances of earthly thoughts, flees the pleasures of the flesh and restrains the wanderings of the senses, reads in the book of life, keeps quiet in the choir of virtues, and contemplates the goodness of the Father. The cloister is decorated with columns of virtues and surrounded by a wall of good works, which, when the door of silence is closed, prohibits the wandering mind from going out (PL 176: 1087D). Hugh goes on to equate the buildings on the four sides with contempt of self, contempt of world, love of God, and love of neighbor. He describes the progress of the soul from the north-facing side (in the cold and darkness of worldly cares and vices) round to the east as the dawn of divine justice bringing an invitation to love of neighbor and through that to love of God, till it comes to bask in the midday sun of perfect charity on the south-facing side. Hugh's fundamental notion of the cloister here is as an architectural space. His spiritual cloister, while imagined as being inside the soul, is also conceived of as a space in which the soul can move around, experiencing various sorts of development.

The cloister of the *Speculum virginum,* on the other hand, has very little spatial reference. Here the primary associations of the cloister are enclosure (of the women) and exclusion (of temptations coming from outside world). The second book is constructed around the subject of enclosure and the dangers of going out into the world. This preoccupation with the necessity for remaining in the cloister is in line with the other advice literature for religious women of the period.[26] Alongside the external enclosure provided by the cloister, the *Speculum virginum* proposes a matching internal claustration. The mind and body are closed to the outside world by keeping a strict guard on the five senses. This state is compared to a house with all its doors and windows shut against incursions by the enemy (*SV* 2.69–73, 9.937–38). Such enclosure is twice associated with the physical enclosure of the convent and once with monastic discipline (*SV* 2.69–73, 180). The few architectural images that are associated with the cloister in the *Speculum*—the inner room, the wine cellar, and the garden— carry strong connotations of enclosure and secrecy, and are equated with the virgin's own body, whose openings to the outside world are through the senses.

The enclosure of the virgin both within the cloister and within her own closed body is not merely negative. The house is not simply locked against intruders; there is something happening inside. This positive value of enclosure is expressed in the *Speculum virginum* through a range of biblical imagery primarily, although not exclusively, drawn from the Song of Songs. The space within which the virgin is enclosed is also the inner room to which one retires to pray to the Father (Matthew 6.6; *SV* 2.65), the dove's nest in the rock (Cant. 2.14; *SV* 2.197), the garden (Cant. 5.1), and the wine cellar of the King (Cant. 1.3; *SV* 2.184). The Bride is herself a closed garden (Cant. 4.12; *SV* 2.98). In short, the virgin's enclosed space is the place in which the kiss of the Bridegroom can be received (*SV* 2.180–84).

The *De modo bene vivendi* incorporates a mixed set of images. In two passages dealing with conversion, the monastery is equated with the land God showed to Abraham (PL 184: 1212B), the mountain to which Lot fled from Sodom, and the desert where the Israelites stayed on their way from Egypt (1212C), and referred to as "God's fortress" *[castrum Dei]* (1229D) and "God's house" *[domus Dei]* (1230D). In a chapter dealing with the necessity of remaining in the cloister, however, the image from the Song of Songs of the closed garden and the sealed fountain is used in the context of the nun's enclosure. The holy soul can be understood as a garden, because when it is nourished by virtues, flowers grow there and bear fruit. It is closed because it has withdrawn from worldly strife and the eyes of men. It is referred to as a sealed fountain because when it thinks assiduously on heavenly things, and stores up the knowledge of Scripture, living waters bubble up from which the thirsty can drink (1297CD). The identification between the enclosure and the virgin herself is not as complete as it is in the *Speculum*. It is made clear that the garden is an allegory of the soul. The senses are not presented as the gates to the enclosure, although the *De modo* does provide teaching about the custody of the senses.[27]

While there are differences in their image of cloister, particularly between the *Speculum virginum* and the *De claustro animae,* there is common agreement on the necessity for remaining inside it. But there, too, there are differences of emphasis within a certain commonality of vocabulary and overlapping of exempla. The story of Dinah (Gen. 34.1–31) is often used in monastic literature to illustrate the dangers of leaving the cloister. Barbara Newman notes that it was primarily used for this purpose in texts for women, while for male readers it was used as a warning against curiosity.[28] It is used in all three texts under consideration here, but the distinction does not hold in quite so straightforward a way.

In the *Speculum* it is certainly used (among other examples) as a warning against going out of the cloister, reinforcing the message that it is better to be kept there by force and saved than to go out and perish. Peregrinus suggests that if Dinah had remained secluded in her tent, instead of being lured out by curiosity, she would not have incurred the loss of her virginity nor brought down the sword of her father on her lover and his people.[29] The message is that venturing outside the safe enclosure brings disaster, but it is Dinah's curiosity that tempts her out. Her story is used at the end of a series of examples of the dangers of going out and "exceeding the condition of one's nature."[30] Adam and Eve were virgins in paradise and merited corruption on leaving. Cain called his brother to go out into the fields, and it led to homicide; he himself was condemned to wander as a fugitive. Those inside Noah's ark were saved; those who remained outside were drowned. Esau lost his birthright by wandering (*SV* 2.87–97). In the *De modo bene vivendi* the story is given a different slant. There, in the context of a discussion about the dangers of the eyes as "heralds of fornication" *[oculi annuntii sunt fornicationis],* Dinah, along with David and Samson, is presented as an example of someone who was ruined because she looked where she should not have. "And thus the unfortunate girl lost her reputation and virginity because she imprudently saw what she should not have seen."[31] Here the danger is clearly presented as sexual, but again it is curiosity, allied with imprudence, that causes the trouble.

While the *Speculum virginum* and *De modo bene vivendi* both use the story as a straightforward example, keeping to the historical sense in exegetical terms, Hugh presents an exegesis of the moral sense of the passage (PL 176: 1087D-88C). His reference to the passage comes at the end of his description of the cloister of the soul as contemplation, closed with the door of silence. "From this cloister Dinah the daughter of Jacob went out."[32] He quotes Gregory the Great's interpretation: Dinah going out from her family's camp is like the mind leaving its own habits and order to become embroiled in external cares. In this state it is easy prey for the devil, as Dinah was for the prince Shechem.[33] Dinah's brothers are like the virile movements against vice of the soul, which battle to expel the devil and root out the major vices, so they can lead home their sister, the mind, violated by carnal desire. Like the women taken captive, the pleasures of the soul are banished from the land of the flesh and released from carnal desires. This is a standard moral exegesis of the passage, applying it to the soul. It warns not so much against physical departure from the cloister, as the author of the *Speculum virginum* does, as against distraction from monastic life. The perceived threat is to the monk's mind and discipline, not to his chastity. However, the vehicle for this threat is not presented as intellectual curiosity but rather as a failure of concentration.

Distraction from monastic life could take the form of physical departure from the cloister, though, and elsewhere Hugh criticizes monks who frequent the courts of princes and run off to Rome to plead lawsuits.[34] All religious who become active in the world are castigated at the end of the second book where, using a passage from Lamentations, "the stones of the sanctuary are strewn at the end of every street,"[35] Hugh interprets the stones as priests and members of religious communities, who are scattered about involved in worldly business and seeking fame instead of praying in their cloister. The use of this passage to condemn worldly clerics goes back to Gregory the Great, but the source here seems to be Paschasius Radbertus' commentary on Lamentations, itself based on Gregory.[36]

The same passage is used in the *De modo bene vivendi,* independently following the same source, in its chapter on the dangers of going out of the cloister. Although this work is addressed to a nun, this part of the chapter gives a view of the dangers of worldly involvement that seem to concern only men, even to the extent of explicitly stating that the male religious should remain in his monastery: "It is necessary that any religious man who desires to be saved despise the world, and enclose himself within the walls of the monastery."[37] But when it comes to the exhortation to the addressee, the language of this text soon changes to that of the garden and the Bride.[38] The reward for remaining in the cloister is expressed not as salvation or perfection but as being loved by Christ, the Bridegroom: "If you enclose yourself in the cloister, you will be loved by Christ."[39]

## Virginity

The importance of virginity during this period in the gendering of models of holiness has been demonstrated.[40] A cursory examination of the three texts under discussion bears out the conclusion that it has come to be regarded as pertaining in a special way to female holiness, for while virginity is central to the *Speculum virginum* and important to the *De modo*, it occupies only a small space in the text addressed to men.[41]

However, between the two texts addressing women, there is a considerable difference of emphasis. Spiritual virginity, qualified as "true," is at the core of the identity constructed for religious women by the *Speculum virginum*. The entire treatise is about what it means to be a virgin betrothed to Christ. It assembles and adds to all of the theorizing and examples provided by the tradition of writing on virginity, creating a synthesis that is at once a reasoned exposition of monastic life and an aesthetic creation, drawing on the bridal imagery of the Song of Songs and Psalm 44. Each part focuses on a different aspect, for example: the three grades of reward for married women, widows, and virgins (part seven); Mary as the model for virgins (part five); the meaning of the parable of the wise and foolish virgins (part six). In the *De modo bene vivendi*, virginity provides the subject matter for only two chapters out of seventy-one, so it could be argued that the author of this text saw it as only one element in the theory of the religious life for women, albeit an essential one. The content of these chapters is conventional, and they contain no ideas that are not also present in the *Speculum virginum*. In comparing the two texts, however, we can see how differently they treat this traditional material.

The chapter on virginity in the *De modo* is organized around the parable of the wise and foolish virgins but expounds only its first verse. The wise are those who are virgins in mind and body: "Virgins in mind and body are not foolish, but prudent: and they can go out to meet the bridegroom, who have oil in their vessels, that is, chastity in their hearts."[42] It stresses the futility of physical virginity if it is not accompanied by spiritual virginity, one of the main themes of the *Speculum virginum*, citing Isidore, Augustine, and Jerome as authorities.[43] Virgins who glory in their merits and seek praise for good works have no oil for their lamps (PL 184: 1238D–39A). The exegesis of the parable concludes with the note that the oil in the wise virgin's lamp is good works, lit with sacred virtues (1239B). The parable's message has more to do with the opposition between wise and foolish behavior than with virginity. It is used in this way at other points in the treatise. In the chapter on silence we are told that the wise virgin says little, while the talkative virgin is foolish (1255B); she who keeps her ears from detractors and her tongue from all wicked speech will be counted among the wise virgins (1257A); and she who maintains humility will rejoice in heaven with the wise virgins (1260D–61A).

The *Speculum* devotes a whole book to the parable of the wise and foolish virgins and expounds the moral sense of each verse, not just the first. This permits a far more subtle and detailed interpretation. The lamps of the virgins, for instance, are good works, but they are further elucidated as examples that draw neighbors to the light (*SV* 6.66–68). The oil the wise virgins carry with them is knowledge of the grace of redemption, and they keep their lamps trimmed by not seeking a reward for their good works here and now (7.118–28). Both interpretations of the parable stress the moral aspect of being a wise virgin and the importance of humility (not seeking praise for her merits or good works).

In the following chapter of the *De modo*, on continence, some nuances appear. It begins with the same thirty-, sixty-, and hundredfold reward for married women, continent widows, and virgins (1239B) as is the basis of the seventh part of the *Speculum virginum*, and praises chastity. "The fruit of chastity is sweet" *[castitatis enim fructus est suavis]* (1239C). The chastity of the married is good, the continence of widows better, and the integrity of the virgin best of all (1240A). The chapter passes on the traditional warning against pride on the part of virgins: A humble widow is more pleasing to God than a proud virgin. This warning is also present in the *Speculum virginum*, where the struggle against pride is a major theme. But it is in elaborating this with continued insistence on the potential for virtue of married women that the *De modo* shows a difference of emphasis. The author warns the reader against despising married women living chastely, or looking down on married women who enter the convent; a virgin who does this has no oil, and her lamp is extinguished (1239D). The virgin should honor these women, and love and serve them like a daughter. He gives examples of holy women who lived some of their lives in the world: Anna the prophetess, who had a husband, and Mary Magdalene, rewarded by seeing the risen Christ and deserving to be called "Apostle of the apostles" (1240A).

Throughout the passages on virginity in the *De modo*, there is no mention of Mary. This is a striking difference from the discourse about virginity in the *Speculum*, where Mary is presented as the leader of virgins and a model for them to emulate.[44] When the *Speculum* introduces the theme of spiritual motherhood for virgins, it is to say that they are to bring forth Christ, joining in the motherhood of Mary (*SV* 6.643–44). The *De modo* appeals to another tradition of spiritual motherhood, according to which the virgin will give birth to virtues, which she will nourish and educate like children (1240BC). Mary is neither promoted as a figure of devotion nor advanced as a model to emulate. Her only appearance is as an example of poverty (1267D).

The *De modo* brings together the teaching on virginity that was current at the time it was written. Consecrated virginity is certainly construed as an important element of the identity of its audience. The reader is often addressed as beloved, venerable or dearest sister" *[soror dilecta/venerabilis/charissima]*, as well as "honest virgin" *[honesta virgo]*. Virginity is not given as much weight in the work's overall plan as love, to which three early chapters are devoted (charity, love of God, and love of neighbor). But if spiritual virginity is not the governing idea of the religious life this author is trying to communicate, what is? I believe a clue can be gained from the recurring phrase that has provided the title of the edition: "to live well" *[bene vivere]*. This is what the sister must do to avoid melancholy (1254B), what she must give an example of to her sisters (1228A), what she must persevere in to be like a cypress or a cedar in the house of the Lord, or to rest in the bosom of Abraham (1237B, 1212B). The centrality of this notion to the author's conception of the work is shown in the epilogue where he says, rather testily: "Now you have been given advice and rules for living well. You do not have ignorance now as an excuse for sin . . . now you have been shown how you should conduct yourself in the house of the Lord."[45] The precepts themselves are summarized at the end of the sixty-third chapter, and include keeping faith and hope, speaking the truth, love of God and neighbor, maintaining chastity, and persevering in good works (1293B). In this scheme of things, the maintenance of interior virginity is one precept among many.

The comparison of these three texts demonstrates the variety of resources available for imagining the religious life in the twelfth and early thirteenth centuries; the mirror of the text could reflect a multiplicity of images, while maintaining a common ground. For their authors some sets of images were indeed gender specific. The concern with interiority that they share is given a different orientation in *De claustro animae* from that of the *Speculum virginum* or the *De modo bene vivendi*. While the possibility of public activity exists for the monk, even if only as a temptation, it does not enter into the vocabulary of the religious life for nuns. Even the figurative space of the interior life presented in the allegorical cloister is wider and less circumscribed than the enclosed garden and the virgin's body that form the core of the imagery of the *Speculum*. The woman's cloister is much less social, less associated with material construction, more individual and personal. While the association of Song of Songs bridal imagery with notions of virginity and enclosure does seem to be regarded as appropriate to a specifically female spirituality, the picture that emerges from these texts is complex. The *De modo* places before the nun both the image of the enclosed garden in which the soul receives the heavenly Bridegroom and the public space in which the misguided representatives of the Church dissipate their spiritual capital. As metaphors for persevering in the monastic enterprise, the *Speculum* and the *De modo* use the traditional ascetic imagery of the battlefield and the athletic contest that is also found in the *De claustro*. And yet the sense of progression through stages in the interior life that the *De claustro* conveys as it moves through the allegorical monastery is absent from the two texts for women. It has been argued that this absence is characteristic of religious advice literature for women; that it lacks dynamism, tending to concentrate on the preservation of virginity rather than on spiritual progress. Yet here, as in the case of the story of Dinah, the distinction needs to be nuanced. Fighting a battle, running a race, and cultivating a garden are certainly not static images, but neither do they convey a sense of progress through stages or of ascent. Again there is the suggestion of multiplicity, that the dynamism of the spiritual life might be imagined differently for women and for men.

It would be unwise to make too much of these differences. In this regard the *De modo* provides a cautionary example. In some ways it looks like a synthesis of the approaches of the other two texts. It shares with the *De claustro* an interest in communicating the practicalities of communal life, prescribing what is to be observed and warning against pitfalls. On the other hand at key points it inserts passages that convey the ideology and language of virginity that inform the *Speculum virginum*. It is tempting to hypothesize that the author, knowing the *Speculum*, either found it not comprehensive or practical enough and supplemented it from other sources or, making a compilation of advice on the religious life from general sources, tried to "feminize" it with material on virginity. Nothing is known of the early history of this text that would allow this hypothesis to be tested, but one manuscript exists that reminds us how much caution is needed when ascribing gender specificity to language and content.

Madrid, Biblioteca Nacional MS 871 is a manuscript, dated to 1267, that contains on folios 1v–142v a copy of the text, under the title *Liber admonicionis*.[46] This copy is addressed to a male audience. Apart from addressing the reader as "brother" [*frater*] rather than "sister" [*soror*], it offers a text very close to that reprinted by Migne. No content has been omitted; the adaptation has been made by simply reversing the gender terms, and as noted earlier, some of the content suggests that the "sister" version is the original.[47] Thus, in the chapter on continence, the brother is warned not to despise men who come to the monastery from the world, having been married and had children. The feminine examples of Anna and Mary Magdalene, however, are retained. The brother is told that as a virgin, he can have seven sons, and the language of childbirth—womb, breasts [*utero, mamillas]*—is used (fol. 60v). The chapter on remaining in enclosure contains the same exhortation, with the image of the enclosed garden. It is only when the vocabulary is examined very closely that there is any evidence to suggest that some of the bridal language of virginity was regarded as gender specific. In phrases where Christ is referred to in the published text as the reader's bridegroom, "Bridegroom" *[sponsus]* is changed to "lord" *[dominus]*. "Bridal chamber" *[thalamum]* is once changed to "kingdom" *[regnum]* (fol. 120v), and once left unchanged. In the chapter on love of God there is a lengthy passage where in the feminine version the reader is addressed directly and given prayers to say that are woven from the words of the bride in the Song of Songs (PL 184: 1221D-22C). In Madrid MS 871 this becomes a dialogue between the Soul *[Anima]* and the Man *[Homo]*, so designated by rubrics in the text (fols. 35–35v), so that the male reader, while presumably expected to identify with the Soul, is not a direct participant in the exchange in the same way as the reader of the female version. Finally, the male reader is never addressed as "virgin," an indication perhaps that while virginity might be a spiritual ideal for men, the social category of "virgin" was perceived as female.

The Madrid manuscript indicates that, at least in the second half of the thirteenth century, the "virginal rhetoric" found in the *De modo* could be considered just as appropriate to men as it was to women, but language that suggested too specifically a gendered relationship between the soul and Christ needed to be modified. The male could think of himself as a mother but not as the bride of Christ. For a woman imagining her relationship with the divine, no distinction needed to be made between the soul, gendered feminine, and the biologically female human being, but for a man such a distinction was necessary.

Set beside the *De claustro animae* and the *De modo bene vivendi*, the *Speculum virginum* emerges as an extraordinary moment in male writing for women on the religious life. The aspects examined in this chapter have shown the author choosing strongly gendered images of virginity and enclosure to place at the center of his construction of female religious identity, while insisting on the value of perseverance in the struggle for spiritual perfection. Yet the comparison with the *De modo* shows that it was only a moment; where the *Speculum* author integrated traditional ascetic teaching into complex intellectual and aesthetic structure governed by the notion of spiritual virginity, the *De modo* author unpacked it again and drew in less gender-specific material. At the same time, that which had been directed specifically toward women was perhaps coming to have a wider application. Most of the twelfth- and thirteenth-century manuscripts of the *Speculum virginum* have been preserved in male monastic libraries; while this has been taken as an indication that the text was primarily for monks who were engaged in the pastoral care of nuns, in the light of the minimal adaptation of the *De modo* for a male audience, it could also have been seen as appropriate spiritual reading for the monks themselves. Thus the gendering of images of the religious life in this period is best seen as dynamic. There are points where sets of images coalesce and are more closely associated with men or with women. Yet as the three texts we have examined here show, images are also constantly shifting, being modified, and exchanged.

### Notes

1. *SV* Epist. 34–38: "Intitulatur autem idem opusculum SPECULUM VIR-GINUM, in quo Peregrinus presbiter cum Theodora Christi virgine tanta contulisse probatur, ut studiosis Christi virginibus sit in eo magnum conservandae castitatis incitamentum, fastidium presentium, formula quaedam celestium appetendorum."

2. *SV* Epist. 47–50: "Sunt enim specula mulierum eloquia diuina visibus obiecta sanctarum animarum, in quibus semper considerant, quomodo sponso aeterno aut placeant decore sanctae conscientiae aut displiceant peccati foeditate." The author is referring here to the women's mirrors used by Moses to make a basin for Aaron and his sons to wash in at the tabernacle (Exod. 38.8, 40.29).

3. This conception of the text as a handbook, grounded in Scripture, is common to the plethora of advice literature produced for monks and nuns in the twelfth and thirteenth centuries. These works include a variety of literary genres: commentaries on existing monastic rules, works that see themselves as rules, treatises, dialogues, and letters. They have been interrogated by Caroline Bynum for differences of emphasis between monks and canons and by Barbara Newman for gender differences. See Caroline Walker Bynum, *Jesus as Mother: Studies in the Spirituality of the High Middle Ages* (Berkeley: University of California Press, 1982); Barbara Newman, "Flaws in the Golden Bowl: Gender and Spiritual Formation in the Twelfth Century," in Newman, *From Virile Woman to WomanChrist: Studies in Medieval Religion and Literature* (Philadelphia: University of Pennsylvania Press, 1995), pp. 19–45.

4. Newman, *Virile Woman*, p. 22. Elisabeth Bos in chapter 9 of this volume argues that the idea of spiritual progress is present in religious advice to women.

5. Hugh of Fouilloy, *De claustro animae*, PL 176: 1017–1182; *Liber de modo bene vivendi*, PL 184: 1199–1306.

6. Seyfarth, pp. 48*–50*. On manuscripts of *SV,* see chapter 2 by Seyfarth in this volume, and for the distribution of manuscripts of the *De claustro,* Henri Peltier, "Hugues de Fouilloy. Chanoine régulier; Prieur de Saint-Laurent-au-Bois," *Revue du moyen âge latin* 2 (1946): 25–44, n. 34.

7. Seyfarth, p. 50*: "Ut igitur ante oculos claustralium quasi speculum quoddam ponam, rotam praelationis in capite presentis opusculi pingam."

8. *SV* 1.989–92: " . . . volo tamen quendam paradisum speculatorium pre
oculis tibi in pictura ponere. . . ." On *pictura speculatorium*, see chapter 5 by
Powell in this volume.

9. This picture cycle is less consistently present in the manuscript tradition
than that of the *Speculum virginum:* see Morgan Powell, "The Mirror and
the Woman: Instruction for Religious Women and the Emergence of Vernacular Poetics 1120–1250" (Ph.D. diss., Princeton University, 1997), pp.
106–7.

10. See Ivan Gobry, "Hugues de Fouilloy" in *Dictionnaire de spiritualité ascétique
et mystique* (Paris: Beauchesne, 1969), 7: 882–38. Some of the 176 known
manuscripts of the *De claustro animae* are listed on col. 882. The relation between Hugh's efforts to reform Saint-Laurent-au-Bois and the writing of
the *De claustro* is discussed at greater length by the same author in his dissertation, '*De claustro anime' d'Hugues de Fouilloy. Edition critique avec traduc-
tion, introduction et notes* (thèse complémentaire de la Sorbonne, Paris,
1965).

11. Little is known about the manuscript tradition of this text. Two manuscripts that contain it are held in the Biblioteca Nacional in Madrid. The
first, Madrid, Biblioteca Nacional MS 871, was completed in 1267 (see n.
46 below). I am indebted to Eric Reiter for alerting me to the existence
of the Madrid manuscript and to Constant Mews for discovering the second manuscript of the text in the Biblioteca Nacional MS 308, fols.
1–116v, which dates from the fifteenth century: *Inventario general de manu-
scritos de la Biblioteca Nacional*, 5 vols. (Madrid 1953–59), 1: 227. There is
also an early fourteenth-century manuscript of the text from Spain, now
in Uppsala University Library (Cod. Ups. C240), which belonged to St.
Birgitta of Sweden: Margarete Andersson-Schmitt and Monica Hedlund,
*Mittelalterliche Handschriften de Universitätsbibliothek Uppsala. Katalog bei der
C. Sammlung. Acta Bibl. R. Universitatis Upsaliensis 26:3* (Stockholm:
Almqvist & Wiksell, 1990), pp. 151–52. The monastery of Clairvaux also
possessed one, listed in the early sixteenth-century catalogue of a small library housed near the dormitory, which probably contained small-format
books that monks could borrow. The present whereabouts of that manuscript are unknown: André Vernet, *La Bibliothèque de l'abbaye de Clairvaux
du XIIe au XVIIIe siècle* (Paris: Editions du Centre national de la recherche
scientifique, 1979), pp. 43, 44, 589.

12. Bridget Morris, "Birgittines and Beguines in Medieval Sweden," in *New
Trends in Feminine Spirituality: The Holy Women of Liège and their Impact*, ed.
Juliette Dor, Lesley Johnson, and Jocelyn Wogan-Browne, Medieval
Women: Texts and Contexts 2 (Turnhout: Brepols, 1999), p. 162.

13. It has been attributed Thomas of Froidmont, a Cistercian active in the early
thirteenth century (an attribution probably first made by Charles de Visch
in his 1656 catalogue of Clairvaux manuscripts: see Vernet, *Bibliothèque de*

*l'abbaye de Clairvaux, p.* 707), but this is untenable on stylistic grounds. For a brief summary of this attribution and its refutation, see Maur Standaert, "Thomas de Beverly (de Froidmont)" in *Dictionnaire de spiritualité ascétique et mystique* (Paris: Beauchesne, 1991), 15: 783. The MSS Madrid 308, Uppsala C240, and the Clairvaux copy all attribute the text to Bernard.

14. Madrid 871, fols. 26v–27: "Nigrum velum castitatis et sanctitatis est signum" [The black veil is a sign of chastity and holiness]. A couple of sentences further on, where the edited text has "just as your veil is consecrated, so let your work be holy," this manuscript has substituted the word *vestimentum* [clothing] for *velum* [veil].

15. "Finito libro sit laus et gloria Christo. Sub era Ma.Cca.Lxa.Viia. idus septembris': Madrid 871, fol. 142v.

16. I have italicized the verbal parallels with *SV: De modo* Praefatio, PL 184: 1199B: "Nunc ergo, charissima soror, hunc librum accipe, et eum ante oculos tuos quasi speculum propone, eumque omni hora velut speculum contemplare. *Praecepta* namque *Dei specula sunt, in quibus se ipsas animae inspiciunt,* et in quibus cognoscunt *maculas,* si quae sunt, *foeditatis;* quia nemo mundus a delicto: et in quibus emendant vitia cogitationum suarum, et relucentes vultus quasi ex reddita imagine componunt: quia dum praeceptis dominicis toto animo intendunt, in eis procul dubio quid in se *coelesti sponso placeat,* vel quid *displiceat* cognoscunt." Cf. *SV* Epist. 47–50: "*Sunt enim specula* mulierum *eloquia divina* visibus obiecta sanctarum animarum, *in quibus semper considerant,* quomodo *sponso aeterno* aut *placeant* decore sanctae conscientiae aut *displiceant peccati foeditate.*"

17. *De modo* 24, PL 184: 1254B: "Soror dilecta, vis nunquam esse tristis?— Frater mi, volo.—Ergo bene vive."

18. *De modo* 20, PL 1237CD: "Quia in monasterio est vita contemplativa, in saeculo est laboriosa: in monasterio est vita sancta, in saeculo est vita criminosa: in monasterio est vita spiritualis, in saeculo est vita carnalis: in monasterio est vita pacifica, in saeculo est vita litigiosa: in monasterio est vita pacifica: in saeculo est vita jurgiis plena: in monasterio est vita casta, in saeculo est vita luxuriosa. . . ."

19. *SV* 3.1–2. See chapter 1 by Mews and chapter 5 by Powell in this volume. This psalm is used in a similar way by Aelred to evoke his sister's decision to become a recluse: Aelred of Rievaulx, *De institutione inclusarum,* lines 464–68, ed. C. H. Talbot, CCCM 1 (1971): 650.

20. For example, a lengthy passage in the chapter on love of God explicitly identifies the reader with the Bride in the Song of Songs: *De modo* 12, PL 184: 1221D-1222C.

21. Augustine of Hippo, *Regula* 1.5, ed. L. Verheijen, *La Règle de saint Augustin* (Paris: Etudes augustiniennes, 1967), 1: 417–37. Reproduced with English translation in George Lawless, *Augustine of Hippo and his Monastic Rule* (Oxford: Clarendon Press, 1987), pp. 80–103.

22. This aspect of religious advice to women is discussed by Elizabeth Bos in chapter 9 in this volume.

23. Isidore, *Sententiarum libri tres* 3.32, ed. Pierre Cazier, CCSL 111 (1998).

24. *De claustro* 1.1, PL 176: 1020A: "Monachi faciunt sibi claustra quibus homo exterior teneri possit; sed utinam claustra facerent quibus homo interior ordinate teneretur!"

25. *De claustro* 1.1, PL 176: 1020AB: "Claustra vero quasi castra Domini alii Domino componunt, et sicut regum ministri turrium instaurata munitione securius fraudes inimicorum excludunt: sic homo interior, et homo exterior intra munimina claustrorum propositi, antiqui hostis insidias, et temporalium rerum fragiles casus effugiunt."

26. See Jane Schulenburg, "Strict Active Enclosure and Its Effects on the Female Monastic Experience (500–1100)," in *Medieval Religious Women 1: Distant Echoes,* ed. John Nichols and Lillian T. Shank, Cistercian Studies 71 (Kalamazoo, MI: Cistercian Publications, 1984), pp. 51–86.

27. This teaching is associated with individual vices: for example, on the tongue in the chapter on contention (*De modo* 17, PL 184: 1229BC) and on the eyes in the chapter on fornication (*De modo* 23, PL 184: 1241C, 1242D-43A).

28. Newman, *Virile Woman,* p. 25.

29. *SV* 2.97–103: "Si Dinam curiositas noxia non emisisset, gemino malo fratres non turbasset . . . . . Jactura floridae pudiciciae, pressura hostilis ruinae. Si Dina quieta, si tabernaculo suo inclusa mansisset, virginitatis damna non incurrisset nec paternum gladium super hostem, carnis amatorem evaginasset."

30. *SV* 2.86–87: "Quantae animae egrediendo egressusque noxio naturae suae statum excedendo perierunt."

31. *De modo* 23, PL 184: 1242C: "Et sic misera puella quia incaute vidit quod non debuit videre, honestatem ac virginitatem suam perdidit."

32. *De claustro* 3.1, PL 176: 1087D: "De hoc claustro egressa est Dina filia Jacob. . . ."

33. Gregory the Great, *Regula pastoralis* 3. 29, ed. F. Rommel, Schr 381–382, 2 vols. (1992), 2: 472.

34. *De claustro* 2.16 and 17, PL 176: 1067A-70C.

35. Lam. 4.1: "dispersi sunt lapides sanctuarii in capite omnium platearum."

36. Paschasius Radbertus, *Expositio in lamentationes Hieremiae* 4.92, ed. B. Paulus, CCCM 85 (1988); Gregory the Great, *XL Homiliarum in evangelia libri duo* 1.17.15, PL 76: 1147AC.

37. *De modo* 66, PL 184: 1297B: "Necesse est igitur ut quisque Religiosus, si salvari desiderat, saeculum contemnat, et sese intra monasterii claustra concludat. Debet Religiosus vir conventus saecularium hominum fugere, et societatem servorum Dei requirere."

38. *De modo* 66, PL 198: 1297C.

39. *De modo* 66, PL 184: 1297C: "Si te incluseris in claustro, amaberis a Christo."

40. See Newman, *Virile Women,* pp. 28–30.

41. It is mentioned in the fourth book, where in the four orders of columns in the monastery of the heavenly Jerusalem, the fourth order, sky-blue/vi-

olet in color, represents virginity. The others are yellow (crocus) representing the Church fathers; red (rose) representing the martyrs; and white (lily) representing the confessors. *De claustro* 4.30, PL 176: 1168CD.

42. *De modo* 21, PL 184: 1238B: "Mente et corpore virgines non sunt fatuae, sed prudentes: et possunt exire obviam sponso, quia habent oleum in vasis suis, id est, castitatem in mentibus."

43. *De modo* 21, PL 184: 1238C, quoting Isidore, *Sententiarum libri tres* 2.40, CCSL 111: 644: "virgo corpore et non mente, non habet praemium in remuneratione;" PL 184: 1239A, attributed to Augustine: "Nihil prodest virginitas carnis, ubi habitat iracundia mentis;" PL 184: 1239A, attributed to Jerome: "Nihil prodest habere carnem virgineam, si mente quis nupserit: nihil etiam prodest corporis virginei custodire virginitatem, si oculos a concupiscentia noluerit refrenare. Virginitas in corpore nihil proderit, si charitas aut humilitas a corde discesserit." The quotations attributed to Augustine and Jerome may in fact be cited from an anthology like the Defensor of Ligugé, in the chapter on virginity, *Liber scintillarum* 13.4 and 27, CCSL 117 (1957): 65 and 67.

44. *SV* 5, and many references through the rest of the text.

45. *De modo* 72, PL 184: 1305BC: "Datum est tibi consilium bene vivendi, et etiam norma. Nulla jam ignorantia a peccato te excusat . . . jam demonstratum est tibi qualiter in domo Dei debeas conversari. . . ."

46. See n. 11 above. According to the catalogue, this manuscript belonged to the Trinitarians (an order founded in the twelfth century to free captive Christians): *Inventario* 2: 481.

47. See n. 17 above.

# CHAPTER 8

# THE *SPECULUM VIRGINUM*
# AND TRADITIONS OF MEDIEVAL DIALOGUE

*Sabina Flanagan*

This chapter situates the *Speculum virginum* within the broader context of dialogue literature in the twelfth century. The genre was employed to provide instruction in a wide range of subjects. The *Speculum* is unusual, however, in that it adapts a literary technique normally employed to instruct boys and young men to an extended dialogue between a spiritual guide and his female disciple. Seen in this light, the *Speculum* emerges as a work of great creative originality that applies the questioning technique of scholastic literature to discussing the religious life for women in an unusually vivid way.

Although its title does not immediately disclose the fact, the *Speculum virginum* belongs among the considerable stock of twelfth-century dialogues. Indeed, while historians of Renaissance thought and literature may have claimed that era as "the golden age of dialogue,"[1] a glance at the Patrologia Latina will show that—especially during what I have come to think of as "the long twelfth century"[2]—a very considerable number of works can be identified as dialogues by the inclusion of such words as *dialogus, conflictus, altercatio,* and *disputatio* in their titles.[3] However, this chapter is not concerned with the relative merits of the dialogues belonging to these two very different epochs but rather with an investigation of the various forms of dialogue written in the twelfth century, with the ultimate aim of seeing where the *Speculum virginum* can be placed among them. Its author also composed a *Dialogue on the Authors*, a relatively simply pedagogic exercise about a range of classical authors; *On Contempt or Love of the World*, a debate between a monk and a clerk contrasting secular and religious life; and a doctrinal debate, the *Altercation of the Synagogue with the Church*.[4] I shall argue that the *Speculum virginum*, whose author seems to have had a particular fondness for the genre, is noteworthy among other twelfth-century dialogues not only in terms of its subject matter, length, and the nature of its interlocutors but also for its assured handling of the form.[5]

## Toward a Definition of the Genre

First, some sort of working definition for the medieval dialogue is required.[6] Put most simply, the term describes the form in which a piece of writing is cast rather than a distinctive literary genre, such as the epic poem or the romantic novel. This may seem counterintuitive in light of the more familiar Platonic dialogue, which suggests that there is such a genre that involves the discussion of a philosophical problem in dialogue form.[7] Writers of the twelfth century, however, had limited direct access to Plato's dialogues even in translation. Thus St. Anselm (1033–1109) describes three of his dialogues *(On Truth, On Freedom of the Will, On the Fall of the Devil)* as "three treatises pertaining to the study of the holy Scriptures . . . alike in that they proceed by question and answer."[8] Quoting St. Jerome, Reimbald of Liège describes his dialogue as "preserving the Socratic form,"[9] while others use such words as "per" or "sub" to indicate the manner in which the work is presented. Walter and Balduin claim to have written "a work against the Jews in the dialogue form"[10] while Otloh of St. Emmeram (1010–ca. 1070) writes his treatise on three theological questions "in the manner of a dialogue,"[11] and Peter Alfonsi (ca. 1060–ca. 1140) says that he has "set forth [his] entire book in the form of a dialogue."[12]

The understanding of "dialogue" on the part of these authors is presumably that advanced by Isidore of Seville in his *Book of Etymologies:* "Dialogue is a conversation involving two or more people."[13] The advantage of this definition is that it allows for a wide range of presentations, including those where the speech of the participants is reported with more or less introduction, elaboration, and scene setting. It also encompasses a range of representations from the formal (as in the case of the catechetical exchanges between a master and a disciple) to the more naturalistic and informal, though in a sense more "literary" productions, where several participants engage in less structured conversation. It also allows for differing degrees of authorial representation within the debate.

Although many twelfth-century authors make use of the form (some indeed on several occasions), they seem less inclined to make theoretical pronouncements about the method. One of the few theoretical discussions of the dialogue in our period, taken from a work that is itself in the form of a dialogue, is by the author of the *Speculum virginum*, presumed to be Conrad of Hirsau. In his *Dialogue on the Authors*, he distinguishes between Cicero's and Boethius' use of dialogue. He notes that in *On Old Age* Cicero was imitating Plato by attributing all the words of the dialogue to a set of characters he portrays in discussion, whereas Boethius, in the *Consolation of Philosophy*, also appears as himself.[14] It is interesting to note here that the Platonic/Ciceronian form, in which all the words are put into the mouths of third persons, real or imaginary, and the author is not present as one of the participating speakers, is actually quite rare in the twelfth century. In fact, the *Speculum virginum* is one of the few, nonallegorical examples extant.

While many dialogues are written in the form of conversations between the author and various real or imagined people, and although it could be said that each person in a dialogue is the mouthpiece of the author (since he has written what they say),[15] a rather closer connection between the principal players is sometimes apparent. Paradoxically, such dialogues often have a term like *Soliloquy* in the title. They also have a long pedigree, deriving ultimately from St. Augustine.[16] The fact that the interlocutor is the alter ego of the author is sometimes made plain by the choice of names: "Petrus" and "Abelard" in Abelard's *Soliloquy*,[17] or "Alfonsus" and "Moyses" in *Dialogues of Alfonsi the Convert with Moses the Jew*, by the Jewish convert Peter Alfonsi.[18] However, it must be said that "Ratio" [Reason] and "Anima" [Soul] in the *Soliloquy* of Adam of Dryburgh are hardly recognizable as two sides of the austere Premonstratensian canon and later convert to the Carthusians who wrote *On the Tripartite Tabernacle*.[19] Complaints of "Anima" to "Ratio" about his/her temptations, such as "I think of a multitude of elegant and beautiful women" [Cogito multitudinem compatrum et pulchrarum mulierum] and that manual work is "unfitting for those who are ordained and lettered" [Non mihi videtur ad ordinatos, et maxime ad litteratos pertinere], might have been better represented as between Magister and Discipulus. The whole text actually presents sage advice from an older canon to a novice struggling to come to terms with his vocation. It seems likely, however, that the choice of names (like the title) refers back to Augustine's *Soliloquies*, where the subject matter is more appropriate to such participants. Peter von Moos argues convincingly that "Everardus" and "Ratius," characters in the *Dialogue of Ratius and Everard*[20] by Everard of Ypres (ca. 1115–ca. 1191), are really projections of different sides of the author himself, even though they are presented in a convincing mise-en-scène, with distinctive psychological profiles.[21] His conclusion is in contrast to Richard Southern's interpretation of the dialogue, which takes Everard's scene-setting much more literally, even suggesting that in Ratius we have the first example of a Greek student attending the schools of Paris.[22]

Partly dependent on the kinds of characters involved in the dialogue is the scale and manner of their interactions. Generally speaking, participants of equal intellectual and social status get roughly equal time to put their point of view. Thus in the *Dialogues* of Anselm of Havelberg (d. 1158), discussions held between himself and Bishop Nicetas of Nicomedia, the two parties are more or less equal and are given more or less equal time, albeit on a rather leisurely scale—the debate being more like a parliamentary debate than a discussion.[23] Other examples can be found where the two speakers are unequal and get very unequal time or space. The most obvious example of this is the simple catechism type of dialogue where the Disciple asks one-line questions and the Master answers at length. Examples of this can be found among the more didactic works of Hugh of St-Victor (d. 1141) and Honorius Augustodunensis (ca. 1080–ca. 1140).[24] However, this is not to suggest that there is a predictable relationship between forms of interaction and the subject matter. While scientific topics can be treated in catechism form, they also can provide the subject matter of "problematized debates," as in the case of Adelard of Bath (fl. 1100–1150). In his *Natural Questions,* the master figure does not have all the answers nor the disciple all the questions.[25] The dialogue form allows for a wide variety of treatments on virtually any topic. Thus theological questions are dealt with quite summarily between Master and Disciple in the *Elucidarium,*[26] whereas real open-ended discussion between equals occurs in the *Dialogue* of Everard of Ypres and, for reasons that are not far to seek, in Abelard's *Soliloquy.*

## Subject Matter

It is now time to investigate the subjects of writings in the dialogue genre. If the distinguishing mark of a dialogue is its form—a form that admits of wide variation in the status of participants, method of discussion, and weight given to speakers—we might expect the subject matter to parallel the subjects treated in contemporary Latin literature in nondialogue form. This indeed seems to be the case. A sampling of the more than seventy dialogues I have found for the twelfth century furnishes examples from the following seven categories[27]:

1. Doctrinal/theological subjects
2. Debates between different orders
3. Saints' lives and miracles
4. Pedagogic dialogues on the liberal arts

5. Natural history/cosmology, etc.
6. History, administration, etc.
7. Spiritual formation

## Doctrinal/Theological Subjects

Not surprisingly, given the avocations of the authors of the dialogues, this is the largest group. The nondialogue equivalent here is the treatise, the commentary, and the sermon. This category includes such well-known dialogues as St. Anselm's *Why a God Man* and *On Truth* and Gilbert Crispin's *On the Holy Spirit.*[28] A large subsection of this class consists of polemical debates between Jews/Christians/Gentiles (or philosophers); among them are works by Abelard, Gilbert Crispin (fl. 1070–1100), Rupert of Deutz (ca. 1070–ca. 1129), and Odo of Cambrai (d. 1113).[29] Interestingly, there do not seem to be a large number of nondialogue treatments of this subject. One such that comes to mind is the treatise (or diatribe) of Peter the Venerable (1094–1156) against the Jews, *Against the Enduring Stubborness of the Jews.*[30]

## Debates between Different Orders

The *Dialogue of Two Monks* of Idung of Prüfening concerns the claims of the relative merits of Cistercians over Cluniacs, while the *Dialogue on the Eating of Fowl,* by an anonymous Benedictine, represents the more limited treatment of particular differences between the orders.[31] Many nondialogue treatises deal with such topics.[32]

## Saints' Lives and Miracles

Examples here are the *Life of Otto Bishop of Bamberg* by Herbord of Michaelsberg and the *Dialogue of Miracles* by Caesarius of Heisterbach.[33] These do not seem to be widely treated topics in dialogue form, despite or perhaps because of the example of Gregory the Great's *Dialogues.*[34]

## Pedagogic Dialogues on the Liberal Arts

Examples here are the *Dialogue on the Authors* on literary history and theory (studied as "grammar" in the trivium) by Conrad of Hirsau, and the more advanced dialogue by William of Hirsau on music, or St. Anselm's introduction to dialectic, *On "Grammarian,"* definitely not for beginners.[35] There are, of course, numerous treatises written on such topics that are not in dialogue form.

### Natural History / Cosmology, etc.

Examples here include Adelard of Bath's dialogues with his nephew concerning natural history and falconry, *Natural Questions* and *Treatise about Birds*, and William of Conches' dialogue between himself as a philosopher and the future Henry II.[36]

### History, Administration, etc.

A large miscellaneous group including dialogues embracing history (including apocalyptic, such as Gerhoch of Reichersberg's *On the Fourth Vigil of the Night*), law (Everard of Ypres, *Synthesis of Questions on the Decretals*), government, and other more or less secular subjects.[37] Particularly interesting, since it treats a subject that was only developed in the twelfth century, is the *Dialogue about the Exchequer* by Richard Fitzneal, dealing with the workings of the Anglo-Norman exchequer.[38]

### Spiritual Formation

Examples, which include expositions of monastic rules, are the *Bridlington Dialogue* (or *Colloquy of a Master and a Disciple on the Rule of Blessed Augustine about the Life of Canons*) and the *Soliloquium* of Adam of Dryburgh.[39] The *Speculum virginum* is also to be placed in this classification.

## Reasons for the Dialogue Form

If twelfth-century authors had a choice between presenting their material as a straightforward treatise or commentary or in dialogue form, what might have been their reasons for choosing the latter? Some clues are given by the practitioners of dialogue themselves. Let us look at what the author of the *Speculum virginum* had to say on the subject.[40] In the *Dialogue on the Authors*, a short introduction to literary history and terminology, Conrad of Hirsau (following the identification of Trithemius) writes: "Every dialogue is made for three motives or reasons: it is either for the sake of greater confirmation, as in the dialogue of Gregory and Peter, or for the sake of recreation and delight, as is found in the poets, or for the sake of authority, so that faith may be placed in the words which a real person speaks."[41]

This passage appears in his introduction to the works of Cicero, and his third category (that of authority) no doubt refers to such works as *On Friendship* and *On Old Age*, where Cicero puts his views on old age and friendship into the authoritative voices of Cato the Elder and Gaius

Laelius.[42] Conrad's first example of the dialogue form, exemplified by the *Dialogues* of Gregory the Great, uses the responses of Peter the Deacon to drive home a point or explain more clearly something that needs to be stressed.[43] He also serves to indicate or sometimes direct a return to the narrative after a digression. Which poetical dialogues Conrad might have had in mind is not clear, although there were several possible twelfth-century examples.[44] Of these, some might be thought to have had a higher moral or intellectual purpose than simply recreation and delight as he suggests. In addition, some of the more accomplished prose dialogues could also be said to delight the reader.

But how far is this theory exemplified in Conrad's own practice? It is difficult to assign his own works to the categories he outlines, except in a very general way. Further, since some of his dialogues, notably the *Dialogue on the Authors* and *On Contempt or Love of the World* lack prefaces (a possible indication of what has been presumed to be their less than finished state), we do not find the expected explanatory justification of the form there. While the *Speculum virginum* does seem to be complete, and is accompanied by a prefatory letter to two anonymous nuns, this introduction also proves disappointing in that it makes little overt reference to the dialogue form. Conrad, in fact, remarks that he has divided the work into twelve parts to make it more acceptable, not that he has put it in dialogue form to make it more engaging.[45]

By contrast, St. Anselm, also the author of several dialogues, explains his choice of the form in the preface to *Why a God Man* in the following way: "And since investigations, which are carried on by question and answer, are thus made more plain to many, and especially to less quick minds, and on that account are more gratifying, I will take to argue with me one of those persons who agitate this subject; one who among the rest impels me more earnestly to it, so that in this way Boso may question and Anselm reply."[46] In this case, although the part of the interlocutor appears to be largely heuristic, Boso was a real person. He had been Anselm's disciple at Bec since 1090, having come originally from Laon in search of solutions to questions that worried him. Around 1093 Anselm summoned him to Canterbury; indeed Richard Southern believes that Boso may have been responsible for getting Anselm to think in new ways about some of the philosophical questions that were exercising him.[47]

Turning to other dialogues of spiritual formation, we find in the prologue to the *Bridlington Dialogue*, the Disciple, who has already asked that the answers be given in writing "for my benefit and it may be for that of the many" [*mee vel multorum utilitati*], setting out the ground rules for the debate: "If, however, any topic of disputation should arise between us, either about the Rule itself or out of our discussion, I implore you not to be irked by my slowness when I either propose some point, or else adduce something by way of contradiction, but rather, out of your forbearance, to give me reasonable, satisfying answers to my inquiries."[48] In his prologue to *On Spiritual Friendship,* Aelred of Rievaulx (1110–1167) mentions the impression made on him by Cicero's dialogue on friendship, no doubt expecting readers to make their own comparisons between the two works.[49] That he has chosen to write a dialogue is not surprising, given his model, although we might note that unlike Cicero, Aelred puts himself into the dialogue, discussing the nature of friendship with three of his monks, first at Wardon and later at Rievaulx. The anonymous Cistercian who wrote *Dialogue about a Dispute between the Love of God and the Lying Tongue,*[50] explains his unusual choice of interlocutors in terms of prosopopoeia rather than dialogue.[51] However, the reasons are similar: "Let us leave the judgment about why we should use prosopopoeia to our predecessors. For they knew by experience that variety in speech lifts the tedium of truth."

Thus the authors of dialogues give various reasons for their choice, including the avoidance of tedium, the pleasures of variety, and their advantages as aids to understanding. Finally, there is doubtless some element of imitation involved, since various degrees of familiarity with earlier models, including those of Plato, Cicero, Boethius, and Augustine are evident.

## The *Speculum virginum* and Twelfth-Century Dialogue

We may now ask where the *Speculum virginum* might be accommodated in the rather protean literary form of dialogue. First, I examine the work from a formal point of view (although form and content are not entirely separable). Then I make some comparisons with those dialogues that are similar in content, that is, the other dialogues that I have classified as dialogues of spiritual formation.

One of the first things to note is the unusual length of the *Speculum virginum* compared to other dialogues, especially those of spiritual formation. Second is that it is conceived in a realistic mode, that is not as a dream vision, as is the case with many of the poetical dialogues. In such works the participants are often allegorical, as Philosophia in Boethius' *Consolation of Philosophy,* Ecclesia in Reimbald of Liège's *Stromata,* Philosophia and Philocosmia in Adelard of Bath's *On the Same and the Different.*[52] The dream vision dialogue also can involve more apparently flesh-and-blood participants, as in Abelard's dialogue between a philosopher, a Jew, and a Christian.[53]

In the *Speculum virginum* these supposedly real people have real names, although not their proper names. If there is a deeper significance to the names "Peregrinus" and "Theodora," beyond their general appropriateness for two religious, it has so far eluded me.[54] Clearly, in terms of particularizing the subjects, this puts them above the Magister/Discipulus category but in a slightly different class from the more common practice where the author uses his own name or initial and is represented in conversation with his real disciples or acquaintances.[55] Examples of this practice are to be found in *Why a God Man* with Anselm and Boso, and in *On Spiritual Friendship*, where Aelred talks with his disciples Ivo, Gratian, and Walter, his subsequent biographer. Odo of Cambrai introduces a person called Leo the Jew as his partner in dialogue, although his translator, Irven Resnick, suggests that that might not have been the real name of the person described in the prologue.[56] Of course, the use of initials might be just for economy of copying, except that Odo makes rather a point of saying that he will use initials in the body of the dialogue, even though he gives the full names elsewhere.[57] Possibly writers thought that it would aid the reader to identify with the participants if the names were not too distinctive.

If the nomenclature of the *SV* falls somewhere in the middle of the scale, we might ask how differentiated the two characters are. That there is no external description of Peregrinus and Theodora is not surprising since this sort of description usually occurs in the more "mixed" form of dialogue (i.e., those that do not consist entirely of direct speech) of which Boethius' *Consolation of Philosophy* is the most famous example. Without going to the extent of Alan of Lille's *On the Lament of Nature,* where fully a third of the work is taken up with the allegorical description of the appearance and clothing of *Natura* before anyone speaks, some dialogues manage to indicate the salient features of the participants by more economical means. In *On Spiritual Friendship,* for example, Aelred's speeches include short but telling descriptions of the behavior of his fellow monks.[58] While the *Speculum* author does not follow this course, we do get some idea of the distinctive personalities of Peregrinus and Theodora through their verbal interactions.

One obvious point of differentiation between the two participants is their gender. The *Speculum virginum* is one of the few nonallegorical dialogues in which there is a female participant. Indeed, there do not seem to be any other twelfth-century Latin dialogues representing a conversation between a man and a woman on a mundane level (if we exclude short poetic dialogues, such as found in the *Carmina burana,* texts of a very different genre). The closest parallel would be the anonymous dialogue that purports to be between St. Anselm and the Virgin Mary, which, despite the exalted nature of the female partner, remains exceedingly pedestrian.[59] However, if we admit that the dialogue is just a technique to be used with any particular topic, then such a male/female dialogue is less remarkable, since the subject matter comprises spiritual direction from male to female, as often attested throughout the medieval period. What is perhaps surprising is that there are not more dialogues that treat this important material.

But let us see how the dialogue handles such matters. Where, for instance, does it stand on the continuum between radical disparity and rough equality between the two interlocutors? It might be parenthetically noted that in some cases the author's persona is the one who takes instruction. The case of Laurence of Durham's *Consolation on the Death of a Friend* is one such, although it is possible that the *Consoler* here is actually another side of the author, since in his other dialogues Laurence takes actual monks, or at least their names—Peter and Phillip—as his interlocutors.[60]

Theodora undoubtedly gets some good lines and is shown as conversant with Scripture, which she quotes extensively. She makes a joke (*SV* 12.20–22) and Peregrinus makes a similar one at end of part twelve (12.440–43). More surprisingly, she is also acquainted with the Latin comedy, *Geta* (2.423).[61] Indeed, despite being a woman, she compares quite well with the male pupils in similar dialogues. She is not cast as a total foil to the Master, unlike the Disciple in some of Honorius' dialogues, where his contribution is confined to asking simple questions and praising the master.

In fact, the expected power imbalance between the male instructor and his female pupil is indicated more by the forms in which they address each other than by their arguments. Although Theodora begins by calling Peregrinus "brother in Christ, Peregrinus" [1.36: *frater in Christo, Peregrine*], this egalitarian mode is soon abandoned for the more hierarchical "venerable brother" [3.8: *frater venerande*] and later intensified as "venerable father [5.908: *pater venerande*], "excellent father" [10.69: *pater optime*], "beloved father" [5.13, 8.736, 10.69: *pater amande*]. Peregrinus calls her "sister" in part one (1.159) but more frequently "daughter" (e.g., 1.566, 669; 2.186, 344, 443, etc.) Quite often she is addressed as Theodora, especially, for some reason, in parts one and nine (e.g., 1.2, 159, 574, 774 and 9.43, 113, 319, 639, 735, etc.). Although she does not refer to him as Peregrinus except at the very beginning (*SV* 1.36), it is possible that she is making a pun on his name at the close of part six: "I gratefully accept from a pilgrim whatever comfort for my pilgrimage and trouble" [6.855: Gratulanter accipio quodcumque peregrinationis et molestie mee solatium a peregrino]. At other points the personal relationship takes second place to the more universal where she is addressed as "virgin of Christ" [3.703, 6.172: *virgo Christi*] and variants. If we compare this with Conrad's *On Contempt or Love of the World*, we find a rough equality between the participants, the monk and the clerk addressing each other as "brother," sometimes with additional epithets such as "beloved brother" [*frater amande*].[62]

That the aims of the dialogue are not as transparent as might at first appear emerges from the fact that Peregrinus sometimes seems to address others beside Theodora. Thus on occasion priests with pastoral care for women seem to be apostrophized (5.1078–80 and 1094). This lends support to the argument of Morgan Powell that the dialogue is intended not just to be read as a discussion between two people but for more programmatic purposes, as a kind of template for priests to use in their instruction of religious women.[63]

The same precarious balance found in the way the participants address each other is illustrated by the nature of their exchanges. Theodora asks questions, often politely (8.537–38; 9.301–302, 721–23), occasionally more abruptly: "Explain what you are saying with an example" [11.830: *Resolve per exemplum, quod loqueris*] or "Indicate by way of a brief definition, how they [knowledge and wisdom] are similar in sound, but different in meaning" [11.430–31: *Discerne igitur brevi diffinitiuncula, quomodo voce similia sensu sint dissimilia*]. Peregrinus also asks questions; some of these are Socratic in the sense that they draw the pupil on to express what she already knows, as in 11.30–35; some are rhetorical where he asks and answers his own questions (3.684–732).

There are also passages where the discussion is sustained through a series of shorter questions and answers. (6.185–98, 483–96, and 7.799–813) In the latter case Theodora asks a question and Peregrinus replies "A good question" [*Iusta inquisitio*] then continues with a question of his own. In 8.115–23 we have a rapid exchange about human resemblances to beasts and angels. Later there is a further exchange where Peregrinus confirms her answers to his leading questions with "nothing truer" [8.323: *nihil verius*]. In part eight (8.421–25) Theodora is allowed to describe the significance of the fifth day of creation and eventually sums up this section of the argument (8.488–92) and is praised for her understanding (8.493–95). However, it must be said that for much of the discussion, Peregrinus favors the imperative mood. Many passages begin with such injunctions as "Wait, Theodora" [1.574, 774; 2.1; 9.753, 1043; 11.407: *Attende, Theodora*] or "Listen" [9.113, 319: *Audi*] or "Believe" [9.753: *crede*] or "Tell me" [9.1141: *Dic mihi*].

As we have seen, the participants in the dialogue are partly differentiated by their unequal relationship as pupil and teacher. However it should be noted that this inequality falls somewhere in the middle of the continuum represented by simple Master/Disciple exercises such as Honorius' *Elucidarium* and the more open-ended and equally matched discussions such as Everard's *Dialogue* or Adelard of Bath's exploration of physical questions with his nephew. Gender is a second factor in the equation and plays a somewhat unusual role. The high allegorical status of most female participants in dialogues (as *Philosophia, Ecclesia, Anima,* etc.) usually serves to mitigate the lowering effects of their gender.

Peregrinus does make some rather sexist remarks, including references to "female curiosity" [1.507 and 7.382: *more femineo curiositate*] and how women are more inclined to sin (9.882–86). Theodora herself refers to "womanly lightness that delights in feminine ornament [3.398–99: *levitas muliebris*] and generally seems to accept these examples of gender stereotyping in silence. An interesting comparison here can be made with the misogynist exclamation of "Love of God" *[Amor Dei]* in the *Dialogue about a Dispute between the Love of God and a Lying Tongue:* "In a way, you are like one of the foolish women" [Modo quasi una ex stultis mulieribus es] in response to "Lying Tongue" pointing out that some powerful people are destined for hell, to which "Love of God" then retorts "I shall not burn less, if I burn with many."[64] This, however, is a particularly vituperative dialogue.

Although the latter exchange does not depend on the question of how Scripture should be interpreted, being based rather on an understanding of the nature of the world, one aspect of the *SV* dialogue (possibly indeed its greatest subtext) is the proper understanding of biblical exegesis. It does not seem to me that here Peregrinus is entirely consistent. Theodora shows herself to be quite capable of understanding the rationale for biblical exegesis. When confronted with the passage from Ecclesiastes 42.14 ("Better the wickedness of a man than the goodness of a woman"), she asks: "Does the letter hide any mystical sense or does it show that it needs to be understood differently [9.348: An aliquem sensum misticum littera celat et aliter intelligendum demonstrat?] In her request for a mystical meaning to reverse a misogynist letter she shows a perfect grasp of the concept of biblical exegesis, although the need for its application to this particular case might not have been approved by the majority of male exegetes. Peregrinus is prepared to go some of the way, however, when he replies: "You do not argue in vain in your defense, you who hope for better and closer things for your salvation in return for the sweat of your effort" [9.351–52: In defensionem tuam non frustra moveris, quae meliora et viciniora saluti pro laboris tui sudoribus speras].

On several other occasions Theodora asks for a nonliteral reading and is sometimes rebuffed for this apparently legitimate request by Peregrinus.[65] On another occasion (5.869), however, Theodora, although conceding the delightfulness on a literal or historical level of the occasion where St. John rested on the Lord's breast during the Last Supper, wonders whether there is a further mystical or allegorical significance to the action. Here Peregrinus agrees, declaring that it is of supreme significance, being symbolic of the delight of the Bride and Bridegroom, the Church and Christ. Thus Peregrinus' outburst in *SV* 12.104–12 when he exclaims, seemingly without justification: "Your ignorance urges you to tricks, so that you defend what you do not know and do not know what you defend. Very many times you revert to the letter, you who always seem to hesitate in the same mire of heedlessness . . ." [Ignorantia tua ad strophas te excitat, ut defendas, quod nescis et nescias, quod defendis. Multotiens tibi littera repetenda est, quae semper in eodem neglegentiae luto hesitare uideris . . .].

In other dialogues of this type the pupil is often allowed to make quite simple requests without being regarded as a simpleton. For example, in the *Bridlington Dialogue* the Disciple, when presented with Hebrews 4.12 "For the Speech of God is living and effective . . ." responds: "This German sounds like Greek if it is not explained." He is then favored with a literal explanation, introduced by the Master with the words "Then we must humor you."[66] In the *Soliloquies about the Instruction of the Soul,* Soul *[Anima]* admits "I have heard these words many times in Isaiah, but I do not know how they are to be understood" when Reason *[Ratio]* quotes Isaiah 14.29.[67] Reason then explains, with no signs of impatience, the terms "serpent," "root," "rule," and "seed" in terms of the mind acquiescing to the suggestions of the devil. In the *Dialogue about the Conflict between the Love of God and a Lying Tongue,* a dialogue already noted for the sharpness of the exchanges, "Love of God" agrees to an explanation of scriptural passages on various levels, when "Lying Tongue" asks, "Explain what you say, if not for me, at least for others," after an initial demurral about casting pearls before swine.[68]

Taking such points into consideration, it seems that the positions represented in the *Speculum virginum,* and the way the parties are depicted in their interactions, accord with what we know from other sources about male attitudes. Even the internalized antifeminism that Theodora expresses on occasion rings somewhat true. If we take one of the aims of the piece as being to delight its readers, I believe that it might well have struck a chord with its intended audience. This audience, I suggest, consisted of male priests with pastoral care for women, presumably with rather more advanced and liberal attitudes toward women than, say, those of Bernard of Clairvaux, and whom we might associate with the reformed orders such as Hirsau or possibly the regular canons.[69]

Finally, to return to the question of why the *Speculum* author chose to write this piece as a dialogue, we might reconsider his remarks on the uses of the genre. Examination of the *Speculum virginum* with the aim of assigning it to one of his three classifications does not in itself get us very far. Rather, the work seems to combine elements from each of his suggested motives for writing in this form. That is, it seems that Conrad chose the dialogue form to enhance the authority of its teaching.[70] He also used it for confirmation, when Theodora asks questions, sums up the arguments, and moves the discussion along. Ultimately, part of his purpose in choosing to write a dialogue appears to have been simply for his own delight. In his convincing portrayal of the complex relationship between a man and a woman, a teacher and a pupil, a monk and a nun, in short, between Peregrinus and Theodora, he has succeeded beyond all expectations.

## Notes

1. See the classic paper of Peter von Moos, "Le dialogue latin au moyen âge: L'exemple d'Everard d'Ypres," *Annales. Economies, Sciences, Civilisations* 44 (1989): 993–1028. In countering this claim, von Moos concentrates on the *Dialogus Rathii et Everardi*, written in defense of the philosophical opinions of Gilbert de la Porée, while allowing that the period produced many other dialogues that never attained such heights.

2. On the analogy of the original "long eighteenth century" and more recently "the long sixteenth century," see Part II of *Beyond the Persecuting Society*, ed. John C. Laursen and Cary J. Nederman (Philadelphia: University of Pennsylvania Press, 1998). My long twelfth century runs from about 1060 to 1220.

3. According to my count over thirty, to which should be added works whose titles are variations on the word *Soliloquium* and others with such non-indicative titles as *Stromata, Cur Deus homo*, or indeed, *Speculum virginum*. My hand list of dialogues for this period contains more than seventy items and is as yet largely confined to published examples. Whether this represents a significant increase in the proportion of dialogues compared to earlier centuries must be based on inexact methods; this is the impression, however, gained by many who have studied the literature of the period; see, for example, Giles Constable, *The Reformation of the Twelfth Century* (Cambridge: Cambridge University Press, 1996), p. 128. Peter L. Schmidt, in the *Repertorium* appended to his article "Zur Typologie und Literarisierung des Frühchristlichen Lateinischen Dialogs," in *Christianisme et formes littéraires de l'antiquité tardive en occident*, Entretiens sur l'antiquité classique 23, ed. Olivier Reverdin (Geneva:Vandeuvres, 1976), pp. 101–80, describes thirty-seven examples of dialogues written between A.D. 412 and 636.

4. R. B. C. Huygens, ed., *Accessus ad auctores. Bernard d'Utrecht. Conrad d'Hirsau, Dialogus super auctores* (Leiden: Brill, 1970), pp. 71–131; Robert Bultot, ed., *Dialogus de mundi contemptu vel amore, attribué à Conrad d'Hirsau. Extraits de l'Allocutio ad deum et du De veritatis inquisitione. Textes inédits*, Analecta Mediaevalia Namurcensia 19 (Louvain: Editions Nauwelaerts, 1966). On these texts and the *Altercatio Synagogae et Ecclesiae*, printed in Cologne in 1534, see Mews, chapter 1 in this volume.

5. While it is possible to query the identification of the author with Conrad of Hirsau and to debate whether Peregrinus was his by-name or a literary

persona, it has been established beyond doubt that the author of *SV* also wrote at least these three other dialogues.

6. This chapter is concerned with the Latin dialogue rather than the vernacular dialogue, which appears to undergo a similar burgeoning at this time. The relationship between Latin and the various vernacular literatures is a problem of some complexity that needs further study. See, for example, the remarks of Rodney M. Thomson, "The Origins of Latin Satire in Twelfth-Century Europe," in his *England and the Twelfth-Century Renaissance* (Aldershot: Ashgate, 1998), pp. 82–83.

7. See Raymond Klibansky, *The Continuity of the Platonic Tradition During the Middle Ages* (London: Warburg Institute, 1950), p. 22. Peter Dronke mentions that the *Timaeus* "was the only Platonic dialogue that was widely diffused" in the twelfth century, while the other translations available (of the *Phaedo* and the *Meno*) "appear to have had scant influence." *A History of Twelfth-Century Western Philosophy* (Cambridge: Cambridge University Press, 1988), p. 2. By contrast, Cicero's dialogues were well-known to twelfth-century writers.

8. Anselm, *De veritate*, ed. Schmitt, *SAOO* 1: 173 (Praefatio 1–5): "Tres tractatus pertinentes ad studium sacrae scripturae . . . consimiles in hoc quia facti sunt per interrogationem et responsionem."

9. *Stromata*, ed. C. de Clercq, CCCM 4 (1966): 42: "hic liber . . . socraticorum consuetudinem servabit."

10. PL 209: 425A: "libellum in Judaeos sub dialogo scripsimus."

11. PL 146: 59A: "more dialogi."

12. PL 157: 538B: "Librum autem totum distinxi per dialogum."

13. *Etymologiae* 6.8.2: "Dialogus est conlatio duorum uel plurimorum, quem Latini sermonem dicunt. Nam quos Graeci dialogos vocant, nos sermones uocamus. Sermo autem dictus quia inter utrumque seritur."

14. Conrad of Hirsau, *Dialogus super auctores*, ed. Huygens, lines 969–72: "Imitatur autem in hoc libro *[De senectute]* ex parte Platonem, ad cuius similitudinem disponit librum sub dialogo et totum introductis personis attribuit sermonem." Compare lines 1151–55: "Tres autem a Boetio inducuntur personae, Boetius miser querens ut consoletur, Philosophia quae consolatur, Boetius auctor qui de utrisque loquitur. Est enim officium eius ostendere quid misero sibi contigerit et quali consolatione Philosophia conquerentem erexerit." He makes a similar comment in *Altercatio Synagogae et Ecclesiae;* see Robert Bultot, "L'auteur de l'Altercatio Synagogae et Ecclesiae Conrad d'Hirsau?" *RTAM* 32 (1965): 268.

15. A possible exception here is the dialogue between Walter and Balduin (*Tractatus sive dialogus magistri Gualteri Tornacensis et Balduini Valentianensis contra Judaeos*, PL 209: 423B-458C) which is apparently jointly written, with Balduin arguing the part of a Jew (PL 209: 426AB).

16. See Augustine, *Soliloquiorum libri duo*, PL 32: 869–904. Augustine explains that this work consisted of "me interrogans mihi qui respondens, tamquam duo essemus ratio et ego, cum solus essem, unde hoc opus soliloquia nominaui"

(*Retractationum* 1.4, l. 1). The novelty of this undertaking is suggested by Ratio's statement in *Soliloquiorum* (PL 32: 891) "novo quidem et fortasse duro nomine, sed ad rem demonstrandam satis idoneo."

17. Charles Burnett, ed., *Studi medievali* 3a ser. 25.2 (1984): 859–94.

18. Peter Alphonsus, *Dialogi Alphonsi conversi cum Moyse Iudaeo,* PL 157: 535C–671A.

19. Adam of Dryburgh, *De tripartito tabernaculo,* PL 198: 843A–872A.

20. Everard of Ypres, *Dialogus Rathii et Everardi,* ed. Nikolaus M. Häring, "A Latin Dialogue on the Doctrine of Gilbert of Poitiers," *Mediaeval Studies* 15 (1953): 243–89, and idem, "The Cistercian Everard of Ypres and his Appraisal of the Conflict between St. Bernard and Gilbert of Poitiers," *Mediaeval Studies* 17 (1955): 143–72.

21. Von Moos, "Le dialogue," 1002.

22. See Richard W. Southern, *Scholastic Humanism and the Unification of Europe,* vol. 1 (Oxford: Blackwell, 1995), pp. 225–30.

23. Anselm of Havelberg, *Dialogi,* PL 188: 1139–1248; Gaston Salet, ed., *Dialogues. Livre 1,* SChr 118 (1966).

24. Hugh of St-Victor, *De Sacramentis,* PL 176: 17B–42B. Honorius, *Scala Coeli Major,* PL 172: 1229C–40A; *Elucidarium,* PL 172: 1109A–76D.

25. Adelard of Bath, *Quaestiones naturales,* ed. and trans. Charles Burnett, *Adelard of Bath: Conversations with His Nephew* (Cambridge: Cambridge University Press, 1998), pp. 81–235. However, this is in contrast to his *De avibus tractatus,* ed. Burnett, pp. 238–74, where the nephew's questions are simply a device to introduce information on various aspects of the care and training of hawks.

26. Honorius Augustudonensis, *Elucidarium,* PL 172: 1109A–76D.

27. My categories are slightly different from those used by Peter Schmidt in his analysis of the early Christian dialogue literature (n. 3 above). He distinguishes five main classes of dialogue, mostly but not entirely in terms of their subject matter: (1) controversy dialogue, subdivided into: (a) Jewish-Christian; (b) gentile-Christian; (c) heretical-orthodox (Manichaean, Arian, Luciferian, Pelagian, Donatist, Monophysite, Nestorian); (2) philosophical dialogue; (3) didactic dialogue; (4) hagiographical dialogue; and (5) self-reflective dialogue. I am leaving to one side a further class of more literary dialogues. These include verse debates, ranging from relatively short and lyrical pieces such as those found in the *Carmina Burana,* to what might be described as cosmological epics, such as Alan of Lille's *De Planctu naturae* and Bernard Sylvestris' *Cosmographia* (actually in the form of *prosimetrum*).

28. *Cur Deus homo,* ed. Schmitt, SAOO 2: 37–133; *De veritate,* ed. Schmitt, SAOO 1: 169–99; *De spiritu sancto,* in *The Works of Gilbert Crispin Abbot of Westminster,* ed. Anna Sapir Abulafia and Gillian Rosemary Evans (London: The British Academy, 1986), pp. 115–24.

29. Such debates raise interesting questions about their intended audience and purposes. It seems that they were aimed as much at furnishing arguments

for Christians as much as at various types of infidels. On this see further
the introduction to Odo of Tournai, *On Original Sin and a Disputation with
the Jew, Leo, Concerning the Advent of Christ*, trans. Irven Resnick (Philadelphia: University of Pennsylvania Press, 1994).

30. Peter the Venerable, *Adversus Iudaeorum inveteratam duritiem*, ed. Y. Friedman,
     CCCM 58 (1985).

31. Idung of Regensberg, *Dialogus duorum monachorum*, ed R. B. C. Huygens,
     *Studi medievali*, 3 ser. 13 (1972): 291–470; [anonymous], *Dialogus de esu
     volatilium*, PL 213: 929A-948B.

32. On these see Giles Constable, *Reformation* (n. 3 above), especially chapter 4.

33. *Vitae Ottonis episcopi Bambergensis*, ed. R. Köpke, MGH SS 12 (1856):
     721–903; *Dialogus miraculorum*, ed. Joseph Strange (Cologne: J. M. Heberle,
     1851).

34. *Dialogorum libri iv*, ed. Adalbert de Vogüé, SChr 260, 265 (1979).

35. William of Hirsau, *Musica*, ed. Denis Harbinson, Corpus Scriptorum de
     Musica 23 (Rome: American Institute of Musicology, 1975); Anselm, *De
     grammatico*, ed. Schmitt, *SAOO* 1: 141–68; see also n. 4 above.

36. On Adelard's dialogues, see n. 25 above; William of Conches, *Dragmaticon*,
     ed. I. Ronca, CCCM 152 (1997).

37. Gerhoch of Reichersberg, *De quarta vigilia noctis*, MGH Libelli de Lite 3:
     503–25; Everard of Ypres, *Summula decretalium quaestionum*, Rheims, Bib-
     liothèque municipale MS 689, fols. 1–74. See S. Kuttner, *Repertorium der
     Kanonistik (1140–1234)* 1, *Studi e Testi* 71 (Rome, 1937): 187.

38. Richard Fitz Nigel, *Dialogus de Scaccario. The Course of the Exchequer*, ed. C.
     Johnson, F. E. L. Carter, and D. E. Greenway (Oxford: Oxford University
     Press, 1983).

39. Robert of Bridlington, *Bridlington Dialogue (Colloquium magistri et discipuli
     in regulam beati Augustini de vita clericorum)*, ed. Sister Penelope (London:
     Mowbray, 1960). For the term "spiritual formation," see Barbara Newman,
     "Flaws in the Golden Bowl: Gender and Spiritual Formation in the
     Twelfth Century," in *From Virile Woman to WomanChrist* (Philadelphia: Uni-
     versity of Pennsylvania Press, 1995), pp. 19–45, esp. pp. 20–21. On Adam's
     treatise, see n. 19 above. For forty-five examples of such works, many in
     nondialogue form, see Newman's Appendix A, "Religious Literature of
     Formation, 1076–1225," on pp. 313–16.

40. Conrad of Hirsau wrote the *Dialogus super auctores*, a relatively simple ped-
     agogic exercise; the *De mundi contemptu vel amore*, a debate between a monk
     and a clerk about the secular versus religious life; the *Altercatio Synagogae
     cum Ecclesia*, a doctrinal debate; and the *Speculum virginum*, a dialogue on
     the topic of spiritual formation. See Mews, chapter 1 in this volume.

41. "Omnis autem dialogus fit tribus modis vel causis: fit enim vel causa
     maioris confirmationis, sicut in dialogo Gregorii et Petri, vel causa recre-
     ationis et delectationis, sicut invenitur in poetis, vel causa auctoritatis ut
     fides habeatur sermoni, quem auctentica persona facit." *Dialogus super auc-
     tores*, lines 972–76.

42. Cf. Cicero, *De senectute* 1.3 and *De amicitia* 1.4–6.
43. Peter's role is indicated by his saying "videor mihi utiliter non intellexisse quae dixeras, quando ex tarditate mea tantum creuit expositio tua." *Dialogi* 2.35, line 72.
44. For poetic dialogues, see the *prosimetrum* of Hildebert of Tours, *Liber de querimonia et conflictu carnis et animae,* PL 171: 989A–1004B, and Alan of Lille *Vix nodosum valeo.* While strictly speaking not a subject category, the themes of these poems (cosmology, etc.) are somewhat similar to, and often take the form of, dream visions. These are the most obviously literary dialogues and are very different from most of the other categories. On the other hand, not all poetic dialogues are like this; Laurence of Durham's *Dialogi* with its description of William Cumin's ravaging of Durham fits better in the historical category.
45. *SV* Epist. 58.
46. *Cur Deus homo* l. 11–15, ed. Schmitt, *SAOO* 1: 48: "Et quoniam ea quae per interrogationem et responsionem investigantur, multis ex maxime tardorioribus ingeniis magis patent et ideo plus placent, unum ex illis qui hoc flagitant, qui inter alios instantius ad hoc me sollicitat, accipiam mecum disputantem, ut BOSO quaerat et ANSELMUS respondeat hoc modo."
47. Richard William Southern, *Saint Anselm: A Portrait in a Landscape* (Cambridge: Cambridge University Press, 1990), p. 203.
48. *Bridlington Dialogue,* p. 2a (n. 39 above): "Siquid autem inter nos natum fuerit questionis sive de ipsa regula, sive de collocutione nostra, ne molestum tibi sit oro tam proponentem quam opponentem tarditatem meam pie tolerare, et tolerando conpetenti mihi ratione respondere, et repondendo satisfacere."
49. *De spiritali amicitia,* ed. C. H. Talbot, CCCM 1 (1971): 287–88.
50. *Dialogus de conflictu amoris dei et linguae dolosae,* PL 213: 851A–864B.
51. PL 213: 851A: "Cur autem prosopopoeia utamur, majoribus judicium relinquamus. Ipsi enim experimento noverunt, quod varietas locutionis tollit fastidium veritatis." Cf. Isidore, *Etymologiae* 2.21.45: "Prosopopoeia est, cum inanimalium et persona et sermo fingitur" presumably refers to "lingua" rather than "amor dei."
52. Everard of Ypres' dialogue, although on one level very realistic, has Ratius (Reason) as one of the chief speakers. For Adelard's *De eodem et diverso* see Burnett, *Adelard,* pp. 1–79 (n. 25 above).
53. Abelard, *Dialogus inter philosophum, Iudaeum et Christianum,* ed. Rudolf Thomas (Stuttgart: Frommann Holzboog, 1970); *Collationes,* ed. and trans. John Marenbon and Giovanni Orlandi (Oxford: Clarendon Press, 2001).
54. While "Peregrinus" is perhaps the more obvious choice to mean pilgrim, the author remarks on the appropriateness of "Theodora" (*SV* 2.437): "Non sine ratione Theodoram te dixerim, quae verbi dei tam studiosa videris, ut, quod futura es, mente precurras et totum visum in eum conuertas." Coincidentally, the twelfth-century English recluse Christina of Markyate was apparently called Theodora before her entry into religion.

55. It is interesting to note that Conrad also seems to be following his penchant for fictitious names rather than putting himself in the dialogue in his *Dialogus de mundi contemptu vel amore*. The debaters are introduced in the prologue as S and R in Bultot's MS *K;* in the Bodleian manuscript, Laud Misc. 377, the debaters appear as N and N in the prologue while the change of speaker in the body of the text is confusingly signaled by three different types of M, apparently doing duty for *matricularius* and *monachus*.

56. See n. 29 above.

57. Odo, *On Original Sin,* Prologue (n. 29 above).

58. For example, in Aelred's *De spiritali amicitia,* Walter's impatience is described at 2.1 (p. 302) in the following way: "et nunc oculos huc illucque vertebas, nunc frontem confricabas manu, nunc capillos digitis attrectabas, nunc iram ipsa facie praeferens. . . ."

59. PL 159: 271A.

60. *Laurentius von Durham: Consolatio de morte amici,* ed. Udo Kindermann (Inaugural-Dissertation der Philosophischen Fakultät der Friedrich-Alexander-Universität Erlangen-Nürnberg, 1969).

61. See Arnold Paeske, *Der Geta des Vitalis von Blois. Kritische Ausgabe* (Cologne [Paeske], 1976). For a translation, see Alison Goddard Elliott, *Seven Medieval Latin Comedies* (New York: Garland, 1984), pp. 26–49, or A. Keith Bate, *Three Latin Comedies,* Toronto Medieval Latin Texts 6 (Toronto: Pontifical Institute of Medieval Studies, 1976). Interestingly, this comedy also seems to be alluded to in the *Dialogue* of Everard of Ypres; see von Moos, "Le Dialogue," 999.

62. *De mundi contemptu vel amore,* ed. Bultot, line 99.

63. Morgan Powell, chapter 5 in this volume.

64. *Dialogus de conflictu amoris dei et linguae dolosae,* PL 213: 855A: "Non minus ardebo, si cum multis ardebo."

65. *SV* 5.284–91: "T.: Viarum istarum inicium gemino sensu ita declarasti, ut ex hoc intelligentiae nostrae nihil resederit ambigui. Vellem autem a te mistico intellectu cognoscere ea, que sequuntur in eadem lectione, ut per occasionem memoriae matris et virginis augeretur in nobis lumen intelligentie spiritalis. P.: Non hoc mihi propositum erat per allegoricos sensus scripturarum perscrutandos ocia nostra terere, sed aliquod exhortationis opusculum ad virgines Christi Christo cudere adiuvante."

66. *Bridlington Dialogue,* p. 133 (n. 39 above): "Teutonicus hoc quasi Grecum sonat, si non exponatur. . . . Morem tibi gerere necesse est."

67. *Soliloquiorum de instructione animae,* PL 198: 846D-847A: "Multoties in Isaia haec verba audivi, sed quomodo intelligenda sint nescio."

68. *Dialogus de conflictu amoris dei et linguae dolosae,* PL 213: 853D: "Si non propter me, saltem propter alios pande, quid dixeris."

69. I would not rule out the possibility that it might also have been intended for a female audience, albeit a restricted one. Because of the peculiar circumstances of medieval German library preservation, it is not sufficient to rule out the possibility of women's houses having copies from the

provenance of surviving manuscripts. Whether women might have derived an equal measure of delight from the piece is another question.

70. Although Peregrinus is not an established authority figure in the manner of Cato, as Powell points out in chapter 5, his words are in some way to be identified with the authoritative teaching of Holy Scripture.

CHAPTER 9

# THE LITERATURE OF SPIRITUAL FORMATION FOR WOMEN IN FRANCE AND ENGLAND, 1080 TO 1180

*Elisabeth Bos*

This chapter explores the extensive literature of spiritual instruction for religious women produced in France and England from the time of St. Anselm to that of Peter of Blois. It considers the question of whether or not spiritual advice for women differed from that provided to men. The chapter argues that far from simply exhorting religious women to maintain an existing state of virginity, such literature encouraged women to pursue interior growth in self-discipline and virtue. Virginity was sometimes used to refer more to religious chastity than to physical integrity. There is a close parallel here with the *Speculum virginum*, although no composition comparable in scale ever circulated in England or France during the twelfth century. There are certainly major differences between the imagery employed for writings addressed to women and imagery directed to men. The underlying spiritual principles, however, were the same.

T he ostensible aim of Peregrinus in the *Speculum virginum* is to offer instruction and encouragement to Theodora, a nun, in her pursuit of the religious life. Together they discuss the aim of the spiritual life and the particular goals to which women ought to dedicate themselves. Although the dialogue between Theodora and Peregrinus is a literary device, it nevertheless represents a relationship with which contemporary audiences would have been able to identify. The extensive Latin literature composed for the spiritual guidance of women in France and England during the late eleventh and twelfth centuries illustrates a range of collaborative efforts between women and their male counselors, similar to those evident in Germany. While no treatise comparable in scale to the *Speculum virginum* circulated in France and England during this period, numerous letters survive illustrating how clerics addressed advice to women with whom they were personally connected: sisters, nieces, mothers, patronesses, or neighboring nuns and friends.[1] The advice offered was often specifically requested by these women and, consequently, was tailored to their individual circumstances and designed to address their specific religious questions and personal struggles.

The men who undertook the considerable labor of composing letters and treatises for the edification of women frequently state that they were motivated to do so by a genuine wish to facilitate the spiritual formation of the women in question. Where affection alone could not be relied on to prompt men to pick up their pens, a sense of duty or obligation appears in some cases to have formed an equally powerful motivation. Gerhoch of Reichersberg (1132–1169), for example, addressed two letters to the nuns of Admont, the first of which presents his apologies to the ladies for having hastened away without satisfying their questions about the meaning of certain passages of Scripture.[2] He subsequently found that he was prevented by circumstances from continuing his journey and attributed this to God's anger at this omission. He therefore proffered his letter in answer to their questions and requested in return that they would pray to God to grant him a swift journey. A third letter, addressed to a nun, shows that Gerhoch maintained a correspondence with this community.[3]

Supportive as these relationships may have been, the extant literature is overwhelmingly of male composition. Teaching was explicitly a male preserve. This hierarchical imbalance between participants in these dialogues affected the way in which they engaged in discussion. Modern scholars examining the relatively large body of literature for the spiritual formation of women have differed in their interpretations of these texts. Jean Leclercq, for example, has argued that the advice which Bernard of Clairvaux addressed to women was not essentially different from the advice he gave to men, on the grounds that he considered women to be equal heirs to God's kingdom.[4] Barbara Newman agrees that there is a significant area of commonality between what she terms the "literature of spiritual formation" for men and that addressed to women, particularly where the central tenets of the monastic life were concerned.[5] Newman nevertheless opposes Leclercq's idea that spiritual advice does not differ according to the gender of the audience. In her impressive comparative study of religious literature addressed to women and to men, she isolates several differences, in particular relating to virginity. Indeed, although the subject of virginity is addressed in literature for both men and women, it was far more often presented to women as an ideal than to men. Newman is not the first to draw attention to the potentially insidious implications of emphasizing virginity as a peculiarly feminine virtue to which women ought to aspire. Marina Warner has argued that the veneration of the Virgin Mary involved proportional devaluation of other feminine roles: Virgins were lauded at the expense of women who did not, or could not, mold themselves to this narrowly defined model of perfection.[6] Certainly virginity seems to have captured the imagination of prominent Christian writers and held an established place in the traditional repertoire of images of spiritual purity.[7]

The problem of how to interpret the emphasis on virginity in twelfth-century literature of spiritual formation for women is complicated by the fact that the word *virgo* was capable of sustaining two different interpretations. It could refer equally to a woman who was physically virginal (sometimes specifically referred to as *intacta*) or to "one whose primary relationship was with God."[8] The texts themselves rarely distinguish between these two possible readings; as a result, the author's precise meaning can only be inferred from the context. Yet to a great extent our understanding of how men regarded the spiritual lives of their female contemporaries depends on which interpretation is favored. For example, if physical integrity was stressed so much more for women than for men, this would suggest that male authors regarded the spiritual goals of women as fundamentally different from their own. Indeed, this is the very conclusion reached by Barbara Newman. Although she recognizes that virginity could refer equally to physical integrity and religious chastity, her conclusions depend on the first, more narrow definition. She argues that, since the highest achievement of a woman's spiritual life was represented by virginity, "hers was a static perfection rather than a quest."[9] Newman contrasts the spiritual dynamism urged on men whereby spiritual excellence was achieved through a process of struggle and progression, which could lead the individual either to greater spiritual heights or cause him to plummet downward through sin. She concludes that the prestige associated with virginity during this period was potentially disadvantageous not only to married women, who suffered by comparison, but even to virgins since it only served to make the condition of consecrated virgins more vulnerable by proportionately increasing the shame of falling from this exalted state.

A closer examination of the literature of formation written for women reveals that where "virginity" was used to refer to religious chastity rather than physical integrity, another interpretation is possible. Many of these texts clearly indicate that women, like men, were subject to God's grace and therefore were capable of spiritual redemption even after the loss of their virginity. Furthermore, even the preservation of physical virginity was considered possible only through grace and was achieved through a process of continual struggle by the individual. Perhaps even more striking than the differences between the literature of spiritual formation—for both women and men—are the great areas of overlap in which the same foundational Christian virtues are recommended equally to both sexes. In this light, the texts relating to virginity, discussed by Leclercq and Newman as well as by other scholars, deserve to be reexamined.

Twelfth-century texts for religious women vary in the importance they attach to virginity.[10] Some authors clearly esteemed physical virginity among women as the highest goal of feminine spiritual endeavor. Osbert of Clare (fl. 1136–1153), for example, dwells on the virginity of all the women to whom he addressed his surviving letters.[11] Other writers allow for a more dynamic interpretation of virginity as a religious profession. Still others do not touch on the subject at all.[12] A survey of the literature about virginity confirms the impression that it is treated differently in different contexts. For example, Idung of Prüfening uses stock misogynist topoi about the fickleness of women in writing for a male audience, while he is respectful in writing to individual women.[13] Again, the treatment of virginity might vary depending on the circumstances of the particular woman being addressed.

The following discussion examines letters addressed specifically to women religious and discusses the values they were urged to cultivate. A central theme underpinning this value system is that of worldly sacrifice, thought to represent proportionate spiritual gain. Given the different social roles of men and women, it is hardly surprising that the pleasures that men and women were seen to sacrifice were different. The emphases that particular subjects receive in literature addressed to women perhaps derive more from assumptions about socially constructed gender roles than from differences in expectation about the spiritual capacities of men and women.

## Letters to Newly Professed Virgins

The praise of physical virginity and of its advantages over marriage was most common in literature for young virgins who had only recently made their religious profession. It may easily be imagined that the preservation of physical virginity, with all it implied of the renunciation of marriage and children, was of most immediate concern to women in this situation. A letter of Peter of Blois (ca. 1135–1204) to the newly professed virgin, Anselma, described her frame of mind in such detail that it seems clear he was responding to concerns that she had confided to him.[14] The resultant picture demonstrates very clearly the anxieties that a newly professed nun might have, particularly concerning the potential delights that she had forgone in order to consecrate herself to God. Peter alludes to the fact that Anselma's parents had destined her for marriage and betrothed her to the (unidentified) nephew of the duke of Burgundy. Her betrothed, Peter wrote, was young and physically attractive; both in his skill at arms and his elegance of form he was held to be astonishing and amazing in the eyes of men. What, asked Peter, could fascinate the mind of a young woman more than this young man who was refined in his words, wealthy, and profusely generous? Moreover, Anselma's prospective husband was pre-eminent among the magnates of his province. Marriage to him would offer not only the chance for affection to flourish but for her worldly eminence to increase.[15] Peter described the life she might have looked forward to: abundant wealth, rich accoutrements, the company of numerous relatives, and the joy of children. He then contrasted these glorious expectations with the prospect that now confronted Anselma, the narrow cloister that she would never be permitted to leave, where all laughter, all playfulness, and all pleasures of the world were removed, where she must wear funereal cloths and undertake continual vigils, where the wine was diluted with water and the food was austere. The contrast Peter drew between the pleasures of the world and the bleakness of the convent is so striking that the reader is left wondering who, faced with such a choice, would choose the convent.

In the second part of his letter Peter reversed this impression of the bleakness of the cloister by representing the spiritual benefits of the choice she had made and attempting to persuade her of the evils of secular life. The pleasures she had forsaken, he wrote, were sterile and uncertain, if indeed they should be considered pleasures at all: "the pomp of the world and the favor of the people is smoke, and gold suddenly vanishes. Add that a woman gives birth in great sorrow and risk; and that most frequently more bitter misfortune interrupts the glory of sons now with weakness, now with captivity, now with death."[16] It was common for treatises written with a young virginal audience in mind to portray married life and motherhood in the most undesirable light, by contrast with virginity, which they represent as not only superior but more comfortable. Works such as *Hali Meidhad* and the letter of Hildebert of Le Mans (1055–1133) to the recluse Athalisa dwell at length on the horrors of married life; the repression of being ruled by a husband; the indignity, pain, and danger of childbirth; and the cares of motherhood.[17] The undisguised aim of male authors in so writing was to encourage such women to persevere in the spiritual life. The lengths to which they go in order to stress these themes suggest that some women, who would have preferred marriage, entered the cloister from necessity rather than choice.

Arnulf, bishop of Lisieux (d. 1182), corresponded with one such nun.[18] Since the age of seven G. had been betrothed to Arnulf's brother. G.'s monastic profession seems to have come about not through any particular piety but through lack of alternatives once her fiancé had died. As with Peter of Blois in writing to Anselma, Arnulf was almost certainly responding to confidences from G. as to her state of mind. His letter provides a glimpse of the kind of troubles most affecting her. G. must have frankly acknowledged her love for Arnulf's brother, her pleasure in the anticipation of their marriage, her physical attraction to him, her hopes for children, and her consequent sense of loss at his death. Replacement of her expectation of a prosperous life of marriage and children suddenly with a life confined to the perpetual and unchanging routine of the convent was traumatic and required considerable adjustment.

Like Peter writing to Anselma, Arnulf attempted to persuade G. that her worldly loss represented a spiritual gain and had come about through God's will and, indeed, by his grace. Arnulf described how marriage would have corrupted G.'s virginity with filth and ground the flower of her youth to dust. Instead, God had generously granted her the chance to remain perpetually pure, to follow him in all things and to ensure her own salvation by singing "that spiritual song with the assigned thousands."[19] Arnulf argued that the physical desire that she felt for his brother needed only to be translated into spiritual desire for God. Moreover, the preservation of her virginity was represented as imperative to ensuring the complete devotion of her soul to God. Therefore, the love that stirred up the passions of the corrupt flesh was to be firmly regulated. Arnulf reassured G. that this would cease in time and be replaced with the incorruptible love of God. Like Abelard writing to Heloise, both Peter and Arnulf dwell on the superiority of virginity in order to persuade Anselma and G. to continue in their religious profession and to reconcile them to their lot.

The significance of physical virginity in this literature was multifaceted. Virginity was thought to represent a condition of unsullied purity that allowed virgins to be more closely united to God. It also indicated the virtuous renunciation of the pleasures of marriage and children as well as an ongoing spiritual struggle against the lusts of the flesh. Marbod, bishop of Rennes (ca. 1035–1123), writing to the nun Agenorid, named this sacrifice as the greatest.[20] The decision to preserve physical virginity was thought to signify certain things about a woman's spiritual condition. Women who had made vows of perpetual chastity were viewed as special recipients of God's grace, which allowed them both to make this vow and which gave them the strength to keep it. Aelred, abbot of Rievaulx (1110–1167), expressed this idea that the vow of virginity was a spontaneous offering in his De institutione inclusarum, addressed to his sister.[21]

Rather than a decision once made that then became easy, the suppression of sexual temptation for both men and women was understood to be a perpetual concern. The process of resisting temptation required continual moral vigor and effort.[22]

## Writing for Women Making Religious Profession after Marriage

Other virtues, apart from virginity, were also available to women who chose to live a life of religious chastity after marriage. Although these women might already have borne children, widows were nevertheless congratulated on the decision to forsake future marriages. For example, in his only surviving letter to Empress Agnes (ca. 1025–1077), Jean de Fécamp (1028–1078) congratulated her on her decision not to remarry and commended her as an example to other widows: "And although nobility, wealth, and age might invite you to seek the marriage bed again, yet you did not wish to incline your heart to the words of men, to the false things of flattering men, rather than to true things; but elevated upwards with girded loins you have stood strongly on your feet."[23] Similarly, victory over sexual impulses was no less virtuous in women who had been married than it was in virgins. Nor was the victory ever complete; chastity, like virginity, was praiseworthy partly because it connoted sufficient moral vigor to continually overcome inevitable temptation. For example, in writing to Heloise, Abelard contrasted her victory with his own situation and described how, although he remained chaste, his victory was not equivalent to hers since he did not have to overcome the same temptation: "for the one who must always strive there is also a crown; and the athlete cannot win his crown unless he has kept to the rules. But no crown is waiting for me, because no cause for striving remains. The matter of strife is lacking in him from whom the thorn of desire is pulled out."[24]

Many of the praiseworthy attributes associated with physical virginity, far from being static, were valued because they connoted a victorious spiritual struggle. This struggle centered on the temptation to indulge in worldly gratification and to succumb to sexual impulses. Virgins and chaste religious women were both praised for what this was thought to imply about their spiritual condition. Both had received special grace from God to make and keep their vows of chastity. The receipt of this grace presupposed individual moral vigor and personal dedication to the service of God. This is illustrated by the fact that the physical virginity of young secular girls was praised only when a vow of perpetual virginity was consecrated to the service of God. Indeed, Jo Ann McNamara draws attention to the medieval understanding that "women who had never known sexual activity *became* virgins by taking a vow of consecration."[25] Women were praised for giving up their generative potential only when their energies were thereby redirected toward something deemed to be productive in spiritual terms. Hildebert of Le Mans referred to this concept in his letter to Athalisa the recluse: "There is no virgin unless she clings [to the Bridegroom]; no chaste woman, unless she may esteem him; no free woman, unless she may serve him."[26] Only when virginity was consecrated as a sacrifice to God and was seen to represent total dedication of the self to God, body and soul, was it considered to be a spiritual advantage.

To overstress the importance attached to physical virginity for men and women by twelfth-century theologians is also to underestimate the contemporary understanding of the working of God's grace to redeem fallen humanity. Aelred's *De institutione inclusarum* operates, on one level, as a confession of his own sinful youth and as a personal testament to his experience of God's redemption.[27] He represents himself and his former licentiousness as the soul who fled from God's love but has now returned, while his virginal sister has always remained in God's love.[28] Aelred's discussion clearly suggests that physical virginity, although a great advantage in spiritual terms, may still be equaled or exceeded by one reformed through the grace of God. He urges his sister to emulate his own dedication to the religious life. She has a spiritual advantage of unsullied sexual purity while Aelred must struggle to atone for the loss of his virginity. Nevertheless, Aelred intimates that zeal such as his was still indispensable to her spiritual development: "How you would have to blush if after all my sins I were found equal to you in the next life. The glory of virginity is often tarnished by vices which make their way in later on, while the reformation of a man's life and the replacement of vices by virtues can cancel the infamy of his former behavior."[29] The import of Aelred's treatise is that "God's grace comes equally to saint and sinner, in this case, sister and brother" and thus does not distinguish according to gender.[30]

### Virginity and Spiritual Progress

The dynamism expected of women's spiritual lives could alter their spiritual status in the eyes of God. Although virgins might theoretically begin with a spiritual advantage over other women, this advantage did not represent a permanent status quo. St. Anselm, for example, sought to persuade Gunhilda, the daughter of King Harold who had left the convent of Wilton to be married, that the loss of her virginity was not an insurmountable obstacle to holiness, provided that she return to Wilton and resume her habit.[31] He explained: "your Lord [is] . . . calling you back so that you may be his lawful bride, and if not a virgin, at least chaste. For we know of many holy women who, having lost their virginity, were more pleasing to God and were closer to him through penitence in their chastity than many others, even though holy in their virginity."[32] Similarly, Peter of Blois addressed a sermon to a community of nuns among whom were women who were not virgins in the physical sense, either because they had been married virtuously or had succumbed to lewd desire. Such women, Peter said, although they might follow the Lamb, according to the depiction of the faithful in Revelations 14.3–4, were lame in one foot and therefore could not equal virgins who had both the "foot of virginity" and the "foot of humility" still intact. Nevertheless, Peter commended these women who were no longer virgins, because they would be more eager to remake what was broken: With as much energy as they had formerly entered into filth and iniquity, they would pursue justice and sanctification.[33]

The preservation of physical virginity alone was not sufficient to secure a woman's spiritual status. Advice to specific religious women warns against complacency on this score. Peter the Venerable selected various excerpts from the works of Augustine, Ambrose, and Jerome, relating to virginity and the rewards of virgins, for the instruction of his nieces, Margaret and Pontia.[34] His concern was aroused by a letter that they had sent to him containing medicinal advice to alleviate his illness. Such concern for the body was, wrote Peter, an unsuitable interest for the virgins of Christ. He reminded them that St. Agatha never offered carnal medicine to her body; and were they not, just like Agatha, handmaidens and brides of Christ? Peter described how greatly he would rejoice if Margarita and Pontia, virgins of his blood, should be found acceptable to serve those great virgins Agatha, Agnes, Faith, and, of course, Mary, as footmaidens. From the hierarchical distinction that he drew between these different virgins, the saints, and his nieces, as well as his emphasis on their need for spiritual progression, it is apparent that Peter did not view physical virginity as perfection in itself.

Peter's discussion makes it plain that virgins could be more or less virtuous depending on the extent to which they had committed themselves to God. Although physical virginity was a great spiritual advantage, Margarita and Pontia needed to be sure that God would associate them not only with a virginal body but with a virginal mind. To this end, they were exhorted to arrange their lives, order their morals, fight the good fight, imitate their sisters and mothers in Marcigny and particularly the beloved memory of Peter's own mother Raingard, who had brought them to that community: "All who are living with you are not virgins in flesh still, they are just as father Augustine says, virgins in faith. . . . Where flesh cannot be whole from sexual intercourse a conscience may be a virgin in faith; according to this the whole Church is a virgin."[35] Similarly, in the letter to

Agenorid mentioned earlier, Marbod of Rennes praised Agenorid's pious intentions to preserve her virginity but nevertheless warned her to pursue holiness diligently by avoiding levity and by cultivating virtue of mind, "because it is praiseworthy not to begin but to perfect."[36]

## The Significance of Monastic Profession

The imperative of continually striving for spiritual progress is a recurring theme in devotional literature for women as well as for men. Although chastity contributed toward sanctification, the demands of the spiritual life were considerably more wide-reaching. Spiritual status depended on the degree to which an individual was thought to have surrendered to the miraculous and transforming grace of God. Dedication to God and personal sacrifice for him were the qualities that informed the value-system according to which religious merit was assessed.

The men who offered women spiritual guidance were unanimous in the opinion that the best manner in which to progress was within a monastic setting, since it allowed for greater personal dedication to God. This opinion is apparent both in their exhortations to certain women to enter convents and in their rejoicing over those who had chosen to make such a profession. That male religious counselors should hold such opinions, given that many of them had made such monastic professions themselves, is not surprising. Yet monastic profession was considered equally spiritually valuable for women as for men. For example, Hildebert of Le Mans' letter to a certain *puella conversa* makes it plain that he considered her profession in the same light as his own: "I have provided this healthy counsel for you from the heart. For I also have retired to flee from those things most frequently with all triumph: in this way there is no dowry more acceptable to the bridegroom than flight."[37] Goscelin reflects a similar attitude in his writing for Eve of Wilton.[38] Since only the monastic vocation represented absolute abandonment of the self to God, it was considered by some to be the most effective way of placing oneself on the path to salvation.

Salvation was not a certainty for all who dwelt in monasteries, but it was a significant goal in the quest for perfection for both men and women. This understanding informs Anselm's guidance to several secular women who, by their pious lives and support of ecclesiastical reform, had won his special respect. In the letter addressed to Countess Matilda of Tuscany, Anselm thanked her for her help in preserving his safety while he was traveling to Rome. He acknowledged that her work in protecting the papacy was invaluable to God's purpose and therefore recognized that she must continue in the world, regardless of the strength of her desire to retire from it.[39] Nevertheless, he cautioned her: "If you see yourself threatened by certain danger of death—which God avert!—give yourself totally to God before you leave this life, and for this purpose you should always have secretly in your possession a veil which you have prepared."[40] It seems clear that Anselm thought the monastic life the best indication of total dedication to God and therefore almost a prerequisite for salvation. Shortly before his death, Anselm composed a particularly affectionate letter to Countess Atla (probably Adela of Blois, sister of Henry I), exhorting her to enter a monastery for the good of her soul: "If only I could hear, before I die, that this has been accomplished by the grace of God. Truly I say to you that my soul would leave my body more happily."[41] In another letter, Anselm addressed a Lady Ermengard whose husband wished to become a monk. He argued that by refusing to allow this, Ermengard was harming her husband spiritually and damaging his chances of salvation. Rather, Anselm prayed that she too would take vows so that she might be equal to her husband in the heavenly kingdom.[42]

Monastic profession, as a total commitment of the self to God, was equally valuable for both sexes. Yet because secular women were usually under the authority of a male family member, they had less freedom to dedicate themselves to the service of God as daughters, wives, and mothers than their sons, husbands, and fathers. Ermengarde, Countess of Brittany (d. 1147), for example, at one time fled from her marriage to Count Alan (d. 1116), which she declared to be consanguineous, and placed herself under the protection of Robert of Arbrissel in Fontevrault. The Church, however, upheld the legitimacy of her marriage and forced her to return to the world. Although he appears to have regarded her spiritual dedication as preferable to this, Robert composed a treatise for Ermengarde, offering instruction on how to progress spiritually in the world.[43] He insists that the pressures of court life need not exclude all time for private prayer, reading, and reflection. Nevertheless, Robert's letter recognizes that the other activities entailed in court life, which included the hearing of petitions and the administration of justice as well as her duties to her family, would clearly limit the degree to which Ermengarde could focus exclusively on God.[44]

Next to virginity, widowhood was represented by twelfth-century male authors as a desirable status for women. After retirement to a convent, widowhood offered a degree of independence, allowing those who wished to, to disengage themselves from worldly cares and concentrate exclusively on God.[45] The negative representations of the conditions and limitations of married women in the literature of spiritual formation have already been noted. The spiritual hierarchy that placed virgins above widows and widows above wives corresponds with the degree of freedom that these women had on a practical level to dedicate themselves to the service of God.

## The Pursuit of Virtue

Not only was the form of religious life similar for women and men but
the spiritual goals to which they were to aspire were essentially the same.
Both monks and nuns were to observe modesty of demeanor and dress.
Both men and women were to pursue Christ-likeness represented by the
virtues of charity, humility, and obedience.[46] It will suffice to give a few
examples of the great many to be found in the twelfth-century literature
of formation for women. Obedience is an important theme in many letters of Anselm, who insists that true obedience cannot be measured by
outward appearances alone.[47] The kind of obedience that Anselm required
of the nuns was absolute and admitted no degrees of commitment.[48] In
one of his sermons to a community of religious women, Peter of Blois af-
firmed that chastity transcended all other virtues. Nevertheless he was
adamant that it was not pleasing to God unless it was combined with
charity.[49] Peter reminded the nuns that the apostle Paul (1 Cor. 7.25) only
recommended chastity to those who were able to bear it and did not instruct everyone to remain chaste. On the other hand, the Gospel (Matth.
18.3–4) stated that humility was a prerequisite for salvation. "Because the
Holy Spirit does not rest except over a humble and gentle man you see
that humility with virginity is more acceptable before God, because without this [humility] no one can be saved. Without the other [virginity] indeed, many can be saved." Peter further reminded his audience of the
words of the Magnificat: "for He has considered the humility of his hand-
maiden." Following the thought of Augustine, Peter reasoned that it was
not Mary's virginity alone that caused her to be exalted, but only her virginity combined with humility.[50] He condemned arrogant virgins and as-
serted that: "there is nothing . . . which also blackens the lily of chastity
more totally than arrogance."[51] Of central importance is charity: "Indeed
you have received the grace of Christ in emptiness, carrying off an empty
lamp, if you do not have the oil of charity, that is, if you do not esteem
Christ from your whole heart."[52]

Humility was an essential aspect of individual spiritual progress. Bernard
of Clairvaux encouraged Hildegard of Bingen to use her prophetic gift
wisely and not to become proud: "I congratulate you on the grace of God
that is in you and admonish you to regard it as a gift and respond to it with
all humility and devotion in the sure knowledge that God flouts the scorn-
ful, and gives the humble man his grace."[53] Commenting on this letter,
Leclercq points out that Bernard's approval of Hildegard's spiritual life was
determined by, and dependent on, her humility. Bernard reminded her that
according to St. James, "God only gives grace to the humble."[54] God could
work through Hildegard only as long as she remained humble.

Modesty of demeanor was another common theme in the literature of spiritual formation for women. Aelred of Rievaulx advised his sister to guard her speech: "Your every word and action should be graced with modesty: it is modesty which bridles the tongue, calms an angry mood and prevents quarreling. Since a recluse should blush to speak even when it is to speak judiciously, how deeply must she blush if she allows resentment or anger to goad her into speaking injudiciously."[55] Indulgence in frivolous talk and gossip were considered signs of a weaker commitment to the monastic life. Bernard severely criticized the former frivolity of a certain nun who, having lived a worldly life for many years, had now told him of her decision to reform: "Why did you feign by the veil on your head a gravity that your impudent glances belied? The veil you wore covered a haughty brow, under the outward guise of modesty you carried a saucy tongue in your head. Your unrestrained giggles, wanton bearing, good attire, were more becoming to a coiffure than a veil!"[56] Bernard praised the reform that this woman had effected in her own behavior and rejoiced that "under the leadership of Christ the old habits have passed away." The fact that she could have behaved in such a manner, Bernard reasons, demonstrates that she had not yet submitted to the Holy Spirit, who "breathes, not only where he will, but also when he wills." Nevertheless, Bernard warned her that now the Holy Spirit had breathed on her, a relapse to her previous ways would be inexcusable.

These concerns were essentially the same as those that exercised men who had taken an equivalent monastic vow. Leclercq has concluded that Bernard's advice to women was not essentially different from the advice he gave men by reason of the fact that he considered women to be equal inheritors of God's kingdom. Steady spiritual progress, by means of careful and continual surveillance of the condition of the heart, is also a recurring theme in Anselm's letters to various female religious houses as well as to monks. In two letters to the community of St. Edward's, Shaftesbury, for example, Anselm offered the nuns advice on how to implement the ideal of spiritual progress in everyday life. Although he explained that no one could be sure of salvation, this hope was stronger for those who daily strove toward an ideal of spiritual perfection:

As long as man lives, he either ascends toward heaven by living a good life or descends into hell by living an evil life. If, therefore, you wish to attain what you vowed, it is necessary that you progress towards it by holy deeds, as if step by step. Therefore diligently examine the course of your life, not only in deeds but also in words, and not only in these but also in your slightest thoughts.[57]

Ten years later he again touched on this theme of the dynamic quality of the religious life: "Your intention should always be to strive for progress and to dread regress with all your heart. For it is written 'that one who despises little things fails little by little.'"[58]

## Conclusion

Underpinning all of these virtues is the theme of worldly sacrifice. Virtues could appear more or less excellent in different individuals according to the degree of personal sacrifice involved. This principle was illustrated earlier in the case of virginity. The consecration of a physical virgin was considered laudable for many reasons, among them the fact that she had demonstrated that her love for God was greater than her desire for the worldly gratification of marriage and children. In the same way, the monastic profession of a noble woman was considered laudable for the renunciation of wealth. Although poverty was expected of all nuns, there does appear to have been some correlation between the degree of earthly glory forsaken by women and the spiritual splendor they thereby attained. To be poor and sacrifice wealth was no sacrifice at all. On the other hand, to disdain all the glory of the world for the love of God was considered highly meritorious.[59] Bernard of Clairvaux's letter to the virgin Sophia is a good illustration of this theme. Praising Sophia on her rejection of worldly glory, Bernard commented on how unusual such devotion was among the nobility, and particularly among noble women: "Moral vigor amongst men is 'a rare bird on earth' but it is even more so among refined and noble women. 'Who will find a vigorous woman?' the Scriptures ask, but it is much harder to find one who is also of high birth."[60] He continued to reason that "God is no respecter of persons" and therefore nobility should not be weighed in the balance, but even so, virtue seemed to him more pleasing in the nobility: He could feel sure that they are being virtuous by choice rather than by simple necessity.

Although theologically insupportable, it is nevertheless easy to understand how the monastic dedication of a member of the nobility might seem a greater sacrifice in comparison with a similar profession from one of lesser rank.[61] The letter of Marbod of Rennes to Vital of Savigny, in which he requested that Vital accept a certain orphan into his new women's foundation, made it plain that this girl could not aspire, by reason of her poverty, to enter an older, more established institution.[62] Neither of her parents was available to take care of her, she had no friends or relatives, and Marbod described her as destitute. Clearly entry into a religious foundation would represent great improvement in fortune to one in this orphan's circumstances. By contrast, the alternatives that noblewomen faced were significantly more appealing and their decision to renounce these delights was considered correspondingly more meritorious.

This correlation between the degree of worldly sacrifice and the proportion of spiritual merit attained also may help to explain certain other differences between the literature of formation for men and women. For example, beauty, like virginity, is much more commonly touched on in literature for women. The earthly glory that women had theoretically surrendered upon entering the religious life was represented as dust and ashes in comparison with the spiritual glory they had thereby attained. In his letter to the recently professed virgin Sophia, Bernard of Clairvaux addressed these issues at some length. He reassured her of the superiority of the spiritual equivalent to the worldly goods that she was forsaking. He dwelt on the spiritual crown that the Lord had prepared for Sophia in eternity and the glory of Christ, her Bridegroom: "If the daughters of Babylon have anything like this, let them bring it forth, whose only glory is their shame. They are clothed in purple and fine linen, but their souls are in rags. Their bodies glitter with jewels, but their lives are foul with vanity. You, on the contrary, whilst your body is clothed in rags, shine gloriously within, but in the sight of heaven, not of the world."[63] Osbert of Clare, by way of preamble in a letter of praise to Matilda of Darenth, wrote: "You shine out among distinguished women by the splendors of birth but you glitter more serenely by the brightnesses of your virtues."[64] Aelred warned his sister not to covet costly jewels or ornament: "Leave such things to people who have nothing within themselves in which to glory and so must seek their pleasure in outward things."[65] Her glory, he said, was in her marriage to Christ and her status as daughter to the King of Heaven. Her ornaments should be chastity, humility, simplicity, prudence, mercy, and justice. In all these things, it was not the outward circumstances of women in themselves that were perceived to be spiritually meritorious but what these circumstances were thought to signify about the inner, spiritual commitment of the individual woman. The monastic profession, for women as well as for men, represented a symbolic renunciation of self, home, family, wealth, marriage, and worldly pleasures that might distract the individual from serving God undividedly. It also created the conditions in which individuals were free from worldly responsibility and the authority of their families.

Women were especially praised for renouncing precisely those things that they were thought particularly to covet. These were the most likely impediments to women dedicating themselves entirely to the service of God. Virginity was virtuous partly because it indicated the pious renunciation of marriage and children, a prospect that many women apparently regarded with great anticipation. A vow of poverty was more virtuous in those of noble birth because it indicated the sacrifice of worldly comfort and the privileges or rank. Most especially for women, the sacrifice of worldly ornament, beauty, jewelry, and costly attire attracted the praise of clerical men. All of these things may be seen to represent the highest ambitions of secular women. Perhaps it is for this reason that they occupy such a prominent place in the literature of formation for religious women but not in that for men.

There is room for both perspectives in relation to the question of whether the literature of formation for women was essentially the same as that addressed to men. As Leclercq argues, the spiritual principle underlying the religious lives of men and woman was seen as essentially the same. Nevertheless, literature for women does dwell at great length on certain subjects, notably virginity, marriage, wealth, children, clothing, and beauty. Newman is right to draw attention to these differences. These differences, however, relate more to social roles and aspirations than to spiritual ideology. These contrasting roles and expectations are reflected in differences in the treatment of certain subjects within the literature of spiritual formation. The spiritual principles underpinning the lives of religious men and women remained fundamentally the same.

### Notes

1. For fuller discussion, see Elisabeth Bos, "Relationships of Religious Guidance Between Men and Women in the Twelfth Century" (Ph.D. diss., Cambridge University, 1999).

2. Gerhoch, Letters 26 and 28, PL 193: 607–11 and 614–18.

3. Gerhoch, Letter 27, PL 193: 611–14.

4. Jean Leclercq, "Does St Bernard Have a Specific Message for Nuns?" in *Medieval Religious Women: Distant Echoes,* ed. J. A. Nichols and L. T. Shank (Kalamazoo, MI: Cistercian Publications, 1987), pp. 276–77. Alcuin Blamires argues that Marbod of Rennes held similar views to Bernard; *The Case for Women in Medieval Culture* (Oxford: Clarendon Press, 1997), p. 20.

5. Barbara Newman, "Flaws in the Golden Bowl: Gender and Spiritual Formation in the Twelfth Century," *Traditio* 45 (1989/90): 113; reprinted in her volume of essays, *From Virile Woman to WomanChrist* (Philadelphia: University of Pennsylvania Press, 1995), p. 21.

6. Marina Warner, *Alone of All Her Sex: The Myth and Cult of the Virgin Mary* (London: Picador, 1990), pp. 77–78.

7. Jane T. Schulenburg, "The Heroics of Virginity: Brides of Christ and Sacrificial Mutilation," in *Women in the Middle Ages and the Renaissance: Literary and Historical Perspectives,* ed. M. B. Rose (Syracuse, NY: Syracuse University Press, 1986), pp. 29–72.

8. Newman, "Flaws in the Golden Bowl," p. 30. Bella Millet and Jocelyn Wogan-Browne acknowledge the importance of this second definition in

their introduction to *Medieval English Prose for Women: Selections from the Katherine Group and Ancrene Wisse* (Oxford: Clarendon Press, 1990), p. xv. Jo Ann McNamara further points out that within the Christian tradition, virginity was "defined by intention and behaviour rather than physical accident." *Sisters in Arms: Catholic Nuns through Two Millennia* (Cambridge, MA: Harvard University Press, 1996), p. 3.

9. Newman, "Flaws in the Golden Bowl," 143 (n. 5 above).

10. Throughout its history, this division of fruitful Christians into the virginal, the widowed, and the married had always referred to both male and female Christians. John Bugge, *"Virginitas": An Essay in the History of a Medieval Ideal* (The Hague: International Archives of the History of Ideas, 1975), p. 67. It is quite unusual, however, to find physical virginity discussed in the context of male spirituality. Exceptions include a lament of a man for the loss of his virginity by St. Anselm, *SAOO* 3: 80–83. Aelred of Rievaulx also lamented the sexual promiscuity of his youth before his conversion in *De institutione inclusarum* in *Aelredi Rievallensis, Opera Omnia*, ed. A. Hoste and C. H. Talbot, CCCM 1 (1971): 673–76. He pointed out that the virginity of both sexes was pleasing to God, consecrated in the Virgin Mary and John, *De inst. inclusarum*, 658–59. If virginity in the physical sense was not an exclusively feminine virtue, Newman is quite right when she points out that "male chastity . . . never evoked either the same rapturous praise for its preservation or the same dire warnings about its loss." "Flaws in the Golden Bowl," p. 28 (n. 5 above).

11. Osbert, Letters 21, 22, 40, 41, and 42, *The Letters of Osbert of Clare:. Prior of Westminster*, ed. E. W. Williamson (Oxford: Oxford University Press, 1929), pp. 89–91, 91–96, 135–40, 140–53, 153–79.

12. See "The *Liber confortatorius* of Goscelin of St. Bertin," ed. C. H. Talbot, *Studia Anselmiana* 37 (Rome, 1955): 1–117. Goscelin deals with many subjects but virginity is not among them.

13. R. B. C. Huygens, ed., "Le moine Idung et ses deux ouvrages: *Argumentum super quatuor questionibus* et *Dialogus duorum monachorum*," *Studi Medievali*, 3rd ser., 13 (Spoleto, 1972), 361; *An Argument Concerning Four Questions*, in *Cistercians and Cluniacs: The Case for Cîteaux*, trans. J. F. O'Sullivan and ed. J. Leahey (Kalamazoo, MI: Cistercian Publications, 1977), p. 176. See also his letter to the Abbess Kunigunde of Niedermunster, "Le moine Idung et ses deux ouvrages," 375–76.

14. Peter of Blois, Letter 35, PL 207: 113–14.

15. On the subject of marriage as a bond characterized by affection, see Jean Leclercq, *Monks on Marriage: A Twelfth-Century View* (New York: Seabury Press, 1982), p. 2, and James A. Brundage, "Sexual Equality in Medieval Canon Law," in *Medieval Women and the Sources of Medieval History*, ed. J. T. Rosenthal (Athens: University of Georgia Press, 1990), p. 71.

16. Peter of Blois, Letter 35, PL 207: 114B.

17. *Hali Meidhad*, in *Medieval English Prose for Women*, ed. and trans. Millet and Wogan-Browne (n. 8 above), pp. 2–43; Hildebert, Letter 21, PL 171: 193–97.

18. Letter 5, *The Letters of Arnulf of Lisieux*, ed. Frank Barlow (London: Royal Historical Society, 1939), p. 8.

19. Letter 5, ed. Barlow, p. 8; Arnulf is referring to Rev. 14.3–4, which speaks of those who are saved on the day of Judgment.

20. Marbod of Rennes, Letter 5, PL 171: 1475.

21. Aelred, *De institutione inclusarum*, CCCM 1: 650; trans. M. P. Macpherson, "A Rule of Life for a Recluse," *Aelred of Rievaulx: Treatises and the Pastoral Prayer* (Kalamazoo, MI: Cistercian Publications, 1971), p. 62.

22. Aelred, *De institutione inclusarum*, CCCM 1: 653; trans. Macpherson, p. 66.

23. "Lettre à l'imperatrice Agnès," *Un Maître de la vie spirituelle au XIe siècle, Jean de Fécamp*, ed. J. Leclercq and J. P. Bonnes (Paris: Vrin, 1946), p. 212.

24. Letter 5, ed. Muckle, "The Personal Letters between Abelard and Héloïse," *Mediaeval Studies* 17 (1955): 93; trans. Betty Radice, *The Letters of Abelard and Heloise* (Harmondsworth: Penguin, 1974), p. 154.

25. McNamara, *Sisters in Arms*, p. 3 (n. 8 above).

26. Hildebert, Letter 21, PL 171: 196B.

27. Marsha Dutton-Stuckey, "A Prodigal Writes Home: Aelred of Rievaulx's *De institutione inclusarum*," in *Heaven on Earth: Studies in Medieval Cistercian History*, ed. E. R. Elder (Kalamazoo, MI: Cistercian Publications, 1983), pp. 36–37.

28. Ibid., p. 37.

29. Aelred, *De institutione inclusarum*, CCCM 1: 676; trans. Macpherson, 95–96.

30. Dutton-Stuckey, "A Prodigal Writes Home," p. 38. Newman interprets this passage differently. She sees Aelred as asserting his (male) capacity for moral progress, which can make up for his former lapses, and contrasting this with his sister's static, although elevated, moral condition which is determined by her physical *integritas*, "her being, not her doing" (Newman, "Flaws in the Golden Bowl," p. 30; n. 5 above). However, there is nothing in Aelred's text to indicate that he does not consider his sister equally capable of progress. He says the opposite; she should be ashamed if she has not progressed, if her virginity comprises the entire measure of her spiritual stature. She ought to outshine him because she has never lapsed and therefore, theoretically, has spent her whole life in progress.

31. For a discussion of these letters, see Rosemary Beare, "Anselm's Letters to Gunhild, Daughter of King Harold," *Prudentia* 28 (1996): 25–35.

32. Anselm, Letter 168, SAOO 4: 43–46; trans. Walter Fröhlich, *The Letters of Saint Anselm of Canterbury*, 3 vols. (Kalamazoo, MI: Cistercian Publications: 1990–94), 2: 66–67.

33. Peter of Blois, Sermon 64, PL 207: 748BC. Aelred of Rievaulx described how his loss of physical virginity had made him more zealous to progress spiritually, *De institutione inclusarum*, CCCM 1: 675–76.

34. Letter 185, *The Letters of Peter the Venerable*, ed. Giles Constable, 2 vols. (Cambridge, MA: Harvard University Press, 1967), 1: 429–33.

35. Ibid., 1: 434.

36. Marbod, Letter 5, PL 171: 1475.

37. Hildebert, Letter 13, PL 171: 178BC.

38. Gopa Roy, "'Sharpen Your Mind with the Whetstone of Books': The Female Recluse as Reader in Goscelin's *Liber confortatorius*, Aelred of Rievaulx's *De institutione inclusarum* and the *Ancrene Wisse*," in *Women, the Book and the Godly: Selected Proceedings of the St. Hilda's Conference 1993*, ed. L. Smith and J. H. M. Taylor (Cambridge: D. S. Brewer: 1995), p. 16.

39. Herbert E. J. Cowdrey discusses Matilda's desire to enter a convent, in *Gregory VII, 1073–1085* (Oxford: Clarendon Press, 1998), p. 624. Matilda's care for Anselm's situation in exile is attested to by her letter of intercession on his behalf to Pope Paschal II, Letter 350, *SAOO* 5: 289–90.

40. Letter 325, *SAOO* 5: 256–57; trans. Fröhlich, 3: 39.

41. Letter 447, *SAOO* 5: 395; trans. Fröhlich, 3: 232. The women living at Bec had not made formal professions, and nor had Gunhilda, but Anselm apparently considered these women to be totally committed to God. See Letters 22, 68, 98, 118, and 147, in which Anselm mentions or sends greetings to Eve, Crispin, and Basilia of Gournay, widows at Bec, *SAOO* 3: 129, 188, 228–29, 255–56, 293–94; trans. Fröhlich, 1: 113, 191, 247, 283, 333.

42. Letter 134, *SAOO* 3: 276–78; trans. Fröhlich, 1: 310–11.

43. "Lettre inédite de Robert d'Arbrissel à la Comtesse Ermengarde," ed. J. De Petigny, *Bibliothèque de L'Ecole des chartes* 15 (1854): 209–35.

44. Ibid.

45. Shulamith Shahar, *The Fourth Estate: A History of Women in the Middle Ages*, trans. C. Galai (London: Methuen, 1983), p. 95.

46. McNamara has dedicated a chapter to discussion the imitation of Christ for nuns during the high Middle Ages in *Sisters in Arms* (n. 8 above), pp. 233–59.

47. Letter 402, *SAOO* 5: 347–48. Anselm urged the nuns of Shaftesbury to "display obedience, not to the eye but in the inmost heart."

48. Letter 402, *SAOO* 5: 347–48; trans. Fröhlich, 3: 167.

49. Peter of Blois, Sermon 63, PL 207: 745C.

50. Joyce E. Salisbury, "The Latin Doctors of the Church on Sexuality," *Journal of Medieval History* 12 (1986): 286.

51. Peter of Blois, Sermon 63, PL 207: 745–46. See also his Letter 36, PL 207: 114–16.

52. Peter of Blois, Sermon 63, PL 207: 745–46. In a letter to Haimeric, Bernard of Clairvaux wrote that "chastity without charity is a lamp without oil. Take away the fuel and you have extinguished the lamp" in Letter 42, *SBO* 7: 108. This phrase also appears in *SV* 5.1004–5.

53. Bernard, Letter 166, *SBO* 8: 385; trans. Bruno Scott James, *The Letters of Bernard of Clairvaux* (London: Burns and Oates, 1953), p. 460.

54. Leclercq, "Does St. Bernard Have a Specific Message for Nuns?" in *Medieval Religious Women*, p. 273 (n. 4 above).

55. Aelred, *De institutione inclusarum*, CCCM 1: 643; trans. Macpherson, 53.

56. Bernard, Letter 114, *SBO* 7: 291–93; trans. James, p. 179.

57. Anselm, Letter 183, *SAOO* 4: 67–68; trans. Fröhlich, 2: 102. This theme also appears in Letter 48 to Basilia of Gournay and informs several of Anselm's letters to men. For example, see Letter 2 to Odo and Lanzo, Letter 35 to the monk Herluin, and Letter 51 to Herluin, Gunduif and Maurice; *SAOO* 3: 98–101, 142–43, 164–65.

58. Letter 153, *SAOO* 5: 347–48; trans. Fröhlich, 3: 168.

59. Brian Golding, commenting on the same sentiment in the *Vita* of Stephen of Obazine, confirms that this idea was commonplace during this period: "Hermits, monks and women in twelfth-century France and England: the experience of Obazine and Sempringham," in *Monastic Studies: the Continuity of Tradition*, ed. J. Loades (Bangor, Gwynedd: Headstart History, 1990), p. 131.

60. Bernard of Clairvaux, Letter 1, *SBO* 7: 1; trans. James, p. 174.

61. André Vauchez in *Images of Sainthood in Medieval Europe*, ed. R. Blumenfeld-Kosinski and T. Szell (Ithaca, NY: Cornell University Press, 1991), p. 26.

62. Marbod, Letter 4, PL 171: 1474–75B.

63. Bernard, Letter 113, *SBO* 7: 287–91; trans. James, pp. 175–76. This also forms a theme of Hildebert's Letters 10 and 21, PL 171: 162–68 and 193–97.

64. Osbert, Letter 41, *The Letters of Osbert of Clare*, ed. Williamson (n. 11 above), p. 140.

65. Aelred, *De institutione inclusarum*, CCCM 1: 657; trans. Macpherson, 71–72.

# CHAPTER 10

# HERRAD OF HOHENBOURG:
# A SYNTHESIS OF LEARNING IN
# *THE GARDEN OF DELIGHTS*

*Fiona Griffiths*

This chapter compares the *Speculum virginum* to the *Hortus Deliciarum* of Herrad of Hohenbourg, a treatise that provides a visual synthesis of scholastic theology, drawn from both reason and scripture. The *Hortus* pays less emphasis to bridal imagery than the *Speculum*, but rather is much more concerned to incorporate the arguments of some very recent authors. The *Speculum* may have provided a precedent in provoking communities of religious women to develop a distinct visual culture. The difference between the *Speculum* and the *Hortus* illustrates a profound shift in sensibility that took place within the twelfth century. The *Hortus* shows what can happen when a woman is no longer simply the disciple but herself becomes the teacher.

Some thirty-five years after the completion of the *Speculum virginum*, a very different kind of illuminated manuscript was produced for the Augustinian nuns of Hohenbourg in Alsace. Created between about 1175 and 1191 under the direction of their abbess Herrad (d. after 1196), the *Hortus deliciarum [Garden of Delights]* provided these women with a synthesis of twelfth-century learning through its integration of broad-ranging textual extracts with rich illuminations.[1] On the basis of her extensive reading, Herrad brought together more than 1,100 texts, drawn from various Christian authors, with 340 miniatures.[2] These she combined in a carefully ordered presentation of salvation history and offered to the women of Hohenbourg as a metaphorical garden of learning.

Herrad's title places the work within a tradition of monastic composition. Monastic authors were drawn to the imagery of the *hortus* because of the spiritual and allegorical possibilities that it suggested.[3] Yet Herrad did not limit herself to traditionally monastic sources or subjects. She integrates monastic learning with that of the emerging intellectual milieu of the Parisian schools. Herrad's major sources included works by the German Benedictine authors Honorius Augustodunensis (d. ca. 1140) and Rupert of Deutz (d. 1129) as well as the Parisian scholars Peter Lombard (d. 1160) and Peter Comestor (d. 1178), whose *Historia scholastica* was completed in Paris between 1169 and 1173, only a few years before work began on the *Hortus*.[4] The magnificence of the original manuscript, its breadth of learning, and its didactic emphasis establish the *Hortus deliciarum* as a critical landmark in the history of women, their education, and involvement in the religious life of the twelfth century.[5]

Like the *Speculum virginum*, the *Hortus deliciarum* represents an important response to the enthusiasm manifested by women for the religious life during the twelfth century. Although Hohenbourg claimed to have been founded in the eighth century, it had been re-founded not long before Herrad's time.[6] Only one generation had elapsed since the devastation of the monastery in the battles of the investiture controversy. Indeed, at the mid-twelfth century, when Frederick Barbarossa, asserting his probable advocacy over the monastery, summoned Herrad's predecessor Relinde (d. ca. 1176) to be its abbess, Hohenbourg was in a state of disrepair.[7] Relinde quickly embarked on the physical and spiritual reparation of the monastery, restoring its buildings, placing it under the Rule of St. Augustine with the support of Bishop Burchard of Strasbourg, and establishing it firmly within the Alsacian network of Augustinian houses by entering into a confraternity with the canons of nearby Marbach.[8]

At the time of Herrad's abbacy in the last quarter of the twelfth century, Hohenbourg was in a practical sense a new foundation for women, with all of the difficulties that this implied with respect to the *cura monialium*, or care of nuns. The reluctance of the nearby Benedictine monks of Ebersheim to provide priests for the altar of Hohenbourg placed the spiritual lives of the women of the monastery in dire jeopardy. Although the monks had traditionally ministered to Hohenbourg, by this time they were engaged with the women of Hohenbourg in a contest concerning land claims which Ebersheim explicitly linked to its provision of spiritual service.[9] In response to this impasse, Herrad founded two new monastic houses, one at St-Gorgon in 1178 with the cooperation of the Premonstratensian canons of Étival and a second two years later at Truttenhausen, with the Augustinian canons of Marbach.[10] These were intended to provide priests who would minister to the spiritual needs of Hohenbourg and were to remain under the authority of its abbess.[11]

Through her foundations at Truttenhausen and St-Gorgon, Herrad freed Hohenbourg from its previous dependence on Ebersheim and reinforced the links established by Relinde between Hohenbourg and the Augustinian canons of Marbach, in whose care Truttenhausen was placed.[12] She also ensured the continuing independence of Hohenbourg from the authority of a male house, rendering the monastery unique as a reformed, yet still autonomous, house for women.[13] The *Hortus*, certainly well under way at Hohenbourg when Herrad established St-Gorgon and Truttenhausen,[14] was a product of the same impulse that had inspired her monastic foundations. Through it Herrad met the spiritual needs of the women of Hohenbourg and provided them with a thorough and orthodox theological education.

Writing perhaps in the late 1130s, the author of the *Speculum virginum* was engaged in a very different enterprise from that of Herrad forty years later. The *Speculum* was designed to provide spiritual guidance for some of the many women who were drawn to the religious life in the mid-twelfth century. From the manuscript history it is clear that the *Speculum* was also used as a guide for priests engaged in the care of women within the new religious climate of the Hirsau reform movement. The author's concern throughout the *Speculum* was to provide the virgin with a mirror that reflected the path of the individual soul in its journey to God. In keeping with this spiritual goal, he avoided discussion of theological issues that might be distracting to his audience. Contemporary Christological or sacramental debates find no place in his work. Instead, the *Speculum* focuses on the ultimate goals of the Benedictine life—simplicity, virtue, and knowledge of God—in a presentation tailored for women. The contents and intellectual influences of the *Speculum* reflect its author's spiritual goal in that while his explanation drew heavily on Scripture and the writings of the Fathers, contemporary influences are rare.[15] Yet, in that it was presented in the form of a dialogue between a woman, Theodora, and a monk, Peregrinus, the *Speculum* implicitly involved women in the questioning and rational intellectual culture of the early twelfth century, in some ways anticipating Herrad's much more active engagement some years later.

Despite their shared agenda of providing religious instruction for women in the twelfth century, the *Hortus* and the *Speculum* are very different works. Herrad's *Hortus*, a product of the last quarter of the twelfth century, reflects a broadening of theological enterprise in the years after the *Speculum* was composed.[16] Unlike the *Speculum* author, Herrad drew as readily on the writings of the schoolmen as she cited the works of traditional Benedictine authors. Her intellectual landscape was also shaped by Byzantine imagery and Christian texts such as the *Summarium Heinrici*, a German reworking of Isidore, that transmitted stories of the ancient world.[17]

Herrad's *Hortus* has more in common with the *Liber floridus*, a work, produced around 1120 by Lambert of St-Omer, that also combined text and miniature, poetry and prose, in a broad-ranging encyclopedia.[18] In his prologue, Lambert likened his work to a bouquet of flowers and stated his intention that "the faithful bees may fly together to them and drink from the sweetness of the heavenly potion."[19] His manuscript reflects an insatiable curiosity for the world in which he lived. History, geography, medicine, theology, astronomy as well as diverse other subjects are included in the more than 300 chapters of the *Liber.* Yet Lambert's work lacks the organization of Herrad's *Hortus*, even though he provided his readers at the outset with a table of contents. As Fritz Saxl observed, Lambert was "obviously an enemy of systematic arrangement," who appears to have incorporated into the *Liber* whatever he had read most recently.[20] Because of its disorganization, Yves Lefèvre has argued that the *Liber* could not have been designed as a work of instruction.[21]

Despite some similarities between the two texts in title, in the use of illuminations, and even in some cases in subject, there is no evidence that Herrad either saw or knew of the *Liber floridus*. All of her major sources postdate the *Liber*, so there is little intellectual overlap between the works. Lambert's interest in local history and contemporary events, which together occupy at least one-quarter of the *Liber*, is not shared by Herrad, who, apart from the prologue and the last four folios of the *Hortus*, does not mention the monastery at Hohenbourg at all.[22] Neither the privileged relationship that Hohenbourg enjoyed with Frederick Barbarossa nor the investiture controversy are mentioned in the text. Although Herrad did not provide an outline of the text in her prologue, or divide it into books and chapters, she nonetheless subordinated her excerpts and miniatures to its master theme, the Christian history of salvation.[23] Her organization and integration of these texts into the schema of the *Hortus* demonstrates her wide reading and careful selection, prior to working on the manuscript.

The lack of an explicit schema indicates that the *Hortus* was not designed as a reference book but as a spiritual manual for use within a contemplative, monastic context.[24] Like her fusion of scholastic with monastic sources, Herrad's omission of the organizational structures common to the works that she cited conflated the distinctions that we have been taught to expect between the two types of learning.[25] She subordinated her material, encyclopedic in scope, to the plan of salvation history. Rosalie Green's examination of the miniatures of the *Hortus* supports this conclusion. She comments that the miniatures appear as "a great triptych whose center is a narrative life of Christ."[26]

Herrad's prologue to the *Hortus* confirms the impression that her goal was to unite the intellectual with the spiritual. As one of the very few pieces in the manuscript that can unequivocally be attributed to her, her prologue provides important insights into her perception of the *Hortus* and its purpose.[27] Dedicating the work to the women of Hohenbourg, she wrote:

> Like a bee inspired by God, I collected from the diverse flowers of sacred Scripture and philosophic writings this book, which is called the *Garden of Delights,* and I brought it together to the praise and honor of Christ and the Church and for the sake of your love as if into a single sweet honeycomb. Therefore, in this very book, you ought diligently to seek pleasing food and to refresh your exhausted soul with its honeyed dewdrops.[28]

Herrad's imagery here is not original. The metaphor that she provided of herself culling texts from the flowers of Scriptures can be found not only in the writings of Jerome, Abelard, and Lambert of St-Omer, as we have seen, but also the prefatory epistle to the *Speculum virginum.*[29] Her image of herself as a bee also drew on traditional ideas concerning women and compilation. As an animal that was thought to procreate without coitus, the bee was typically a symbol of chastity. It was in this vein that Ambrose presented the bee as a symbol of purity in *De virginibus.*[30] The coupling of the bee imagery with the assembling of wisdom in women appears in Aldhelm's *De virginitate,* a text written for the English nuns of Barking in the late seventh or early eighth century. Aldhelm described the women as bees, "roaming wildly through the flowering fields of Scripture."[31] The bee gathering honey was also used as an image of diligence and industry.[32] In the context of monastic composition, the image of the bee, collecting nectar from flowers and producing honey, may also suggest exegesis of Scripture and patristic texts.[33] Herrad's imagery is striking in that it suggests that she saw herself engaged in the production, and not simply the collection, of theology.

A further innovation is that she presents herself as collecting texts not only from the flowers of Scripture but also from works of philosophy. Brought together in the *Hortus,* the combination of philosophy and Scripture is presented to the women of Hohenbourg by Herrad as a source of enjoyment. In the poem that preceded her prose dedication, Herrad writes to her nuns: "May this book be useful and delightful to you, may you never cease to study it in your thoughts and memory."[34]

Herrad's use of the term "philosophy" to describe the works that she has consulted in her project is puzzling, especially as she included in the

*Hortus* no overtly philosophical works. She did not draw on the writings of the ancient philosophers, although she was certainly aware of them; Plato and Socrates appear in a full-page miniature of Philosophy and the liberal arts on fol. 32r.[35] Here *Philosophia* is shown in the center of two concentric circles, wearing a crown out of which protrude three heads identified as *ethica, logica,* and *phisica,* the Platonic divisions of learning. Socrates and Plato sit below Philosophy's throne at the center of the miniature while around them are shown the seven liberal arts in the second concentric circle. An inscription in the ring between philosophy and the arts establishes Philosophy as their ruler.[36]

Within her presentation of salvation history, the liberal arts are shown by Herrad as guides for the soul on its path to Divine Wisdom, a Christianised *Philosophia.*[37] Plato and Socrates, although not Christian, appear under the aegis of philosophy as Divine Wisdom, while outside this realm Herrad depicts poets and magicians drawing inspiration from blackbirds that hover above their shoulders. A text warns against the inappropriate use of study.[38] Herrad taught her nuns that philosophy was the goal of wisdom and the knowledge of all things both human and divine, a conception that was confirmed through text and image. Philosophy holds a banner asserting the divine origins of all wisdom, while an inscription to her left advises that the Holy Spirit is the inventor of the seven liberal arts. [39] Herrad wanted to teach her nuns that all knowledge leads to God.

As abbess of Hohenbourg, Herrad's ultimate concern was for the salvation of the nuns in her care, a fact reflected in the Christocentric organization of the *Hortus.* Yet she was never as absorbed in the individual soul as the author of the *Speculum virginum* had been. Interested primarily in wider spiritual and theological issues facing the Church, she did not hesitate to address difficult theological issues, balancing care of the spirit with awareness of the intellectual curiosity of her audience. Herrad encourages the women of Hohenbourg to seek salvation in the text that they might secure "the things that last forever in happiness and pleasure."[40] She presents learning and study to her nuns as a route to this ultimate goal.

Apart from the first and last folios of the *Hortus,* addressed to the women of Hohenbourg, Herrad's text is not marked by any special attention to women. Unlike works for female audiences that emphasized heroic women of the past, especially those virgins who had been martyred for their faith, the *Hortus* offers a model of women who had gained salvation through study. Only once in the *Hortus,* in an excerpt from Honorius Augustodunensis' *Speculum ecclesiae [Mirror of the Church],* are female saints and their martyrdom specifically discussed.[41] But added to Honorius' list of female saints are names that would have been more familiar to the women of Hohenbourg. Herrad altered the list to include the legendary founder of the monastery and patron saint of Alsace, Odile, as well as Waltpurg and Brigid. Her rationale for emphasizing these women is that they had also entered into the community of saints through pious study *[per pia studia]*.[42]

The content, organization, and sources of the *Hortus* confirm the impression that Herrad intended her work to be used as a teaching tool within a spiritual context. Although the manuscript was not explicitly divided into books or chapters, the texts of the *Hortus* are organized according to a fourfold schema: the history of salvation through the Old Testament, the person of Christ, *Ecclesia* as the *sponsa Christi,* and Last Things with miscellanea.[43] This design shares much in common with the organization of Honorius' *Elucidarium* and Peter Lombard's *Sententiae,* texts of central importance to Herrad. There is a similar organization in the *De sacramentis fidei christianae* of Hugh of St-Victor, a work that Herrad did not cite in the *Hortus* and may not have known.[44]

Section one of the *Hortus* presents the Old Testament, historically and allegorically. Fol. 2r through fol. 68r deals primarily with the old covenant established between God and the Israelites. Two subsequent sections summarize the Old Testament message: fols. 68r–72v, allegorically, according to the *Speculum Ecclesiae,*[45] and fols. 73r–80r, historically, according to *Chronicorum tomi II* of Freculph of Lisieux (fl. 825–52).[46] The second section of the *Hortus,* which encompasses at least one-third of the entire manuscript and formed its central part, introduces the message of salvation and the person of Christ. Fols. 80v to 133v provide a genealogy of Christ and the story of his birth and early ministry. The history of his betrayal, crucifixion, resurrection, and ascension into heaven is presented in fols. 138r to 167r. Fols. 167v to 199r detail the events of Pentecost from the Acts of the Apostles. These texts are followed by the famous *psychomachia* cycle of miniatures, which depict the virtues and vices in battle (fols. 199v–204r).[47]

Fols. 222v to 240v comprise the third section of the *Hortus,* in which the place of the Church in the history of salvation is presented. Shown alternately as Bride, Virgin, and mystical body of Christ, the Church is discussed in long excerpts from Honorius Augustodunensis' *Gemma animae* and *Speculum ecclesiae.*[48] A miniature on fol. 225v shows *Ecclesia* as a queen enthroned and surrounded by ecclesiastical dignitaries, laymen and women, hermits, recluses, and young women *[adolescentule].*[49] Above the building in which they are shown, angels, pictured with shields and swords, face the bows and arrows of the demonic forces in a vivid depiction of spiritual warfare.

The fourth section of Herrad's text, fols. 241r to 263v, is set aside for eschatological discussions. Twenty folios contain miniatures that depict in gruesome detail the Antichrist, the Last Judgment, and the torments that await the impious. Until fol. 263v the text and miniatures of the *Hortus* follow a plan, which, if it seems at times disordered, is in general coherent.

The final folios of the manuscript break away from the salvation history that guided the first part of the text. Three large sections of text, drawn from three different authors, are here presented not so much as encyclopedic excerpts but as selections coherent in themselves. Fols. 264r to 294r are devoted to Peter Lombard's *Sentences*, in relation to the sacraments and Last Things. Fols. 295r to 308v are taken from the pseudo-Clementine *Recognitiones*. Unidentified texts on fols. 309r to 315v discuss the regular life and the superiority of canons to the rest of the clergy[50]; unfortunately, these were not copied before the destruction of the manuscript in 1870.

With few digressions, the *Hortus* follows this broad four-part organization in which the central focus of the text, the story of salvation through the person of Christ and the role of the Church, is framed by the old covenant and the discussion of Last Things. However, in keeping with her desire to educate her nuns, Herrad intersperses the history of salvation with aspects of secular learning, presented largely through visual images and excerpts from writings of Honorius or the *Summarium* of Heinricus. Following her initial discussion of God, the Trinity, the angels, and the fall of Lucifer, Herrad introduces cosmology, including the zodiac, astrology, and geography (fols. 10r–15v).[51] The creation of the first man allows her to present a miniature depiction of the human microcosm on fol. 16v. Old Testament history up to the story of Noah and the Flood is followed by a discussion of pagan learning (fols. 30v–33r), including the miniature of *Philosophia*. The second section of the manuscript maintains a greater degree of pictorial and thematic integrity, without digressions in its treatment of the life of Christ.[52] The section closes with a depiction of the Wheel of Fortune (fol. 215r) and three miniatures devoted to the history of Ulysses and the Sirens (fols. 221r–v). In this way Herrad places the learning of the ancient world alongside the Christian history that formed the essence of her work.

Herrad's sources reflect her twin goals: the education and edification of the women of Hohenbourg. Several texts she draws from were traditionally cited within the monastic context. While the Scriptures provide her with continuous inspiration, patristic and early medieval texts did not feature heavily. Excerpts drawn from St. Gregory, Bede, and Eusebius appear, but Ambrose, Augustine, Jerome, Cassiodorus, John Chrysostom, and Boethius are primarily mentioned only in marginal and interlinear glosses. Just two authentic Augustinian texts are included in the *Hortus*, and only one from Jerome.[53] Herrad probably lifted these isolated texts from a compilation.

Without question, the most striking aspect of the *Hortus* is Herrad's reliance on contemporary texts: twelfth-century works of theology, biblical history, and canon law. Herrad's inclusion of Peter Comestor's *Historia scholastica,* the poetry of Walter of Châtillon (d. 1202/3), and a sermon ascribed to Geoffrey of St-Thierry (ca. 1200) place the *Hortus* firmly within the intellectual milieu of the late twelfth century. It was to the *Speculum ecclesiae* of Honorius Augustudonensis that Herrad turned most often, although she never mentioned him by name. Some 300 texts in the *Hortus* were drawn from Honorius' *Speculum,* 250 from Peter Lombard's *Sententiae,* and some 74 from writings of Rupert of Deutz, particularly his *De divinis officiis.*

Herrad ensured the pastoral aspect of the *Hortus* by her reliance on the writings of Honorius. In addition to the *Speculum ecclesiae,* Herrad included sixty-two texts from his *Elucidarium,* and about thirty from his *Gemma animae.*[54] Little is known of Honorius's origins. He was certainly an ardent supporter of the ecclesiastical reform movement and was probably a disciple of Anselm of Canterbury (d. 1109).[55] His writing was designed to guide priests and provide them with an orthodox theological program to support them as they furthered the cause of church reform.[56] Honorius described his first work, the *Elucidarium,* as a *summa totius theologiae* in which he presented, in dialogue format, all the knowledge that he thought necessary for the understanding of salvation.[57] Herrad cited this work almost in its entirety. Honorius' later projects, the *Speculum ecclesiae* and *Gemma animae,* were planned as complementary guides to the liturgy of the church.[58] In the *Gemma animae* he explained the liturgy and outlined the liturgical year, while in the *Speculum ecclesiae* he provided relevant sermons. Herrad recast these works in the *Hortus,* excerpting those parts that fitted her design. The *Speculum ecclesiae,* for instance, became for Herrad a source of symbolic interpretations that inspired the miniatures of the *Hortus* rather than sermons as Honorius had intended.

Honorius was more interested in pastoral issues than he was with contemporary theological debates.[59] Herrad's incorporation of the writings of Rupert of Deutz, particularly his first major work, the *De divinis officiis* (1112),[60] complemented her reliance on Honorius. Rupert was also a staunch supporter of the papal reform movement, but unlike Honorius, his aim was to provide an edifying work for priests within a monastic context. His *De divinis officiis* was designed more as a spiritual aid for the personal use of priests than as a guidebook for them in their pastoral responsibilities. As such, he allowed digressions in his text in order to treat major theological issues of the day. Rupert began his work with the daily service performed by ordained monks rather than with a more general discussion of the mass or of the church year and then proceeded to discuss the various theological controversies that occupied contemporary monks and schoolmen, evidence of what John van Engen has called Rupert's "theologizing tendency."[61]

Herrad also drew on Peter Lombard's *Sententiae* and, to a lesser extent, on Peter Comestor's *Historia scholastica,* writings that became standard texts within the schools.[62] Although she copied almost all of the *Elucidarium,* Herrad omitted Honorius' discussion of the Eucharist, baptism, and marriage, choosing rather to deal with these subjects according to Lombard, whose discussion was more current. [63] In choosing Honorius as her major source, Herrad embraced his simple, pastoral aim, which she then combined with Rupert's theologizing and the scholasticism of Peter Lombard. Influenced by the encyclopedic style of Honorius, she chose to transform his model through the integration of Parisian school texts, such as the *Sententiae,* with theological works like those of Rupert. Herrad brought them together in a manuscript, richly illuminated with miniatures, designed to appeal to a wider audience than were any of her original sources.

Herrad was more than a bee collecting nectar from various flowers. In taking texts written for priests and students of theology and incorporating them into a didactic work designed for women, she claimed a body of knowledge for the women of Hohenbourg from which, as the universities became more entrenched, women would increasingly be marginalized. As Susann El Kholi observes in her study of women's monastic libraries, many of the authors that Herrad cites within the context of the *Hortus* do not appear in any other works available within female monastic communities during this period.[64] Indeed, books owned by female houses, or copied or commissioned by them, tended to be of a liturgical or a devotional rather than a theological nature.[65] The *Hortus* is in this sense unique as an indication of women's potential access to education and reading patterns within the monastery.

Herrad's choice, organization, and integration of texts within the schema of the *Hortus* demonstrates a real understanding of the content of the works that she included. No mere copyist, she read and assimilated information before sifting out those aspects that she felt would contribute to her educational design. Her reliance on Lombard's sacramental theology, in preference to that of Honorius, is only one example of her editorial intervention. Although the four-part design of the *Hortus* reflects that of Honorius' *Elucidarium* and Peter Lombard's *Sententiae,* excerpts from these works were rearranged to her new design. Herrad's editorial input also extended beyond reorganization. With Honorius' *Speculum ecclesiae* and *Gemma animae,* and Rupert's *De divinis officiis,* for example, she incorporated material not according to liturgical context but by subject.

Herrad was a teacher. Her goal was not only to create an anthology of important theological texts but to present them in a way that would captivate her students.[66] She interspersed prose, poetry, sermons, miniatures, and German glosses throughout the folios of the *Hortus.* By relying on Honorius' *Elucidarium,* the *Hortus* also included substantial sections of dialogue. Many of the poems of the *Hortus,* a handful of which are unique to the manuscript, were accompanied by musical notation, evidence that they were sung aloud at Hohenbourg.[67] The most important manifestation, however, of Herrad's didactic purpose are the numerous illuminations throughout the manuscript.[68] Some of these were designed as moral lessons, such as the ladder of virtues (fol. 215v), the *psychomachia* cycle (fol. 199v–204r), and the lurid depiction of hell (fol. 255r). Most were designed to educate and entertain her readers: for instance, the depiction of *Philosophia* with the seven liberal arts, Plato and Socrates (fol. 32r), the Wheel of Fortune (fol. 215r), and the history of Ulysses and the Sirens (fol. 221r–v).

Unfortunately, the actual composition of the manuscript cannot be known with certainty. The 1979 Warburg reconstruction allows some observations and tentative conclusions concerning the purpose of the miniatures and the integration of word and image within the original manuscript. Few folios of the *Hortus deliciarum* were devoted exclusively to either text or image. Herrad included images that reinforced the messages contained in textual extracts, often through their direct illustration of the text. Indeed, her reliance on Honorius may have been due to the fact that his theological lessons were easily translated onto a visual level.[69] His *Speculum ecclesiae* furnished Herrad with inspiration for many of the miniatures of the *Hortus.* The *scala virtutum* (fol. 215v), inspired by Honorius's description of the ladder in the *Speculum,* is only one example. Here Herrad explicitly linked the text from Honorius with the image of the ladder by including the relevant sections from the *Speculum ecclesiae* on the folio facing its visual representation. The importance of the miniatures in providing explanations of the text is reinforced by the fact that some of the miniatures, such as the depiction of the Journey of the Israelites on fol. 51r, may even have been designed specifically to accompany a text in the *Hortus* as no pictorial precedent is known.[70]

Herrad's integration of text and image extended to her inclusion of texts within the miniatures of the *Hortus.* These texts function as written glosses on the visual message and frequently direct the reader's attention to links with textual extracts included at other places in the manuscript. Biblical excerpts, rarely acknowledged, are the most common type of text to be placed in a miniature. Herrad also included in the miniatures sections, some quite long, that she explicitly associated with the *Speculum ecclesiae* (*HD* Cat. Nos. 28, 101, 205, 211, 245, 307), *Gemma animae* (*HD* Cat. no. 45, 235, 241), *Elucidarium* (*HD* Cat. no. 14, 207), *Sententiae* (*HD* Cat. no. 5, 8, 14, 16), or to Rupert of Deutz (*HD* Cat. no. 101, 191). The link between text and image is made explicit from the beginning of the manuscript. Miniatures on fols. 3v and 8r contain the exhortation: *Hic lege.*[71]

It is probable, as Rosalie Green has observed with respect to the illustration on fol. 176v, that in the production of the manuscript, the tasks of writing and illuminating were carried out in tandem. Green suggests that the outline of the miniature was first drawn onto the folio, after which the scribe copied the text, and only then did the artist paint the outlined miniature.[72] Herrad rarely refers to the place or purpose of the miniatures in the *Hortus*,[73] but when she introduced her summary of the Old Testament, which she based on Honorius' *Speculum*, she commented, "here begin the mysteries of the Old Testament which the previous pictures illustrate."[74] Clearly, the pictures must have been planned, if not already completed, before the scribe began to write. The only other explicit reference in the *Hortus* to the use of pictures appears in an extract from Honorius: "there are three reasons for a picture: first, because it is the literature of the laity, second, that the house might be honored with such decoration, and third, in order to bring to mind the lives of those who have gone before."[75] This reference to memory is central to the overall didactic purpose of the *Hortus*. The pictures included in the manuscript functioned as mnemonic devices, intended to reinforce lessons learned and perhaps to prompt a retelling of them from memory by the women of Hohenbourg. Herrad encouraged the women to memorize pieces of the text; as we saw earlier, she presented the *Hortus* to them with the wish that they study it always in their memory.[76]

The place and purpose of the miniatures in the *Hortus deliciarum* highlight some of the differences between Herrad's work and the *Speculum virginum*. In both works text and image function together as teaching tools. However, in order to understand the pictures of the *Hortus*, it was often necessary to understand the texts that accompanied them. The extensive glossing of the miniatures indicates that their purpose was not simply to provide for those within the monastery who were less learned than others. The pictures could quite literally also be "read."[77] By contrast, the twelve illuminations that accompany the text of the *Speculum virginum* represent the ascent of the individual soul and seem to encourage an identification of the female audience with their subject.[78] The most striking example of the difference in emphasis between the *Hortus* and the *Speculum* lies in the depiction of the *scala virtutum* in each manuscript. Herrad's ladder (fol. 215v) shows the ascent and temptations of various different groups within Christian society. The laywoman, knight, cleric, monk, nun, recluse, and hermit are each distracted from the ultimate goal: the crown of life. A young woman is shown reaching that goal, but Herrad's inscription indicates that she is only a symbol meant to represent the holy and the elect. The *Speculum* ladder (plate 12 in Seyfarth's edition) depicts a single virgin at various points in her ascent, indicating that the author's concern lay primarily with the growth in virtue not of the Church as a whole but of the individual virgin.

The differences between the *Speculum virginum* and the *Hortus*, in content, structure, and use of miniatures, reflect the many changes that had taken place in the forty years that separate the two works. Writing in the late 1130s, the *Speculum* author had extended to women many of the same ideas that he had addressed to a male audience in his *Dialogus de mundi contemptu vel amore*. In this way he was responding to concerns raised in other contexts by such women as Heloise, whose request for a history and rule for nuns prompted Abelard's rule for religious women. The presence of a manuscript of the *Speculum virginum* during the twelfth century at the Augustinian house of Frankenthal indicates the intersection of Benedictine and Augustinian reform at this time.[79] Even though the *Speculum* author was Benedictine in his training, he nonetheless referred to the Augustinian concept of the common life, suggesting intellectual cross-fertilization between the two orders. That a copy of the Benedictine-authored *Speculum* existed at Frankenthal and probably also at Andernach suggests that the *Speculum* was alone in the 1140s in addressing the religious life for women in the Rhineland. By the 1170s Herrad was able to provide through the *Hortus* a more theological and intellectual response than the *Speculum* to the need for a religious literature for women, this time within the framework of an Augustinian community.

Did Herrad know the *Speculum virginum*? Certainly there are some similarities in the emphases of the *Speculum* and the *Hortus*. Herrad, like the *Speculum* author, stressed contempt for the world in the excerpts that she chose for inclusion in the *Hortus* and in the poems that may be attributed to her.[80] The *Hortus* opens and closes with exhortations that the nuns of Hohenbourg should flee the snares of this world in order that they might receive the rewards of the next. "Scorn, scorn the world!" Herrad encouraged them in her introductory poem, warning that Christ "hates the blemishes of sin."[81] In another place she prayed that her readers would triumph over the passing pleasures of the world and, in the closing miniature of the *Hortus*, encouraged the Hohenbourg women to "hasten to heaven, after despising earthly dust."[82]

However, it is not in their shared emphasis on the *contemptus mundi* but rather in the *psychomachia* cycle of the *Hortus* that the possible influence of Conrad of Hirsau on Herrad is most visible. The longest section of miniatures in the manuscript without accompanying text, the cycle vividly depicts the battle between virtues and vices (fol. 199v–204v).[83] Drawn originally from the early fifth-century poem of Prudentius, the *psychomachia* tradition explores the conflict of spirit and flesh, virtue and vice. Herrad's depiction seems to draw less on Prudentius than on *On the Fruits of the Flesh and of the Spirit,* a work erroneously printed among the writings of Hugh of St-Victor but in fact by the author of the *Speculum virginum*.[84] Its influence on Herrad's depiction of the virtues and vices is seen primarily in her presentation of Humility, backed by the virtues, against Pride, backed by the vices. Herrad may well have known *On the Fruits of the Flesh* even if she was not familiar with the text of the *Speculum virginum*.

Two final observations concerning the *Hortus* underline the differences between it and the earlier *Speculum virginum*. The first relates to the evidence that the *Hortus* provides for women's education at Hohenbourg, the second to cooperation between men and women within the Augustinian order during the twelfth century. Herrad's *Hortus* suggests a culture of both female teachers and female pupils as well as of intellectual engagement between men and women of a nonhierarchical kind. The *Hortus* indicates the very high degree of learning possible within a female monastery. The depiction of *rhetorica* on fol. 32r holding a *stilus* and a *tabula* is one of the few medieval pictorial indications of female scribal activity. It suggests that Hohenbourg did have an active *scriptorium* at this time, although, apart from the *Hortus,* few manuscripts are thought to have been produced there.[85]

Herrad was, of course, a teacher. But she was not the sole witness to the intellectual vitality of Hohenbourg in the twelfth century, as she herself makes clear in the *Hortus:* "Herrad abbess of Hohenbourg, appointed and instructed according to the admonitions and examples of Relinde."[86] Although this short tribute provides the only information that we have as to her intellectual formation, it suggests that Herrad had been educated at Hohenbourg. Relinde's involvement in Herrad's education may have been matched by her active participation at least in the early stages of the *Hortus* project, which began before Herrad became abbess.[87] Facing miniatures on fols. 322v–323r outline the history of Hohenbourg's foundation by St. Odile's father, Duke Eticho (or Adalric), and depict the nuns who inhabited the mountain at the time of the creation of the *Hortus.* Herrad and Relinde are here shown symmetrically, each holding scrolls containing poetry, and standing on either side of the assembled women.[88] If Relinde was the author of the poem that she presents, and it was not simply imputed to her by Herrad, then it seems likely that Relinde was indeed actively involved in the creation of the *Hortus.*

A second monument to the cooperation of Relinde and Herrad exists in a stone sculpture that can still be seen at Hohenbourg.[89] The stone contains carvings on each of its three faces. On the third face, Relinde and Herrad are shown prostrate at the feet of the Virgin and Christ child, presenting to them an open book. There has been much debate over its content. Josef Haupt cited it as evidence for association of a German paraphrase of the *Song of Songs* with the monastery of Hohenbourg.[90]

Christine Bischoff posits that the book could represent either the foundation charter of the monastery or, more interestingly, the manuscript of the
*Hortus*.[91] If the book was meant to represent Hohenbourg's foundation
charter, which we lack, then Herrad and Relinde are shown together as
the monastery's second founders. If it was intended to denote the *Hortus
deliciarum*, then Relinde was thought of as an author of the project. In either case, Relinde is seen in the *Hortus* as Herrad's teacher, collaborator,
and partner, providing an exception to the model of male guidance and
scribal support, as in the case of Hildegard of Bingen (d. 1179) and Elisabeth of Schönau (d. 1164).[92]

Yet while the *Hortus* indicates the level of education available within a
female monastery, it also suggests intellectual collaboration of men and
women within the Augustinian reform movement extending beyond the
teacher-student relationship assumed in the *Speculum virginum*. In addition
to her partnership with Relinde, Herrad must have benefited from scholarly cooperation from outside Hohenbourg. Where might Herrad have
found her books?[93] Male monastic houses would have received news of the
latest intellectual developments in the schools from canons or monks who
were able to travel in order to study. Evidently this is how the library at
Frankenthal grew.[94] The women of Hohenbourg could not travel to Paris
to get copies of Peter Comestor's *Historia*. Who then would have alerted
Herrad to the existence of such recent texts?

The *Hortus deliciarum* may itself hold the answers to these questions. Two
poems on the penultimate folios of the manuscript address the monastery
of Hohenbourg directly. The first, entitled *Rithmus de monte Hohenburc*, is
attributed to *Conradus;* the second, *item rithmus de monte Hohenburc*, to *Hugo
Sacerdos*. Although the identity of Conrad and Hugo cannot be known
with certainty, it is likely that they were canons from either St-Gorgon or
Truttenhausen. Herrad ensured that both houses were to remain firmly
under the control of the abbess of Hohenbourg. She had been the instiga-
tor rather than the founder of St-Gorgon, whereas Truttenhausen was constructed under her direct guidance. The foundation of Truttenhausen was
part of the preexisting and ongoing relationship between Hohenbourg and
Marbach that had been established during the abbacy of Relinde.

The fraternity between Hohenbourg and Marbach might provide the
final clue as to the origin of Herrad's sources. By the time of Herrad's abbacy, Marbach had already gained a reputation for cooperation, both intellectual and spiritual, with female monasteries. One manuscript in particular
bears witness to this singular cooperation.[95] The *Codex Guta-Sintram* dates
from 1154 and is preserved in the library of the Grand Séminaire in Strasbourg.[96] The text was the work of Guta, a nun of Schwartzenthann, while
the miniatures were completed by Sintram, a canon of Marbach. The codex

attests to both the high level of literacy of women associated with Marbach and the willingness of the canons of Marbach to enter into projects with women of neighboring houses. This apparent openness to intellectual collaboration with women may have been a part of the culture of Marbach from its foundation in the late eleventh century. Richard of Poitiers tells of a certain philosopher named Manegold whose wife and daughters were so learned in the Scriptures that, although they were women, they had students of their own. This figure may be Manegold of Lautenbach (d. 1103), the first provost at Marbach.[97] In any case, it seems likely that the Augustinian canons of Marbach encouraged Herrad in her erudite project.

The image of women teaching women that is suggested in the *Hortus* is very different from the model of female learning presented in the *Speculum*. As we have seen, if Herrad did have a primary intellectual partner in the creation of the *Hortus*, it was Relinde and not a canon from Marbach or Étival. But what in many ways is more interesting than the indications provided by the *Hortus* of female intellectual vitality during the twelfth century is the existence of a nonhierarchical collaboration between religious men and women during this period that the text implies. That Conrad and Hugo contributed only a single poem each to the *Hortus* without involving themselves more directly in the project indicates that Herrad managed to include men in her project without sacrificing her own editorial authority. The witness of the relationship between Marbach and Schwartzenthann bears out the model of male-female intellectual cooperation implicit in the *Hortus*.

The *Hortus deliciarum* is Herrad's lasting testament to the intellectual activity of religious women in Alsace during the last quarter of the twelfth century. As it was never disseminated beyond the monastery of Hohenbourg, it seems that the text was only ever intended for domestic use. Herrad does not separate the spiritual from the intellectual. Instead her work celebrates in grand style the marriage of the two. She presented study and the liberal arts as a way for the women of Hohenbourg to liberate themselves from the world and open themselves up to knowledge of the Creator.[98] She interspersed secular learning with the history of salvation in order to give her nuns a comprehensive education as a background to their faith. In so doing, she became the first woman to compile a theological encyclopedia (if we exclude Hildegard's *Scivias* as a visual encyclopedia). In the *Hortus*, Herrad selected and adopted for the education of women texts that had been written by men for men.

In her prologue, Herrad depicts herself as a divinely inspired bee selecting flowers from the Scriptures and philosophy to be included in her garden of delights. But she also provides a further metaphor: The *Hortus*, and the treasury of knowledge it contained, should be to the women of

Hohenbourg as sweet honeydrops, nourishing and pleasing them at the same time. Herrad's title reflects her attitude toward learning. The *hortus* evoked the three different gardens of the Bible: Eden, the garden of paradise; the garden of pleasure in the Song of Songs; and Gethsemane, the garden of Christ's agony. It was particularly relevant for Herrad's female monastic audience as the *hortus conclusus* of the Song of Songs, most frequently used to denote virginity.[99] Within Herrad's didactic program, however, the *hortus deliciarum* represented the first of the biblical gardens, the earthly paradise.[100] The book of Genesis (2.8–9) records that in the garden of Paradise, God made many trees grow that were both pleasing and helpful. In the center of these was the tree of the knowledge of good and evil. Herrad's choice of title was appropriate for a work that presented knowledge within a moral framework. She believed that learning would be for her nuns a garden of delights. More important, she was confident that through study, they would achieve that garden that is Paradise.

## Notes

I am greatly indebted to Constant Mews for his helpful comments on earlier drafts of this chapter, as well as for his continuing discussion with me concerning women's religious and intellectual lives during the twelfth century.

1. Herrad of Hohenbourg, *Hortus Deliciarum*, ed. Rosalie Green, Michael Evans, Christine Bischoff, and Michael Curschmann, 2 vols. Studies of the Warburg Institute, 36 (London: The Warburg Institute, 1979); hereafter referred to as *HD*. Texts and miniatures of the reconstructed *Hortus* (vol. 2) are designated as "*HD* nos." and "*HD* fols." respectively. Citations from the *Commentary* (vol. 1) will be designated by the author's name followed by "*HD*, p.";  descriptions of miniatures in the *Commentary* according to "*HD* Cat. no."

2. Most of the images of the *Hortus* were patterned on earlier pictorial models, drawn from either Byzantine or Western sources. For specific art historical studies of *HD*, see J. Zellinger, "Der geköderte Leviathan im Hortus deliciarum der Herrad von Landsberg," *Historisches Jahrbuch* 4 (1925): 161–77; Otto Gillen, *Ikonographische Studien zum Hortus deliciarum der Herrad von Landsperg* (Kiel: B. Krause, 1929); Frances Godwin, "The Judith Illustration of the *Hortus Deliciarum*," *Extrait de la Gazette des Beaux Arts* 36 (1949): 25–46; Rosalie Green, "The Adam and Eve Cycle in the *Hortus Deliciarum*," *Late Classical and Medieval Studies in Honor of Albert Mathias Friend, Jr.*, ed. Kurt Weizmann (Princeton, NJ: Princeton University Press, 1955), pp. 340–47; Gérard Cames, *Allegories et symboles dans l'Hortus deliciarum* (Leiden: Brill, 1971); Robert Will, "La Reconstruction des Miniatures de l'*Hortus Deliciarum*," *Cahiers Alsaciens d'Archéologie d'Art et d'Histoire* 26 (1983): 99–113, and 30 (1987): 207–10.

3. Bernard of Clairvaux interpreted the *hortus* as the human soul in his *Sermones super Cantica canticorum* 23, *SBO* 1: 138–50. Rupert of Deutz read it as the Virgin Mary in his *Commentaria in Canticum canticorum*, ed. R. Haacke CCCM 26 (1974). Honorius Augustodunensis associated paradise, which he called the *hortus deliciarum*, with the Church, in his *Speculum ecclesiae*, PL 172: 833.

4. James Morey, "Peter Comestor, Biblical Paraphrase and the Medieval Popular Bible," *Speculum* 68 (1993): 6–35.

5. Unfortunately, the original manuscript was destroyed in the Prussian siege of Strasbourg in 1870. Only copies of the manuscript made by scholars during the nineteenth century have survived.

6. A thirteenth-century document places the original foundation of Hohenbourg in 738; *Archives départémentales du Bas-Rhin*, G 1613 (8).

7. *Archives départémentales du Bas-Rhin*, G 28 (2) (1185), ed. Johann Schoepflin, *Alsatia aevi Merovingici, Carolingici, Saxonici, Salici, Suevici diplomatica*, 2 vols. (Mannheim, 1772–75), 1, no. 335. Robert Will, "Les origines de l'abbesse Relinde de Hohenbourg," *Archives de l'église d'Alsace* n.s. 21 (1974): 1–12.

8. Schoepflin, ed., *Alsatia diplomatica*, 1, no. 335. François-Auguste Goehlinger provides a general history of Marbach; *Histoire de l'abbaye de Marbach* (Colmar: Éditions Alsatia, 1954). Concerning the Augustinian reform in Alsace, see Henri Dubled, "Recherches sur les chanoines reguliers de Saint-Augustin au diocèse de Strasbourg," *Archives de l'église d'Alsace* n.s. 16 (1967–68): 5–52.

9. *Chronicon Ebersheimense*, ed. L. Weiland, MGH SS 23: 427–53.

10. Herrad's foundation of St-Gorgon is attested in a charter of 1178, edited in Stefan Würdtwein, *Nova subsidia diplomatica*, 14 vols. (Heidelberg: T. Goebhardt, 1788–89), 10: 65. Her foundation charter for Truttenhausen has been lost but was confirmed by Duke Frederick V in 1181 and by Pope Lucius III in 1185; ed. Schoepflin, *Alsatia diplomatica*, 1, no. 335; Würdtwein, *Nova subsidia* 10: 107.

11. Würdtwein, *Nova subsidia* 10: 65.

12. Schoepflin, ed., *Alsatia diplomatica* 1, no. 335.

13. See chapter 3 by Julie Hotchin in this volume.

14. *HD* no. 1160 contains the only certain date in the *Hortus: facta est hec pagina anno MCLXXV.*

15. On patristic allusions in the *Speculum*, see chapter 4 by Kim Power in this volume.

16. Fritz Saxl, "Illustrated Medieval Encyclopedias 2. The Christian Transformation," in *Lectures*, (London: The Warburg Institute, 1957), pp. 242–54, p. 254; Christine Bischoff, *HD*, p. 42.

17. Michael Curschmann discusses the *Summarium Heinrici*, the source to which Herrad turned most consistently, if not extensively, *HD*, pp. 63–80. Herrad cited no pagan authors in the *Hortus*, although certain sections are reminiscent of Ovid, whose work she may have known, probably at secondhand (*HD* no. 43).

18. Albert Derolez, *The Autograph Manuscript of the Liber floridus: A Key to the Encyclopedia of Lambert of St-Omer,* Corpus Christianorum Autographa Medii Aevi 4 (Turnhout: Brepols, 1998); Albert Derolez, ed., *Lamberti Audomarensis canonici Liber floridus* (Ghent: In aedibus Story-Scientia, 1968). Yves Lefèvre, "Le Liber floridus et la littérature encyclopédique au Moyen Âge," *Liber floridus Colloquium, Papers Read at the International Meeting Held in the University Library Ghent on 3–5 September 1967,* ed. Albert Derolez (Ghent: E. Story-Scientia, 1973), pp. 1–10; Saxl, "Illustrated Medieval Encyclopedias."

19. Cited in Saxl, "Illustrated Medieval Encyclopedias," p. 242.

20. Saxl, "Illustrated Medieval Encyclopedias," p. 242.

21. Lefèvre, "Le *Liber floridus,*" 8. This is a conclusion that Derolez argues is perhaps too harsh; see his note to Lefèvre's article, p. 8.

22. Albert Derolez, "British and English History in the *Liber floridus,*" *Liber floridus Colloquium,* ed. Derolez, pp. 59–70; R. van Caenegem, "The Sources of Flemish History in the *Liber floridus,*" ibid., pp. 71–83.

23. Some of the subjects within the *Hortus* are delineated through the use of *incipit* and *explicit*. Michael Evans, *HD,* p. 2.

24. On scholastic presentation of texts, see Malcolm Parkes, "The Influence of the Concepts of *Ordinatio* and *Compilatio* on the Development of the Book," *Medieval Learning and Literature: Essays Presented to Richard William Hunt,* ed. J. J. G. Alexander and M. T. Gibson (Oxford: Clarendon Press, 1976), pp. 115–41.

25. Jean Leclercq, *The Love of Learning and the Desire for God: A Study of Monastic Culture,* trans. Catherine Misrahi (New York: Fordham University Press, 1985), translation of *L'Amour des lettres et le désir de Dieu. Initiation aux auteurs monastiques du moyen âge* (Paris: Editions du Cerf, 1957). The sharpness of Leclercq's dichotomy between monastic and scholastic culture has recently been questioned by Constant Mews, "Monastic Educational Culture Revisited: The Case of Hirsau and Zwiefalten," *Monastic Education and Formation,* ed. George Ferzoco (London: Leicester University Press, 2001), pp. 182–97.

26. Rosalie Green, *HD,* pp. 24–25.

27. Herrad's own words survive only in her prose prologue (*HD* no. 2) and in four of the sixty-seven poems that appear in the text: *Salve cohors virginum* on fol. 1v (*HD* no. 1), *De primo homine* on fol. 109v (*HD* no. 374), *Rithmus de Domino* on fol. 166v (*HD* no. 595), and *Beata illa patria* on fol. 244r (*HD* Cat. no. 317). The texts included in the facing-page miniature featuring Hohenbourg on fols. 322v–323r are probably also by Herrad (*HD* Cat. nos. 345–46): *Vos quas includit, Esto nostrorum pia merces,* and *O nivei flores dantes. O pie grex* on fol. 322v may have been composed by Relinde. Herrad's poetry has been discussed by Johannes Autenrieth, "Einige Bemerkungen zu den Gedichten im Hortus deliciarum Herrads von Landsberg," *Festschrift Bernhard Bischoff zu seinem 65. Geburtstag,* ed. Johannes Autenrieth and Franz Brunhözl (Stuttgart: A. Hiersemann, 1971), pp. 307–21; and Fiona Griffiths, "Herrad of Hohenbourg and the Poetry

of the *Hortus deliciarum: Cantat tibi cantica,*" in *Women Writing in Latin,* ed. Laurie Churchill (New York: Garland Press, forthcoming).

28. *HD* no. 2.

29. Jerome, Letters 65.2, 122.4, 130.9, ed. Isidore Hilberg, CSEL 54 (1910): 618, and CSEL 56 (1918): 69, 188. Abelard, "Rule for Religious Women," ed. T. P. McLaughlin, *Mediaeval Studies* 18 (1956): 241–92, p. 243; *SV* Epist. 58–64 and 1.505.

30. Ambrose, *De virginibus* 1.8.41, ed. F. Gori, *SAEMO* 14.1 (1989): 100–240.

31. *Aldhelm: The Prose Works,* trans. Michael Lapidge and Michael Herrin (Cambridge: D. Brewer, 1979), p. 61.

32. Peter the Venerable encouraged Heloise to be, like Deborah, a bee; Letter 115, *The Letters of Peter the Venerable,* ed. Giles Constable, 2 vols. (Cambridge, MA: Harvard University Press, 1967), 1: 305; trans Betty Radice, *The Letters of Abelard and Heloise* (New York: Penguin Books, 1974), p. 280.

33. Seneca's use of the bee metaphor in his *Epistulae morales* is discussed by Ann Moss, *Printed Commonplace-Books and the Structuring of Renaissance Thought* (Oxford: Clarendon Press, 1996), p. 12.

34. *HD* no. 1

35. *HD* Cat. no. 33.

36. *HD* Cat. no. 33.

37. L. D. Ettlinger, "Muses and Liberal Arts: Two Miniatures from Herrad of Landsberg's *Hortus deliciarum,*" *Essays in the History of Art presented to Rudolf Wittkower,* ed. Douglas Fraser, Howard Hibbard, and Milton J. Lewine (London: Phaidon Press, 1967), pp. 29–35.

38. *HD* no. 124.

39. *HD* no. 115; see also *HD* no. 36 and Cat. no. 33.

40. *HD* no. 2.

41. *HD* no. 700

42. *HD* no. 700. Bischoff, *HD,* p. 42, n. 15.

43. Bischoff, *HD,* pp. 38–41.

44. Bischoff, *HD,* p. 41. Barbara Newman has already commented on the similarities between Hugh's *summa* and Hildegard of Bingen's encyclopedic *Scivias* in her introduction to Hildegard of Bingen, *Scivias,* trans. Mother Columba Hart and Jane Bishop (New York: Paulist Press, 1990), p. 23.

45. Honorius Augustodunensis, *Speculum ecclesiae,* PL 172: 807–1108.

46. Freculph Lexoviensis, *Chronicorum tomi II,* PL 106: 917–1258.

47. See n. 83 below.

48. *Gemma animae,* PL 172: 541–738.

49. The *adolescentule* are representative of all Christians, *HD* Cat. no. 302.

50. *HD* no. 1131.

51. Green argues that fols. 10–16 formed an "intrusive" quire, *HD,* p. 28.

52. Green, *HD,* p. 25.

53. *HD* nos 855, 86, 174.

54. *Elucidarium,* Yves Lefèvre, *L'Elucidarium et les lucidaires,* Bibliothèque des Ecoles françaises d'Athènes et de Rome, fasc. 180 (Paris: E. de Boccard,

1954); *Speculum ecclesiae*, PL 172: 807–1108; *Gemma animae*, PL 172: 541–738.

55. Valerie Flint, *Honorius Augustodunensis*, Authors of the Middle Ages 2 (Aldershot: Ashgate, 1995), pp. 89–183. See pp. 180–83 for a bibliography of secondary works concerning Honorius.

56. Valerie Flint, "The *Elucidarius* of Honorius Augustodunensis and reform in late eleventh-century England" *Revue bénédictine* 85 (1975): 699–721; Flint, *Honorius Augustodunensis*, pp. 129–32 (n. 55 above).

57. Marcia Colish, *Peter Lombard*, 2 vols. (Leiden: Brill, 1994), pp. 37–41.

58. Flint, *Honorius Augustodunensis*, pp. 135–39.

59. Colish, *Peter Lombard*, p. 41.

60. John van Engen, *Rupert of Deutz* (Berkeley: University of California Press, 1983), pp. 58–67.

61. Van Engen, *Rupert of Deutz*, p. 65.

62. On Peter Comestor, see Beryl Smalley, *The Study of the Bible in the Middle Ages*, 3rd ed. (Oxford: Blackwell, 1983), p. 179 and Morey, "Peter Comestor," p. 6 (n. 4 above).

63. Bischoff, *HD*, p. 47.

64. Susann El Kholi, *Lektüre in Frauenkonventen des ostfränkisch-deutschen Reiches vom 8. Jahrhundert bis zur Mitte des 13. Jahrhunderts*, Würzburger Wissenschaftliche Schriften 203 (Würzburg: Königshausen und Neumann, 1997), pp. 118–20.

65. Michel Parisse makes a similar observation in *Les Nonnes au Moyen Age* (Le Puy: C. Bonneton, 1983), p. 166. David Bell studies English nunneries during the later period; *What Nuns Read: Books and Libraries in Medieval English Nunneries* (Kalamazoo, MI: Cistercian Publications, 1995).

66. Until the thirteenth century, women were allowed to teach within female monastic communities. Nicole Bériou, "The Right of Women to Give Religious Instruction in the Thirteenth Century," in *Women Preachers and Prophets through Two Millennia of Christianity*, ed. Beverly Kienzle and Pamela Walker (Berkeley: University of California Press, 1998), pp. 134–45, p. 143 n. 17.

67. *HD* nos. 1, 327–333, 374, 816, 1162–3. Kenneth Levy, "The Musical Notation" in *HD*, pp. 87–88.

68. Saxl, "Illustrated Medieval Encyclopedias," p. 253 (n. 16 above).

69. According to Emile Mâle, Honorius' work provided "one of the perennial sources of inspiration for medieval art." *The Gothic Image: Religious Art in France of the Thirteenth Century*, trans. D. Nussey (New York: Harper & Row, 1972), p. 105.

70. *HD* Cat. no. 67. Other miniatures that are singular to the *Hortus* include Ulysses and the Sirens on fols. 221r–221v (*HD* Cat. nos. 297–99) and the miniature of Christ appearing to Peter and James on fol. 160v (*HD* Cat. no. 220). Rosalie Green has discussed the miniatures in *HD*, pp. 17–36.

71. *HD* Cat. nos. 4, 6.

72. Green, *HD*, p. 29.

73. Herrad provides no justification for the appearance of pictures in the *Hortus*. For a discussion of the use of images in the teaching of the illiterate, see Celia Chazelle "Pictures, Books, and the Illiterate: Pope Gregory's Letters to Serenus of Marseilles," *Word and Image* 6 (1990): 138–53.

74. *HD* no. 229.

75. "Ob tres autem causas fit pictura: primo, quia est laicorum literatura, secundo, ut domus tali decore ornetur, tercio, ut priorum vita in memoriam revocetur." *HD* no. 789, from Honorius' *Gemma animae*.

76. *HD* no. 1.

77. Rosamond McKitterick discusses the ways images presuppose knowledge of the written word in "Text and Image in the Carolingian World," in *The Uses of Literacy in Early Mediaeval Europe*, ed. McKitterick (Cambridge: Cambridge University Press, 1990), pp. 297–318.

78. On the prevalence of visual imagery in later medieval women's devotional practices, Jeffrey Hamburger has commented that "corporeal images proved uniquely suited to the somatic character of female spirituality," in "A *Liber Precum* in Sélestat and the Development of the Illustrated Prayer Book in Germany," *Art Bulletin* 73 (1991): 209–36, 233. See also Hamburger, "The Use of Images in the Pastoral Care of Nuns: The Case of Heinrich Suso and the Dominicans," *Art Bulletin* 71 (1989): 20–46; *Nuns as Artists: The Visual Culture of a Medieval Convent* (Berkeley: University of California Press, 1997); and *The Visual and the Visionary: Art and Female Spirituality in Late Medieval Germany* (New York: Zone Books, 1998).

79. See Mews, chapter 1 in this volume.

80. *Contemptus mundi*, or contempt for the world, is the theme of *HD* nos. 125, 359, 715, 732f, 741, 750, 1164, 1165.

81. "Sperne, sperne seculum"; "Christus odit maculas." *HD* no. 1.

82. "Exoptat in dies, ut leta victoria vincas transitoria." *HD* no. 1. "Pulvere terreno contempto currite celo, que nunc absconsum valeatis cernere sponsum." *HD* Cat. no. 346.

83. T. McGuire, "Psychomachia: A Battle of Virtues and Vices in Herrad of Landsberg's Miniatures," *Fifteenth Century Studies* 16 (1990): 189–97.

84. *HD* Cat. nos. 258–85. Adolf Katzenellenbogen, *Allegories of the Virtues and Vices in Medieval Art* (London: The Warburg Institute, 1939), pp. 10–11.

85. Green has established a positive link between the *Hortus* and British Library Add. MS 42497, known as the *flabellum* of Hohenbourg, on the basis of the similarities between miniatures of both manuscripts. Rosalie Green, "The Flabellum of Hohenbourg," *The Art Bulletin* 33 (1951): 153–55. Rosamond McKitterick has argued that the *vita Odiliae* (MGH SS rerum merovingicarum 6: 24–50) was produced by a woman at Hohenbourg; "Women and Literacy in the Early Middle Ages," *Books, Scribes and Learning in the Frankish Kingdoms, 6th–9th Centuries* (Aldershot: Variorum, 1994), p. 28. See also Lesley Smith, "*Scriba Feminea*: Medieval Depictions of Women Writing," in *Women and the Book: Assessing the Visual Evidence*, ed. Lesley Smith and Jane Taylor (Toronto: University of Toronto Press, 1996), pp. 21–44, 21.

86. "Herrat Hohenburgensis abbatissa post Relindam ordinata ac monitis et exemplis ejus instituta." *HD,* fol. 323r.

87. Green, *HD,* p. 24–25.

88. *HD,* fol. 322v.

89. Photos of the second and third faces of the stone appear in *HD* figs. 349–50.

90. Josef Haupt, *Das hohe Lied, übersetz von Williram, erklärt von Rilindis und Herrat, aus der einzigen Handschrift der Hoffbibliothek zu Wien* (Vienna: W. Braumüller, 1864); Helmut de Boor and Richard Newald, *Geschichte der deutschen Literatur,* vol. 1 (Munich: Beck, 1949), p. 118. The *Sankt Trudperter* (or Hohenburger) *Hohe Lied* was largely based on the work of Willeram, abbot of Ebersberg.

91. Bischoff, *HD,* p. 12.

92. For a discussion of the involvement of male scribes in shaping women's writings, see Anne Clark, "Repression or Collaboration? The Case of Elisabeth and Ekbert of Schönau," in *Christendom and its Discontents: Exclusion, Persecution and Rebellion, 1000–1500,* ed. Scott Waugh and Peter Diehl (Cambridge: Cambridge University Press, 1996), pp. 151–67.

93. Although nothing is known of the Hohenbourg library, Susann El Kholi assumes that the works cited by Herrad in the *Hortus* were available to her there, in *Lektüre in Frauenkonventen,* p. 306 (n. 64 above).

94. Aliza Cohen-Mushlin, "The Twelfth-Century Scriptorium at Frankenthal," in *Medieval Book Production Assessing the Evidence,* ed. Linda L. Brownrigg (Oxford: The Red Gull Press, 1990), pp. 98–100.

95. A second manuscript was the result of cooperation between Marbach and Schwartzenthann. The *Evangeliary of Marbach-Schwartzenthann,* which contains the second part of the *Annales Marbacenses* and the chronicle of Hohenbourg-Neuburg, was produced in the mid-twelfth century; Joseph Walter, "L'Evangélaire de Marbach-Schwartzenthann du commencement du XIIIè Siècle," *Archives Alsaciennes d'Histoire de l'Art* 9 (1930): 1–20. The Evangeliary is now preserved as Codex Jenensis Bos 9.6 (MS 550) in the Bibliothèque municipale at Laon.

96. *Le Codex Guta-Sintram MS 37 de la bibliothèque du Grand Séminaire de Strasbourg,* ed. Beatrice Weis (Lucerne: Editions Facsimiles, 1983).

97. More work is needed to substantiate such an identification. See François Chatillon, "Recherches critiques sur différents personnages nommées Manegold," *Revue du Moyen Âge Latin* 9 (1953): 153–56; and Constant Mews, "Hildegard and the Schools," in *Hildegard of Bingen: The Context of her Thought and Art,* ed. Charles Burnett and Peter Dronke (London: The Warburg Institute, 1998), p. 94, n. 33.

98. *HD* no. 115.

99. The *hortus conclusus,* mentioned twice in Herrad's text, represents both the *domicilium virginitatis* and the Virgin Mary. *HD* nos. 314, 769.

100. Isidore of Seville, *Etymologiae* 14.3.2.

CHAPTER 11

THE SECOND BLOSSOMING OF A TEXT:
THE *SPIEGHEL DER MAECHDEN*
AND THE MODERN DEVOTION

*Urban Küsters*

*(translated by Adrian Anderson)*

This chapter explores a new vogue of influence of the *Speculum virginum*
in the fifteenth century through a widely copied translation into Middle
Dutch. It traces the early diffusion of manuscripts of the Middle Dutch
translation to dependencies of the Utrecht chapter of the sisters of the
common life, in particular to the influence of Wermbold of Buscoep,
who became known as "the common Father of devout women in Holland." Women inspired by the ideals of the Modern Devotion occupied
a precarious position in canon law, as they were not formally attached to
a religious order. The *Speculum virginum* provided them with a sanctioned
way of life, obedient to the instruction of a male spiritual adviser. The
translated version offered practical guidance to women in communities
that in the fifteenth century were increasingly taking on the characteristics of an institutionalized religious order.

It is quite remarkable that a medieval religious text should experience as
it were two phases of popularity, separated by a mere two and a half centuries, and that this text should be the subject of interest in two periods of
religious reform that are quite independent of each other. In the twelfth
century the Latin text of the *Speculum virginum* played a significant role
within the monastic reform movement of the time. While its presumed

Hirsau origin has been disputed, its early transmission since the middle of the twelfth century was certainly within the circles of the Canons Regular and Cistercians in the region of the middle Rhine. It was above all the Cistercians who promoted the spread of the text in the fourteenth century. The *Speculum virginum* became the manual for the spiritual adviser involved in the monastic pastoral care of nuns *[cura monialium]*. Through its theological basis and practical orientation toward feminine piety, it sought to rectify the lack within the monastic life of a rule for religious women, just as Abelard had attempted within his writing for the Paraclete.

Two and a half centuries later, from around 1400, the *Speculum virginum* experienced anew a strong revival—but now through a vernacular translation. The Middle Dutch translation, of which twenty-five verified witnesses have been identified, significantly enlarged the reception of the work in the late Middle Ages. Indeed, the *Spieghel der Maechden [Maidens' Mirror]* became a leading text of the major movement of religious reform that issued from the Netherlands and encompassed most of northwestern Europe, known as the *Devotio Moderna* or Modern Devotion. Despite its significance for late medieval piety, the vernacular version of the *Speculum virginum* has been relatively little studied. The writings of Matthäus Bernards certainly uncovered important themes within the Latin text but did not facilitate access to the vernacular translation.[1] Furthermore, the edition produced by Jutta Seyfarth has now taken research into the Latin text to a new level.[2] In an entry in *Die deutsche Literatur des Mittelalters. Verfasserlexikon,* I was able to document a further six manuscripts of the vernacular translation, in addition to the nineteen listed by Bernards, and to sketch the first indications of the historical involvement of the text in the Modern Devotion.[3] In the meantime, the Middle Dutch text was published by Irene Berkenbusch, on the basis of the relatively late Darmstadt manuscript.[4]

In what follows, I want to demonstrate some likely contemporary cultural and social functions of the *Speculum virginum,* with reference to the development of religious women's communities in the circles of the Modern Devotion. By taking into consideration pastoral care for religious women in the early stage of the movement, around 1400, new light can be shed on the circumstances of its creation and the possible author of the translation. It will be argued that the expansion of a systematically organized congregation and its offshoots of religious communities substantially assisted in the diffusion of the text of the *Spieghel der Maechden.* From a historical perspective, it was the female tertiaries of the Utrecht chapter in northwest Holland who were initially important in the first half of the fifteenth century. Augustinian nuns and sisters of the common life became significant in southern Holland and northwestern Germany after 1450.

The sisters of the common life originated from the vicinity of Windesheim. These communities of sisters illustrate the basic dilemma of the Modern Devotion, being always in a precarious position midway between the cloister and the world, while also eager for the integration and institutionalization of the "common life" into the framework of ecclesiastical law. The *Speculum virginum* became important once again precisely for this reason, as a programmatic text for female monastic life.

### The *Spieghel der Maechden,* Wermbold of Buscoep (d. 1413), and the Utrecht Chapter

Contrary to an early opinion of Matthäus Bernards, the *Spieghel der Maechden* was an original Middle Dutch translation of the *Speculum virginum* (and certainly not based on one in German). The *Speculum* was later translated into Low German and Ripuarian—in or adapted to the written dialects of Geldern. I shall not enter here into the philological questions concerning the exact manuscript of the Latin text used for the Dutch translation. Such questions could be elucidated further on the basis of the new edition from Jutta Seyfarth.

The *Spieghel der Maechden* certainly originated as a translation some time late in the fourteenth century, as indicated by the St. Petersburg fragments, dated by Lievens to between 1380 and 1400.[5] Its origin is therefore contemporaneous with the beginnings of the Modern Devotion in the last quarter of the fourteenth century.[6] Deacon Geert Grote (1340–1384), born in Deventer, is regarded as the founding father of the movement of religious awakening. Grote, together with Florentius Radewijns (1350–1400), guided the first houses of the brethren of the common life in Deventer, Kampen, and Zwolle. These communities consisted of clerics (often not ordained) and laity, who lived together after the ideal of the primitive apostolic church, initially without taking a vow, following the Rule of an order, or being attached to an order. This precarious semireligious position within ecclesiastical law was even more pressing for the countless religious women who became attracted by the preaching of the Devout and who wanted to live in a community.[7] The early communities of sisters were distrusted by the Inquisition and could not be distinguished from the Beguines, who since the thirteenth century had led a controversial pattern of life in towns in the northwest of Europe, straddling between the cloister and the world.

In order to escape ecclesiastical criticism, the Devout tended to adopt monastic rules and to form monastic associations. The congregation around the Augustinian prebendary monastery of Windesheim is worth mentioning in particular, as this group's influence radiated out into many communities that had not made a formal connection with it. There were also smaller reform groups, such as the chapter of Zion. Although not as famous as the Windesheim congregation, the Utrecht chapter was every bit as influential, with well over one hundred dependencies.[8] These communities—in strong contrast to the Windesheim chapter—consisted almost exclusively of female convents. If one considers the manuscript tradition of the *Spieghel der Maechden* in the fourteenth century, one notices that at least six copies of the text, perhaps as many as nine, can be assigned to tertiaries of the Utrecht chapter. In Easter 1399 this congregation, formed of communities of sisters and of brothers, was founded by a group of priests in Amersfoort. Shortly thereafter, in the years 1399 to 1401, many communities in the town and diocese of Utrecht and in northern Holland joined them. They took vows of obedience to the Order of Penance, accepted the so-called third Rule of St. Francis, and chose a "General Minister," the priest and notary Wilhelm Hendricks from Amersfoort. This reform initiative was supervised by the bishop of Utrecht and supported by privileges from Pope Boniface IX, from 1399 to 1401.[9]

The central founding figure was the chaplain and preacher, Wermbold of Buscoep, namely of Utrecht, a leading thinker among the Devout, who deserves special attention in reference to the creation of the *Spieghel der Maechden*.[10] Nothing is known about his social background. He was, however, a personal friend of Geert Grote and also had contact with Radewijns, and the circle of the Devout in Deventer. His pastoral activities spanned the period between 1380/90 and his death in 1413. Wermbold was a well-known popular preacher, committed to the pastoral care of women. He became the spiritual adviser to numerous communities of sisters. For this reason he received from the Devout, as did Gerart Zerbolt of Zutphen, the honorary title "common Father of devout women in Holland" *[communis pater devotarum in Hollandia]*. Indeed, he was called the "Apostle of Holland."

By 1392 he was appearing as confessor, procurator, and founder of a large number of communities of Beguine and religious sisters in the town of Utrecht. The basis from which he started out was the convent of St. Cecilia in Utrecht, of which he was administrator, possibly already since 1383 but certainly by 1392. There he worked closely together with the widow Aleid Cluten, who, as leader or "mother" of the convent, supervised the access to confession of the sisters and was also herself active in the taking of the confessions. The convent of St. Nicolas, formerly a house of Beguines, also came under Wermbold's leadership from 1394, as did the convent of St. Ursula, the convent "In den Wijngaard" [In the Vineyard], subsequently a Birgittine house, and the convent of St. Agnes. In 1399 the sisters of St. Nicolas in Utrecht seem to have adopted the third Rule and were ceremoniously given their habit in the convent of St. Cecilia.[11] Around 1399 Wermbold founded the community of female tertiaries at Vreedendael near Utrecht, which adopted the Augustinian Rule in 1417. The Utrecht female communities seem to have subordinated themselves to the "mother" of the convent of St. Cecilia, Aleid Cluten. Wermbold officiated as the supervisor and confessor of the entire group, an office that after his death was handed down to the confessor of St. Cecilia. The chronicle of the convent of St. Nicolas reports the following:

> Soe hebben wi ons volkomeliken overgegeven onder her Warmbout ende onder de moeder van sint Cecilien, horen raet in allen te volgen. Des ghelikes haben oec die ander conventen gedaen. . . . Ende di tot sinte Cecilien biechtvader was, die was over al. Ende dit duerde lange jaren oec nae her Warmboutes doet.[12]

> [So we all completely submitted ourselves to Wermbold and to the mother of St.Cecilia, to follow their advice in everything. The other communities also did similarly. . . . And the person who was confessor of St. Cecilia, was confessor everywhere else. And this continued for many years after Wermbold's death.]

Wermbold reached out with his reforming efforts toward north Holland from the convent of St. Cecilia in Utrecht and reformed, among others, various women's communities in Delft, Rhenen, Gouda, Amersfoort, and Weesp. His concern was to effect the regularization of "untamed" communities of women that previously had known neither commitment to an order, nor Rule, nor vow, nor an equivalent to a Mother Superior. Sources from the St. Agatha cloister in Delft, which Wermbold reformed in the year 1400, reports the following: "Doe brochten si (die fratres) ons ersaemlic bi dat we noch nie mit rehter ordonancien noch regel noch professie noch moeder noch anwisinge der ghemeenen susteren gehabt en hadden." [There the brothers advised us that we never had a right order of life nor rule nor profession nor mother nor instructions for the common sisters.][13] With the reform, the third Rule was introduced, the ecclesiastical rule of the brethren was accepted, and a superior or "mother" was taken on by the women's community from St. Cecilia in Utrecht. Profession was also made in Utrecht. Clearly, Wermbold, together with Aleid Cluten, had thought of the St. Cecilia convent in Utrecht as a center of reform or mother house of a multitude of women's communities. The decisive organizational elements were set up by Buscoep in 1399, with the founding of the Utrecht chapter. This gave an official form and hierarchical structure to the groups of women's communities and made the third Rule obligatory. After St. Francis had founded the order of the Minors (first order) and the order of the Clares (second order), he established the third order, for people in the world, namely for women and men, both married and single. These were the "tertiaries" or "brothers and sisters of the third Rule of Penance" *[fratres et sorores tertiae regulae de penitentia]*. The Rule, which was considered less strict than Rules of other orders, was formally approved in the year 1289 by Pope Nicolas IV in the bull *Supra montes*. Together with other papal privileges of 1399 and 1401, this bull was followed in religious communities. In addition to the third Rule, convents pledged themselves to statutes that were likewise formally approved by the pope, and also to resolutions of the chapter.[14]

The convents were changing from semireligious women's communities to regular nunneries. Measured by monastic standards, the way of life was not so very rigorous. The regulations governing fasting and prayer were not very strict, and the vow of silence was limited to a few hours per day. Handicrafts and textiles were made, so that the convents became a commercial force within an urban environment. Steps toward further monastic institutionalization can be discerned, however. Profession, together with taking the habit, was celebrated after a trial period of one year. From 1401 the brothers and sisters were allowed to take the vow of chastity. By contrast, the vows of poverty and obedience were not strictly compulsory. Also, the great majority of the convents were "enclosed." In other words, the sisters were secluded from the world in a formal ceremony.[15]

In addition to a confessor whom they could choose, the women had a mother *[mater]*, who in particular supervised access to confession. At the head of the entire chapter stood a General Minister, who annually called together the confessors of the communities to a chapter meeting. The convents were to be visited once each year, and where possible by a visitor from the Order of St. Francis. Although the communities of sisters did not belong officially to the Franciscan Order, a link to the Franciscans was achieved through this process. Moreover, many convents had as confessors priests from the houses of brothers from the circle of the reformed Windesheim communities, so that contact also existed with this better-known reform group.

Convents of tertiaries spread from Utrecht and Delft into north and northwest Holland until the middle of the fifteenth century. In around 1450 there were well over one hundred communities. In the earlier period, the number had been even greater, but under ecclesiastical pressure and influenced by the Windesheim Reform, some of these adopted the Augustinian Rule after 1418.

Wermbold of Buscoep seems to have played an important role in the creation and diffusion of the *Spieghel der Maechden*. It can be proven that the text was known to the tertiaries of the Utrecht chapter from at least 1424. The important early London manuscript (British Library, Add. 38527) also points to this connection. This manuscript is the only one in which the

*Spieghel der Maechden* is illustrated. In later manuscripts there are only indications to miniatures that were not executed. The London manuscript is clearly shown to be an early text through its significant illuminations and its careful, well-formed script, and can be dated to 1410.[16] A rubric (fol. 143v) confirms that it comes from Utrecht: "dit boec hoert tot den susteren bi onser vrouwen in de wiyngaert t'Utrecht" [This book belongs to the sisters of Our beloved Lady, In the Vineyard, of Utrecht]. The Birgittine convent "In the vineyard" was originally a convent of sisters.[17] The community was founded about 1407, and reformed and guided by Wermbold of Buscoep, the "common Father of devout women in Holland" and founding father of the Utrecht chapter. The convent "In the vineyard" was closely connected to the Utrecht center of St. Cecilia and its mother superior, Aleid Cluten. The sisters from "In the vineyard" probably took the monastic habit there and committed themselves to the third Rule.

We encounter the *Spieghel der Maechden* at the beginning of the fifteenth century in the group of reformed women's communities that formed the nucleus of the Utrecht chapter. It was then disseminated further among the tertiaries of the chapter. This raises the suggestion that the Middle Dutch translation of the *Speculum virginum* was made in Utrecht, and indeed within a small circle around the spiritual leader, Wermbold of Buscoep.

There is another significant clue to this connection between Wermbold and the *Speculum virginum:* Two manuscripts of the *Speculum virginum*, copied around 1450, were preserved in the community of tertiaries of St. John in Weesp (Oude Hof), founded in 1396. One of these was a complete text; the other was an extract of the work. Wermbold had close contacts and was much revered there. In the memorial book of the community of sisters (The Hague, Koninglijk Bibliotheek, MS 73 G 1, fol. 40v), he is commemorated at length as a preacher and "leader of the Devout": "Heer Wermbolt toe Utrecht tot Sinte Cecilien, een groet predicaer en hoeft alrer devoter menschen" [Mr. Wermbold of Utrecht, at St. Cecilia, a great preacher and leader of all devout men].[18]

The period when the *Spieghel der Maechden* was produced coincides with the period when Wermbold was active (1380/90–1413). The early manuscript tradition of the *Spieghel der Maechden* corresponds very precisely to the region of Wermbold's pastoral influence, with the communities of sisters in the town of Utrecht and in the Utrecht chapter. Wermbold of Buscoep may have been the person who commissioned or indeed translated the *Speculum virginum*. He was also associated with other translations of Latin texts. J. Deschamps sees in Wermbold the author of the second Middle Dutch translation of the *Verba seniorum*, the fifth and sixth books of the *Lives of the Fathers*. According to Thomas à Kempis, Wermbold had translated into Dutch "certain sayings of the saints" *[quedam dicta sanctorum].*[19] Furthermore, there is evidence that other parts of the *Lives of the Fathers* were translated at the Utrecht convent of Vreedendael, founded by Wermbold.[20] There was obviously a need in the circle around Wermbold and the devout sisters for translation of Latin texts that would provide a systematic foundation of the monastic way of life.

Wermbold, preacher and confessor, was dedicated specifically to the pastoral care of women through the founding, nurturing, and reforming of communities of sisters. So he would have known the Latin text of the *Speculum virginum,* the most important manual for pastoral care of women. Those partners in literary dialogue, Peregrinus and Theodora, may even have provided a role model for the spiritual friendship between Wermbold, the pastoral adviser, and Aleid Cluten, the mother superior of St. Cecilia in Utrecht. The translation of the Latin text into the vernacular enabled it to be made known to the sisters entrusted to his care, who were according to their educational status the most unlettered. Wermbold's involvement in the creation of its text would also explain its further diffusion among the tertiaries.

In any case, it can be shown that the diffusion of the *Spieghel der Maechden* coincides both chronologically and geographically with the affiliation of communities of tertiaries to the Utrecht chapter until the middle of the fifteenth century. I provide here an overview of this process:

> Monikendam, O.L. Vrouwe [Our beloved Lady]
> Utrecht, Universiteitsbibliotheek MS 1021; 1424.
> Doesburg, St. Catharina
> Brussels, Bibliothèque royale, MS II 4748; 1457.
> Amsterdam, St. Clara
> Weert, Provincialarchiv van de Minderbroers, MS 1; mid-15th century
> Weesp, St. Johannes (Oude Hof)
> 1.  The Hague, Koninglijk Bibliotheek, 73 G 16; mid-15th century
> 2.  The Hague, Koninglijk Bibliotheek, 73 G 17); 2nd half of the 15th century
> Delft, St. Ursula (in't Oesteynde)
> Leiden, UB Letterk. 342; mid-15th century[21]

Apart from six manuscripts of known provenance, two Leiden manuscripts come from convents that may have belonged to the tertiaries:

> Leiden, UB Letterk. 341; mid-15th century: this is assigned to a community of sisters of St. Catherine, in Rosendael near Gouda; if this convent is identical with the tertiary convent of St. Catherine, then a connection with the Utrecht chapter would be revealed.[22]

Leiden, UB Letterk. 222; 1458 [extracts]. Probably comes from Delft; it is still to be clarified whether its specific origin is the tertiary convent of St. Barbara, St. Agatha, or St. Ursula.

A number of the communities of tertiaries that owned copies of the *Spieghel der Maechden* possessed relatively large libraries. The statutes provided for a "keeper of books" who was to supervise the library and the orthodoxy of the texts.[23] The community of St. Barbara in Delft had many religious legends, treatises, and sermons, most of them written in Dutch.[24] The library of the community of St. John in Weesp, which owned two manuscripts of the *Spieghel der Maechden*, contained at least 110 volumes, according to its catalogue.[25] In addition to patristic works, scholastic and mystical literature, it also contained some classical authors.

Books were made available to women in these convents mainly by priests and relatives in the form of gifts or bequests. Because the majority of the women were unlettered, books in the vernacular were preferred to those in Latin. Since the women had a limited ability to write, texts were written mainly by external scribes, who were in fact clerics. In some cases, however, texts were written mainly by women in the community. The manuscript of the *Spieghel der Maechden* from Monikendam was written in 1424 by Dirk Adams, the son *[Dirc Adams zoen]* (fol. 126c). One of the manuscripts from Weesp (The Hague, Koninglijk Bibliotheek 73 G 17, fol. 134r) asks for an Ave Maria "for the scribe" *[uor den scriuer]*. By contrast, a manuscript from the community of St. Clare in Amsterdam mentions someone, obviously a sister, as the writer: "Read for the [female] scribe an Ave Maria for God's will" [Leest voer die scrijfster somwijls en ave maria um gods wille] (fol. 114 v).

A literary preference for Dutch translations of ecclesiastical Latin texts can be seen in these book collections.[26] They frequently included texts of the Bible, Passion tracts, legends of the saints (martyrdoms, the *Golden Legend*), the *Lives of the Fathers* and the related *Conferences* of John Cassian, the *Bonum de apibus* of Thomas of Cantimpré, and the works of Jordan of Saxony. The *Spieghel der Maechden* belongs to this group of translated literature; its pragmatic significance as "mirror literature" for the instruction of female religious life is to be noted.

## The Windesheim Reform, Augustinian Nuns, and the Sisters of the Common Life

While the early circulation of the *Spieghel der Maechden* was in the region of Utrecht and north Holland, among the circle of tertiaries of the Utrecht chapter, its center of diffusion in the second half of the fifteenth century moved into new areas. These later manuscripts come more from south Holland, in particular the region of Rhine and Maas (Nijmegen, Geldern), the Rhineland (Cologne), as well as north and northwest Germany (Frenswegen, Hannover, Lübeck). This area corresponds exactly to the region of influence of the Modern Devotion. It became transmitted by the communities of brethren and of sisters in the vicinity of the Windesheim congregation, which had taken the vow of the Augustinian Rule. The Windesheim reform had been expanding since the early fifteenth century. The Modern Devotion found within its framework a stable monastic organizational form. Many women's communities of the Devout accepted the Augustinian Rule under the influence of Windesheim. Johannes Brinkerinck, who developed the convent in Diepenveen into an ecclesiastical center, played a significant role.[27] Again we can observe the tendency to integration and institutionalization of this movement of religious women.

Distinct stages in the forming of connections to the monastic life are evident. No more than sixteen nunneries in Belgium, Holland, and Germany were officially incorporated into the Windesheim association of communities.[28] The great majority remained communities of sisters without formal association and followed more or less exactly the Augustinian Rule and appropriate Windesheim statutes. Brothers from Windesheim were often active as confessors, helpers, and procurators.

After 1450 or so, practically all the manuscripts of the *Spieghel der Maechden* come from convents of female tertiaries or from convents that were connected with Windesheim. This group includes male monasteries that were incorporated in the chapter, such as those of Bredevoort and Frenswegen, as well as a nunnery incorporated in 1457, namely the community of Marienburg in Nijmegen.[29] It also includes male and female Augustinian houses like that of Jerusalem, at Venray.[30] As in many communities of female tertiaries, priests from male monasteries functioned as confessors. Their influence was important in making the *Spieghel der Maechden* well known and popular. The close connection of the *Speculum virginum* to the Windesheim reform is evident from the fact that not only was the vernacular translation known at Frenswegen, an important center of the Windesheim reform, but at least by 1430 the original Latin text was known as well.[31]

The sisters of the common life in the Rhineland and northwest Germany played an important role in the diffusion of the text in Germany. Gerhard Rehm has shown how in individual convents, stages of "monastification," namely a process of monastic integration and institutionalization, can be identified.[32] The St. Michael convent in Lübeck was originally a Beguine house, then a convent of sisters. It first accepted the Augustinian Rule only late in the fifteenth century. The *Spieghel der Maechden* circulated in the following communities of sisters in Geldic (the local dialect of the town of Geldern), Ripuarian, and Low German versions:

Geldern, convent of Nazareth
Berlin, Staatsbibliothek Preussischer Kulturbesitz, MS germ.oct. 352; 1465 (Geldic); the texts and extracts in the following manuscripts may also come from Geldern:
Berlin, Staatsbibliothek Preussischer Kulturbesitz, MS germ. fol. 1028; 1482 (Ripuarian)
Hamburg, Staats-und Universitätsbibliothek, St B theol. Qu. 1535; 15th century (Ripuarian): "Dit boeck hoert te nazareth bynnen Gelreden beslaten regularissen" [This book belongs to the enclosed regular sisters at Nazareth, in Geldern].
Eldagsen, convent of Marienthal
Hannover, Niedersächsische Landesbibliothek, MS I 237; 1482 (Low German)
Lübeck, probably convent of St. Michael
Lübeck, Stadtbibliothek, MS theol. germ. 30); 15th century (Low German)
Cologne, convent of St. Cecilia
Darmstadt, Hessische Landesbibliothek MS 466; 16th century (Middle Dutch, with Cologne dialect)

We are relatively well informed about the library of the community of sisters of St. Nazareth in Geldern through recent research.[33] It can be shown that it owned the writings of Dutch reformers, such as Jan van Ruusbroec and Gerart Zerbolt of Zutphen. It also owned mystical and ascetic literature from the region of south Germany, such as by Meister Eckhart and Suso. Most of these texts are preserved in the local script of Geldern. There was evidently no independent text production; rather, books from other communities were copied out and adapted to the Geldern script. The Berlin anthology from 1465, which includes excerpts from the *Spiegel der J‍oncfrowen,* is accordingly written in the Geldern script. In addition, this collection provides extracts from leading texts of the Modern Devotion, such as *Geestelike brulocht [Spiritual Marriage]* by Jan van Ruusbroec and texts of Jordan, his fellow brother.

## Enclosure and the Programmatic Function
### of the *Spieghel der Maechden*

The traces of the manuscript transmission of the *Spieghel der Maechden* in the early fifteenth century have pointed initially to Utrecht, to the community of sisters called "In the vineyard," and to the Utrecht chapter of the tertiaries. At this stage it can be firmly argued that the Middle Dutch translation of the *Speculum virginum* arose in the confined circle around the Utrecht reformer Wermbold von Buscoep, the spiritual guide and founding father of these female communities of the Devout in Utrecht, and his spiritual friend, Aleid Cluten. Wermbold was celebrated as a translator by Thomas à Kempis (ca. 1380–1471) and therefore has been connected with the (second) Middle Dutch translation of the *Lives of the Fathers* by J. Deschamps.[34] Around 1400 there was obviously a great interest in Utrecht in the translation into the vernacular of Latin monastic literature by which the sisters could become engaged with a monastic way of life.

The author of the translation may even have been Wermbold himself, and he and Aleid Cluten may have recognized each other as Peregrinus and Theodora. The Latin version of the *Speculum virginum* corresponds very closely to the spiritual profile and pastoral interests of Wermbold, who dedicated himself from 1380 to 1413 as "father of the devout women" *[pater devotarum]*, specifically to the pastoral care of sisters. He also founded and reformed many communities of sisters in Utrecht and in other cities in north Holland, and in 1399 he gave these a firm organizational structure with the chapter of Utrecht. The translation of the *Speculum virginum* into the vernacular responded to the needs of the unlettered sisters.

While the convents of female tertiaries were mainly responsible for the transmission of the text between 1400 and 1450/60, it was the Augustinian sisters and communities of sisters in the vicinity of the Windesheim Reform who were the main bearers of the text after 1450. An important characteristic of its transmission is that while the Latin *Speculum virginum* was disseminated virtually exclusively through male monasteries, the manuscripts of the Dutch *Spieghel der Maechden* come from women's houses in the great majority of cases. Convents of female tertiaries, such as St. John in Weesp and of Augustinian sisters such as Nazareth in Geldern, had large libraries. Their books consisted primarily of Middle Dutch texts, often translations of Latin literature. We can observe a substantial production of manuscripts by the Devout, just before and even within the growing the influence of the early phase of book printing. The manuscripts of the *Spieghel der Maechden* were, for the most part, preserved in female convents, although they were not necessarily written there. Scribes from outside the cloister are named in the manuscripts of the tertiaries from Monikendam and Weesp; these were in fact priests. The manuscripts from Amsterdam and Geldern, however, were actually written by the sisters themselves.

The diffusion of the *Spieghel der Maechden* permits the following conjecture: If the Latin text was a kind of manual for male pastoral advisers, then the Dutch text was received directly inside the women's communities. In this connection, we can imagine the text being read during the afternoon collation. This use of the text is confirmed by the presence of excerpts within collation books, a genre of religious literature typical of the Modern Devotion.[35]

The *Spieghel der Maechden* was a guiding text of the Modern Devotion, as the presence of excerpts from the work in anthologies and collation books demonstrates. It is not by accident that it is often handed down together with the main works of the Dutch mystics. For example, it is found with Jan van Ruusbroec's *Geestelike Brulocht [Spiritual Marriage]*[36] and Hendrik Herp's *Spieghel der Volcomenheit [Mirror of Perfection]*.[37] What makes the text attractive for the communities of sisters is certainly its clear and pragmatic structure. The literature of the Modern Devotion is less oriented toward theological speculation and more toward practical action.[38] It seeks to establish instructions, standards, and rules for the actual conduct of the religious life. In this way the preference of the Modern Devotion for *Mirror* literature is explained; book titles like *Mirror of Christian Faith, Mirror of Perfection, Mirror of Sins,* and *Mirror of Eternal Life* confirm this.[39]

The *Speculum virginum* also belongs in this context, for through this text a binding program of the female common life is presented and elucidated. It is not by accident that the collation books choose excerpts from parts eight and nine of the *Speculum virginum*—the section that differentiates the condition of the religious from that of the married woman and widow. This section of the *Speculum* also offers examples of Christian and classical feminine piety, debates practical questions of the sumptuary laws, develops an ethical teaching concerning the core concept of conscience, and thereby values spiritual nobility over inherited nobility of blood.

Excerpts from part nine appear in the Nijmegen anthology, *Collatieboek over het huwelijk en de eerbaarheit der weduwen [Collation book concerning the marital life and the dignity of widowhood]*.[40] In its context, this extract also is concerned with establishing the ethical and religious basis of a way of life for women.

In particular, the *Spieghel der Maechden* has pragmatic significance in relation to the extension of "monastification" of the communities of sisters. The convents indeed sought to move from a semireligious way of life to a monastic order of life, by commitment to rules, the vow, and enclosure. It was of course a central preoccupation of pastoral concern for women that sisters should become familiar with the demands of a monastic communal life. In this respect, the *Speculum virginum* was comparable to the *Bonum de apibus* or *Book of the Bees [bijen-boec]* of Thomas of Cantimpré, often encountered in the circle of communities of sisters. The translations of the *Lives of the Fathers,* evidently made in the circle around Wermbold of Buscoep, served a similar purpose. In all these texts the life of a religious community is introduced, described, and legitimated.

The pragmatic function of the *Spieghel der Maechden* is very evident in the example of enclosure, an important step in the path to a monastic way of life for communities of sisters *[besloten susters]*. Enclosure signifies strict separation from the influence of the world of the laity. In a formal ceremony the tertiaries were given their habits and received into the enclosure. Numerous hostile examples are told of sisters who broke out of the strict enclosure and fled.[41] It is therefore all the more important to establish the value of such enclosure. The entire second part of the *Speculum virginum* is dedicated to the benefits of enclosure.

In its new lease of life within the context of the communities of sisters of the Modern Devotion, the *Speculum virginum* found a new historical "Sitz im Leben" as a key text within the movement of reform. Translated into Middle Dutch as the *Spieghel der Maechden [Spieghel der Maechden]* and closely connected to the person of Wermbold von Buscoep, this pedagogical dialogue became once again a guiding programmatic document in the reforming concerns of the Devout for the pastoral care of women.

### Notes

1. Matthäus Bernards, *Speculum virginum. Geistigkeit und Seelenleben der Frau im Hochmittelalter* (Cologne-Vienna: Böhlau, 1955; 2nd ed. 1982), pp. 8–9. Bernards assumed that there was originally a Low or even a High German translation. For corrections, see the review of Kurt Ruh, *Zeitschrift für deutsche Philologie* 77 (1958): 317–20.
2. See the description of the Middle Dutch manuscripts, based on my own research, in Seyfarth, pp. 109*–123*.
3. Urban Küsters and Jutta Seyfarth, "Speculum Virginum," in *Die deutsche Literatur des Mittelalters. Verfasserlexikon,* 2nd ed., 9 (Berlin: de Grayter, 1992): 67–76, especially 72–76.
4. Irene Berkenbusch, *Speculum virginum. Mittelniederländischer Text. Edition, Untersuchungen zum Prolog und einleitende Interpretation,* Europäische Hochschulschriften 1/1511 (Frankfurt: Peter Lang, 1995).
5. Warsaw, MS Dutch O.V.I, n. 8 (formerly St. Petersburg, Imperial Library, returned to Warsaw in 1924, but destroyed in 1944); photographs preserved in Ghent (Seyfarth, p. 117*) are studied by R. Lievens, *Middelnederlandse Handschriften in Oost-Europa* (Ghent: Secretariaat van de Academie, 1963), p. 181, no. 136.
6. For an overview, see R. T. M. van Dijk, "Geert Grote en de Moderne Devotie," in *Moderne Devotie. Figuren en Facetten. Catalogus* (Nijmegen: Katholieke Universiteit, Afdeling Hulpwetenshappen van de geschiedenis 1984), pp. 11–43.

7. See A. G. Weiler, "De intrede van rijke weduwen en arme meisjes in de leefgemeenschapen van de Moderne Devotie," *Ons Geestelijk Erf* 59 (1985): 403–20.

8. For what follows on the Utrecht chapter, see the fundamental work of Dalmatius van Heel, *De Tertiarissen van het Utrechtse Kapittel* (Utrecht:Van Rossum, 1939), and more lately Florence W. J. Koorn, "Hollandse nuchterheid? De houding van de Moderne Devoten tegenover vrouwenmystiek en -ascese," in *Ons Geestelijk Erf* 66 (1992): 97–114, especially 108ff. and ibid., "Het Kapittel van Utrecht," in *Windesheim 1395–1995. Kloosters, Teksten, Invloeden*, ed. A. J. Hendrikman et al. (Nijmegen: Centrum voor Middeleeuwse Studies, 1996), pp. 131–42. More recently, a research group at the University of Amsterdam has been studying the Utrecht chapter. See Kees Goudriaan, "De deerde orde van Sint Franciscus in het bisdom Utrecht," in *Jaarboek voor Middeleeuwse Geschiedenis* 1 (1998): 205–60, in which a new list of 166 convents is given, revising the older list of 82 convents, documented by van Heel.

9. The privileges and statutes of 1399 to 1401 are edited by van Heel (n. 8 above) in an appendix.

10. On Wermbold's career, see van Heel, *De Tertiarissen*, p. 10 and especially Koorn, "Hollandse nuchterheid?" pp. 108ff. (n. 8 above).

11. P. J. Vermeulen, "Kronijk van het S. Nicolaas-Klooster te Utrecht," in *Tijdschrift voor Oudheden, Statistiek, Zeden en Gewoonten, Regt. Genealogie en andere deelen der geschiedenis van het bisdom, de provincie en de stat Utrecht* 4 (1852): 71–100, 76f.

12. Ibid., 77.

13. N. C. Kist, "De oorsprong en opkomst van et S. Aagteklooster te Delft," in *Nieuw Archief voor Kerkelijke Geschiedenis* 2 (1854): 377–93, 381.

14. On the statutes and their transmission, see van Heel, pp. 16ff. and Koorn, "Het Kapittel van Utrecht," p. 139 (n. 8 above).

15. According to van Heel, pp. 16ff. (n. 8 above), almost all the convents were enclosed after a short period. By contrast, Koorn, "Het Kapittel van Utrecht," p. 140 (n. 8 above) puts the question of how strict enclosure could be reconciled with their economic activity.

16. Erwin Panofsky, *Early Netherlandish Painting*, 2 vols. (Cambridge, MA: Harvard University Press, 1953), 1: 99; illustration in 2: 119.

17. Koorn, "Hollandse nuchterheid?" 108 (n. 8 above) draws on Vermeulen (n. 11 above) and Utrecht, Gemeentearchief, bibliotheek, no. 1840, fol. 124; see now Goudriaan, "De deerde orde," 244, no. 147 (n. 8 above).

18. Koorn, "Hollandse nuchterheid?" 109 (n. 8 above).

19. J. Deschamps, *Middelnederlandse handschriften uit Europese en Amerikaanse Bibliotheeken,* 2nd ed. (Leiden: Brill, 1972), p. 176, no. 59, in relation to Utrecht, *Erzbischöfliches Museum* MS 51.

20. Ibid., p. 174, no. 57; this is an anthology of 1417 from Vreedendael (Utrecht, Universiteitsbibliotheek MS 7 N 25) containing Timothy of

Alexandria, *Historia monachorum in Aegypto* (*Vitae patrum II*), and Palladius of Hellenopolis, *Historia Lausiaca* (*Vitae patrum VIII*).

21. Seyfarth, p. 116*, no. 14, speaks incorrectly of St. Ursula in Ostend, when it is actually the "Ostende" (east end) of Delft; see van Heel, p. 323 (n. 8 above).

22. G. I. Lieftinck, *Codices manuscripti V codicum in finibus Belgarum ante annum 1550 conscriptum, qui in Bibliotheca universitatis asservantur,* vol. 1 (Leiden: Brill, 1948), p. 263.

23. Van Heel, pp. 45ff. (n. 8 above).

24. W. Moll, *De boeken van het St. Barbara-Klooster te Delft* (Amsterdam, 1857), following The Hague, Koninglijk Bibliotheek MS 130 E.24.

25. T. H. G. van Iterson, "De bibliotheek van het oude konvent der zusteren in het St. Johansklooster te Weesp," in *Nederlands Archief voor Kerkgeschiedenis* 7 (1837): 177; van Heel, pp. 46ff., 125ff. (n. 8 above).

26. See the extensive overview of the collections by van Heel, pp. 315ff. (n. 8 above); see also the overview of the manuscript collections, arranged according to Order by Karl Stooken and Theo Verbeij, *Collecties op Orde,* 2 vols. (Louvain: Peters, 1998).

27. On pastoral care of women at Windesheim and Diepenveen, see Weiler (n. 7 above).

28. Individual communities of the congregation are listed in W. Kohl, E. Persoons, and A. G. Weiler, *Monasticon Windeshemense,* 4 vols. (Brussels: Association des archivistes et bibliothécaires de Belgique, 1976–84); for more recent studies, see the collective volume *Windesheim 1395–1995* (n. 8 above); on the incorporated women's communities, see the study of Wybren Scheepsma, *Deemoed en Devotie. De koorvrouwen van Windesheim en hun geschriften* (Amsterdam: Prometheus, 1997).

29. Description of the manuscript, Nijmegen, Gemeentearchief, MS 25, in *Catalogus: Moderne Devotie. Figuren en Facetten,* p. 269ff, no. 99 (A. J. Geurts); see n. 6 above.

30. Lucidarius Verschueren, "Handschriften afkomstik uit het Klooster Jerusalem te Venray," in *Publications de la Société historique et archéologique dans le Limbourg* 85 (1949): 693–730, especially 703ff., no. IV.

31. Frenswegen owned the manuscripts Cuyk, Kreuzherrnkloster St. Agatha, MS C 124, fols. 181v–186v, 194r–195v (1452/53), with excerpts from the *Spieghel der Maechden;* and Burgsteinfurt, Bibliothek der Grafen von Bentheim, MS 4 (1430), with the Latin text of the *Speculum virginum.*

32. Gerhard Rehm, *Die Schwestern vom Gemeinsamen Leben im nordwestlichen Deutschland* (Berlin: Duncker & Humblot, 1985).

33. Monika Costard, "Predigthandschriften der Schwestern vom Gemeinsamen Leben. Spätmittelalterliche Predigtüberlieferung in der Bibliothek des Klosters Nazareth in Geldern," in *Die deutsche Predigt im Mittelalter,* ed. Volker Mertens and H. J. Schiewer (Tübingen: Max Niemeyer Verlag, 1992), pp. 204–20; Hartmut Beckers, "Die volkssprachliche Literatur des

Mittelalters am Niederrhein," *Xantener Vorträge zur Geschichte des Niederrheins* 18 (Duisburg, 1995), 17ff.

34. See n. 19 above.

35. On collation practice, see Küsters, *Der verschlossene Garten. Volkssprachliche Hohelied-Auslegung und monastiche Lebensform im 12. Jahrhundert*, Studia Humaniora 2 (Düsseldorf: Droste, 1985), pp. 27ff.; on collation books, see Thom Mertens, "Posthuum auteurschap. De collaties van Johannes Brinckerinck," in *Windesheim 1395–1995*, pp. 85–97 (n. 8 above).

36. Jan van Ruusbroec, *Die Geestelike Brulocht*, ed. J. Alaerts, CCCM 103 (1988): 98ff, 101, 117; on the significance of Ruusbroec, see Kurt Ruh, "Jan van Ruusbroec. Versuch einer Würdigung von Person und Werk," in *Zeitschrift für deutsches Altertum* 125 (1996): 1–50.

37. Hendrik Herp, *Spieghel der Volcomenheit*, ed. Luciduis Verschueren, vol. 1 (Antwerp: Neerlandia, 1931), p. 68.

38. Nikolaus Staubach, "Pragmatische Schriftlichkeit im Umkreis der Devotio Moderna," in *Frühmittelalterliche Studien* 25 (1991): 418–61.

39. Petty Bange, *Spiegels der Christenen* (Nijmegen: Centrum voor Middeleeuwse Studies, 1986), p. 263; see also Urban Küsters, Angelika Lehmann-Benz, and Ulrike Zellmann, eds., *Kulturnachbarschaft. Deutsch-Niederländisches Werkstattgespräch zur Mediaevistik* (Essen: Item Verlag, 1997), pp. 142ff.

40. Contained in Nijmegen, Berchmanianum, Bibliotheek van de Jezuiten, MS 12 B 1, fols. 93v–94r, 148v–152r; description of the manuscript in *Moderne Devotie. Figuren en Facetten*, pp. 162ff., no. 54 (P. Bange); see n. 6 above.

41. Van Heel, pp. 25ff. (n. 8 above).

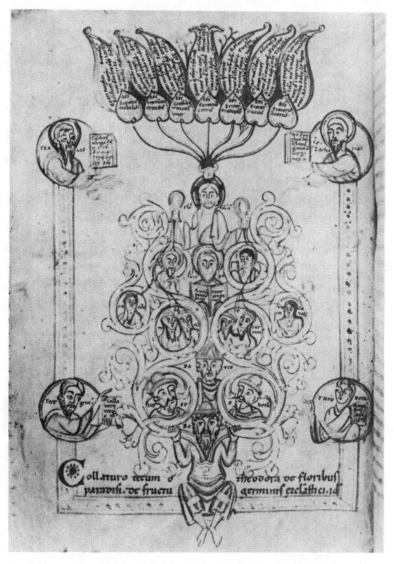

Fig. 1 Tree of Jesse, beginning of *SV* 1 (London, British Library, Arundel 44 f. 2v)

Fig. 2    Tree of Vices, beginning of *SV* 4 (London, British Library, Arundel 44, f. 28v)

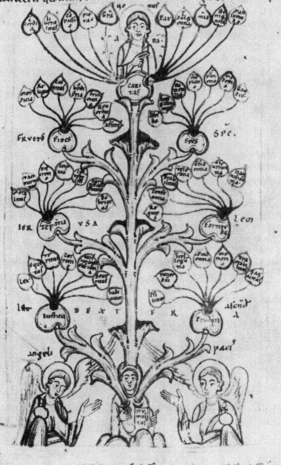

Fig. 3    Tree of Virtues, beginning of *SV* 4 (London, British Library, Arundel 44, f. 29r)

Fig. 4    Humility conquering Pride, *SV* 4 (London, British Library, Arundel 44, f. 34v)

Fig. 5    Flesh and Spirit, beginning of *SV* 8 (London, British Library, Arundel 44, f. 83v)

Fig. 6    Temple of Wisdom, beginning of *SV* 12 (London, British Library, Arundel 44, f. 114v)

# APPENDIX

## *SPECULUM VIRGINUM:* SELECTED EXCERPTS

### *(translated by Barbara Newman)*

Note: *All biblical citations refer to the Latin Vulgate. The language and numbering of verses, especially in the Old Testament, often differ from that found in English Bibles.*

### Letter of Dedication; *SV* Epistula 1–105

From C., the least of Christ's poor, to the holy virgins N. and N.: may you attain the joy of blessed eternity!

Because every human being is drawn by a certain natural order to seek her beginning, that is, her Creator, she should be admonished by the guidance of nature itself to be attentive, and to hold temporal things of little worth in comparison with eternal. But this advice especially suits those who are sealed by the sacraments of the Church for the kingdom of heaven, and who have learned from the doctrines of sacred law to value the temporal less than the eternal. I rejoice with you all the more sweetly, daughters vowed to Christ, because with a willing spirit you have preferred the eternal to the transient, as I now see that for the love of Christ you have trampled underfoot your homeland, your family, and—what is most difficult—the beauty of your blooming youth. "Great is my confidence in you," as Paul said; "great is my boasting on your account. I am filled with comfort, I abound with joy in all my tribulations" because of you [2 Cor. 7.4].

Therefore I continually beseech the divine mercy that your beginning may be crowned with a still happier ending, for both kinship and the double obligation of charity demand that my affection alone watch over you, although age and time and distance divide us. Nor should you think the presence of relatives or friends a thing greatly to be desired—you who bear Christ, your bridegroom and your brother, in your hearts. In him and through him you possess all things, as Paul said: "All things are yours, whether the world or life or death or the present or the future—all are yours, but you are Christ's" [1 Cor. 3.21–23]. And in another passage: "Christ died for all, that even those who live might live no longer for themselves, but for him who died for them and rose again. From now on, therefore, we know no one according to the flesh. Even if we once knew Christ according to the flesh, we no longer know him thus" [2 Cor. 5.15–16]." Therefore, daughters, possessing all things in Christ to whom you have fled, do not look back at the things you despised for his love.

But since love is never idle, I have sent you a little book as a kind of token of mutual love. In it you may exercise your mind, grow in the grace of the eternal bridegroom, and grieve the less at my absence. This little work is entitled *The Mirror of Virgins*. In it a priest, Peregrinus, holds a dialogue with Theodora, a virgin of Christ, to provide Christ's studious virgins with a great incentive for the preservation of chastity, an example of disdain for the present life, and a model of desire for heavenly things. The title indicates the usefulness of the following material, so that by a kind of analogy, you may learn how to seek what is invisible.

Virgins hold mirrors before their eyes to see whether their beauty has increased or diminished. For the beholder's image is reflected in the mirror, and even though the gaze and its reflection are distinct, the beholder's mind is informed about what it wishes to know. We read that Moses, God's confidant, "made a laver from the mirrors of the women who watched at the door of the tabernacle" [Exod. 38.8] in which "Aaron and his sons might wash" [Exod. 40.29]. Now the mirrors of the women are divine words set before the eyes of holy souls, in which they may see at all times how they either please the eternal bridegroom with the beauty of a holy conscience or displease him with the ugliness of sin. The women are said to "watch at the door of the tabernacle" because, as long as they remain in this flesh, they do not enter the holy of holies of our celestial mother Jerusalem. When the "enigma and mirror" by which we know God in part has passed away, what is now sought invisibly in the Scriptures will be seen "face to face" [1 Cor. 13.12]. So, blessed virgins of Christ, wash your conscience in this laver constructed from the divine law, so that God's image in you may shine the more brightly and what is now hidden from mortals, being divine, may appear more radiant than the noonday sun.

Finally, because varied reading gives pleasure while a monotonous, unbroken treatise aggravates and weakens the reader's attention, I have divided this little work into twelve parts. When the virgin of Christ, eager for the divine word, browses in these sections as if in adjoining meadows, delighting in the different flowers—that is, in the mystical senses—she may boast that she has woven a multicolored crown for her head from the Word of God.

The first part, then, is about the mystical flowers of paradise proceeding from the unique "flower of the field and lily of the valleys" [Cant. 2.1], that is, the sacred virgins of Christ nourishing their flower and fruit in Christ's love, and the form of paradise with its four symbolic rivers, which are the four evangelists and doctors, watering the whole Church with their word and example. The second part is about the usefulness of enclosure and the danger of straying, and it warns that cloistered virgins should keep the matter of sin away from their five senses, for by guarding themselves they shut off access to the enemy. It also tells the story of a certain cleric who broke into a cloister of virgins and perished at once by the just judgment of God. The third part is the Holy Spirit's address to the daughter of the Church on the mystical garment of virginity, which adorns the daughters of Zion. Unless they are humbled by grace, they can easily be despoiled. The fourth contains a diagram of pride and humility, vices and virtues, and after the example of Jael and Judith—women who conquered the enemies of Israel—the virgins of Christ rejoice in triumph when pride is conquered by humility. The fifth part is about the chief of virgins, Mary, together with her Son and the two Johns [the Baptist and the Evangelist], who are like a team of four horses drawing a chariot. By their example, those who seek the fruit of merit through the flower of virginity may be lifted from the depths to the heights. This section also deals with good and bad teachers of virgins. The sixth concerns the ten foolish and wise virgins, and the discretion with which they ought to keep watch [Matt. 25.1–13]. The seventh is about the three ranks of married people, widows, and virgins, and the thirtyfold, sixtyfold, and hundredfold fruit. The virtue of women under paganism is also held up as an example. The eighth part concerns the fruits of flesh and spirit, their growth, and their differing qualities, and makes the point that, from the beginning of the world, those who have spiritually departed (or will depart) from their native land have been (or will be) pleasing to God. This section also correlates the works of the six days of creation with the progress of the six ages of history. The ninth part treats the mighty ascent of virgins on the ladder to heaven, and contains exhortations on patience and other virtues. It teaches that the perfection of virginity is revealed above all through humility and patience. The tenth section is a thanksgiving. The eleventh contains an exposition of the sevenfold gifts of the Spirit, with its appendices, and a rationale for the seven sevens from the testimony of Scripture. The twelfth is an exposition of the Lord's Prayer with a contemplative epithalamium.

After you have received this little gift, then, virgins of Christ, make the Lamb that you follow [Apoc. 14.4] propitious toward me by your prayers, so that he who is denied the grace of following the Lamb with you may not be denied that of imitating the Lamb's perfect followers in virtue. Scrutinize the faces of your hearts in the mirror I sent, and if you cannot understand all that is written there, it is no small part of knowledge to listen to and love one who does understand. *Here ends the letter of dedication.*


### SV 1.1–171

*[Peregrinus].* I will converse with you, Theodora, about the flowers of paradise and the fruit of the Church's crop—that is, the holiness of the virginal life and the consummation of chastity in Christ's members. As the subject or starting point of our dialogue, let us take that flower that said, "I am the flower of the field and the lily of the valleys" [Cant. 2.1]. From that flower come fruits of such marvelous sweetness and beauty that, in comparison with them, whatever is sweet or blooming in this worldly garden seems bitter, whatever is precious grows vile. In the root of this flower, or the flower of this root, is a double grace that offers itself to the lovers of chastity in its fruit: namely that the flower of virginity, preserved now for the sake

of Christ, may in the future yield the special fruit of virgins in the paradise of God. For you find this in the prophet: "To my eunuchs," says the Lord, "I will give in my house and within my walls a place and a name better than sons and daughters" [Isa. 56.4–5], for in the future when different rewards are given to different ranks, none shall equal the virgins. "For they follow the Lamb wherever he goes" [Apoc. 14.4].

The bride of Christ herself, the Church, is therefore compared to paradise as "a fountain sealed, a garden enclosed" [Cant. 4.12]—a fountain to water the garden, a garden to multiply fruit; a fountain of water leaping up to eternal life, a garden of aromatic wood exuding eternal fragrance; a fountain that gratifies the thirsty with its draughts, a garden that refreshes those who toil in hunger for the sacred word. This garden, blossoming with delicious increase, bears the shoots of varied spices, the teeming fruits of peace and justice; in it grow flowers of different kinds, diverse in color and fragrance. There the white lily of chastity shines, the crocus of charity burns, the violet of humility glows; there the rose of modesty blushes, the spikenard breathes a fragrance of spiritual discipline; there the slender stalks exude balsam, there thousands of virgins multiply the hues of ardent love in the sight of God; and in short, this garden bears as many delightful perfumes are there are virtuous practices in the religious life. Whenever the bridegroom strolls in this spiritual garden, like a flower more charming than the rest, and rambles among the flowers, enhancing each by his grace, receiving from them no increase of his own native glory, he says, "I have gone down to the nut garden to see the fruits of the valleys" [Cant. 6.10]. The soul plants a nut garden for God, with delicious fruits of the valleys, when it desires to please God in humility of mind with the unshakable holiness of chaste morals.

*Theodora.* Chastity is the chief among virtues, Peregrinus, my brother in Christ, without which no one will see God [Hebr. 12.14]—who according to the apostle presented the Church to himself all glorious, without spot or wrinkle [Eph. 5.27]. So nothing pleases me more, and I think nothing more suitable at this time, than to converse with you about chastity—especially since that ancient Babylonian furnace is kindled even now with naphtha, pitch, and resin [Dan. 3.46]. Not only Daniel and the three young men, but even the sons of the Church—if anyone protected by still greater innocence could be found among them—even they could escape its burning fire only by the great power of God. So to cool the furnace of the frail body, and to overshadow with the power of the Most High [Luke 1.35] the heart boiling with the filth of vices, let us use our dialogue to celebrate the healing shade of that flower, with its fruits, that it may offer hope of health and salvation, and the blazing heat may be eased. But why did the Father and Creator of all flowering and fruit-bearing plants, and of everything that is born, call himself a flower of the field? First explain in a few words why he compared himself to so trivial a thing; and then we should investigate what fruit is produced by that flower. The explanation of mysteries, of course, is progress in understanding.

*Peregrinus.* When you hear analogies that compare the rational creature or the Creator himself to senseless or irrational things, this is the reason: that the human mind may be aroused by the beauties flashing forth from the native splendor of God's unity to seek things even more beautiful, and may advance from the lesser to the greater.

*Theodora.* Say then what this flower is, the virtue of blooming flowers, the "lily of the valleys" [Cant. 2.1].

*Peregrinus.* This is the flower born of a flower, the virgin Christ of a virgin mother, the beautiful bridegroom of his bride the Church; the flower fairer than its root, more charming than its stalk; forever alluring beholders' eyes with its radiance and delighting their taste with its marvelous savor; sweet to the smell, pleasing to the touch, delightful to the ear, and always desirable to maidenly disciplines. This flower, hidden at first in the field of the patriarchs, budded more openly on the stalk of the prophets and kings and yielded the fruit of blessed eternity, from which come the fruits of life for all who follow the Lamb in the footsteps of chastity. What else is this flower of the valleys but Christ?—and the beauty and glory of humble minds, which, having received the rain of spiritual grace in the soil of submissive devotion, preserve the gift they have received, so that the fruit of virtues may spring up in them the more abundantly, the more tenaciously the valley of the yielding mind retains that heavenly moisture. For rain cascading down from the mountains always flows onto lower ground, because on the steep slope of the mountain it finds no place to rest. Take this as a reference to proud hearts! But the valleys in which this lily grows can also be understood as the humble parentage of Christ, from which the flower and fruit that timelessly created the world, and all times, have come down to our own time.

*Theodora.* The great poverty of Christ's parents is clear from the fact that, instead of offering a lamb, they were barely able to sacrifice pigeons or turtledoves [Luke 2.24].

*Peregrinus.* O how beautiful is that flower, the lily that sprang up pleasantly in the valley of the world, as it is written: "The fields of the wilderness have sprouted" a shoot of fragrance for Israel [Joel 2.22]. The field of the wilderness is uncultivated earth—the virginal integrity of Mary. Fertile without a cultivator, from that shoot she brought forth in human sight a flower and its fragrance, proclaiming to the bridegroom and the bride: "Draw me after you, we will run in the fragrance of your ointments" [Cant. 1.3]. Now Isaac is known to have expressed many of the Church's sacraments figuratively in words and actions. Is it not of this flower's fragrance that he speaks when he says, "Behold the smell of my son, like the smell of a full field that the Lord has blessed" [Gen. 27.27]? But what is the fullness of this field except Mary, "full of grace, blessed among all" with a singular blessing [Luke 1.28, 42]? For although Christ himself is the full field, "in whom all the fullness of deity dwells bodily" [Col. 2.9], Mary too is shown to be this field, just as she is the sun—like her Son. Yet in a different sense she is the moon, like the Church, and by analogy she is also the star of the sea, watching over those who are in peril in this world. All these titles she draws from this flower of hers, which she produced as a branch from the stem of Jesse. This then is the flower the maidens passionately love [Cant. 1.3], embrace, and follow in adoration while Mother and Son go before them, that they may flourish with these flowers and gather the fruit of eternity in blossoming chastity.

*Theodora.* Although a flowering field may be a sign that some of the seed has perished, this is not something that virginal flowers need to fear, because fruits are produced along with flowers in divine fields that have received no generative seed.

For where a flower grows without seed, it is fitting that the fruit should be like the flower, growing by spiritual increase.

*Peregrinus.* As we are discussing the flowers of the Church, that is, virginal disciplines, would you like to consider that song the Holy Spirit composed as an invitation for those who follow the Lamb—addressing divine fruits and bringing forth flowers, roses and lilies?

*Theodora.* Because our discourse has begun with a flower unique in all ages, it is right for whatever is said in praise of virgins to resound in the heavenly marriage song. Proceed with the order of that song, so that we may plainly see how useful our enclosure is.

*Peregrinus.* It allows us to celebrate songs to the bridegroom in due order, and to grasp the setting and occasion of this song.

*Theodora.* Speak, then.

*Peregrinus.* "Hear me, divine fruits," it says, and so forth [Ecclus. 39.17]. Just as a fruit comes after its flower, so virgins follow the virgin Christ; so the disciples of chastity, the friends of truth, the chaste brides of the chaste bridegroom, follow the Lamb. Let the virgins of Christ, then, hear what fruits are truly divine; let them hear the voice of one who shows where and how they may bear fruit, and with what praise they may preserve the fruit they have borne. For they are truly "divine fruits" if they dedicate what they have received to the praise of Christ above. "For what do you have that you did not receive?" [1 Cor. 4.7].

*Theodora.* Since the progress of every soul can be understood, not unjustly, as divine fruit, I wonder why you have ascribed this fruit to virgins alone, as you seem to have excluded other orders—even those of great merit. For what is conceded to one alone is denied to many. Surely you will not deny that the fruit of the Spirit, which the apostle sets forth distinctly as "charity, joy, peace, long-suffering" [Gal. 5.22], is divine fruit. Paul does not refer this fruit specifically to virgins alone, but extends it generally to all who are making progress "in faith that works through love" [Gal. 5.6]. And in another passage he says, "The fruit of light is found in all goodness, justice, and truth" [Eph. 5.9]. Therefore every virtue related "to the end of the law, which is Christ" [Rom. 10.4], is seen to be divine fruit by which a person of any order will be saved, if he perseveres in bearing good fruit.

*Peregrinus.* Indeed, the progress of every soul, as you say, is proven to be fruit of justice. Yet I have referred to the glory of the virginal life, springing from the aforesaid flower, as "divine fruit" by a special privilege, for a life intent on chastity is closer than others to divinity. "Not all can receive this word," as the Lord says, "but those to whom it is given" [Matt. 19.11]. It is given to all good people in common to do good works; it is not given to all to flourish and bear fruit in the virginal life. It is granted to many, daughter, to grow in faith within the fellowship of the Church; it is only given to a few to bloom with the rose of virginity. Hear the prophet Zechariah: "What is the goodness of God but a wine that sprouts virgins?" [Zech. 9.17]. What does this mean? How could wine with its liquor sprout anything, since it has no root, no flower, and no leaf?

*Theodora.* I would not easily believe the divine word to contain any error, since everything it reveals in words and things always rests on the rationality of truth.

*Peregrinus.* There is nothing truer. God, therefore, who is supremely good and "the beauty of justice" [Jer. 31.23], is the "bread that strengthens man's heart and the wine that gladdens the heart" [Ps. 103.15] of one who makes progress toward him—and this is the wine that sprouts virgins. Truly, sister Theodora, the savor of this wine makes virgins into divine fruits, for the soul seduced by the taste of this wine rejects carnal intercourse and tends with a special purity toward the life of angels. For no virtue comes so close to angelic purity as the splendor of chastity, when a human being—by nature unlike an angel—attains by virtuous effort what was given to the celestial spirits from eternity as their natural condition. When the treacherous Pharisees asked about the seven brothers who had one wife, wishing to know whose wife she would be in the resurrection, Jesus replied that those who are counted worthy of an eternal reward will be equal to angels, nor will they be bound by the law of any carnal intercourse [Luke 20.27–36]. Hence it appears that the virginal life is a proof of the angelic life, and a pledge of the future resurrection.

### SV 1.953–1000

*Peregrinus.* Look! While browsing through the meadows of Scripture, we have at the same time gathered flowers to weave a crown for the virgin's head, until we are able to cover the rest of her body as well with mystical garments—so that, beautifully adorned, she may proclaim to her bridegroom, "He has clothed me with the garment of salvation, he has covered me with the robe of justice" [Isa. 61.10]. For contemplation of the divine Scriptures is like a mystically flowering paradise, in which the little blossoms of the varied sayings breathe forth a supremely sweet fragrance for readers, and a delight in works worthy of God. Just as, in the beginning of creation, a fountain is said to have burst open in the midst of paradise and watered four rivers with its abundant streams [Gen. 2.10], so Christ, the fountain of all wisdom set in the midst of the Scriptures, made the four evangelists flow from himself, as from an abyss of evangelical teaching, like the four rivers of the world. With their superabundant flowing streams, he watered the flowers of heavenly disciplines, and after the flowers, he multiplied the fruit, like apples from a tree of delight, in the hearts of believers. Do you not have a prophetic speech about these rivers where the Lord says, "I will open rivers on the sloping hills, and fountains in the midst of the fields; I will make the desert into pools of water, and the trackless wilderness into springs of water" [Isa. 41.18]? And "you will draw water with joy from the springs of the Savior" [Isa. 12.3], and much more in that vein.

Yet in this paradise of the Church, there are still found transgressors of the divine command, just like Adam and Eve in the first paradise—even though they have now come by the Mediator's grace into the freedom of the children of God [Rom. 8.21], and the bondage of the former servitude is abolished. Notice how "paradise" has a threefold meaning. First is the earthly paradise, abounding in delights of every kind—flowers, perfumes, fruits—in which Adam and Eve were created and ensconced. We know that the second paradise, signified by the first, is the present Church, varied in splendor with its fixed orders—married people, teachers, the continent—adorned in their degrees with the fruits of diverse virtues. The third is the heavenly paradise, the most sure reward of those who are predestined to eternal life. In that paradise, everyone will have as many never-ending ornaments of peace and glory as she once wore badges of virtue in this paradise below. There the order of married persons, the lowest of the three, will have ornaments suited to its merits; the order of widows—higher than the first but lower than the last—will be allotted what it has earned; but the virginal order, as it excels in the contest, will also be supreme in the increase of its rewards.

In every painting or work of art, the conception surpasses the execution, and the artist is greater than the thing he has made. Yet I wish to set before your eyes, like a painting, an image or reflection of paradise in which the fountain, with its intelligible rivers rushing in their fourfold courses, minister drink to holy virgins as if to "doves who dwell beside plentiful streams" [Cant. 5.12], that they may drink of the Gospel springs and the Church's doctrines, and so have the strength to imitate the eight beatitudes and the four cardinal virtues, in which lies the rationale of every spiritual discipline; and thus, steeped in celestial disciplines, they may arrive at the celestial paradise by way of this one, composed of mystical reasoning. Be attentive, then, that you may progress through the mystical painting, if more slowly through the written text. *Here ends the first part.*

## SV 2.253–475

*Peregrinus.* Since we have touched on a few points concerning your enclosure and your double gates, would you like me to insert a story about the entrance and exit of a certain man who came from the north, so that you may know how to spare your modesty when you see and converse with the male sex?

*Theodora.* When argument is enlivened by examples, the studious lack nothing they need to learn a discipline. Speak, then.

*Peregrinus.* It is said that there was in a certain monastery a congregation of nuns, who feared God and righteously fulfilled their vows under the discipline of the Rule. On the side there were also stipendiary clerics who served the nuns in divine ministry, especially in the office of the holy altar, fulfilling the duties of their office in mutual charity. "But when the sons of God came before the presence of God, Satan also was among them" [Job 1.6], and a new Judas, a twig of the Antichrist, appeared among the disciples of Christ. For one of the clerics, young and confused in the blindness of his mind, forgetting shame and especially the honor of his own order, cast a profane gaze upon the prioress of that monastery, who held second place in the discipline and governance of the cloister. Utterly casting aside the fear of God, the man explored every means of entrance in order to fulfill his lust. The cunning deceiver searched for a time and place, for the least occasion to see or converse with the holy virgin or indeed, if an opportunity offered itself, to reveal his intention—but she suspected nothing at all, for her spirit was united with Christ and she would rather have endangered her life than her chastity.

What more can I say? At last the insolent madman broke into the dormitory of Christ's virgins with furtive steps, I don't know exactly where or how, but it was early morning at the time of Lauds. Unobserved, he climbed into the bed of the virgin he wickedly loved and lay in wait there, ready to carry out his pernicious plan at once if he were able. But divine vengeance instantly checked his rash enterprise. For he was "handed over to Satan for the destruction of his flesh" [1 Cor. 5.5]. Strangled by the very angel who had tempted him to filthy love, he expired at once. When the solemnities of Matins were over, the virgins of Christ went up to the dormitory to refresh their weary bodies with sleep. But the aforesaid virgin remained behind. Being second to the mother and zealous for discipline, she checked every corner as usual with her lantern, then returned to her bed with her sisters to rest a little. As soon as she saw and recognized the cleric, she trembled; seeing that he was dead, she groaned; at the sight of his corpse, she shuddered. Yet to avoid disturbing the virgins' brief interval of quiet with a loud noise, she concealed for a while the extraordinary crime she had witnessed.

When morning came, the throng of nuns came running at her call. They marveled at the cleric's audacity, praised the jealous vengeance of the supreme Judge, and rejoiced that the virgin's chastity had been defended. Without delay they cast the ignoble corpse out of their holy dwelling, and henceforth they blocked up every door through which men could gain access to their private quarters. As for the enemy of chastity, he was delivered for burial, but according to the deserts of a sinner, not according to the office for a priest. Having become an example of tighter security for holy virgins, indeed for all orders of the Church, the unworthy man was stripped of all grace, even human mercy. Wretched and miserable is he whom neither respect for due measure nor the eyes of the terrible Judge could deter!

*Theodora.* Frequent access of men to women, even those who are dead to the world, fans sparks into flame.

*Peregrinus.* Concerning such matters, the fathers say plainly that women living beside men will breed thorns and stab their innermost minds with sharp swords. But it is surprising that banter with virgins, or the reckless exchange of gossip, should delight monks or clerics. What is safer than to love Christ? What is wiser than to fear him? What is sweeter than to delight in him, remember him, worship and venerate him? To converse with him is no cause of suspicion or offense, but rather of grace and healing.

*Theodora.* I would like to know if any hope of salvation could relieve the unhappy man, since he did not carry out the intent of his wicked will in action.

*Peregrinus.* Who could pierce the inscrutable abyss of divine judgments? Who knows whether God might not judge twice in the same case, or whether the sudden sentence of death might have purged the guilt of the intended sin? Perhaps the death of the defiled spirit was reversed by the death of the body, lest the dead man be punished by the ruin of perpetual death. Accept this without doubt: If a perverse mind obtains what it has sinfully desired, the completion of the intended wrong is very near to death, and for this reason, when prompt punishment of a sin about to be committed prevents the actual crime, it is a proof of divine mercy, not a sign of eternal damnation. You need not believe this of all people, I think, but only of the vessels of mercy—those whose earthly lives are so ordered as to be preserved in eternal honor, not in the disgrace of eternal ruin. The proof of this is obvious. For the nun, taking pity on the man who had perished because of her beauty, which was not her fault, ministered to the deceased with amazing compassion. Along with the other virgins, she tortured herself in penance to win his absolution so long that, for a whole year, she offered God the sacrifice of the Lord's prayer daily on bare and bended knees, to blunt in some way the spear of divine vengeance that had pierced the cleric. Nor was this in vain. For when a year had passed, the dead man appeared in a vision to a woman of no small merit, joyfully intimating that he had received communion. He said that every day at a fixed time, a certain person had passed by and offered golden alms to God for his assistance, so that his torment diminished from day to day, until a change of the right hand of the Most High [Ps. 76.11] gave him full and complete remission of his sufferings.

*Theodora.* How wonderful is the providence of God's purpose toward the children of Adam, which so moderates and tempers the mystery of his judgments in this life! Thus the Church, forever rising and falling in her children, may recognize a Father as well as a judge, so that mercy may always attend man along with punishment—for scarcely, if at all, can anyone pass through this temporal life without guilt.

*Peregrinus.* Every occasion of falling, daughter, must be removed from a weak conscience. Let no cause for blasphemy be given to the wicked; let no cause to suspect evil of you be given to anyone. The frail conscience of a brother should find nothing in you that may offend his eyes. Think of Susanna. If the holy woman had bathed in her house with her servants, she would have given no occasion for slander to her enemies, nor would she have fallen prey to such terrors and imperiled her life with the swords of her accusers. Admittedly, the holy woman's conscience was pure, yet we may be allowed to ask if it was fitting for a noble daughter of Israel to refresh herself with a bath in a place of pleasure? For orchards are places of pleasure. Was it proper for her to be seen naked beneath the naked sky, to send her maids away, to be found alone, to seek ointments while under the yoke of bondage? How many religious men would have shunned these things, let alone a chaste and noble matron! For even though the apostle tells how a virgin seeks to please Christ, while a bride seeks to please her husband [1 Cor. 7.32–34], this is no way to please husbands if it scandalizes the weak and gives occasion to stray. What am I saying? Do I convict the holy woman of any lewdness or transgression? By no means! This question arises for us because the apostle says, "Take thought for what is good not only in the sight of God, but also in the sight of all men" [Rom. 12.17].

*Theodora.* Beyond a doubt, if the holy woman had not appeared in the orchard, the profane elders would still have had their lust, though without occasion to fulfill or even reveal it.

*Peregrinus.* So, in order that the thoughts hidden in the elders' hearts might be revealed, she whom they wickedly desired was set before their eyes, by the just permission of God, so that their lurking iniquity might be detected and the woman's innocence tested, and from then on she might learn to be more careful on account of the chastisement. From this lesson, let the faithful learn to accept discipline in their private lives, and praise and glorify God at all times in all his judgments.

*Theodora.* It is absolutely clear that virginity ought to be circumspect, so that all its good may lie in the love of God and careful protection of that good in the sight of the neighbor.

*Peregrinus.* We have set out to speak about the glory of virginity and its reward. Since no virtue surpasses virginity in the struggle that must be fought to win it, none is more highly rewarded in the victory. Yet no virgin could ever gain as much glory from her victory as she would earn shame from her ruin if she fell.

Now the grace of virginity, or rather the glory of all virgins, proceeded in the first age of grace from the virgin mother Mary—even though we read that Elijah and Elisha and many sons of the prophets were virgins. Mary, cleansing herself from every defilement of flesh and spirit and winning sanctification [2 Cor. 7.1], gave birth to the Holy of holies, indeed to holiness itself, truth itself—for "truth sprang up from the earth" [Ps. 84.12], bequeathing an inviolable heritage of chastity to its sons and daughters. Mary is spiritually the mother of the universal Church, as she is corporeally the mother of Christ. For Mother Church, visited by the same Spirit that made Christ's Mother pregnant to conceive and bear the Word of God, continually conceives and gives birth to Christ. "You are my little children," Paul says, "to whom I give birth once again until Christ be formed in you" [Gal. 4.19]. If Christ, then, is formed in the Church through the instruction of the doctors, he is also born in the Church every day. A marvelous exchange! Mary is the bride, mother, and daughter of Christ; she is also the mother and daughter of Christ's Church.

*Theodora.* Explain this more clearly.

*Peregrinus.* Mary is the Church's mother because she gave birth to the Church's brother, who said, "Go and announce to my brethren" [Matt. 28.10]. And David said, "No brother will ransom [him]; a man will pay the ransom" [Ps. 48.8]. She is also the daughter of the Church because she herself was regenerated by Mother Church. For even though Mary was the mother of Christ, she nevertheless needed Christ's grace, "for all have sinned and fall short of the glory of God" [Rom. 3.23]. For this reason Mary, like Mother Church, needed the regeneration common to all by the grace of her Son who regenerates; for it profited her more to be incorporated in Christ and the Church in the Holy Spirit, through faith, than to have Christ as her son through kinship in the flesh. "Mary is more blessed," Augustine said, "in receiving the faith of Christ than in conceiving the flesh of Christ" [*De sancta virginitate* 3]. Thus the Gentiles who believed in Christ were closer kin to him than his relatives, who did not wish to recognize that Christ was God. In the former, faith prevailed over kinship; in the latter, neither blood relationship nor familial love acknowledged his rights.

Now our catholic mother is a virgin in all her members, although not all possess integrity of the body. Yet all her children are virgins in that they deserve praise for perfect faith, while some are graced with the glory of physical virginity.

*Theodora.* The mother of virgins rightly surpasses all, both in her example and in her crowning reward. For no one will ever be able to follow the Lamb as well as she who bore the Lamb and remained a virgin.

*Peregrinus.* It was she who so pleased the Son of God, as all agree, that he chose to be born of her. But do you think she drank from that fountain mentioned earlier—the one that said, "Learn from me, for I am gentle and humble of heart" [Matt. 11.29]?

*Theodora.* How could she drink, when she had not yet seen or heard the one she bore in her womb?

*Peregrinus.* Why then did she say she was pleasing on account of humility, if she had heard nothing about the virtue of humility?

*Theodora.* You make me out to be a ridiculous barbarian, pretending in jest that I am totally ignorant of the power of the Holy Spirit! As if she could not have drunk from the fount of the prophet: "On whom does my Spirit rest [Isa. 11.2], if not the one who is humble and peaceful and trembles at my words?" [Isa. 66.2]. Or as if the Holy Spirit could not be the invisible teacher of the Virgin, he who guarded her virginity from her mother's womb! Have I not learned from your own teaching that the sacraments have a double meaning, visible and invisible? One part is accomplished by the ministry of the Holy Spirit alone; the other is fulfilled by human offices, though not without the Holy Spirit. Jeremiah and John the Baptist, as well as Moses, the patriarchs, and many of the saints "were consecrated in their mother's womb" [Ecclus. 49.9, Jer. 1.5, Luke 1.41]. Without the administration of any blessing, they were granted the effect of the sacraments. How much more did she especially deserve the anointing of the Holy Spirit, she who bore the author of all sacraments?

*Peregrinus.* Not without reason have I called you Theodora, since you appear so zealous for the Word of God that you anticipate what you are to become and turn your gaze entirely toward it. There is nothing in this life more blessed than the prudence of virgins! When their purity is assisted by the Word of God, their minds are illumined by him just as a crystal is lit up by a ray of sunlight. Humility alone preserves whole in a virgin the gifts she is given from on high. Do not boast then, daughter, that you have the name of a virgin. But rejoice greatly in this, that you have offered yourself to him who is both a virgin and the reward of virginity. You deserve praise not merely because you are a virgin, but because you made a vow to keep your flesh and spirit pure for him who is the son of a virgin and the bridegroom of virgins. Otherwise, if the mere name of virgin deserved a reward distinct from that of the married, exceptional holiness could be ascribed to an infinite number of virgins who are simply waiting for their wedding day. How many virgins have lived among their families with admirable continence, but died before their nuptials! Yet they obtained only a small reward because, in their minds, they were already married to their future husbands.

*Theodora.* As I see it, the only kind of virginity that deserves praise and reward is that which a chaste life commends to the heavenly Bridegroom in a stable vow, without hypocrisy.

*Peregrinus.* How rightly you said "without hypocrisy"! For pretended love excludes real love. You take away from God whatever you have done for the love of another.

*Theodora.* Who could doubt that in our time, the Christian profession is wavering in many people, men and women alike? When a person pays no attention to what he is and what he was made for, when people who are not yet trained in the fear of God socialize freely, exchanging glances, conversations, and little gifts, what evil lurking in the heart is revealed!

*Peregrinus.* If you apply flame to straw, what will happen? Of course the fire will ignite the dry material. Be on your guard, then, against what you find displeasing in the lives of others. Avoid frequent conversations with anyone who is not of your profession. In fact, limit your contact even with people you know, for very often a close friendship, abusing the privilege of familiarity, has led to illicit deeds. Now the desire for sin is a near neighbor to death. Have you not read, "the waters wear away the stones, and gradually the land is consumed by floods" [Job 14.19]? So, when unlike persons mingle in frequent conversation, the hearts of those who converse are necessarily in danger at times. But since Paul asserts that the single collective "virgin" he gathered from both sexes is "betrothed to one husband" [2 Cor. 11.2], it is to this collective virgin that the Holy Spirit says, both universally and individually, "Listen, daughter, and see" [Ps. 44.11]. Let us begin the next book with this locution, renewing our strength after a pause. *Here ends the second part.*

## *SV* 3.1–116

*[Peregrinus].* "Listen, daughter, and see, and incline your ear, and forget your people and your father's house. And the king will desire your beauty" [Ps. 44.11–12]. Listen, daughter of holy Church, betrothed and sealed as a chaste virgin to one husband, Jesus Christ. Listen to your bridegroom calling you to eternal gifts, see him showing you the rewards, follow him as he goes before you. "Listen," I say, by paying attention to the divine laws; "see" by obeying those laws fervently, not by force or necessity but by reason, free will, and love. Listen to what your bridegroom commands and see what he promises, so that you may be directed to the commands by which you will attain to the promises. For Christ seeks ears to hear [Matt. 13.9], he seeks eyes to see, so that what the outward voice commends may dwell within, and what is perceived through physical sight may bear fruit in the mind's eye. Listen, daughter! See, unique one! Attend, bride and dove, sister and beloved!

"Listen, daughter." Do you want to know whose daughter? The daughter of the king of kings, daughter of the ruler of creation, bride by faith of the immortal bridegroom, unique by the singularity of love, dove by the grace of simplicity, beautiful by the gift of chastity, sister of Christ by grace and nature alike, and ever beloved in the covenant of spiritual grace. Listen, daughter of the apostles! Listen, darling child of all the Catholic teachers, who have begotten you by faith, established you by action, and adorned you by the love of virtues, and who by their teaching show you the bridal bed of sweet delight that will be yours in eternal beauty, so that you may seek your beginning by preserving the virtues, you who entered this wretched world because of the righteousness lost by our forefathers.

What, then, does Christ exhort his virgin to hear and see? "Forget your people," he says, "and your father's house." It follows most rightly that, if the bride happens to have heard her beloved speaking or seen him going before her, she will promptly forget her father and her fatherland. For she proclaims, "My soul melted as my beloved spoke: draw me after you" [Cant. 5.6, 1.3]. To have listened to Jesus inwardly is to have left the house of one's kin; to have seen him is to have sought him. Thus the mind inspired by God knows no paternal home on earth, awaiting a house in the heavens not made with hands [Hebr. 9.11]; and having forgotten her earthly father, she who was old becomes new, she who was vile becomes fair, she who was frail becomes strong, adding beauty to beauty, that is, love of the eternal to her native reason, by despising the allure of the world. So, when the virgin of Christ has begun to turn away from the arrogance of the proud world, from the very outset of her heavenly discipline she already begins to please the supreme king, who sees in his virgin what he has created or added to his creature.

What is the surpassing beauty of this virgin, so esteemed by the royal gaze? What beauty does this king, who is the creator of heaven and earth, desire in the virgin? What is this beauty that God seeks in you? Would you like to know? It is the beauty of righteousness, the form of a praiseworthy life, the light of understanding, the grace of heavenly discipline, the love of God, the hatred of the world, or anything else of that kind that the rational soul acquires through longing for virtues or hatred of vices.

*Theodora.* It seems to me, reverend father, that there is no small profit for the holy virgin in this divine calling, if she hears what is commanded and sees what is promised, if she obeys what she has heard and follows what she has seen. But I wonder why the love of this king is especially aroused if this daughter forgets her kin and her homeland, when even there, this beauty could have been preserved and cherished.

*Peregrinus.* There is no space now to discuss these questions, but in their place, it will be appropriate to show in a few words that a common life can scarcely be led without common vices, and one who is turned toward the dust is often stained with its squalor. But since we have been created, redeemed, beloved, and called by the grace of God, daughter, it is fitting that we direct our life, our knowledge, and our abilities toward heaven in thanksgiving, so that what seems to have illumined us in a good beginning may be commended by holy perseverance. Indeed, the completion of a holy work commends the fruit of a good beginning and encloses the whole of the reward in eternal salvation, as the Lord himself says: "He who endures to the end will be saved" [Matt. 10.22]. For you appear to have blessedly renounced the seductions of the world in habit and in spirit, to have offered the flower of your virginity to God along with Mary, to have attended the Lamb wherever he wanders, and to have transcended the temporal by a leap of faith with a view to eternity. What then? Remain content with this blessed rank, I beseech you. Remain in your most honorable order by right of your virginal flower, lest the higher you appeared to stand, the more deeply you might fall, shaken by the wind of seductive vanity and frivolity. For the higher the rank, the lower the fall.

We will speak somewhat in the following section about the three orders—the married, the continent, and the virgins—which are to be regarded as good, better, and best. Your own order surpasses all because the virginal Son of the Virgin consecrated this order alone to himself. Married fidelity and widowed continence hasten forward according to the law of their vows, but virginal integrity is always intent on spiritual disciplines, with an observance all the stricter inasmuch as it contends for rewards that surpass the others. For holiness in the lower order will be given the common bliss of all the saints, but the virginal order will be crowned with glory upon glory. For it is fitting that what excels temporally in discipline and labor should excel eternally in the honor of its reward.

*Theodora.* You persuade me, reverend brother, that the noble lineage of virginity should be cultivated in the love of Christ; but there are few who grasp this flower, from which such glorious fruit is proven to grow. For in this flower can be found beautiful honor and honorable beauty, an angelic way of life upon earth, and, so it seems to me, progress beyond nature.

*Peregrinus.* Have you not heard the Lord say of this fruit, "Not all can receive this word, but those to whom it is given" [Matt. 19.11]? For it is truly a special and not a universal gift, given to few indeed, rewarded with not a few gifts. For because there are few who can follow the Lamb wherever he goes [Apoc. 14.4], the value of the reward corresponds to its rarity, and the greatness of the prize compensates for the small number who receive it. Thus Christ supplies the dignity of this singular order with abundant grace and blessing, and as he has made only a few to follow the narrow way, he multiplies their reward.

*Theodora.* Because this flower, which can be found with such difficulty, should be kept with great diligence, I ask you by the eternal flower—he who said, "I am the flower of the field and the lily of the valleys" [Cant. 2.1], and whom we have discussed above—try to show in this dialogue of ours how the grace of blooming integrity should be sought, found, and preserved. Then, with a sequence of arguments and collected exempla, set it like a mirror before Christ's virgins. By looking in this mirror, let them see who, what, and how they shall become, and let them know how to judge between night and day, between the shade of this present life and the light of the life to come, as they progress from one to the other.

*Peregrinus.* Truly, daughter, you have rightly evaluated this dialogue by asking for a rule or mirror in which to examine yourself. For the knowledge of one's own frailty is a great thing and the first degree of virtue; and the contemplation of worldly vanity is a light by which we can behold the truth to come. With Christ's help, then, I will do what you ask, conversing with you to the best of my ability about the glory of chastity, its preservation, and its singular crown—not in learned words of human wisdom, but comparing spiritual things with spiritual [1 Cor. 2.13]. I will offer solid food to the mature and infants' milk to babes, so that according to the intellectual capacity of each, my pen may shape a mode of discipline. "If anyone among you seems to be wise," the apostle says, "let him become a fool that he may be wise, for the wisdom of this world is folly with God" [1 Cor. 3.18–19].

### SV 5.1–234

*[Peregrinus].* As an example of this heavenly garment, consider the Lord's mother—the ornament of sacred beauty, the mirror of holy virginity. By her distinction in the twin virtues of humility and virginity, she deserved to conceive him whom heaven and earth do not contain, enclosing in the shrine of her womb the Word begotten without beginning by the Father, who came forth for the salvation of all. As this mother and virgin—the mother of mothers and virgin of virgins—incurred

no loss of her chastity in giving birth, so after birth she remained constant in her integrity. This is Mary: the root of an eternal flower, the flower and fruit of eternal blessing. Imitate this chief of virgins as far as possible, virgin of Christ, and you too, with Mary, will seem to give birth spiritually to the Son of God.

*Theodora.* Since you propose the chief of virgins, the queen of heavenly virtues, as a model for imitation, beloved father, I beg you to linger awhile in her praise. For it is impossible for the handmaids of so great a lady to go astray when, from her praise, they may see the path of truth and purity lying open to her followers.

*Peregrinus.* What you ask is beyond my strength, and I will sink beneath the burden if I presume to lift the heavy weight of speech about her, as you request. If I tried to say anything about the Lord's Mother it would be an act of reckless presumption rather than learning. For the magnitude of grace divinely granted to Mary exceeds my faculty of speech, since she was chosen before she was born to conceive the eternal Word, and crowned once born with the perfection of all blessings. It is written, after all, "Do not seek what is above you or scrutinize what is greater than you, but think always of what God has commanded you, and do not be curious about the multitude of his works" [Ecclus. 3.22]. Yet, governing my pen by divine grace, I will not fail you in this inquiry. So let us say a little in our dialogue about a patroness so great that we could by no means speak of her worthily.

*Theodora.* I will accept this gratefully, father, for the pious memory of such a virgin is the way and the life to her virgin followers [John 14.6].

*Peregrinus.* Through this virgin of whom you ask, the sacraments of divine mercy were consummated. For her sake the heavens were bowed down, "fountains of water appeared and the foundations of the earth were laid bare" [Ps. 17.6]. This means that when Christ was born of her, the apostles were chosen, through whom the earth received drink as from inexhaustible fountains; and when prophecy had been laid bare, the world could be brought to faith and established on an unshakable foundation. She then is the bride of the eternal king; she is daughter, mother, and virgin; dove, sister, and beloved [Cant. 5.2]; unique mother of the unique Son of God, foreordained in heaven before she was born to be the Mother of God's Son. She is the joy and glory of angels, for she is the mediatrix who made peace between the heights and the depths. She is the dawn, the sun, the moon, and the star: the dawn preceding the Sun of justice in its rising; the sun in whom the Creator himself set the tabernacle of his body, and came forth like a bridegroom from his chamber [Ps. 18.6]; the moon radiant from its Creator's splendor, though changeable in this life by the law of its own creation; and the star of the sea, because she is the path, the harbor, and the life of sailors in this worldly darkness.

In paradise she is the flower and fruit of trees that exude the finest balsam, and the green shoot of all spices. Among the patriarchs, she is that stock and root from whom the seed and flower of eternal blessing burst forth for all who are foreordained to life. Since she is mother and virgin, she is revealed by a mystic figure in the bush that burned and was not consumed [Exod. 3.2]. In the tabernacle of Moses, fashioned with such variety of materials and such marvelous art, she is supremely figured in the branch of Aaron and the golden urn. She is the dry branch that flowered among the other dry branches [Num. 17.2–8], bearing flower and

fruit before the whole mass of humankind which had withered in sin, and yielding the sweetness of nuts with no root or moisture of human coupling, i.e., giving
birth to Christ, the power of God and the wisdom of God [1 Cor. 1.24]. The
golden urn which preserved the manna [Exod. 16.33–34] symbolizes the purity of
her mind and body in its gold, displaying the manna—that is, the Word of God,
"the food of angels" [Wisd. 16.20]—to all the faithful. Do you see that all the labor
of the wondrous tabernacle and its most precious hangings—"in gold and silver,
purple and linen, twice-dyed scarlet" and every precious stone [Exod. 25.3–4]—
pertained to those four things [the tabernacle, the ark, the golden urn, and the
branch of Aaron] in which the future mysteries of the Mother and Son were
chiefly hidden for our future age? For the tabernacle is the Synagogue, the ark is
the Church; the golden urn is Mary and the manna is Christ, the Word of God;
and the flowering branch is again Mary. All these things, wrapped and veiled in
symbolic foreshadowings, have been revealed to our age more clearly than light by
the gracious gifts of heaven.

What is more glistening than gold, and what is more precious to the greedy
world than this metal—not because of its substantial quality, but because of the
price it fetches? What do believing minds find more acceptable than manna as a
symbol, or sweeter to the palate? What is more beautiful than the Virgin Mother's
fertility or more splendid than her chastity? What is more wholesome and delightful than the body of Christ on which we feed? The golden urn once preserved the
manna that had been collected and passed it down as a kind of memorial to instruct posterity. Mary provided Jesus Christ, the Word of God whom she conceived
and bore, to the Church as a nourishment. Now the flower and fruit of the dry
branch represent the miraculous childbearing of the Virgin, a thing unheard-of in
all prior ages.

*Theodora.* It is a most fitting and spiritual affair that all the most profound and
noble sacraments granted to the ancient people should pertain to the beauty and
glory of Mary, who visibly bore "the beauty of justice" [Jer. 31.23] "in whom all
the fullness of deity dwells bodily" [Col. 2.9].

*Peregrinus.* You find Mary among the judges in the fleece that was dry at first, but
then flowing with celestial dew [Judg. 6.36–40]. You find her hidden in the royal
stock and designated by great and marvelous sacraments among the prophets: Isaiah
proclaimed that a virgin would give birth [Isa. 7.14]; Ezekiel revealed the closed gate
that would open for none but the prince [Ezek. 44.2]; Daniel tells of a stone hewn
from the mountain without hands [Dan. 2.45]; Jeremiah states that "the Lord will
do a new thing on the earth: a woman will enclose a man" [Jer. 31.22]. Indeed, you
will find many things proclaiming and bearing witness to the Lord's Mother in the
prophets' writings and miracles, and if we were to scrutinize and discuss every one
of them, our dialogue would exceed all bounds. For what speech can contain her
whom the Son of God chose before the commencement of time to be his temple,
about whom a serious question was raised between God and man at the beginning
of the world, and who alone was preserved to redeem humankind?

If then you seek Mary with a subtle understanding, you will find her in heaven
before all creation; you will see her in paradise and in Noah's ark in the flood; you

will see her among the patriarchs and wandering with the people of God in the desert; you will find her among the judges and kings, coming forth from the royal stock and blooming among the Jews like a rose among thorns. You will marvel at her speaking with angels to renew the world. You will see the queen of heaven ministering to Elizabeth, lying amazed beside the stable of her Son, and later receiving the gifts of the Magi with her child, and rejoicing with a spirit of surpassing sweetness over the infant at her bosom: "Let him kiss me with the kiss of his mouth!" [Cant. 1.1]. "My beloved is to me a little bundle of myrrh; he will lie between my breasts" [Cant. 1.12]. "Behold you are fair, my beloved, and lovely!" [Cant. 1.15]. "Like an apple tree among the trees of the wood, so is my beloved among the sons" [Cant. 2.3]. "My beloved is mine and I am his" [Cant. 2.16]. And this too: "I have found him whom my soul loves; I will hold him and not let him go until I have brought him into my mother's house, and into the chamber of her that bore me" [Cant. 3.4]. "I am a wall and my breasts are like a tower; therefore I have become in his sight as one who finds peace" [Cant. 8.10]. You will also find her remaining with her Son from birth until his passion, when she stood beside him at the cross and grieved at her beloved Son's passion as if transfixed by a sword. After his ascension, you will find her assumed into heaven at the time and in the manner that pleased her Son.

*Theodora.* Truly is she "blessed among all women" [Luke 1.42], who from the beginning of the world until its end has received and granted blessings! Yet I do not understand what you say about her being conceived before time and remaining in heaven, or how a question was raised about her in paradise at the beginning of creation.

*Peregrinus.* She herself will answer you in my place—the creature who bore the Creator. Let her speak in my stead—the mother chosen before the foundation of the world. "The Lord possessed me in the beginning of his ways," she says, "before he made anything from the beginning. I was ordained from eternity and from of old, before the earth was made. The abysses did not yet exist, and I was already conceived" [Prov. 8.22–24], and so forth.

*Theodora.* Explain, then, how these things should be understood as pertaining to her.

*Peregrinus.* The providence of God, in which "the treasures of all wisdom and knowledge are hidden" [Col. 2.3], comprehends all things simultaneously, containing, perfecting, encircling, and ruling all things past, present, and future, but especially those like human beings whose reason or nature tends toward eternity, and is destined at last, by divine gift, to transcend all the instability of its own nature and of time. Therefore, since all things existed within the wisdom of the Word of God, waiting to be unfolded as and when God willed, according to their nature, manner, order, and species, how could the Mother not preexist with the Son, in whose conception and birth turned the hinge that opened the door for the whole rational creation to be sanctified, unified, and restored to peace? How could she be absent, in whom an eternal decree had laid the foundation of an eternal building, the celestial Jerusalem? Did not the whole visible creation, formed for the sake of humanity, emerge before man himself was formed, so as to serve him in a manner fitting the nature and dignity of him for whose sole benefit it seems to have been made? How then could the Mother ordained from of old, from eternity, not pre-exist with her Son in a mysterious unity? Did not the primal origin of all divine works lie hidden in them invisibly, with the perfect fullness of the eternal will and the supreme goodness, to be unfolded at the foreordained time?

Scripture says that God "has made" things that are yet to be, showing on one hand his immutable will, on the other the completion of his work. For it lies within the power of divine reason that things may be at the same time "made" and "still to be made," nor does any interval of time fall between the will and the potency of God, who knows neither past nor future. That his mother was chosen, that Christ was conceived, born, and died, that he rose again and ascended—these events were planned before all creation, and divine wisdom, simultaneously comprehending the whole, foresaw what would come to pass in its own time. Now the cause of human creation exists before and above all things that arose in time and were ordained before time. For if God made all things for the sake of humanity, man is the cause of all temporal things. That for which man himself was made is prior to man, and exists long before all the things it precedes through causation.

*Theodora.* These truths are profound and beyond the strength of my intellect. But tell me, I beg you, how to understand that certain things which can be said specifically of the Son of God can also be applied generally to the Lord's Mother, the Church, or indeed, the soul of any righteous person.

*Peregrinus.* The divine word, adapting itself to the grasp of our intellect and descending to our level, in this way embraces and includes sometimes the Mother with the Son, sometimes his bride the Church, and sometimes the soul of every just person, in a sacramental unity, so what is said about any of these, it seems, can be said about them all. Although there are many, indeed countless traits that the Son alone has from the Father by nature, yet to commend the sacrament of unity, he communicates them universally to the Church by grace, to the point that he may call himself bride as well as bridegroom, and her bridegroom as well as bride. So just as the head and the body are united, there may be one spirit in both by prevenient grace, as it is written: "He who clings to the Lord is one spirit" [1 Cor. 6.17]. Nothing more certain, nothing more holy than this degree of unity could be uttered or heard or even imagined, because the author of creation created all things that this sacrament might be eternally consummated. Listen to the Scripture: "For this reason," it says, "a man shall leave his father and mother and cleave to his wife, and they will be two in one flesh" [Gen. 2.24]. "This is a great sacrament," says the apostle, "and I refer it to Christ and the Church" [Eph. 5.32]. But who would dare to enter or lay bare the depth of the divine dispensation, especially since "God has made darkness his hiding place" [Ps. 17.12], and the little spark of our understanding barely comprehends the fact that God is incomprehensible? Mary, then, was ordained from eternity with her Son—not by quality of time but by reason of divine foreknowledge; not by the form of bodily substance but by an image of subsistence, to be revealed in her time foreordained before the ages.

*Theodora.* You have done justice to my question in all respects. But certain points in the same lesson remain to be explored.

*Peregrinus.* Say what you wish.

*Theodora.* The same Scripture that can refer to Mary may also refer to eternal Wisdom, that is, "The Lord possessed me in the beginning of his ways, before he made anything from the beginning" [Prov. 8.22]. In each case—in the Wisdom of God and in Mary—what are the mystical meanings of these "ways"? Add an explanation of both to what you have already written, I ask, for our mutual progress.

*Peregrinus.* You set the Word of God as a lantern before your feet [Ps. 118.105] when you inquire so subtly about the beginning of these ways. Let us seek together, then, as Christ illumines our darkness. The eternal God, incomprehensible in majesty, inconceivable in divinity, was never without his Son, never without his Wisdom. He always was, always is, and always will be, and as it is written, he was never "without his Word, without his Son, without his Wisdom," which are all one [Augustine, *De trinitate* 2.5]. "The beginning of his ways" was a certain immutable and invisible procession by his Word to form things visible and invisible, heavenly and earthly, mutable and mobile, and a certain revelation of himself to the rational creation through his works, coming forth with the movement of time. Indeed, humanity would never have known the power and greatness of God if God, the creator of man, had not made himself known to man through creation. "For the invisible things of God are perceived through those that are made" [Rom. 1.20], and the Creator is known through creation. As Solomon says, therefore, "although Wisdom herself is one, she can do all, and in herself unchanging, she makes all things new, and throughout the nations she enters into holy souls" [Wisd. 7.27]. Changelessly retaining what she is, she renders souls capable of divine understanding, "reaching from end to end mightily and ordering all things sweetly" [Wisd. 8.1]. So God in his eternal goodness has always willed, and in his eternal wisdom has always planned, what he did at a particular time in his eternal power. And the goodness, the wisdom, and the power existed simultaneously, nor could those attributes which were substantially always the same be divided or separated from one another in time. Thus as these three properties exist in God, namely will, wisdom, and power, the primordial causes proceed from the divine will, are directed by wisdom, and brought forth by power. Will moves, wisdom plans, power unfolds. These are the eternal foundations and the first principle of all causes; they are ineffable and incomprehensible to all creation. For although these three exist in God [power, wisdom, and will], yet to God it is one thing to be able, to know, and to will. Reason distinguishes what nature does not divide.

So much for the beginning of the invisible ways of the invisible God—the ways that the Son of God somehow walked when he proceeded invisibly, or rather immutably and ineffably, to create all things. It remains now to show how the beginning of these ways may apply to the Lord's Mother, whom we are discussing, and to consider how the new creation had its origin through her.

## SV 5.908–1069

*Theodora.* [In the image of the chariot,] reverend father, you promise an ascent to holy virginity that is marvelous indeed, but quite unequal to our stature. If we are given the opportunity to contemplate its course, I should think it sufficient for us to follow at a distance.

*Peregrinus.* I will add yet more examples of virgins of the same company, if not of the same merit. Not only the splendor of vernal chastity, but also the distinction of a noble and constant spirit makes these virgins worthy of imitation. I speak of Agnes, Lucy, Cecilia, and Agatha, who conquered the impure world with pure minds and, having rejected and overcome carnal bridegrooms and tyrants, followed the Lamb who led them into life. The first of these, Agnes, had reached the age of girlhood and was intent on her school studies when, by her beauty, she unwittingly aroused a furious enemy to fall in love with her. After she had repressed the impudence of his reckless presumption and her enemy lay dead, she made a brothel into a chapel and restored him to life by prayer through the true Bridegroom. Broken by fire and pierced by the sword, she was plucked like a little rose from a thornbush and passed into the fragrance of eternal sweetness, a pure victor over the world.

*Theodora.* This was a girl of truly virile constancy! In a victory of double virtue, she confounded the enemy of virtue, prostrated the man she had confounded, and compassionately raised him who lay prostrate.

*Peregrinus.* Listen, daughter. Nothing should seem great to man except God. A human being, therefore, who has no one but God above herself, is greater than all creation and should courageously despise whatever is beneath her among creatures. Love your Creator, daughter, and any hostile force beneath him will be more a witness to your virtue than a reason for your fall.

The second virgin, Lucy, was to be drawn by wild oxen at a tyrant's instigation for his sport. Though dragged by many pairs of oxen, she could not be moved, and so offered a spectacle worthy to be venerated not only by those present, but by all ages, past and future. The maiden's constancy tore at the punitive tyrant's bowels and made his mind swell and blaze with furious wrath. Drenched with boiling oil and liquid pitch, yet unharmed, she gave her spirit up to the Lord at last, a sword plunged into her bowels.

What shall I say of the third, Cecilia? A true follower of the true Lord and an energetic servant of Christ's poor, her persuasive arguments won her bridegroom and his brother to the faith of Christ. Her responses to questioning, full of constancy and seasoned with the salt of wisdom, confounded the pagan foe Almachius; angels spoke with her and brought blossoming crowns from paradise for the blooming recruits of Christ. At last, after transmitting the fruit of her sacred learning and example, with vigils and abstinence, to the virgins of all times who seek Christ and follow the Lamb with unfailing steps, she dedicated her virginal flower to the Lord and was slain by the sword, and thus she pierced the heavens to reign together with Christ.

Who could offer sufficient praise to celebrate the life and struggle of the virgin martyr Agatha? For her, the endurance of protracted torture for Christ's sake supplied the most delicious feasts, and the weakening of her limbs only strengthened her vigilant spirit. She was stretched on the rack, imprisoned, wounded with iron hooks, and rolled on the sharp edges of potsherds. When her breast was cut off, she deserved to be healed by an apostle; and after she had died and entered into life,

she sent the ringleader of her tormentors to hell by drowning. Although she was
exalted by a noble lineage, she accepted the name and duties of a servant in devout
humility, for she burned with love for her most noble king.

To these virgins you may add those who stand like a heap of testimony to be
honored through all the ages—the eleven thousand virgins with their eleven leaders, who lay hold of the heavenly bridal bed after deceiving a carnal bridegroom
and exulting over the world like victorious eagles, with the Holy Spirit as their
guide. By engaging in mock battles at sea, they deceived the lovers of their flesh
and managed to evade the forces arrayed against them. After completing their sacred journey, they fell like snowy-fleeced lambs among savage wolves and, mangled
by their raging cruelty, they rose up to heaven like flowers, to be crowned as victors with eternal flowers. But if we wanted to hold up every single example of virginity as a mirror for holy virgins, we would exceed the rule of brevity, for both
under the law and under grace, such a multitude of virgins of both sexes have followed the Lamb that the most eloquent tongue would scarcely suffice to expound
them all. Some of these have adorned their heads with crowns of white lilies; others have decked their right hands and their heads alike with crimson roses.

*Theodora.* It is not clear to me why you distinguish these flowers, or whether
you relate the different species to a difference in merits.

*Peregrinus.* Lilies are compared to pure virginity in peacetime, roses to martyrdom. But the two mutually complement each other, so you can have roses blushing
without bloodshed in the peace of the Church and lilies gleaming under persecution in the peace of Christ. For the Lord says, "in the world you will have tribula-
tion; have peace in me" [John 16.33]. In shedding her blood, then, a virgin of Christ
is adorned outwardly with a rosy crown; in the peace of her mind, she is decked inwardly with lilies. Conversely, in the absence of persecution by the sword, if struggles rage in her breast but do not vanquish her, she deserves a rose for her mind and
a lily for her chaste body. For when the soul is tempted by the fire of lust or any
other vice, but does not consent to the flesh for illicit deeds and preserves the body
unstained, it plants a whole garden for God, roses and lilies alike. So when the flowers of chastity spring up from the soil of our flesh, which is accustomed to breed the
thorns of vices, they produce a garland interwoven with red and white for our
supreme Head. Would you like me to weave you a garland with just a few flowers?

*Theodora.* Which ones?

*Peregrinus.* Lilies, roses, and violets—that is chastity, charity, and humility. If one
of these three species is lacking, the beauty of the woven crown will not endure.
Take charity away from chastity, or humility from both, or take either one from humility, and all the flowers that seemed charming individually will wither at once.
What is more beautiful than chastity, which makes a fragile human being conceived
from impure seed into a pure vessel, and somehow turns an enemy into a servant
and a human being into an angel? The virtue of chastity is natural to an angel; for
a human being, it is a cause of virtue and the glory that will follow, resplendent
with the beauty of a flower. "This is your sanctification," the apostle says, "that you
abstain from fornication, so that each of you may know how to possess her vessel
in holiness and honor, not in passionate desire, like the Gentiles who do not know

God" [1 Thess. 4.3–5]. But unless you love, your chastity has neither value nor merit. For what good is chastity if it is not accompanied by perfect love? Chastity without charity is a lamp without oil. Take away the liquid and you have quenched the lamp. But it is a grace of marvelous splendor, and a lamp of double grace, when the virgin of Christ is zealous for chastity so that she may know how to cherish her Bridegroom above all things and all people, and to cherish in him those whom she loves.

*Theodora.* O how beautiful is the virgin's crown, more precious than any badge of royal dignity!

*Peregrinus.* Listen, daughter. A chaste life among the stings of temptation enjoys the delights of roses and lilies at all times. And surely, if the examples of virgins are not enough to spur your progress, the thousands of holy widows or even the life of married women, diligently studied, will urge the virgin of Christ to follow the Lamb for the glory of continence and the immaculate bridal bed. Among all of these, to mention two inferior to the dignity of your order, Judith and Susanna come to mind. The first, a chaste conqueror, slew with her own sword the invincible tyrant, the foe of chastity, the rebel against God, the lustful adulterer. The second snuffed out the unchaste elders, who were wolves in sheep's clothing, by choosing death to preserve her chastity rather than neglecting herself and the fear of God. For if that blessed woman, victorious over impudence and unchastity, had violated the faith of her marriage bed by accepting adulterers—if, terrified by the judgment of her accusers, she had yielded to the lust of strangers—she would have incurred mortal sin and lost the praise of everlasting glory for her triumph, nor would she have exposed the enemies of Israel to just punishment by a sentence of death.

This passage is a fearful one for Christ's virgins. Or rather, the flowers of paradise suffer grave anxiety lest the pastors of Christ's handmaids prove to be wolves rapacious for souls, slaying with the swords of incontinence those whom they feed with the word of truth. What evil or vice can ever be likened to so great an evil? What death can be compared to this death, when the master of Christ's virgins, the guardian of eternal vessels, the teacher of Zion's daughters and tutor of celestial brides, should forget the fear and love of God and be so blinded by the shadow of lust as to look with illicit love on his own daughter, when he ought rather to have died himself to preserve her chastity? What more detestable thing, I ask, could be heard or uttered, than that a senior bridegroom of the Church, a vicar of Christ, should be dissolved in the excess of youthful debauchery and, straying from justice and truth, take delight in the rotten flesh? Truly this is a seed of Canaan and not Judah, this man whom beauty deceives and the fantastic error of illicit passion bends to treacherous madness, so that he fulfills what the Lord said to Job about the ancient enemy: "He will throw gold beneath himself like mud" [Job 41.21]. And then "the stars will fall from heaven" [Matt. 24.29], and "the sun become like sackcloth" [Apoc. 6.12]—and many similar passages, in which the mark of their own disgrace is branded onto these foul and perfidious masters who give rise to scandals.

*Theodora.* As for the gold turned into mud, the fall of the stars, and the mutation of the sun, this comparison of unlike things instructs my understanding well enough. But I beg you, open up the allegorical sense.

*Peregrinus.* Gold is turned into mud when the understanding and wisdom of a teacher sink down to the filthy love of the flesh. A star falls when the light of his virtues is darkened by the shadow of vices. The sun takes the appearance of sackcloth when a soul resplendent with faith and works is blinded by the cloud of temptation and, losing the rays of divine charity, defiles itself with the squalor of grave sin. Many teachers of sacred virgins are proven to be masters when it comes to discipline, but not to guardianship, as Paul says: "You may have ten thousand teachers, but not many fathers" [1 Cor. 4.15]. For he loved those he fathered in Christ.

Woe is me! How many monasteries of virgins in our times do we see plagued by this evil, so that the judges and elders of the ancient world appear to live again. Holy virgins, deceived by their passion and perverted lust, win everlasting reproach and punishment through the very men whose teaching and example should have given them hope of gracious light and glory. Because the guilty love is the same in both sexes, death then swallows both in the same destruction. O how lamentable to the whole Church is this fall, when the very highest ranks in the Church are cast into the abyss! Young and old are scandalized, God's name is blasphemed, and the whole body of the Church is shattered in hateful ruin. Woe to the blind and profane master by whom this scandal comes! It would have been better for him if he had not been born [Matt. 26.24].

## SV 9.503–59

*Peregrinus.* I exchanged some thoughts with you earlier about patience and wisdom, which are inseparable companions, according to the text, "A man's wisdom is known by his patience" [Prov. 19.11]. It remains now to set forth a few brief moral exhortations about false and true nobility, and generally about the progress and setbacks of the soul, so that wherever your eyes may light on the page, you will see something edifying.

A few remarks should be made about nobility, then. As there is a great difference between flesh and spirit, between the old Adam and the new, so is there between false and true nobility. The greatest nobility of a human being is a noble spirit, one that cultivates virtues and resists vices. If you consider the flesh, it is a wonderful nobility, a wonderfully distinguished family, in which worm is born from worm and corruption is praised by dust! Hear the apostle: "Not many," he says, "are wise according to the flesh; not many are powerful, not many noble; but God has chosen what is foolish in the world to confound the wise, and what is weak to confound the strong, and what is ignoble and despised in the world, even things that are not, to destroy those that are, so that no flesh might boast in his sight" [1 Cor. 1.26–29]. A high-born spirit, then, is one that pays no attention to what it hears about the nobility of its lineage. For all the nobility of earthly stock belongs to the old man rather than the new; it pertains to what is born carnally, not what is reborn spiritually. It follows from this that the honor of the greatest nobility lies within us, not outside us. True nobility, then, should be measured in the spirit rather than in the glory of one's parents. She who exults in the flower of her carnal stock, which will soon perish, does not realize that she is the daughter and bride of the eternal king. Now to be wise or puffed-up according to the flesh is the chain of death. "But where the Spirit of the Lord is, there is freedom" [2 Cor. 3.17]. "For what person knows a man's thoughts except the spirit of the man that is in him? So also, no one knows the things of God except the Spirit of God. We have received not the spirit of this world, but the Spirit which is from God" [1 Cor. 2.11–12]. And elsewhere: "the natural man does not perceive the things of the Spirit" [1 Cor. 2.14]. Why would the apostle make this argument about the Spirit and freedom unless the spirit of the flesh, derived from noble lineage and impelling the soul to blindness, differed from the Spirit that proceeds from the freedom of the children of God and illumines the mind? The nobility of the flesh is a framework of vices; the dignity of the new man is the glory of virtues.

*Theodora.* Yet how often, in the lives of saints of great merit, the praise of their nobility is added to their virtues, so that even what is said about the glory of their lineage may prefigure merit, and a title derived from their parents' glory may somehow become a proof of holiness.

*Peregrinus.* Although the dignity of birth is sometimes mentioned even in saints' lives, this praise is transferred to the praise of God, whose love the saints prefer to all worldly glory. For contempt of nobility is a proof of divine love, and for this reason, when a title of nobility is added to the saints' praises, the spirit's virtue is proclaimed by its contempt for carnal lineage. True nobility, then, is revealed not by the flesh but by wisdom, which fashions a beautiful spirit and forms it in the virtues. The best kind of labor nurtures spirits in true nobility; idleness makes them degenerate. Daughter of Zion, "do not turn aside to the right or to the left!" [Josh. 1.7]. Whether you are descended from the lineage of kings or of peasants, you have come to the true Bridegroom; may you remain one and the same. What does the man who is noble in the gates [Prov. 31.23] say to the holy soul? "I will glorify those who glorify me," he says, "but those who despise me will be despised" [1 Kings 2.30]. "Those who are led by the Spirit of God are the children of God" [Rom. 8.14], "who are born not of blood, nor of the will of the flesh, but of God" [John 1.13].

*Theodora.* Let this conclusion, far removed from worldly nobility, suffice to extinguish it, for "what is born of the flesh is flesh, and what is born of the Spirit is spirit" [John 3.6].

*Peregrinus.* "Walk by the Spirit, then, and do not fulfill the desires of the flesh" [Gal. 5.16].

### *SV* 9.699–744

*Theodora.* She who transcends the flesh, while still living in her flesh, is not unjustly compared by analogy to him who is above all. Compare the creature to the Creator by analogy, then, since you cannot do so by equivalence.

*Peregrinus.* It is said by those who know how to probe the subtleties of nature, that is, by scientists, that a virgin of elegant beauty surpasses the shrewdest hunters in skill inasmuch as she can ensnare the unicorn—a savage and ferocious beast that all the labor of hunters is powerless to catch.

*Theodora.* I have often heard this, as it happens. But I beg you, do not hesitate to discuss it here.

*Peregrinus.* The unicorn is not a beast of great size, but it is of such ferocity, restlessness, and strength that it may seem unconquerable, and cannot be captured by any trick of the hunters. For it engages in single combat with the elephant—not to mention beasts of lesser or equal strength—and sometimes vanquishes it by stabbing the elephant's belly with its horn. Although the smaller beast could be devoured by the larger one in a moment, yet it attains the victory by its incomparably superior nature.

*Theodora.* Well then? By what skill could such mighty strength be subdued?

*Peregrinus.* A girl of elegant beauty, attractively dressed, is prepared and set down in a place where the unicorn frequently roams. As soon as it has seen her, the untamed beast runs up immediately and grows gentle. Setting aside its fierceness, it folds its limbs and lays its furious head in the virgin's lap. In this way the beast is captured with a trap the hunters have prepared—nor does the virgin experience any harm.

*Theodora.* Do not hide the significance of this from me, I beg you, for I can hardly believe that this animal's nature is without some great mystery.

*Peregrinus.* Understand this virgin as a type of divine Wisdom, and recognize in the beast the image of worldly princes. For what patriarch, what prophetic sermon could vanquish the rabid cruelty of such princes, or who could tame them, until the Wisdom of God appeared incarnate on the broad plain of this world and in the wild forest of the nations? Who could bend or conquer the savage ferocity of the Roman empire—the unicorn—until Christ, symbolized by this beautiful virgin, laid the snares and nets of apostolic doctrine before this madly raging beast? So the world, once it recognized Christ, hastened to him humbly without delay, set aside its fierce temper and its pride, and with its cruelty pacified, laid its head—or rather, its mind—in the virgin's lap, that is, in the mystery of divine Wisdom. Thus the unicorn, who would not yield to any human skill or bestial strength, yielded to the virgin.

Now the dignity of virgins could be demonstrated by many other examples, if we had not already wandered far enough from our purpose. But to draw a lesson from the literal meaning of this one, notice how the brutality of the beast is diminished by the sight of a virgin, whereas the insanity of men is sometimes aroused to perverse love. So a sensible virgin should, in one sense, fear the company of a dog or a wild animal less than that of a rational creature.

### SV 9.1151–1206

*Theodora.* You are creating for Christ's virgins a garden of delights with a floral chain of arguments, wherein the varied scent and color of the flowers may the more sweetly delight those who pluck the blooms by reading.

*Peregrinus.* The flowers and fruits of a holy conscience supply delicious banquets amid spiritual disciplines. Who knows the worth of the treasury of a good conscience? Who can number its riches? A mind that is conscious of virtue feeds at all times on holy delights; it is nourished without weariness on heavenly dishes, always exulting in that guest whose mere presence gives inexhaustible delight to the delicate soul. But let it suffice, Theodora, to have plucked flowers from the Lord's meadow up to this point. We are now drawing near the end of our work, for it is not appropriate for the sun to set on a man and a woman talking together, even if kinship, by God's grace, removes all suspicion of evil talk. It will be gratifying, though, to append the degrees of the virginal life, as it were fruits of the flowering branch, to what precedes, and to number these degrees in accordance with the five prudent virgins. In this conclusion, let us sum up our whole conversation.

*Theodora.* Nothing could be more pleasing.

*Peregrinus.* The first rank of virginal glory, then, consists of integrity in mind and body and a desire to please the eyes of God alone, according to the apostle's saying: "A virgin of the Lord thinks about the things of the Lord, that she may be holy in body and spirit" [1 Cor. 7.34]. The second degree of the virginal profession is to renounce all the pomps of the world, the delights of the flesh, homeland, and family with a willing mind, and so to become just as contemptible to the world as she herself holds the world in contempt, as the apostle says: "Far be it from me to boast except in the cross of our Lord Jesus Christ, through whom the world has been crucified to me and I to the world" [Gal. 6.14]. "For those who are in the flesh cannot please God, for if anyone does not have the Spirit of God, he does not belong to God" [Rom. 8.8–9]. The third order of virginity is to bend heart and body to prompt obedience for the love of Christ, to precede other members of the community in affectionate service, and to persevere in holy humility and chastity with steadfast faith, following the example of the Lord's Mother—for after she conceived the Lord, his mother began at once to serve an older matron. As the apostle advises, "Outdo one another in showing honor" [Rom. 12.10]. The fourth distinction of virginal glory is to open yourself to the divine Word with a purified heart, to strive for a quiet mind, and to treasure the words of life in your heart as the Lord's Mother did, and, having gathered the Lord's words by sitting at his feet with the other Mary, to prepare potent weapons against the assaults of the enemy's wickedness. The fifth degree, when you have nearly completed the lengthy course on the racetrack of your holy vow, is not to become dissolute through excessive confidence, but to fear and shrink back at the uncertainty of perseverance, like one who will gain no profit from the course she has already run unless she completes what is left, as the apostle said: "Brethren, I do not consider that I have attained the goal" [Phil. 3.13], and so forth. For there are some who, presuming on the long preservation of their virginity even as the end of life drew near, have negligently lost the chastity they had consecrated to Christ through their whole previous lives. What profit was there in climbing the ladder to the highest rung, only to fall back to the bottom in a headlong plunge? What good would it be to have run beyond your strength, if you could not cross the finish line with the others?

The condition of our mortal life should be held in the greatest suspicion by these souls, who are like pregnant women about to give birth. Walking on rough and hilly slopes, they fear a miscarriage at every moment. Or, if a cargo ship laden with great merchandise is shaken by a tempest, it risks the loss of goods and human life even though the shore be near. The progress of a holy virgin is not to be measured by the negligence or levity of others, then, but she should heed this saying: "Each will receive her own reward according to her labor" [1 Cor. 3.8].

### SV 9.1286–99

*Peregrinus.* Look, Theodora! Insofar as divine grace has permitted, you have what you sought. Gather the little flowers in this labor of ours, flee the world, seek Christ, and do not be slow to walk in the fragrance of his ointments [Cant. 1.3]. A runner does not delay when fear goads her forward, grace allures, love invites, and a reward awaits. But when you have arrived, this goad of fear will cease and the sweetness of love will remain. Arrival takes away fear; holy joy increases love. You will find a haven after a stormy voyage, rest after labors, a home after travel, gracious light after darkness—nor will you be sorry to have run with such exertion when you find so much at the journey's end. And here is the end of our dialogue and all our work, completed with a thanksgiving and a prayer, so that in case you recall to memory something we have omitted, you may be edified anew—for you neither would nor could ever have enough of the divine word. So offer a sacrifice of thanksgiving to God on high, by whose gift you were created, that you have been found worthy to become his bride and his beloved. *Here ends the ninth part.*

# CONTRIBUTORS

ELISABETH BOS graduated from Sydney University in 1994, where she studied medieval history with John O. Ward. In 1998 she completed her Ph.D. dissertation, "Gender and Religious Guidance in the Twelfth Century," at the University of Cambridge. Her research has focused predominantly on the evidence of letter collections from the late eleventh and twelfth centuries.

SABINA FLANAGAN is the author of *Hildegard of Bingen: A Visionary Life* (London: Routledge, 2nd ed. 1998) and *Secrets of God: Writings of Hildegard of Bingen* (New York: Shambhala, 1996). She is currently completing a study of twelfth-century doubt as an ARC Fellow in the Department of History, University of Adelaide.

FIONA GRIFFITHS is assistant professor at Smith College, Northampton, MA. She earned her Ph.D. from Cambridge University in 1998 with a dissertation entitled "Female Spirituality and Intellect in the Twelfth and Thirteenth centuries: A Case Study of Herrad of Hohenbourg." She has since published a translation of Herrad of Hohenbourg's poetry as well as an article on the place of history in the *Hortus deliciarum*. Her current research addresses the education of women within the monastery during the twelfth century.

JULIE HOTCHIN completed her M.A. in medieval history at Monash University and is now engaged upon a Ph.D. dissertation on the history of religious women in twelfth and thirteenth century Germany at the Australian National University, Canberra, Australia. She has published articles on Hildegard of Bingen and her social, intellectual and monastic contexts.

CATHERINE JEFFREYS completed her Ph.D. at the University of Melbourne in 2000 with a dissertation entitled "Melodia et Rhetorica: The Song Repertory of Hildegard of Bingen." She has published several papers on music associated with Hildegard of Bingen.

URBAN KÜSTERS is lecturer in medieval literature in the Department of German Literature (Abteilung Ältere Germanistik) at the Heinrich-Heine-University of Düsseldorf, Germany. He has published books on the medieval tradition of the Song of Songs and on personal relations in the Middle Ages. He has also published a number of articles on religious and mystical literature, the history of grief and emotions, semiotics, patterns of the marked body, and concepts of "body-writing" in medieval culture.

CONSTANT J. MEWS is director of the Centre for Studies in Religion and Theology and senior lecturer in the School of Historical Studies at Monash University, Australia. He has written *The Lost Love Letters of Heloise and Abelard: Perceptions of Dialogue in Twelfth-Century France* (New York: St. Martin's Press, 1999) as well as a number of papers relating to Hildegard of Bingen and religious thought in the twelfth century.

BARBARA NEWMAN is professor of English and religion at Northwestern University in Evanston, Illinois. She has written extensively about Hildegard of Bingen and other medieval religious women. Her most recent book is an edited volume, *Voice of the Living Light: Hildegard of Bingen and Her World* (Berkeley: University of California Press, 1998). Her translations of medieval Latin texts include Hildegard's *Symphony* and the *Life of Juliana of Mont-Cornillon*.

JANICE M. PINDER is a graduate of Melbourne and Oxford universities and is now an honorary research associate of the School of Historical Studies at Monash University, Australia. She has published articles on French vernacular hagiography of the twelfth and thirteenth centuries and edited a thirteenth-century French life of St. Francis: *The Life of Saint Francis of Assisi: A Critical Edition of the MS Paris, Bibl. Nat. fonds français 2094* (Rome: Archivum Franciscanum Historicum, 1995).

MORGAN POWELL completed his Ph.D. at Princeton University in 1997 with a dissertation entitled "The Mirror and the Woman: Instruction for Religious Women and the Emergence of Vernacular Poetics 1120–1250," which he is currently revising for publication. He is assistant professor of modern languages at Franklin College Switzerland and a Getty Postdoctoral Fellow in Art History and the Humanities during 2000/01.

KIM E. POWER obtained her Ph.D. from La Trobe University, Melbourne, in 1997 with a dissertation entitled "The Secret Garden: The Meaning and Function of the *Hortus conclusus* in Ambrose of Milan's Homilies on Virginity." A senior Fulbright scholar-in-residence at the College of Notre

Dame of Maryland during 1997/98, she has published several articles on the body, sexuality, and gender in early Christian thought, and *Veiled Desire: Augustine's Writing on Women* (New York: Continuum, 1996).

JUTTA SEYFARTH is professor of art history of the Middle Ages at the University of Cologne. She has published the *editio princeps* of the *Speculum virginum* (CCCM 5, 1990) as well as studies of monastic culture in the twelfth century and of art history in Cologne in the seventeenth century. Her bilingual (Latin/German) edition of the *Speculum virginum* is appearing in 2001 in the series Fontes Christiani, Band 30.1–3.

# INDEX

CPSIA information can be obtained at www.ICGtesting.com
Printed in the USA
LVOW090215260512

283419LV00004B/2/P